D0759685

COLONIAL ENCOUNTERS

COLONIAL ENCOUNTERS

Europe and
the native Caribbean,
1492–1797

Peter Hulme

METHUEN: London and New York

First published in 1986 by
Methuen & Co. Ltd
11 New Fetter Lane, London EC4P 4EE

Published in the USA by
Methuen & Co.
in association with Methuen, Inc.
29 West 35th Street, New York, NY 10001

© 1986 Peter Hulme

Printed in Great Britain
at the University Press, Cambridge

British Library Cataloguing in Publication Data
Hulme, Peter
Colonial encounters: Europe and the
native Caribbean, 1492–1797.
1. Caribbean Area – Relations – Europe
2. Europe – Relations – Caribbean Area
I. Title
303.4'821821'04   F2178.E85

ISBN 0 416 41860 0

Library of Congress Cataloging in Publication Data
Hulme, Peter.
Colonial encounters.
Bibliography: p.
Includes index.
1. Indians of the West Indies – Government relations.
2. Indians of the West Indies – First contact with
Occidental civilization.   3. Indians in literature.
4. Indians of the West Indies – Public opinion.
5. Public opinion – Europe.   I. Title.
F1619.3.G68H85   1986   972.9'02   86-8708

ISBN 0 416 41860 0

*For my father
and in memory of
my mother*

Looking through a map
of the islands, you see
that history teaches
that when hope
splinters, when the pieces
of broken glass lie
in the sunlight,
when only lust rules
the night, when the dust
is not swept out
of the houses,
when men make noises
louder than the sea's
voices; then the rope
will never unravel
its knots, the branding
iron's travelling flame that teaches
us pain will never be
extinguished.

(Edward Brathwaite, Islands, 1969)

Contents

List of figures		x
Preface and acknowledgements		xiii
Introduction		I
1	Columbus and the cannibals	13
2	Caribs and Arawaks	45
3	Prospero and Caliban	89
4	John Smith and Pocahontas	137
5	Robinson Crusoe and Friday	175
6	Inkle and Yarico	225
Afterword		265
Notes		267
Bibliography		329
Index		341

List of figures

page

1 'America' (*c.* 1600); an engraving by Jan van der
Straet (Stradanus). Reproduced by permission of
the British Museum (BM ref. C.62 P/A J.
Stradanus).   xii

2 The extended Caribbean.   4

3 'Columbus in India primo appellens, magnis ex-
cipitur muneribus at Incolis'; from Theodore de Bry,
(*Grands Voyages*) *Americae Pars Quarta*, I. Feyrabend:
Frankfurt, 1594, plate ix.   14

4 Columbus's route through the Caribbean, 1492–3.   23

5 Columbus's probable conception of eastern Asia;
adapted from Hermann Wagner, 'Die Rekonstruk-
tion der Toscanelli-Kartz vom J. 1474 . . .', *Nach-
richten von der Königl. Gesellschaft der Wissenschaften
zu Göttingen, Philologisch-historische Klasse*, 1894,
no. 3.   24

6 Columbus's course off eastern Cuba; from a map
drawn by Erwin Raisz in S.E. Morison, *Admiral of
the Ocean Sea: A Life of Christopher Columbus*, Little,
Brown and Company: Boston, 1942, p. 269.
Copyright 1942, © 1970 by Samuel Eliot Morison.
Reproduced by permission of Little, Brown and
Company in association with The Atlantic Monthly
Press.   25

7 Columbus's fleet attacked by cannibals; an engraving
in Honorius Philoponus, *Nova typis transacta naviga-
tio novi orbis Indiae Occidentalis*, Venice, 1621, between pp. 32 and 33.   44

8 The conventional anthropological classification of

Amerindian societies in pre-Columbian South
America; adapted from the *Handbook of South American Indians*, ed. J. Steward, Smithsonian Institution
Press: Washington, DC, 1946, 6 vols, I, p. 12.
Reproduced by permission of Smithsonian Institution Press from Bureau of American Ethnology
Bulletin 143.   52

9 'The Enchanted Island: Before the Cell of Prospero'
   (1803); engraved by P. Simon from a painting by H.
   Fuseli. Reproduced from *The Boydell Shakespeare
   Prints*, intro. A.E. Santaniello, Arno Press: New
   York, 1979, plate iv.   88

10 'Valboa Indos nefandum Sodomiae scelus commit-
   tentes canibus objicit dilaniandos'; from Theodore
   de Bry (*Grands Voyages*) *Americae Pars Quarta*, I.
   Feyrabend: Frankfurt, 1594, plate xxii.   113

11 The 1622 'massacre' of the Virginia settlers; from
   Theodore de Bry (*Grands Voyages*) *Decima tertia pars
   America*, M. Merian: Frankfurt, 1634, p. 28.   136

12 'The baptism of Pocahontas' (1840) a painting by
   J.G. Chapman. Reproduced by kind permission of
   the Architect of the Capitol.   171

13 'Rescue of the Spaniard'; drawn by Gordon Browne
   in *The Life and Surprizing Adventures of Robinson
   Crusoe*, Blackie and Son: London, 1885, p. 243. Reproduced by permission of the British Library (BL
   ref. 012804 cc 27).   174

14 'Un Anglais de la Barbade vend sa Maitresse'; an
   engraving by Jean-Marie Moreau le Jeune for G.-F.-
   T. Raynal, *Histoire philosophique et politique des
   établissements et du commerce des Européens dans les deux
   Indes*, Jean-Leonard Pellet: Geneva, 1780, 4 vols, III,
   frontispiece. Reproduced by permission of the
   British Library (BL ref. 147b 3–6).   224

15 St Vincent 1700–73; adapted from Michael Craton,
   *Testing the Chains: Resistance to Slavery in the British
   West Indies*, Cornell University Press: Ithaca, 1982,
   p. 148. Copyright © 1982 by Cornell University
   Press. Used by permission of the publisher.   243

AMERICA.

Americen Americus retexit, & ··· Semel vocauit inde semper excitam ··· .

Figure 1 'America' (*c.* 1600); an engraving by Jan van der Straet (Stradanus). In line with existing European graphic convention the 'new' continent was often allegorized as a woman and surrounded with the paraphernalia seen as typically American: parrots, tapirs, bows and arrows, and cannibal feasts. The sexual dimension of the encounter with Vespucci is both visually and linguistically explicit.

Preface and acknowledgements

Europe encounters America. Clothed and armed Europe encounters naked America. Jan van der Straet's remarkable engraving (Figure 1) epitomizes a meeting whose narrative European discourse has repeated over and over to itself ever since the end of the fifteenth century. Columbus and the cannibals, Prospero and Caliban, John Smith and Pocahontas, Robinson Crusoe and Friday, Inkle and Yarico: this book is structured by those five versions of the encounter between Europe and that primordial part of America, the Caribbean. It studies the structure of those narratives, addresses the significance of their repetitions, and attempts to contextualize them within the broader paradigm of colonial discourse. But repetitions are never identical, and the five versions also trace willy-nilly the story of an encounter between Europe and the native Caribbean that lasted 305 years, beginning with Columbus's landfall on Guanahani on 12 October 1492 and effectively ending with the deportation of the Black Caribs from St Vincent on 11 March 1797.

The matrix of the book must therefore be considered historical, but it is not written by a historian and it deals with an area about which there has been little historical writing in the general understanding of the term. Two of the book's chapters also discuss texts usually considered as significant works of literature: here, while by no means read as historical documents in any simple sense, their status as 'literary' texts is put into suspension. This allows them to be seen as moments in a developing discourse which was attempting, in a variety of ways, to manage Europe's understanding of its colonial relationships with native Caribbean societies. In summary form, then, this is the book's project and terrain. Some of the issues that arise from this description are pursued further in the Introduction.

Two points however should already be apparent. The chapters of the book stand or fall as textual analyses: they deal persistently, perhaps obsessively, with narrative structures, tropes, phrases, even single words, in the belief that these can be revealed as sites of political struggle. Yet the texts analysed and the matters raised, although all related to my particular definition of 'the Caribbean', range widely across the conventional boundaries of disciplinary practices. This disregard for disciplinary limits has made me especially dependent on both published scholarship and the help and advice of friends. So I must acknowledge as fully as possible the assistance I have received in writing this book.

For financial support I thank the British Academy and the Research Endowment Fund of the University of Essex. This enabled me to carry out research during the winter of 1982–3 at a number of libraries, to whom I am also grateful: the Biblioteca Ángel Arango, Bogotá; the library of the University of the West Indies, St Augustine, Trinidad; the Public Libraries of Kingstown, St Vincent and St George's, Grenada; the library of the University of Texas at Austin; the Folger Shakespeare Library and the Library of Congress, Washington, DC. I also worked at the libraries of the Institute of Commonwealth Studies and the Royal Commonwealth Society, and at the Public Record Office (Kew), all in London. However, the majority of the research was carried out in the British Library and in the library of the University of Essex, where I thank Jane Brooks and Terry Tostevin for many years of patient and skilful assistance.

I have learned a lot over the last few years from responses to seminars and lectures given on the topics of this book at: the Universities of York and East Anglia; University College, Cardiff; the Institute of Latin American Studies, London; the Museum of Mankind; the Université d'Alger; two Centre for Social History conferences in Oxford; and two Sociology of Literature conferences at Essex. In particular, presenting this material on the Sociology of Literature MA at Essex has acted as a constant reminder that teaching is the most effective test for ideas developed in the solitude of research.

Some of the material in Chapters 1, 3 and 4 first appeared in, respectively, the *Ibero-Amerikanisches Archiv*, and the two sets of Essex Conference proceedings entitled *1642: Literature and Power in the Seventeenth Century* and *Europe and Its Others*. Chapter 3 also draws on ideas that developed in an essay jointly written with Francis Barker as a contribution to *Alternative Shakespeares*, edited by John Drakakis (London, 1985). Full details of all four are given in the Bibliography.

The material production of the book owes a great deal to the work put into it by Sylvia Sparrow and Dorothy Gibson at Essex. I thank them for their care and their skill.

I am grateful for the invaluable encouragement and assistance given to the book at Methuen by Janice Price, Jane Armstrong and Sarah Pearsall.

Particular intellectual debts are referred to in the notes, but I want here to acknowledge the pervasive influence of a number of writers. The model of textual analysis employed owes much to the works of Louis Althusser, Pierre Macherey and Fredric Jameson. Edward Said's *Orientalism* helped clarify my thoughts about the discourse of colonialism. And I am indebted to four great Caribbeanist scholars, Carl Ortwin Sauer, Gordon W. Lewis, José Juan Arrom and Roberto Fernández Retamar.

This book was conceived and developed within the framework of the School of Comparative Studies at the University of Essex and owes its existence to that comparative ideal, whose light still illuminates some dark days. I have received help and support from too many friends and colleagues in all the departments of the School to list them individually, but I would like to mention – from Essex and elsewhere – Dawn Ades, Catherine Belsey, Homi Bhabha, John Drakakis, Robert Clark, Valerie Fraser, Richard Gray, Charles Gullick, Terence Hawkes, Margaret Iversen, Elaine Jordan, David Musselwhite and Jonathan White. All have helped even more than they know.

Finally, and especially, Francis Barker, Gordon Brotherston and Diana Loxley have given so generously of their time and knowledge and friendship over the last eight years that no acknowledgement could fully convey the extent to which this book is indebted to them. I give them my thanks none the less.

Wivenhoe
September 1985

Introduction

Language is the perfect instrument of empire
(Bishop of Avila to Queen Isabella of Castile, 1492)[1]

1

Jan van der Straet's engraving (Figure 1) will stand more reading as an emblem of this book's themes. In a variety of ways the 'discovery of America' has been inscribed as a beginning. It is the first of the great 'discoveries' that form the cornerstones of the conventional narrative of European history over the last five centuries: America is, typically, the 'New World' or later the 'Virgin Land'. The temporal adverbs of van der Straet's motto carry the same message: 'semel ... inde semper ...' (once ... from then always ...). Yet this very insistence on the novelty of the 'New World' evidences an anxiety, some of whose manifestations are charted in the chapters that follow. Put in its simplest terms that anxiety concerns the relationship between European, native and land – what is called in Chapter 4 the classic colonial triangle. The engraving figures a strategy of condensation: 'America', the single allegorical character, combines the terms 'native' and 'land' to create an identity that dissimulates the existence of any relationship at all between the two at the moment of their encounter with Europe. The gesture of 'discovery' is at the same time a ruse of concealment. That the gesture, which is always also a ruse, should then be repeated over a period of three centuries, giving a series of narratives of the 'first' encounter between European and native Caribbean, provides the

particular formulation of that colonial anxiety which is the
subject of this analysis.

2

The general area within which this study operates could then be
named colonial discourse, meaning by that term an ensemble of
linguistically-based practices unified by their common deployment
in the management of colonial relationships, an ensemble that
could combine the most formulaic and bureaucratic of official
documents – say the Capitulations issued by the Catholic Monarchs to Christopher Columbus early in 1492 – with the most
non-functional and unprepossessing of romantic novels – say
Shirley Graham's *The Story of Pocahontas*. Underlying the idea of
colonial discourse, in other words, is the presumption that during
the colonial period large parts of the non-European world were
produced for Europe through a discourse that imbricated sets of
questions and assumptions, methods of procedure and analysis, and
kinds of writing and imagery, normally separated out into the dis-
crete areas of military strategy, political order, social reform, imaginative literature, personal memoir and so on.[2] But, as a case
study, this book operates on a particular geographical and ideological terrain within that general area, which is to say that there
is no presumption that the key tropes and narratives analysed here
would play as central a role within colonial discourse in general.
For one thing, not sufficient work has been done to support such
generalizations.

To say geographical and ideological terrain is to register two
particular possibilities. One is that a central division within
colonial discourse separates the discursive practices which relate to
occupied territory where the native population has been, or is to
be, dispossessed of its land by whatever means, from those
pertaining to territory where the colonial form is based primarily
on the control of trade, whether or not accomplished through or
accompanied by a colonial administration. America and India can
exemplify very roughly this division. The other possibility
concerns a discursive divide between those native peoples perceived as being in some sense 'civilized' and those not, the indices
of such 'civilization' being at different times and in different

circumstances stone buildings or literacy or an ancient heritage. It is true that Christianity never formulated a classification corresponding to the Islamic distinction between 'peoples of the book' and pagans proper; and equally true that the indices were often destroyed or explained away or both. But this proved difficult where the buildings or language were themselves claimed as part of a European or Christian heritage; as in Greece and the Holy Land, and later India. Such a claim hardly prevented the deployment of the language of 'savagery' but it did attenuate it, whereas in America that language was honed into the sharpest instrument of empire. This gives a trope whose various lineaments the following chapters will be concerned to trace: the topic of land is dissimulated by the topic of savagery, this move being characteristic of all narratives of the colonial encounter.

Discursively the Caribbean is a special place, partly because of its primacy in the encounter between Europe and America, civilization and savagery, and partly because it has been seen as the location, physically and etymologically, of the practice that, more than any other, is the mark of unregenerate savagery – cannibalism. 'Cannibalism' – and it will, until satisfactorily made sense of, be held in those inverted commas – is the special, perhaps even defining, feature of the discourse of colonialism as it pertained to the native Caribbean. As such it will play a special part in all the chapters here, particularly the first, since the word itself comes to us via Columbus's log-book and letter, and the third, where 'canibal' – the contemporary English spelling – makes an anagrammatic appearance on the Jacobean stage as Caliban.

Caliban's struggle against Prospero in *The Tempest* is one moment of a larger discursive conflict in which a Mediterranean discourse is constantly stretched by the novelty of an Atlantic world. Time and again these Caribbean texts are set against or have introduced into them the terms of reference of a classical or Biblical text, and time and again those Mediterranean reference points are rejected or turned back against themselves. That conflict, visible again in van der Straet's engraving, will be a constant theme in what follows.

Since place and territory are crucial matters in the book it should be made clear that by 'the Caribbean' is meant not the somewhat vague politico-geographic region now referred to by that term, but rather what Immanuel Wallerstein calls 'the

Figure 2   The extended Caribbean showing many of the places referred to in this book.

extended Caribbean', a coastal and insular region that stretched from what is now southern Virginia in the USA to the most eastern part of Brazil (see Figure 2).[3] Textually this region incorporates at its northern boundary John Smith's 'rescue' by Pocahontas (near Jamestown) and at its southern boundary Robinson Crusoe's plantation (near Bahia). As an entity its logic clearly owes nothing to subsequent political boundaries nor even to sixteenth- and seventeenth-century national spheres of interest. Instead it emphasizes those features, environmental and ideological, that lay beyond national differences. The Caribbean is then the tropical belt defined ecologically or meteorologically, rather than astronomically, as, say, the most suitable area for growing the 'tropical' crops of cotton, tobacco and sugar; or it is the belt of American coastline that lay within range of that other and equally frightening characteristic phenomenon, the hurricane.

The area could also be viewed as a discursive entity, given the resemblances amongst the narrative and rhetorical strategies found within the relevant Spanish, Portuguese and English texts – resemblances that outweigh, or at least weigh equally with, those found between texts in the same language dealing with areas in the same sphere of interest, say Virginia and New England or Hispaniola and Mexico.

Equally important (and the three definitions obviously interconnect) this was the area where, broadly speaking, the native population was replaced by slaves brought from Africa. In other words the extended Caribbean is essentially an historical entity, one that came into being in the sixteenth century and that has slowly disappeared. However, it is worth remembering both that English colonial policy in America in the seventeenth and eighteenth centuries still had the Caribbean as its focus – as shown by the priorities of the Treaty of Paris (1763); and that the area's major socioeconomic feature, the plantation, produced a transnational legacy whose effects are still palpable.

4

What follows is, then, a case study rather than a theoretical work on the subject of colonial discourse. Nevertheless, several theoretical questions demand explicit, if brief, mention. This book has been produced within a generally Marxist framework. Such a statement is not made in order to foreclose theoretical problems, but the political impetus behind the book does have particular consequences. For one thing it means that the colonial discourse studied here cannot remain as a set of merely linguistic and rhetorical features, but must be related to its function within a broader set of socioeconomic and political practices: it must be read, that is to say, as an ideology.

But to use the word ideology is inevitably to introduce a whole series of epistemological issues that have underlain much of the recent debate about the nature, or indeed possibility, of Marxist history.[4] Briefly, it has been argued that ideology always stands, in Michel Foucault's words, 'in virtual opposition to something else which is supposed to count as truth',[5] truth being taken in this argument as a concept fatally undermined by the demonstration, most closely associated with the name of Jacques Derrida, that it always relies on unspoken and ungrounded assumptions, on some master signifier, whether God or Experience or History, that must keep itself out of range of deconstructive analysis in order to guarantee the veracity of statements made under its aegis. In purely philosophical terms this post-structuralist demonstration is difficult, perhaps impossible, to counter, and it has much to teach – particularly in Derrida's own work – about the rigour with which one's own conceptual framework must be examined. Politically, though, such a position can lead only to quietism, since no action at all can be validated from its theoretical endpoint, or to a false radicalism which engages in constant but ultimately meaningless transgression of all defended viewpoints.

Foucault's work has suggested that what counts as truth will depend on strategies of power rather than on epistemological criteria. To meet this challenge the starting point for any radical writing of history must be the political agenda set by the present. In this instance that would involve the observation that international politics is clearly still moulded by the recent era of the great colonial empires, a legacy most apparent in the new national entities and frontiers created in this century. Equally obvious is that the 'end of empire' has concealed signal continuities in the power-relationships still pertaining between different parts of the world – in a word, neo-colonialism. The world of multinational corporations and the international labour market might seem a long way from the relative simplicities of the sixteenth century, but it is important to keep in mind both that the conquest of America, begun in 1492, is still being pursued to completion in Central America and Brazil, and that the United States has inherited the imperial mantles and tactics of England and Spain in the Caribbean and Central America. In both cases the operative discourse has changed little from that studied here. Ronald Reagan's inaugural invocation of the Puritan 'city on the hill' is merely the most recent indication of that constant felt need to hark back to supposed 'beginnings' in defence of present violence.

That, in brief, is the political context which places the study of this area of colonial discourse on the agenda. And equally it is within this political context that the answers – no doubt, but inevitably, *provisional* answers – to theoretical and epistemological problems must be sought.

To return then to the question of ideology. Much of the recent sophistication of the concept of ideology, associated with the names of Gramsci and Althusser, is in any case irrelevant in the present context because we are dealing not with a consensual model of the social formation in which ideology can be seen as fully pervasive, almost constitutive of social and civil life itself, but rather with a model of division in which ideology is a discourse whose mode is largely textual in the narrow sense and whose address is largely internal, towards that group in society most directly concerned with colonial matters. The single notable exception, the *requerimiento* – pronounced, in Spanish, at a safe distance (sometimes of many miles) from its addressees – only proves the point.[6] In other words, if the notion of ideology employed here seems less nuanced than that, say, of hegemony, the crudeness of some of the early colonial manoeuvres, discursive and otherwise, needs recalling.

A further argument would address more directly Foucault's point about 'virtual opposition'. Truth has another conventional opposite: fiction. Indeed the post-structuralist argument must conclude that all statements are in a certain sense fictions inasmuch as no particular form of words can, on epistemological grounds alone, claim access to reality superior to any other form of words. This is useful as long as it is taken as a starting point rather than as the last word. What should follow is a careful examination of the claims and assumptions implicit within different statements, an examination that would involve attention to such elements as genre, rhetoric, pragmatics and so on: a politics of discourse. Only then could it be seen that matters of verification – seemingly made irrelevant by the universality of 'fiction' as a discursive mode – return in a minor key where a statement *claims* veracity. These somewhat abstract issues take on considerable importance in the colonial context since certain of the particular discourses involved – narrative history, historical linguistics, ethnography – stand or fall by their truth-claims. It is therefore in the first instance politically rather than epistemologically important to retain the prerogative to undermine their claims; and ideological analysis remains an essential tool for Marxism because it enables us to say not just that a particular statement is false, but also that its falsity has a wider significance in the justification of existing power-relations. This does not, *pace* Foucault, provide a term in 'virtual opposition' to a transcendental Truth as ultimate guarantor and arbiter. Its antonym is a small and relative and provisional truth, one that eschews the naïvety of any supposedly *direct* access to reality but claims an explanatory superiority over its rival versions, particularly since it includes within its analysis an explanation of why those rival claims might appear plausible. This whole procedure, practised so effectively by Marx in his reading of classical political economy, is known as critique. Its aims and methods will be adopted in the readings that follow.

5

A radical history presenting a new version of the past will usually draw on new sources, even though those sources might well be 'new' only in the sense that the dominant version had repressed them by never even considering them as sources. Within this model of radical history there are then two interdependent but separable moments: first, a critique of existing versions, partly dependent upon, second, the presentation of alternative and contradictory evidence. This model has its anti-colonial equivalent in the rediscovery of native sources that offer a different and revealing light on colonial events and issues. None of this is as simple as it sounds, but it is relatively straightforward when compared with a situation in which there are virtually no alternative sources at all, a state of affairs brought about partly by our inability to read such 'documents' as do survive from the native Caribbean, and partly by the devastating speed and scale of the destruction of its societies in the period following 1492.[7] The only evidence that remains, in other words, are the very European texts that constitute the discourse of colonialism. The European engraved by van der Straet is appropriately enough not Columbus but Amerigo Vespucci, not the first European to stand on the shores of the continent previously unknown to Europe but the first European to give that land a name, a European name, his own, feminized.[8] Such a monologic encounter can only masquerade as a dialogue: it leaves no room for alternative voices.

In this instance therefore, the burden of the radical task necessarily falls upon the protocols of critique. Procedurally, the first aspect of critique concerns the choice of texts. Given the focus on colonial beginnings and the geographical restriction to an extended Caribbean, the texts studied here largely chose themselves. Others could no doubt be added, but the aim is a detailed study of representative texts rather than any attempt at coverage of the whole area.

Even so, the five European stories are very different *kinds* of text, or at least texts that are usually seen as generically distinct. One point needs careful making in this connection. It is probably not accidental that two of the texts considered here (*The Tempest* and *Robinson Crusoe*) are 'literary' inasmuch as they have become essential parts of 'English Literature' in its current form. To focus on these texts is therefore in one sense to introduce into a singular discourse a rhetorical plurality or heteroglossia that might be seen to compensate for the absence of critical parallax noticed above. But there should be no suggestion that such 'literary' texts, *qua* 'literary', produce any internal distantiation or implicit critique of the supposedly 'purer' ideological texts. A different presumption operates here: that whilst all the texts have their generic particularities that require careful attention – log-book, play, historical memoir, novel, anecdote, to mention only the major texts – no intrinsic discursive significance attaches to their current classification as 'literary' or otherwise. Even within current conventions that borderline would be almost impossible to draw: Columbus's log-book has been read 'as literature'; Smith's account of his rescue has sometimes been seen as a fictional embellishment to his history of Virginia; Yarico begins her career embedded as an anecdote in a biographical/historical memoir and is transferred by means of an 'essay' to the whole gamut of 'literary' genres. It may be significant that answers to pressing ideological problems should be sought through recourse to largely imaginative narratives – and obviously inevitable that this should be the case once the original historical circumstances had been left so long behind – but it is still essential, and therefore the first line of approach here, that colonial discourse operates certain strategies and tropes that can be seen at work in texts whose superficial differences –

according to current classifications – might appear very striking. This is another way of saying that questions of textuality and rhetoric will be central.

Differences of emphasis inevitably occur between chapters simply because some parts of the material are much better known than others. Familiarity has been presumed in the cases of *The Tempest* and *Robinson Crusoe* (Chapters 3 and 5) but not with Columbus's *Journal* (Chapter 1) or John Smith's accounts of Pocahontas (Chapter 4), let alone with the once popular but now completely unread story of Inkle and Yarico, or the contemporary and equally unknown wars between England and the native Caribs of St Vincent (Chapter 6).

6

Forty years ago, in *The Idea of History*, R.G. Collingwood developed an analogy between the historian and the natural scientist:

> As natural science finds its proper method when the scientist, in Bacon's metaphor, puts Nature to the question, tortures her by experiment in order to wring from her answers to his own questions, so history finds its proper method when the historian puts his authorities in the witness-box, and by cross-questioning extorts from them information which in their original statements they have withheld, either because they did not wish to give it or because they did not possess it.[9]

The analogy may not work, but its failure is revealing. Collingwood offers three densely woven figures: Bacon's analogy between the procedures of natural science and the inquisitorial method; his own analogy between the procedures of history and the adversary method; and a comparison ('as ... so ...') between natural science and history which is tightened into an analogy by the similarities of phrasing ('wring ... extorts ...'). But even if we let Bacon's extraordinary metaphor for the protocols of natural science stand, it should be apparent that history lacks not only an experimental method that would 'torture' its authorities, but even (and perhaps especially) a resuscitative method that would give those authorities a voice with which to answer the historian's questions. Within the terms of Collingwood's figure, historical documents, put to the question or cross-examined, will always tell the same story, word for word. What is interesting about the paragraph is that its dual metaphorical structure veils the internal contradiction: in other words the statement embodies, à rebours, its own point about what can be hidden within original statements. Collingwood's expression is flawed, one might say, because it is working against the grain of language, that far-from-neutral medium. Seeking to escape the traps of positivism and empiricism he is driven up against the ideological limits of a language that always encodes knowledge in terms of consciousness.

Fredric Jameson, confronting the same problem, takes a surprisingly open resuscitatory line: the past, 'like Tiresias drinking the blood, is momentarily returned to life and warmth and allowed once more to speak, and to deliver its long-forgotten message in surroundings utterly alien to it'; only to recognize that, in practice, the Tiresian message needs considerable piecing together:

> It is in detecting the traces of that uninterrupted narrative, in restoring to the surface of the text the repressed and buried reality of this fundamental history, that the doctrine of a political unconscious finds its function and its necessity.[10]

So the historian here is some kind of picture-restorer, scraping off excrescences to reveal the 'fundamental history' that lies beneath – although of course texts no more have 'depth' (and therefore 'surface') than they have 'voice'. It is not difficult to 'detect' beneath the 'surface' of Jameson's text the repressed operation of a model in which the revealed narrative of class-struggle is so well known in advance that the picture-restoring is devoid of any suspense. But, as in Collingwood's case, the residual model reasserts itself only by dint of the power of linguistic inertia, here to be foiled at the last by the fine oxymoron of 'a political unconscious'.

The point of this final introductory excursus is to show how difficult it is to develop the kind of critical vocabulary necessary for textual interrogation. Jameson's 'political unconscious' is important because, drawing on Althusser and Macherey, it recognizes that Freudian theory offers the one model of reading we have that can claim to make a text speak more than it knows. Within psychoanalysis that speaking is again dependent upon a 'cross-questioning' of the subject (the knowing consciousness rather than the knowing text), so 'the textual unconscious' is just one more metaphor, but it is the one wagered on here: hence the vocabulary of symptom, trace, the unconscious and so on, torn from their analytic context to bolster the scandal of putting texts to the question.[11]

In particular, following Macherey's deployment of the Freudian model, the chapters of this book will work to identify key locations in a text – *cruces*, to extend a conventional term – where the text stutters in its articulation, and which can therefore be used as levers to open out the ideology of colonial discourse, to spread it out, in this text, in an act of explication. The venture, it should be said, is archaeological: no smooth history emerges, but rather a series of fragments which, read speculatively, hint at a story that can never be fully recovered.

1

Columbus and the cannibals

[S]ome strangers had arrived who had gabbled in funny old talk because they made the word for sea feminine and not masculine, they called macaws poll parrots, canoes rafts, harpoons javelins, and when they saw us going out to greet them and swim around their ships they climbed up onto the yardarms and shouted to each other look there how well-formed, of beauteous body and fine face, and thick-haired and almost like horsehair silk, and when they saw that we were painted so as not to get sunburned they got all excited like wet little parrots and shouted look there how they daub themselves gray, and they are the hue of canary birds, not white nor yet black, and what there be of them, and we didn't understand why the hell they were making so much fun of us since we were just as normal as the day our mothers bore us and on the other hand they were all decked out like the jack of clubs in all that heat ... and we traded everything we had for these red birettas and these strips of glass beads that we hung around our necks to please them, and also for these brass bells that can't be worth more than a penny and for chamberpots and eyeglasses ... but the trouble was that among the I'll swap you this for that and that for the other a wild motherfucking trade grew up and after a while everybody was swapping his parrots, his tobacco, his wads of chocolate, his iguana eggs, everything God ever created, because they took and gave everything willingly, and they even wanted to trade a velvet doublet for one of us to show off in Europeland.[1]

Figure 3 Columbus greeted by native Caribbeans; from Theodore de Bry's *Grands Voyages*. The primal encounter tended to be depicted either as this kind of idealized tribute, or as fierce hostility (cf. Figure 7).

1

Human beings who eat other human beings have always been placed on the very borders of humanity. They are not regarded as *in*human because if they were animals their behaviour would be natural and could not cause the outrage and fear that 'cannibalism' has always provoked. 'Cannibalism': the word comes easily and unproblematically; a straightforward word without troubling ambiguities, more familiar (and easier on the tongue) than the

alternative, 'anthropophagy'. Both words exist in English as
nouns describing 'the practice of eating the flesh of one's fellow-
creatures', to quote the *Oxford English Dictionary*'s entry on
'cannibalism', but both words once existed as proper nouns
referring to whole nations who were to be characterized by their
adhesion to such a practice. So, originally, rather than 'cannibalism' or 'anthropophagy', 'Cannibals' and 'Anthropophagi'. But
the histories of the two words are very different. 'Anthropophagi'
is, in its original Greek, a formation made up of two pre-existing
words ('eaters / of human beings') and bestowed by the Greeks on
a nation presumed to live beyond the Black Sea. Exactly the
opposite applies to 'Cannibals', which was a non-European name
used to refer to an existing people – a group of Caribs in the
Antilles. Through the connection made between that people and
the practice of eating the flesh of their fellow-creatures, the name
'Cannibal' passed into Spanish (and thence to the other European
languages) with that implication welded indissolubly to it.
Gradually 'cannibal = eater of human flesh' became distinguished from 'Carib = native of the Antilles', a process only
completed (in English) by the coining of the general term
'cannibalism', for which the first *OED* entry is dated 1796 – a date
that will gather resonance in the final chapter of this book.

One of the ways in which ideologies work is by passing off
partial accounts as the whole story. They often achieve this by
representing their partiality as what can be taken for granted,
'common sense', 'the natural', even 'reality itself'. This in turn
often involves a covering of tracks: if something is to appear as
simply 'the case' then its origin in historical contingency must be
repressed. Generally speaking this repression can take two forms:
the denial of history, of which the most common version is the
argument to nature; or the historical alibi, in which a story of
origins is told. The power of this second form is that it usually
offers a true story, in the restricted but powerful sense of true as
'not false'. It might indeed offer several true stories but these
would never be in conflict because they would be isolated from
one another in separate compartments, often called 'disciplines'.
Here the most pertinent disciplines are ethnography and historical
linguistics, and it is the latter that seems to have provided what
will look, at least for a while, like a real beginning, the first
encounter.

2

The primary *OED* definition of 'cannibal' reads: 'A man (*esp.* a savage) that eats human flesh; a man-eater, an anthropophagite. Originally proper name of the man-eating Caribs of the Antilles.' The morphology or, to use the *OED*'s word, form-history of 'cannibal' is rather more circumspect.[2] The main part of its entry reads:

> (In 16th c. pl. *Canibales*, a. Sp. *Canibales*, originally one of the forms of the ethnic name *Carib* or *Caribes*, a fierce nation of the West Indies, who are recorded to have been *anthropophagi*, and from whom the name was subsequently extended as a descriptive term . . .)

This is a 'true' account of the morphology of the word 'cannibal' in English, yet it is also an ideological account that functions to repress important historical questions about the *use* of the term – its discursive morphology, perhaps, rather than its linguistic morphology. The trace of that repression is the phrase 'who are recorded to have been', which hides beneath its blandness – the passive tense, the absence (in a book of authorities) of any *ultimate* authority, the assumption of impartial and accurate observation – a different history altogether.

The tone of 'who are recorded to have been' suggests a nineteenth-century ethnographer sitting in the shade with notebook and pencil, calmly recording the savage rituals being performed in front of him. However unacceptable that might now seem as 'objective reporting', it still appears a model of simplicity compared with the complexities of the passages that constitute the record in this instance.

On 23 November 1492 Christopher Columbus approached an island 'which those Indians whom he had with him called "Bohio"'. According to Columbus's *Journal* these Indians, usually referred to as Arawaks:

> said that this land was very extensive and that in it were people who had one eye in the forehead, and others whom they called 'canibals'. Of these last, they showed great fear, and when they

saw that this course was being taken, they were speechless, he says, because these people ate them and because they are very warlike. (*J* 68–9)[3] [la cual decían que era muy grande y que había en ella gente que tenía un ojo en la frente, y otros que se llamaban canibales, a quien mostraban tener gran miedo. Y des que vieron, que lleva este camino, dice que no podían hablar porque los comían y que son gente muy armada.][4]

This is the first appearance of the word 'canibales' in a European text, and it is linked immediately with the practice of eating human flesh. The *Journal* is, therefore, in some sense at least, a 'beginning text'.

But in just what sense is that name and that ascription a 'record' of anything? For a start the actual text on which we presume Columbus to have inscribed that name disappeared, along with its only known copy, in the middle of the sixteenth century. The only version we have, and from which the above quotation is taken, is a handwritten abstract made by Bartolomé de Las Casas, probably in 1552, and probably from the copy of Columbus's original then held in the monastery of San Pablo in Seville. There have subsequently been various transcriptions of Las Casas's manuscript. So the apparent transparency of 'who are recorded to have been' is quickly made opaque by the thickening layers of language: a transcription of an abstract of a copy of a lost original. This is chastening, but to some extent contingent. More telling is what might be called the internal opacity of the statement. Columbus's 'record', far from being an observation that those people called 'canibales' ate other people, is a report of other people's words; moreover, words spoken in a language of which he had no prior knowledge and, at best, six weeks' practice in trying to understand.

Around this passage cluster a whole host of ethnographic and linguistic questions, some of which return in the next chapter. But the general argument here will be that, though important, these questions take second place to the textual and discursive questions. What first needs examination, in other words, are not isolated passages taken as evidence for this or that, but rather the larger units of text and discourse, without which no meaning would be possible at all.

3

To write about the text we call 'el diario de Colón' (Columbus's journal) is to take a leap of faith, to presume that the transcription of the manuscript of the abstract of the copy of the original stands in some kind of meaningful relationship to the historical reality of Columbus's voyage across the Atlantic and down through the Caribbean islands during the winter months of 1492–3.

It would be perverse and unhelpful to presume that no such relationship exists, but credulous and unthinking to speak – as some have done – of the *Journal*'s 'frank words, genuine and unadorned'.[5] Circumspection would certainly seem called for. Yet if the *Journal* is taken not as a privileged eye-witness document of the discovery, nor as an accurate ethnographic record, but rather as the first fable of European beginnings in America, then its complex textual history and slightly dubious status become less important than the incredible narrative it unfolds.

This is not an argument in favour of somehow lifting Columbus and his *Journal* out of history. Just the opposite in fact; and gradually, throughout this chapter, the *Journal*'s contexts will be inscribed on to the text. But it is an argument in favour of bracketing particular questions of historical accuracy and reliability in order to see the text whole, to gauge the structure of its narrative, and to chart the interplay of its linguistic registers and rhetorical modalities. To read the *Journal* in this way is also to defer the biographical questions: the Columbus of whom we speak is for the moment a textual function, the 'I' of the *Journal* who is occasionally, and scandalously, transformed into the third person by the intervention of the transcriber's 'I'.

The *Journal* is generically peculiar. It is in part a log-book, and throughout records the navigational details of Columbus's voyage. Commentators have usually accepted that it was written up almost every evening of the six-and-a-half-month journey, not revised or rewritten, and not constructed with a view to publication. It certainly gives that impression, which is all that matters here: Columbus is presented by the *Journal* as responding day by day to the stimulus of new challenges and problems. Yet if its generic shape is nautical the *Journal* is also by turns a personal memoir, an ethnographic notebook, and a compendium of European fantasies about the Orient: a veritable palimpsest.

4

'From whom the name was subsequently extended as a descriptive term'. Linguistic morphology is concerned only with the connection made between the term 'cannibal' and the practice of eating human flesh. We have seen how the very first mention of that term in a European text is glossed with reference to that practice, and for the linguist it is satisfactory, but not of intrinsic interest, to note how that reference is always present, either implicitly or explicitly, in any recorded use of the word 'cannibal' from Columbus's on 23 November 1492 onwards. It was adopted into the bosom of the European family of languages with a speed and readiness which suggests that there had always been an empty place kept warm for it. Poor 'anthropophagy', if not exactly orphaned, was sent out into the cold until finding belated lodging in the nineteenth century within new disciplines seeking authority from the deployment of classical terminology.

All of which makes it even stranger that the context of that beginning passage immediately puts the association between the word 'cannibal' and the eating of human flesh into doubt. Las Casas continues:

> The admiral says that he well believes that there is something in this, but that since they were well armed, they must be an intelligent people [gente de razón], and he believed that they may have captured some men and that, because they did not return to their own land, they would say that they were eaten. (*J* 69)

This passage is of no interest to linguistic morphology since Columbus's scepticism failed to impinge upon the history of the word. Ethnographically it would probably be of scant interest, showing merely Columbus's initial scepticism, and therefore making him a more reliable witness in the end. Even from the point of view of a revisionist ethnography that wanted to discount suggestions of native anthropophagy the passage could only be seen as evidence of the momentary voice of European reason soon to be deafened by the persistence of Arawak defamations of their traditional enemy. Attention to the discursive complexities of the text will suggest a different reading.

The great paradox of Columbus's *Journal* is that although the voyage of 1492–3 was to have such a devastating and long-lasting

effect on both Europe and America, and is still celebrated as one of
the outstanding achievements of humanity, the record itself tells
of misunderstandings, failures and disappointments. The greatest
of these – that he had not reached Asia – was too overwhelming
for Columbus ever to accept. The minor ones are in some ways
even more telling.

According to the account given by the *Journal* the Spaniards
arrived with a whole series of objectives and expectations, and
plied their native hosts with questions. For the most part
Columbus gives the impression of fairly straightforward communication with the natives, but this was hardly the case. The
Spanish ships carried only one interpreter, Luís de Torres,
specially chosen because he spoke Hebrew, Aramaic and some
Arabic; so there is no reason to think that there was any initial
communication at all. The natives presumably remained baffled
but gave (largely by way of signs) what seemed to be the right
answers to expedite their visitors – pointing enthusiastic index
fingers at the horizon; the Spaniards, pleased to find that whatever
they had asked about was so near, thought they were understanding each other famously. On 11 December, three months after the
first landfall, Columbus admits: 'Every day we understand these
Indians better and they us, although many times there has been
misunderstanding' (*J* 93). This is just about credible, even if there
is little subsequent indication of improved communication in the
months that follow. From October to December (the months at
issue here) there is no evidence and no reason to suppose that what
Columbus presented as a dialogue between European and native
was other than a European monologue: Las Casas has a marginal
note by one of the entries under consideration (23 November
1492) commenting on Columbus's misunderstanding of the word
'bohio' (in fact 'house') as the name of an island: 'this shows
how little he understood them'.[6] And yet the monologue is in no
sense simple or homogeneous: Columbus's initial scepticism is to
be explained not as the flickering light of European reason, but
rather as the result of a discursive conflict internal to that
European monologue itself.

In brief, what a symptomatic reading of the *Journal* reveals is
the presence of two distinct discursive networks. In bold outline
each discourse can be identified by the presence of key words: in
one case 'gold', 'Cathay', 'Grand Khan', 'intelligent soldiers',

'large buildings', 'merchant ships';[7] in the other 'gold', 'savagery', 'monstrosity', 'anthropophagy'. Even more boldly, each discourse can be traced to a single textual origin, Marco Polo and Herodotus respectively. More circumspectly, there is what might be called a discourse of Oriental civilization and a discourse of savagery, both archives of topics and motifs that can be traced back to the classical period. It is tempting to say that the first was based on empirical knowledge and the second on psychic projection, but that would be a false dichotomy. There was no doubt a material reality – the trade that had taken place between Europe and the Far East over many centuries, if intermittently. In pursuit of, or as an outcome of, this trade there were Europeans who travelled to the Far East, but their words are in no way a simple reflection of 'what they saw'. For that reason it is better to speak of identifiable discourses. There was a panoply of words and phrases used to speak about the Orient: most concerned its wealth and power, as well they might since Europe had for many years been sending east large amounts of gold and silver. Marco Polo's account was the best-known deployment of these topoi.[8] The discourse of savagery had in fact changed little since Herodotus's 'investigation' of Greece's 'barbarian' neighbours. The locations moved but the descriptions of Amazons, Anthropophagi and Cynocephali remained constant throughout Ctesias, Pliny, Solinus and many others.[9] This discourse was hegemonic in the sense that it provided a popular vocabulary for constituting 'otherness' and was not dependent on *textual* reproduction. Textual authority was however available to Columbus in Pierre d'Ailly and Aeneas Sylvius, and indeed in the text that we know as 'Marco Polo', but which is properly *Divisament dou Monde*, authored by a writer of romances in French, and itself already an unravellable discursive network.[10]

In the early weeks of the Columbian voyage it is possible to see a certain jockeying for position between these two discourses, but no overt conflict. The relationship between them is expressed as that between present and future: this is a world of savagery, over there we will find Cathay. But there are two potential sites of conflict, one conscious – in the sense of being present in the text; the other unconscious – in the sense that it is present only in its absence and must be reconstructed from the traces it leaves. The conscious conflict is that two elements, 'the soldiers of the Grand

Khan' from the discourse of Marco Polo and 'the man-eating savages' from the discourse of Herodotus, are competing for a single signifier – the word 'canibales'. Columbus's wavering on 23 November belongs to a larger pattern of references in which 'canibal' is consistently glossed by his native hosts as 'man-eater' while it ineluctably calls to his mind 'el Gran Can'. In various entries the phonemes echo each other from several lines' distance until on 11 December 1492 they finally coincide:

> it appears likely that they are harassed by an intelligent race, all these islands living in great fear of those of Caniba. 'And so I repeat what I have said on other occasions,' he says, 'the Caniba are nothing else than the people of the Grand Khan [*que Caniba no es otra cosa sino la gente del Gran Can*], who must be very near here and possess ships, and they must come to take them captive, and as the prisoners do not return, they believe that they have been eaten.' (*J* 92–3)

The two 'Can' are identified as one, the crucial identification is backdated, and 'canibal' as man-eater must simply disppear having no reference to attach itself to.

Except of course that it does not disappear at all. That would be too easy. In fact the assertion of the identity of 'Caniba' with 'gente del Can', so far from marking the victory of the Oriental discourse, signals its very defeat; as if the crucial phonetic evidence could only be brought to textual presence once its power to control action had faded. To understand this it will be necessary to look back in some detail at the course of Columbus's voyage through the Caribbean (see Figure 4).

5

Gold was not simply the one element common to both the Oriental discourse and the discourse of savagery; it was in each case the pivotal term around which the others clustered. Oriental gold and savage gold would prove to be very different animals but in the early weeks of the voyage they happily share the single signifier which guided Columbus like a magnet through the bewildering archipelago of the Bahamian islands:

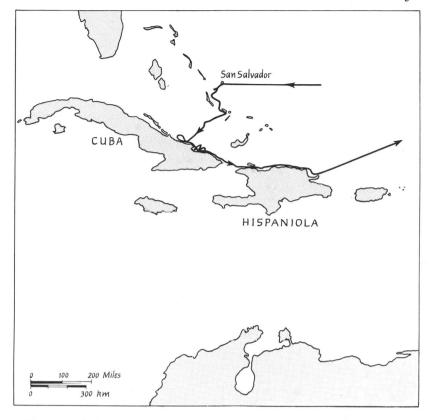

Figure 4 Columbus's route through the Caribbean, 1492–3.

MONDAY, OCTOBER 15TH ... These islands are very green and fertile and the breezes are very soft, and it is possible that there are in them many things, of which I do not know, because I did not wish to delay in finding gold, by discovering and going about many islands. (*J* 30)

TUESDAY, OCTOBER 23RD ... I did not delay longer here ... since I see that there is no gold mine .... I say that it is not right to delay, but to go on our way and to discover much land, until a very profitable land is reached. (*J* 42)[11]

Gold was the object of desire but 'gold' could be articulated by both discourses. What is more, at this stage both discourses pointed

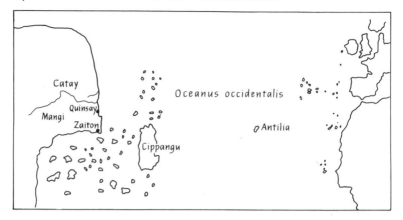

Figure 5 Columbus's probable conception of eastern Asia, based on a reconstruction of the chart drawn for the King of Portugal by Paolo Toscanelli, with whom Columbus corresponded.

in the same direction. According to the medieval geography of Oriental discourse the coastline of Cathay ran from NNW to SSE, and the large island of Cipangu (Japan) had to its north-east a cluster of smaller islands (see Figure 5). So the initial landfall on Guanahani was not problematic; it was clearly one of these smaller islands. A course south-west would take him to Cipangu or, if he missed Cipangu, to the coast of Cathay. As it happened the native fingers pointed south-west too, no doubt for their own reasons,[12] but serving to buttress the traditional link between the sources of gold and the tropics:

> WEDNESDAY, NOVEMBER 21ST .. From this heat, which the admiral says that he experienced there, he argued that in these Indies and there where he was, there must be much gold. (*J* 68)

On 21 October Columbus first hears of Cuba:

> I wish to leave for another very large island, which I believe must be Cipangu, according to the signs which these Indians whom I have with me make; they call it 'Colba'. They say that there are ships and many very good sailors there . . . . But I am still determined to proceed to the mainland and to the city of Quinsay and to give the letters of Your Highnesses to the Grand Khan, and to request a reply and return with it. (*J* 41)

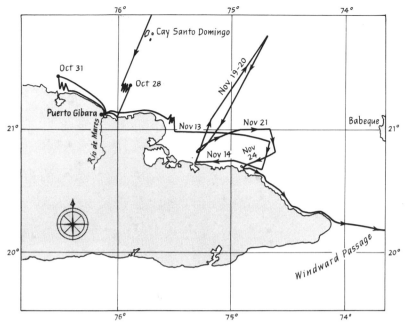

Figure 6 Columbus's course off eastern Cuba, showing his change of direction.

The determination is still to go beyond the island to the mainland. They steered west-south-west and reached Cuba on 28 October:

> The Indians said that in that island there are gold mines and pearls; the admiral saw that the place was suited for them. And the admiral understood that the ships of the Grand Khan come there, and they are large; and that from there to the mainland it is ten days' journey. (*J* 46).

Columbus immediately sets off north-west up the Cuban coast, but his geographical notions quickly lose their assurance (see Figure 6). This is not one of the smaller islands but neither, evidently, is it the rich and civilized island of Cipangu:

> TUESDAY, OCTOBER 30TH . . . After having gone fifteen leagues, the Indians who were in the caravel *Pinta* said that behind that cape there was a river, and that from the river to Cuba it was four days' journey. The captain of the *Pinta* said he understood that this Cuba was a city, and that land was a very extensive

mainland which stretched far to the north, and that the king of
that land was at war with the Grand Khan . . . . The admiral
resolved to go to that river and send a present to the king of
that land, and send him the letter of the Sovereigns . . .; and he
says that he must attempt to go to the Grand Khan, for he
thought that he was in the neighbourhood, or to the city of
Cathay, which belongs to the Grand Khan, which, as he says, is
very large, as he was told before he set out from Spain. (*J* 49)

The refusal of the Caribbean islands to conform to 'Oriental'
expectations is by now becoming embarrassingly evident. Yet
Martín Alonso Pinzón's interpretation of his guides' remarks
offers a way out. If Cuba is a *city* then this must be the mainland
and Quinsay not too far to the north (given that it supposedly has
the same latitude as the Canaries). There then follows an
extraordinary series of events, which will be given in outline
before being discussed in detail.

Columbus begins by saying, quite reasonably since he now
imagines himself to be on the mainland, 'that he must attempt to
go to the Grand Khan'; yet in the same sentence he announces that
he is 42° north of the Equator, an evidently ludicrous assessment
of his position. The next day he makes one desultory effort to sail
north-west:

> WEDNESDAY, OCTOBER 31ST All night, Tuesday, he was
> beating about, and he saw a river where he could not enter
> because the mouth was shallow. . . . And navigating farther
> on, he found a cape which jutted very far out and was
> surrounded by shallows, and he saw an inlet or bay, where
> small vessels might enter, and he could not make it, because the
> wind had shifted due north and all the coast ran north-north-
> west and south-east. Another cape which he saw jutted still
> farther out. For this reason and because the sky showed that it
> would blow hard, he had to return to the Río de Mares. (*J* 49)

The next day he potters around on shore but announces firmly
' "that this is the mainland, and that I am," he says, "before Zaiton
and Quinsay, a hundred leagues, a little more or less, distant from
one and another" ' (*J* 51). Amazingly, the next day, rather than
sailing north-west again, he sends his embassy inland. Cuba, he
had discovered after all, was only four days' inland from the river,
but not *this* river (Río de Mares), rather the one north-west

beyond the cape. The ambassadors are primed in all seriousness
and dispatched; Columbus takes his latitude again, this time with
a quadrant, and again comes out with 42° north. He then spends
four days waiting for the embassy to return, trying all the while
to communicate with the natives:

> SUNDAY, NOVEMBER 4TH ... The admiral showed to some
> Indians of that place cinnamon and pepper – I suppose some of
> that which he had brought from Castile as a specimen – and
> they recognised it, as he says, and indicated by signs that there
> was much of it near there, towards the south-east. He showed
> them gold and pearls, and certain old men replied that in a
> place which they called 'Bohio' there was a vast amount, and
> that they wore it round the neck and on the ears and legs, and
> also pearls. He further understood that they said that there were
> large ships and merchandise, and that all this was to the south-
> east. He also understood that far from there were men with one
> eye, and others with dogs' noses who ate men, and that when
> they took a man, they cut off his head and drank his blood and
> castrated him. The admiral determined to return to the ship to
> await the two men whom he had sent, intending himself to go
> in search of those lands if they did not bring some good news of
> things they sought. (J 52)[13]

The following night (November 5/6) the men return having
found no Oriental city. Columbus relates their story and then
makes a statement. Las Casas, catching the portentous tone,
quotes the words directly:

> 'They are,' says the admiral, 'a people very free from wicked-
> ness and unwarlike; they are all naked, men and women, as
> their mothers bore them. It is true that the women wear only a
> piece of cotton, large enough to cover their privy parts and no
> more, and they are of very good appearance, and are not very
> black, less so than those of the Canaries. I hold, most Serene
> Princes,' the admiral says here, 'that having devout religious
> persons, knowing their language, they would all at once
> become Christians, and so I hope in our Lord that Your
> Highnesses will take action in this matter with great diligence,
> in order to turn to the Church such great peoples and to
> convert them, as you have destroyed those who would not
> confess the Father and the Son and the Holy Ghost, and after

your days, for we are all mortal, you will leave your realms in a
most tranquil state and free from heresy and wickedness, and
you will be well received before the eternal Creator, Whom
may it please to give you long life and great increase of many
kingdoms and lordships, and the will and inclination to spread
the holy Christian religion, as you have done up to this time.
Amen. Today I refloated the ship and I am preparing to set out
on Thursday in the name of God, and to go to the south-east to
seek for gold and spices and to discover land.' (*J* 57)

In six days an absolute determination to sail north-west has been
transformed into an equally absolute determination on the
rectitude of sailing in precisely the opposite direction.

The crucial nature of this decision for Columbus can be gauged
by the almost manic accumulation of explanations he offers for it.
In addition to the *Journal* entry, he gives over a large chunk of his
later *Letter* – addressed to the Spanish monarchs but the document
through which the 'discovery' became known to all Europe – to a
justification of the change:

> When I came to Juana [Cuba], I followed its coast to the
> westward, and I found it to be so extensive that I thought it
> must be the mainland, the province of Cathay. And since there
> were neither towns nor villages on the seashore, but small
> hamlets only, with the people of which I could not have speech
> because they all fled immediately, I went forward on the same
> course, thinking that I could not fail to find great cities or
> towns. At the end of many leagues, seeing that there was no
> change and that the coast was bearing me northwards, which I
> wished to avoid, since winter was already approaching and I
> proposed to make from it to the south, and as, moreover, the
> wind was carrying me forward, I determined not to wait for a
> change in the weather and retraced my path as far as a
> remarkable harbour known to me. (*J* 191–2).

It should be noted that 'many leagues' was in fact two days'
sailing, and that the rest of the *Letter* is almost totally devoid of
navigational detail. Carl Sauer points out the illogical nature of
Columbus's reversal:

> Columbus made too many excuses for not continuing to the
> land of the Great Khan, whose seaports lay at ten days' sail or at

a hundred leagues. Coastline, wind, and current all led west. A purely local change of coast to the north was construed into a continuing change of direction. The passage of cool northern air for several days he interpreted as the arrival of winter cold, although he wrote at the same time about his delight in the tropical verdure. A brief change in wind became the adversity of head winds out of the north.[14]

The wanton dispatch of the embassy into the Cuban interior has also provoked much comment. Las Casas speculated that when Columbus produced a gold object the natives pronounced the word 'Cubanacán' (mid-Cuba) – a district where a limited quantity of gold existed – and pointed up river to the interior; Columbus, of course, immediately connected Cubanacán with 'el Gran Can'.[15] Alternatively, Morison suggests that the natives 'simply mistook the Spaniards' dumb-show of imperial majesty for a desire to meet their cacique'.[16] In the event Luís de Torres was entrusted with the Latin passport, the Latin letter of credence from Ferdinand and Isabella, and a royal gift. As the Arabic speaker of the expedition he was supposed to make direct contact with the Grand Khan. All of this proved superfluous. The party travelled 25 miles up the valley of the Cacoyuguin where they found, not even a walled city, let along Quinsay (Hangchow), at that time the biggest city in the world, but a village of fifty houses. They were treated with deference but saw no signs of the civilization they expected.

But the most interesting (and most problematic) piece of evidence concerns Columbus's ridiculously inaccurate assessment of his position. Las Casas was clearly sceptical when reporting the 30 October reading: 'In the opinion of the admiral, he was distant from the equinoctial line forty-two degrees to the north, if the text from which I have copied this is not corrupt' (J 49); but the figure is twice confirmed: on 2 November when Columbus takes the latitude with a quadrant, and on 21 November, by which time an element of doubt has crept in ('it was . . . his opinion that he was not so far distant' (J 67)). Puerto Gibara, on the estuary of Columbus's Río de Mares, is in fact 21°06' north. Having plotted a course due west from the Canaries and then sailed south-west through the Bahamas, Columbus must have known that he could not have been more than 25° or 26° north even allowing for some error in navigation. The reasons for this seemingly inexplicable mistake have much exercised the commentators; arguably it is the most disputed textual crux in the whole Columbian corpus. One commentator has postulated an imaginary quadrant that read double. Another has argued that Columbus was trying to throw the Portuguese off the track. Las Casas suggested that the scribe copied 21 as 42 – an unlikely error, particularly on three separate occasions. Morison believed he had found the explanation:

> The real explanation is simple: Columbus picked the wrong star. He was 'shooting' Alfirk (β Cephei), which in November bore due north at dusk; mistaking her for Polaris, whose familiar 'pointers' were below the horizon.[17]

But a description of what happened is not an explanation. A simple error, twice repeated, seems unlikely for such an experienced navigator in calm and relatively clear weather.[18] But if the *desire* is to sail south-east then the 42° north would certainly provide a good excuse since Quinsay and Zaiton could not possibly lie that far north, and Marco Polo could therefore be appeased. This of course is the one reason Columbus does *not* offer for his change of direction, although it would on the surface be the most convincing. This seems to indicate that the positional error was not the *reason* for Columbus's alteration of course, but rather a *post hoc* justification to himself for that alteration. It could not be a fabrication: Columbus's conscious mind must have known perfectly well that it was wrong, and anyway such an inconsistently held fabrication could have convinced nobody. Rather Columbus wanted to sail south-east instead of the obvious north-west (obvious, that is, if he were seeking the Grand Khan's cities), and the faulty latitude reading enabled him to convince himself that he was taking the correct and logical course. Once the decision was irrevocable he could voice his own doubts and put the mistake down to a faulty quadrant (*J* 67).

These pages of the *Journal* offer, then, a series of traces that mark the site of a discursive conflict. The commentators have been exercised by these traces but handicapped by attempting to interpret them as a series of individual problems (an accident here, a change of mind there), and, more seriously, as an unmediated reflection of Columbus's mental processes.

A reading of the whole discursive conflict might look like this.

In simple terms the traces mark the defeat of the Oriental discourse as the articulating principle of the *Journal*. Until 29 October 1492 Columbus had, at least to his own satisfaction, been able to get positive enough answers to his Marco Polo-based questions to operate that interpretative grid. More to the point, the directions indicated by Marco Polo coincided with where both Columbus's received notions and native fingers pointed towards gold. On the coast of Cuba Columbus immediately, without hesitation and without comment, sailed north-west before, in this flurry of explanations, strange manoeuvres and nonsensical assessments of position, changing direction. The basic point, as Sauer recognized, is that when the terrain made a south-westerly course no longer possible and forced a choice between north-west and south-east, Columbus chose south-east because he was more likely to find gold in that direction: not of course the gold of Cathay, but exploitable mines of 'savage gold'. This was not just a difficult decision, it was one that could not be brought to textual consciousness, for to do so would have been to admit that the whole discursive structure of the Columbian enterprise had been in vain. As a result the text has to be studded with convincing reasons for the decision to sail south-east but, like Freud's example of the neighbour who fails to return the borrowed kettle, Columbus gives just *too* many. The meteorological points are adequately covered by Sauer's comment: they enable the text to *suggest* that moving northwards in winter (on the coast of Cuba!) might be unwise, but they need firmer support. This is provided by the unconsciously deliberate mistaking of Alfirk for Polaris.

In this light the embassy can be seen not so much as a genuine attempt to locate an Oriental court as Columbus furnishing himself with a decisive piece of empirical proof as to the absence of Oriental courts. Nobody had even suggested there were any inland from the Río de Mares – the earlier news had been of a city inland from a more westerly river; there was no reason at all for supposing there were any large cities to be found. But by creating the sense of expectation and therefore subsequent disappointment the text can produce, as it were, a smokescreen behind which the direction of Columbus's departure will not seem of significance. In other words the embassy was sent with such excessive solemnity *in order that it return a failure*. The incident is given extensive coverage in the *Journal*. The *Letter* can afford to be laconic:

> I sent two men inland to learn if there were a king or great cities. They travelled three days' journey, finding an infinity of small hamlets and people without number, but nothing of importance. For this reason they returned. (*J* 192)

The departure of the embassy creates a space of four days that prove to be the still centre of the *Journal*. The relentless forward momentum of the enterprise is halted. Time is almost suspended. These are the pages of the *Journal* richest in description of the natural world. It is the first European idyll in the tropics. Textually, too, a space has been opened up into which the Herodotean discourse can unfold itself, particularly (since this is what concerns us most here) its darker side, because it is while the embassy is away, while, as it were, the Oriental discourse is occupied elsewhere, that we read for the first time of 'men with one eye, and others with dogs' noses who eat men' (*J* 52): deployment of the standard Mediterranean teratology.

Again it is no accident that at the end of this idyll (in fact as a way of announcing the end of it) Columbus presents his most important policy statement so far, quoted in direct speech by Las Casas. It begins as an argument for the natural goodness of the Antillean natives ('very free from wickedness and unwarlike . . . naked . . . not very black'); trusts that Ferdinand and Isabella will be well received by their Creator for having converted so many pagans (trying to salvage at least something from the goldless and spiceless and Khanless month since the first landfall); prays for the life and empire of his sovereigns; and only then can say what the last four days and innumerable words have been building up to:

> Today I refloated the ship and I am preparing to set out on Thursday in the name of God, and to go to the south-east to seek for gold and spices and to discover land. (*J* 57)

These words were written on Tuesday 6 November. The entry ends on a note of unparalleled bathos:

> All these are the words of the admiral, who thought to set out on the Thursday, but, as he had a contrary wind, he was not able to set out until the twelfth day of November. (*J* 57)

So much for the onset of the northerly winds of winter. There are no more entries at all until the wind changes.

6

During this period of stasis on the coast of Cuba the Oriental discourse is displaced as the articulating principle of the Columbian text by the Herodotean discourse of savagery. The far-reaching nature of this displacement, evident only in the textual upheavals, is disguised to some extent by the continuity apparently given by the signifier common (and indeed pivotal) to both discourses: 'gold'. But the shift can in the end be charted by the gradual displacement of the metonyms of Oriental gold by those of savage gold. In October Columbus was hearing of 'a king who had large vessels of it and possessed much gold' (*J* 26), of 'very large golden bracelets on the legs and arms' (*J* 29), and of 'bracelets on their arms and on their legs, and in their ears and noses and around their necks' (*J* 30). After October this becomes natives digging gold (*J* 58), or sieving and smelting it (*J* 107), or collecting grains as large as lentils (*J* 142), as large as grains of wheat (*J* 140), or larger than beans (*J* 140). (One can note a displaced concern with sustenance in the language.) As a result Quinsay is no longer mentioned as a destination; the Grand Khan and his merchant ships make occasional appearances still, but only at moments where there is no danger of empirical contradiction. Displaced as an articulating discourse, Oriental terminology remains only as vestigial.

The shift in the dominant signified of 'gold' is, it should be emphasized, determinant. One of its effects is to determine the outcome of the struggle over the signifier 'canibal', but an immediate resolution could hardly be expected in so fraught a text. The glossing of 'canibal' as 'soldier of the Khan' fights a rearguard but essentially diversionary action (23 November), and the phonetic equivalence, its most powerful weapon though not brought into play until 11 December, is in essence a Parthian shot, a gesture as empty as the Cuban embassy. There is nothing now to prevent the 'canibales' assuming their role as man-eating savages. On 26 December, just fifteen days after the supposedly 'decisive' phonetic connection, Columbus promises the destruc-

tion of the 'people of Caniba' without it now appearing worthy
of mention that they may be the soldiers of a civilized potentate.

7

This then, in considerable but necessary detail, is the discursive
morphology of the word 'canibal', demonstrating just how it
becomes attached to that 'meaning' of 'man-eating savages', a
process which, although in constant response to the events of
Columbus's voyage through the Caribbean islands and to his
interchange with their native inhabitants, has nothing at all to do
with simple observation or record. The 'historical principles' of
the *Oxford English Dictionary* serve here to occlude history.

But this kind of 'internal' analysis can never be purely formal
or autonomous in the sense of being generated solely by the level
of the textual operations that are laid bare. Any political reading
must interpret the narrower textual conflict in terms of larger
politico-narrative units – must see it, in Medvedev's word, as an
ideologeme, whose significance only becomes apparent in the
larger context. But neither does this imply giving explanatory
priority to that broader level. The interplay should be
dialectical.[19]

For particular purposes the focus here has been fixedly on the
level of vocabulary; but one of the wider issues must also be
broached, since it will prove to be a theme of some importance in
almost all the succeeding chapters. Over the last five centuries
many of the intellectual and political debates about America have
centred on the question of how to approach its 'novelty': whether
the categories of the Old World are sufficient to contain the New
World within them, or whether that novelty needs recognizing
by the formulation of 'new', more appropriate categories. Similar
debates have taken place within natural history, archaeology,
political theory and many other areas, always haunted by the
impossibility of inventing purely 'new' categories, and by the
radical difficulties in understanding the indigenous American
categories on their own terms.

Within the terrain of colonial discourse the problems have
always been slightly different to the extent that novelty, as will be
seen in Chapter 3, has always played a limited and very particular

role, while the main thrust has always been to relate America to the established norms of the Old World. This tendency has several aspects of which the legal was probably the most crucial since it was obviously important that America should be subsumed under the *jus gentium* used to establish European rights to possession of land. Imaginatively, too, it was probably understandable that points of comparison and contact should be sought with the experience of the Old World, but here the relevant discourses have tended to be those which already dealt with worlds other than Europe. As the European nations, especially England, took on their imperial roles, the classical world of the Mediterranean grew in importance as a repository of the images and analogies by which those nations could represent to themselves their colonial activities. Much, as we will see in Chapter 6, turns on an unlikely comparison between St Vincent and Carthage. The court party in *The Tempest* and Robinson Crusoe both follow – or are taken on – triangular courses, from Europe to Africa to America, as if in part to facilitate this discursive transference that will help manage the fearful novelty of the New World.

Of course this Mediterranean discourse (conjoining the classical and the Biblical) had not stood still since classical times, even though, since one of its purposes is to stereotype otherness, the discourse does not often have an openly historical dimension. The threat from Islam was obviously a factor, although it does not impinge significantly on the story here. And we have already seen how the classical image of the Orient was, though not contradicted, given a significant new input of detail and imagery by the western travellers who had taken advantage of the Tartar peace (1241–1368).

The large historical irony, though, whose consequences Columbus never escaped, was that however fantastic the teratologies of classical discourse, however wonderful the riches of Cathay, however much, in a word, we read these discourses as telling more of the collective fantasies of Europe than of the cultures of the Nubians, the Scythians or the Tartars, the products of the Far East did reach Europe: the spice trade was material evidence that could not be gainsaid.

For centuries Genoa and Venice had been competing in the import of Oriental products. The routes from the East were long and difficult, the middlemen many. During the Tartar peace the prospect was opened, briefly but tantalizingly, of a more direct commerce that would lower prices and raise profits. A Genoese expedition had attempted the western circumnavigation as early as 1291.[20] The fall of Constantinople (1453) and tight Turkish control of the Middle Eastern trade routes made that task more vital. Columbus himself was deeply implicated in the Genoese commercial network: Cipolla calls him quite simply the 'agent of Genoese capital'; his chief supporters and financial backers were certainly Genoese.[21] But this search was − as a commercial enterprise − doomed to failure. For one thing it was based on a profound ignorance of Asia: no one in Europe knew that the Mongols had been expelled from China by the Ming dynasty in 1368. For another, European supplies of gold, the traditional payment for eastern spices, had been almost exhausted.[22] China had always scorned even the best European merchandise; Columbus with a ship full of cheap baubles was hardly likely to make much impression on Chinese entrepreneurs. It was obvious, at least in retrospect, that Europe needed either sufficient arms to force an entry into Eastern trade, or an alternative source of gold to ensure the continuity of the traditional exchange. Portugal managed for a while to follow both these options at the same time, diverting at least part of the ancient trans-Saharan gold trade away from the North African coast towards the Lower Guinea coast, while forcing a violent entry into the East Indian spice trade.[23] Spain, having had to forswear a share of the African trade, had little option but to pursue the western route, either, as the Genoese wanted, to find a direct sea route to Asia, or, as the Castilian pattern suggested, to follow through the acquisition of land and natural resources in the Atlantic; after all medieval geography populated the Ocean Sea with plenty of land, some of it gold-bearing.[24]

The discourses which conflict within the text of the *Journal* are therefore imbricated with, and not finally comprehensible apart from, these commercial concerns. Oriental discourse was the only available language in which the project of Genoese commerce could find its articulation. The Herodotean discourse of savagery which, in however refracted a way, deals with issues of disputed land and fractious indigenes, was appropriate to an emergent Castilian expansionism which had already begun its westward translation with the conquest of the Canary Islands and their native Guanches, probably a more significant precedent to their American adventure than the less clearcut relationship with Andalusian Islam.[25]

Columbus's change of direction on the Cuban coast can therefore be seen in this broader perspective as, if not the end then at least the beginning of the end of a particular Genoese dream. The last straw would come with Sebastian Cabot's abortive 1525 voyage which confirmed that Spain had lost too much ground to the Portuguese to be able to compete for the trade of the East.[26] The Genoese had to content themselves with controlling Spanish trade with the New World and developing their finance capitalism into the complex web that entangled the Spanish monarchy. Fernand Braudel has seen all this as a defensive action on the part of the Mediterranean world to hold off what, after the event, can be seen as the inevitable rise of the Atlantic economies, with the consequent move northwards of the pivot of European capitalism.

To some extent all this rephrases a very old and vexed question concerning Columbus's 'motive'. The vexation comes at least in part because of the difficulty of finding concrete evidence for something as tenuous as 'motive'. Nevertheless, it could be that the position outlined here would reconcile some traditionally antagonistic views. The Columbus of the *Journal* and the *Letter* 'believed' he had reached Asia. But Henry Vignaud and Cecil Jane were making valid observations in suggesting, respectively, that 'those Islands and Mainlands which . . . shall be discovered or acquired in the said Ocean Seas' (the formula of the Capitulations agreed between Columbus and the Catholic monarchs)[27] is an odd way of referring to the Cipangu and Cathay of Marco Polo, and that it would have been 'an entirely fatuous undertaking' to send practically unarmed vessels to take control of a powerful and reputedly friendly kingdom.[28] Totally fanciful, though, are the hypotheses that Vignaud and Jane construct regarding Columbus's 'real motive' of reaching unknown lands, with their subsequent need to denounce the authenticity of the correspondence with Toscanelli and even to question Columbus's ability to read at all in 1492.[29] But many of these differences can be defused if the language of the Capitulations is seen as necessarily ambiguous, precisely to embody two different sets of possibilities that came into a tenuous and ultimately tortuous compromise. 'Compromise' is not in fact the right word: it sounds too deliberate and in any case implies a third position between two incompatible ones. The difficulty is again that of having to use words against their intentionalist grain. 'Ambiguous' is wrong too, if unavoidable, since it is a question of variable referents rather than variable signifieds: 'Islands and mainlands' could refer, within Orientalist discourse, to China and Japan; but it could also refer to whatever might be discovered, Antilia perhaps, or another cluster of islands like the Azores. Perhaps it could be said, paraphrasing Nietzsche, that the whole point of language, particularly the language of legal agreements, is that it enables you *not* to specify what you mean, so that the two sets of commercial assumptions and the two discourses associated with them could happily, for a while anyway, share the same signifiers. It was in the end a question of a form of words which temporarily allowed two incompatible positions to proceed as if they were not incompatible.

To say more than this would be to enter the murky waters of psychological speculation. It would hardly be over-bold, in the light of supporting textual evidence, to suggest that Columbus 'had in mind' China and Japan, while Ferdinand and Isabella were more concerned with the possibility of finding other Atlantic islands. But any statements of intentionality – that Columbus framed the Capitulations to allow that very compromise, or that Ferdinand and Isabella deliberately took advantage of Columbus's obsession to embark on a gamble by which they had little to lose and possibly much to gain – remain purely hypothetical.[30]

It is difficult too, but proper, to resist the single step that separates the unconscious textual processes analysed here from the unconscious processes of its author – 'Columbus' the character produced by the text from the 'real' Columbus. At the heart of my explanation of how 'canibal' came to take on the 'meaning' that it has since borne in the major European languages is the suggestion that the discourse of savage gold – the discourse that articulates Castilian expansionism – is in the last analysis the controlling motor of the *Journal* despite the fact that the enterprise had been initiated and framed within the discursive parameters of Genoese commerce. It is easy for us to see why that had to happen and why therefore, in part, the *Journal* is such a fraught text: the crossing of such a large expanse of unknown ocean could only ever have been accomplished by someone convinced, if for entirely the wrong reasons, that he was going to find land as relatively quickly as Columbus did – quickly, that is, bearing in mind the actual distance of the Asian coastline from the western coast of Europe. Such an achievement could *only* be based on a profound misapprehension of the nature of the enterprise. And yet, while all the evidence suggests that Columbus remained convinced to the end of his life that he had achieved what he set out to achieve, it has been argued here that the *Journal*, unconsciously, is articulated by a quite radically incompatible principle. It would be easy, but meaningless, to talk of Columbus's 'unconscious motives', of an unconscious internalizing of Castilian values:[31] such motives are forever out of reach. Yet the textual analysis finds its support in a strange place. Discursively the Columbian enterprise is seemingly a product of the Genoese dream of an Oriental trade but, although that discourse finally flounders on the 'northerly-inclining' coast of Cuba, the enterprise has, unrevealed to the text, been carrying the seeds of its own destruction within it, literally within it, since what kind of trade with the great and powerful Khan of Cathay could be carried out on the basis of the few chests of baubles kept in the holds of the three ships – 'these brass bells that can't be worth more than a penny'?

The baubles offer themselves for interpretation. As an embodiment of the new economic order of colonialism growing within the husk of medieval commerce. As a sign that Columbus really 'knew' that the Genoese dream was a fantasy. But perhaps they should just be seen as a mark of the growing power of the new European states, leaving Columbus – the 'Columbus' of the *Journal* – as the index of a discursive transformation whose consequences will be traced in the chapters that follow.

8

Columbus's last anchorage of the first voyage was on the northern coast of Hispaniola at a harbour just east of a point still called Las Flechas (The Arrows):

SUNDAY, JANUARY 13TH ... He sent the boat to land at a beautiful beach, in order that they might take *ajes* to eat, and

they found some men with bows and arrows, with whom they
paused to talk, and they bought two bows and many arrows,
and asked one of them to go to speak with the admiral in the
caravel, and he came. The admiral says that he was more ugly
in appearance than any whom he had seen. He had his face all
stained with charcoal, although in all other parts they are
accustomed to paint themselves with various colours; he wore
all his hair long and drawn back and tied behind, and then
gathered in meshes of parrots' feathers, and he was as naked as
the others. The admiral judged that he must be one of the
Caribs who eat men [*que debía ser de los caribes que comen los
hombres*]. (J 146)

This is the first of many descriptions of 'cannibals' that will be
quoted in this book. Modern ethnography is of the opinion that
the man was not a Carib, but rather a Ciguayo Arawak, a small
group separated culturally and linguistically from the Taino
Arawak with whom Columbus had had most contact.[32] But
irrespective of who the native *really* was (and this is one of the
issues considered in the next chapter) what is of most interest is the
process whereby Columbus arrives at his attribution. The man is a
native American but uglier in appearance than the natives already
encountered. 'Ugly in appearance' is glossed in such a way as to
make it clear that what is being referred to is not intrinsic physical
characteristics but rather extrinsic cultural features. From these
alone – charcoal stain and parrots' feathers – Columbus 'judges'
that the native is a man-eating Carib.

The encounter then follows the classic pattern. Columbus asks
about gold, the native points east towards the next island in the
chain, Borinquen (Puerto Rico): 'The Indians told him that in
that land there was much gold, and pointing to the poop of the
caravel, which was very large, said that there were pieces of that
size' (J 146). If one could postulate a direct correlation between
the natives' desire to see the back of the Spaniards and the size of
the gold nuggets to be found on the next island then the Ciguayos
were *very* keen to be left alone. This would be confirmed by the
fact that the first skirmish between Spaniards and Amerindians
followed directly upon this exchange, occasioned (according to
the report received by Columbus, who was not among the
landing party) by a Ciguayo attack on seven Spaniards during a
trading session:

Afterwards the Christians returned to the caravel with their boat, and when the admiral learned of it, he said that on the one hand he was sorry, and on the other hand not, since they would be afraid of the Christians, for without doubt, he says, the people there are, he says, evil-doers, and he believed that they were those from Carib and that they eat men. (*J* 148)

The soldiers of the Grand Khan are no longer even worth a mention. 'Carib' could not exactly be said to *mean* 'anthropophagous' as yet, but it is very clearly a place, and the most prominent characteristic of its inhabitants – indeed the only one worth mentioning at all – is that 'they eat men'. Once again this process takes place in a discursive vacuum at some distance from what it purports to refer to. There is no evidence that these people are 'caribes' or 'canibales' other than Columbus's unsupported supposition; there is no evidence at all that they eat men. Two things have changed. The words 'carib' or 'canibal' are now being used consistently with the ever-present and unqualified gloss 'those who eat men'. And those whom the Spaniards consider as 'caribes' have demonstrated a capacity for resistance.

Gold now lies to the east: to the east are the lands of Carib. What more could Columbus want?: to find gold and to confirm the teratology of Herodotus at one and the same time. On Tuesday 15 January 1493 he seems to hesitate: the island of the 'caribes' is difficult to visit 'because that people is said to eat human flesh' (*J* 150). On Wednesday the nettle is grasped: 'He set out from the gulf . . . to go, as he says, to the island of Carib' (*J* 152). But the wind blew stronger than his determination and the course was set for Spain. The *Journal* is a wonderfully rich and strange text but nothing in it can compete with the final irony that desire and fear, gold and cannibal, are left in monstrous conjunction on an *unvisited* island.

9

Before its rediscovery in 1791 only a handful of people had read Columbus's *Journal*; many thousands however had read the letter, written on the homeward voyage, in which Columbus summarized and simplified the complexities of the longer document. Dated 15 February 1493, the *Letter* was given wide publicity. The original was printed in Barcelona in April 1493, and over the next four years translations were published all over Europe in Latin, French, German, Italian and Catalan.[33]

The *Letter*, addressed in different editions to various high officials although its contents are invariable, stresses the fertility of the Caribbean islands and the tractability of their inhabitants. As would be expected in a document of this kind – which was basically a publicity brochure to attract further investment – the tortuousness of the *Journal* has been ironed out into simple findings. For obvious reasons the emphasis is now on the guilelessness and generosity of the natives of Juana (Cuba) and Hispaniola:

> They refuse nothing that they possess, if it be asked of them; on the contrary, they invite any one to share it and display as much love as if they would give their hearts. They are content with whatever trifle of whatever kind that may be given to them, whether it be of value or valueless. I forbade that they should be given things so worthless as fragments of broken crockery, scraps of broken glass and lace tips, although when they were able to get them, they fancied that they possessed the best jewel in the world.(J 194)

This was especially good news since on Hispaniola 'there are many spices and great mines of gold and of other metals' (J 194).

Possible drawbacks and dangers are not dwelt on but the Caribs do make a late and rather tentative appearance:

> Thus I have found no monsters, nor had a report of any, except in an island 'Carib,' which is the second at the coming into the Indies, and which is inhabited by a people who are regarded in all the islands as very fierce and who eat human flesh. They have many canoes with which they range through all the islands of India and pillage and take whatever they can. They are no more malformed than are the others, except that they have the custom of wearing their hair long like women, and they use bows and arrows of the same cane stems, with a small piece of wood at the end, owing to their lack of iron which they do not possess. They are ferocious among these other people who are cowardly to an excessive degree, but I make no more account of them than of the rest. (J 200)

Columbus's engagement at Las Flechas is not mentioned and there is no trace of the discursive struggle over the signifier 'Carib': the people of 'Carib' are unproblematically the 'monsters' — due to their anthropophagy — that many people, he says, expected that he would find. They correspond to Herodotean expectations and are firmly locked into that grid by the confirmatory evidence of the island of women ('Matinino'), the Amazons of classical ideology.[34] Their ferocity is, in other words, fully containable: 'I make no more account of them than of the rest.' It is via the *Letter*'s condensation of the *Journal*'s complexities that the basic contrast within the native Caribbean population between the guileless and the ferocious enters European consciousness, with the ferocity exemplified by anthropophagy and sutured to the word 'Carib' and its cognates.[35]

Insule Canibalium

Figure 7 Columbus's fleet attacked by cannibals: a fanciful Venetian illustration of cannibalistic ferocity in action.

2

Caribs and Arawaks

At the time of their discovery the West Indian Islands were found to be inhabited by red-skinned people of altogether peculiar character.[1]

1

Columbus's account of his voyage through the Caribbean gives the first chapter to many histories. The theme here is the figure of the native Caribbean within the discourse of European colonialism. That discursive history, internal to European texts, could strictly speaking be written without reference to the historical Caribbean and its inhabitants, but only at the cost of refusing engagement with the most challenging of historiographic and political problems, and only, in addition, by repeating the self-enclosing move typical of the workings of ideology, already in this story startlingly apparent in those concluding moments of Columbus's first sojourn in the Caribbean islands. So, however difficult the exercise, and however tenuous the answers, some questions have here to be faced about the 'historical reality' of the native Caribbean.

The European history of the area consists of four often intertwined strands. There are the 'first-hand' reports of colonists, missionaries and travellers, from Columbus onwards, who have written accounts of the native Caribbean inevitably coloured by their own purposes and predispositions. The lengthiest and most valuable of these accounts are those written by the Dominican and Jesuit missionaries who lived on good terms with the Island Caribs over many years, and whose work has considerable ethnographic value. There are also the many histories of the European nations in the Caribbean which, while sometimes drawing on first-hand accounts, usually rely on the official documents and reports lodged in European archives, where the native cultures tend to exist, at best, in the margins. And then there are the two 'scientific' strands – often in practice overlapping – which share native history: a developing but still relatively small-scale Caribbean archaeology with a terminus of 1492; and an anthropology which, in the virtual absence of contemporary native societies to use for comparative purposes, has had to rely on an interpretation of accounts of the native Caribbean written exclusively by Europeans in its attempt to reconstruct the integument of native society on the eve of conquest. All these works contain valuable empirical material, much of which is made use of here.[2] None the less, in different ways and to different degrees, they are all part of that fabric of colonial discourse that is the *subject* of study here, so there can be no question of considering them the independent and objective accounts they usually present themselves as.

This chapter offers towards a history of the native Caribbean merely the interrogation of these texts of colonial discourse, in other words a continuation of the activity of critique, a reading athwart the articulating acts of colonial power in order to effect an ideological analysis which, at the same time, will open up a different terrain, a different set of historical and political questions. That is the most that can be hoped for. Here, then, is no narrative of colonial encounter, as in the other chapters. Instead the two names, Carib and Arawak, mark an *internal* division within European perception of the native Caribbean, a division variously articulated in all European accounts, from Columbus's first jottings in his log-book to the historical and anthropological works written today. An investigation of that central and pervasive couplet provides the framework for this chapter.

It should, however, be made clear just what topics are being addressed here. Not at issue is the substance of the empirical archaeological, anthropological, and linguistic work that has, especially in recent years, greatly enhanced our understanding of the kinds of native societies that existed in the Caribbean. The question, as so often, is rather one of terminology. The distinction Carib/non-Carib (later Arawak) has from the very first been used as the key to understanding the native Caribbean, a key whose importance is testified to by its use in a wide variety of texts. The implications of the previous chapter were clearly that the entry of the word 'canibal' into European discourse with the meaning 'man-eating savage' was, despite appearances, unsupported by what would legally be accepted as 'evidence', and that the role finally played by that word in Columbus's log-book could best be explained by an internal conflict within that European discourse. Indeed the radical dualism of the European response to the native Caribbean – fierce cannibal and noble savage – has such obvious continuities with the classical Mediterranean paradigm that it is tempting to see the whole intricate web of colonial discourse as weaving itself in its own separate space entirely unaffected by any observation of or interchange with native Caribbean cultures.[3]

But even if some such argument were granted, historical questions would still inevitably remain concerning the nature and extent of the interchange between that pre-existing European discourse, that is Columbus's grid of expectations and preconceptions, and what actually took place during those months in the Caribbean. Must not Columbus have heard something very like the phonemes of the word 'Carib'? Surely, despite the linguistic barriers, the natives of Cuba and Hispaniola conveyed to him their genuine fear of their neighbours to the east? Is the widespread use of the word 'Carib' in northern South America and the Caribbean not evidence that Columbus heard correctly a common and important ethnic term? Questions like this, offering to ground that European discourse in a solid, pre-existent 'real' must be explored, with care.

2

European accounts of the Caribbean, historical or anthropological, always tell the same basic story. In outline it goes like this. The Caribbean islands had been populated first by the gentle agriculturalists Columbus had met on his first voyage, who turn out to have been called Arawaks; and then by the fierce, man-eating and nomadic Caribs, who were renowned for stealing Arawak women, and who over several centuries had chased their enemies up the chain of islands as far as Puerto Rico. The Island

Arawak proved too fragile to resist the adversities of the Spanish presence, falling victim to the twin evils of new virus and enforced slavery, and rapidly died out. However the militant Island Carib defended their islands so ferociously that the Spaniards left them alone and turned their attention to Mexico. There is probably not much truth at all in this story, but its real interest lies in its wording, which maintains a remarkable consistency. This for example is almost all that the standard modern history of the West Indies has to say about the Amerindian population:

> The Arawaks . . . were a kindly and peaceful people. They had no reason to be otherwise . . . . In Columbus's time the Arawaks occupied all the greater islands of the Caribbean; but in the easternmost island, Puerto Rico, they were already suffering from the raids of an intrusive and far more warlike people, to whom the Spaniards gave the name of Caribs. Carib means cannibal; and cannibalism . . . was one of the characteristics of these canoe-borne marauders who were pushing north along line of the lesser Antilles and enslaving or destroying the earlier inhabitants in their way.[4]

Deployed here are many of the characteristic devices of ethnocentric rhetoric, especially the value-laden terminology ('canoe-borne marauders', 'an intrusive and . . . warlike people') and the notions of population movements ('pushing north along the line of', 'in their way') that seem to belong to some nineteenth-century discourse of racial destinies. And we are told that 'Carib' *means* 'cannibal' – a statement that is literally meaningless. Even the revisionist histories of the post-colonial period tend to an unproblematic acceptance of earlier terminology. George Brizan sees Grenada's history as marked by conflict from the very beginning:

> The first conflict arose in the pre-Columbian era (pre-1492) between the relatively peaceful Arawaks and the hostile and warlike Caribs. By the time Columbus arrived, Grenada was firmly under Carib control;[5]

a version that again subsumes the Amerindians into a model of conflictual relationships that probably has very little relevance to pre-1492 history.

The *Handbook of South American Indians*, published in 1946–50 but still the standard anthropological reference book for the area, constantly works in terms of, and therefore buttresses, the conventional dualism:

> The *Carib* relied more upon fishing than agriculture; their villages were only semi-permanent; they had more elaborate canoes; placed greater emphasis upon warfare, choosing their leaders by prowess in fighting rather than by inheritance; lacked elaborate ceremonies; had no worship of idols; and were cannibals . . . . The *Carib*, like the *Arawak*, were South American in origin. According to their traditions, they came into the West Indies no more than a century before the arrival of Columbus; by his time they had succeeded in conquering all the Lesser Antilles and probably also the northeastern part of Trinidad, exterminating the *Arawak* men who formerly lived there and taking their wives as slaves . . . . The *Carib* were more robust than the *Arawak*. They had well-developed, flexible bodies and broad buttocks and shoulders. Their height was medium, the skin olive-coloured, and the hair and eyes black. When at ease they tended to be melancholy; when aroused they became truculent and vindictive.[6]

Some of the anthropological procedures evident in such an account will be examined later in the chapter, but the loaded vocabulary is again worthy of note. To what extent, for example, could societies of this level of organization be said to engage in 'conquering' or 'exterminating'? What might it mean to say that the Carib, *as a whole*, had 'flexible' bodies? And, perhaps most telling of all, what anthropological sense can it make to call the average Carib height 'medium'? What scale is being silently evoked?

What we have, in other words, in texts that claim historical and scientific accuracy, is the elaboration and corroboration of ethnic stereotypes, more powerful for being embedded in contexts which convey a certain amount of historical and ethnographic information – though arguably not in this instance a great deal. As always, the stereotype operates principally through a judicious combination of adjectives which establish characteristics as eternal verities immune from the irrelevancies of historical moment: 'ferocious', 'warlike', 'hostile', 'truculent and vindictive' –

these are present as innate characteristics irrespective of circum-
stance; and of course they 'were' cannibals, locked by the verb
into a realm of 'beingness' that lies beyond question.[7]

This stereotypical dualism has proved stubbornly immune to
all kinds of contradictory evidence. For one thing the terrible
devastation inflicted on the native population of Hispaniola has
tended to reinforce the stereotype of the 'gentle Arawak' despite
the extent of the military struggle that took place there. The
cacique Guarocuya, who was given the name Enrique by his
Franciscan mentors, is only the best-known leader of the native
resistance, so successful that the Spaniards had to let him establish
an independent enclave. Enriquillo was later elevated to the role
of national hero of the Dominican Republic, largely through the
influence of Galván's novel of that title.[8]

The Ciguayo, who made a brief appearance towards the end of
Chapter 1, provide another interesting example. A group of
Amerindians at the Bay of Las Flechas on the north coast of
Hispaniola were, it will be remembered, identified as Carib by
Columbus purely on the basis of their appearance − which he
considered threatening − and of a brief skirmish with a Spanish
landing party. Anthropologists subsequently rejected the Carib
hypothesis but, since the image of the Arawaks was gentle and
peace-loving, a *separate* group − 'the Ciguayo' − had to be
posited, to maintain the purity of the Arawak/Carib division.[9]

The task, then, of the remainder of this chapter must be to find
ways of questioning those hard-held stereotypes, examining how
and why they came into being and have survived, while at the
same time ascertaining what kind of relationship to some notion
of 'historical truth' they might be said to hold; inevitably offering
in the process a rather different interpretation of the 'evidence' on
which such stereotyping is based. Beginning by looking at the
place occupied by the Island Carib within the discourse of South
American anthropology, the analysis will gradually move back to
the sixteenth century to uncover the roots of the relevant
terminological complexities.

3

Perhaps the most striking characteristic of the Island Carib as they
have featured within various anthropological discourses is their

tendency to occupy an anomalous and disquieting position, this despite them being one of the first and most constantly known of native American peoples, at least until the end of the eighteenth century. The *Handbook of South American Indians* divides its material according to the classificatory principle of the 'culture-area': in other words South America is divided geographically into areas which are seen to contain within them a relatively homogeneous culture as compared to that of groups on the other side of the dividing line. The major typological divisions deployed in the *Handbook* are Marginal culture, Tropical Forest culture, Circum-Caribbean culture, and Andean civilization (see Figure 8). One sympathetic commentator noted three aims behind this classification:

> (1) to classify tribes or other culture-carrying units on the basis of certain typical cultural traits; (2) to distinguish broad cultural strata or levels and to indicate the developmental interrelationship of these levels; and (3) to determine, in so far as possible, the concrete historical processes by which these developments have taken place.[10]

Clearly the editor of the *Handbook*, Julian Steward, faced monumental difficulties in ordering the vast amount of ethnographic material provided by some ninety contributors, but it is not clear that the use of one terminology for three very different approaches – typological, developmental and historical – could in the end have been anything but misleading. Typological classification is at best a useful heuristic technique in ethnology that can highlight similarities and differences and can result in the positing of a culture area to concentrate the mind – in another context Kirchhoff's construction of 'Mesoamerica' has proved particularly fruitful.[11] But this can only ever be one moment in a dialectical process since such classifications are almost always arbitrary – unlike, say, those of botany or historical linguistics, where the typologies are also genealogies. At worst the gathering of 'cultural traits' can result in a purely empiricist collection of data.

As typology, the classification could be regarded as adequate for the *Handbook*'s editorial purposes. The difficulties begin when it is made the basis for hypotheses about developmental inter-

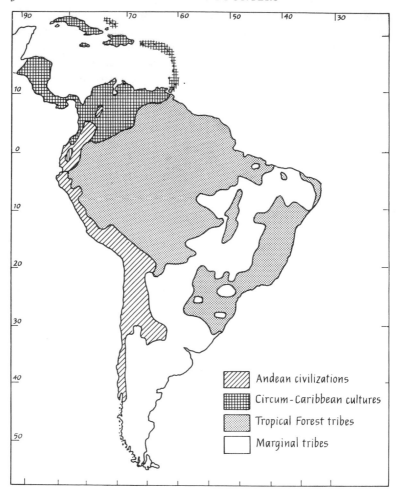

Figure 8 The conventional anthropological classification of Amerindian societies in pre-Columbian South America.

relationships and concrete historical processes. Although the classification claims validity through its scientific objectivity, it carries with it, as the terms 'marginal' and 'civilization' attest, a set of unexamined evolutionary premisses.[12] It is these premisses alone – rather than the examination of any actual historical evidence – that set in motion the four categories and enable the editor to speculate about the historical processes that resulted in their configuration at the beginning of the sixteenth century. Archaeological evidence now contradicts these speculations, but they were always founded on invalid theoretical premisses.

Here as elsewhere it is the Island Carib who best reveal the inconsistencies of the attempted classification. Tropical Forest and Circum-Caribbean are primarily *geographical* culture areas, and clearly the Carib and Arawak of the islands fall into the latter category – or should do. But Steward's collation of geographical culture areas with evolutionary stages – Tropical Forest designating a relatively primitive village-based farming/hunting economy, and Circum-Caribbean a more advanced agricultural mode with a political and religious organization of some complexity – results in the anomaly of the Island Carib being analysed as a typically Tropical Forest 'tribe', despite living in the middle of the Circum-Caribbean area. The implicit suggestion, carried by the overt anomaly and fully in keeping with the moralistic tone of the descriptions looked at earlier ('intrusive', 'marauding', 'exterminating'), is that the Carib are out of their 'proper' place, that they really 'belong' in South America just as they 'belong' to the Tropical Forest classification, and that their presence in the Caribbean is therefore an intrusion. This, after all, is a common colonialist topos, already found in Columbus, whereby one group of natives – who have shown themselves more aggressive – are designated as intruders with respect to a more docile group, the colonizers gallantly and unselfseekingly taking upon themselves the task of protecting the docile by removing the intruders. The anthropological language, no doubt sharpened by the recent fight against expansionism in Europe, carries at least a hint of this topos.

The inherent anomalies of the whole 'culture-area' concept, largely glossed over in discussion of the rest of the subcontinent, are here forced to the surface in order to maintain, and indeed foreground, the Carib/Arawak dualism. That could no doubt be read as evidence of an important ethnological division – which marks two kinds of culture in the native Caribbean – forcing its way through an inherently flawed classificatory system. But it could also be argued that there must be other, ideological, reasons for maintaining that dualism in such flagrant despite of the classificatory system being employed.

4

Culture-area classification, while no longer central to American ethnology, was symptomatic of a division within the anthropological purview that could not be more fundamental to its disciplinary status, and which has particular and important effects for discussion of the native Caribbean.

According to the historians of the concept, definition of the term 'culture' by Edward Tylor in 1871 was the founding gesture of modern anthropology: 'the list of all the items of the general life of a people represents that whole we call its culture.'[13] Or to take a modern textbook definition:

> the term culture refers to a particular set of people in a particular environment who exhibit certain characteristic behaviors with the aid of a particular material culture, and in reference to a particular cultural tradition.[14]

This peculiarly obtuse and resolutely circular definition at least serves to demonstrate the universal *claims* of anthropology: according to such a definition no group of people anywhere in the world could be without culture, a usage of the term that dates from Herder's broad and generous relativism at the end of the eighteenth century.[15]

Under this visionary conception anthropology is, quite simply, as its name proclaims, the study of human kind. In practice it has been rather less than this, as the range of meanings within the term 'culture' clearly demonstrates. Operating in a direct line of descent from Tylor's restatement of the comparative method, culture-area methodology employs a typology drawn up on the basis of shared 'cultural' traits – for example: 'the killing of captives and ceremonial cannibalism; animal sacrifices; medicinal blood-letting; sitting and urn-burial; feminine dress and pederasty among male witch-doctors; the child's cradle; the hereditary chieftancy, and peace and war chiefs' – in other words a conglomeration of material effects, social practices, and political organization very different from anything that Matthew Arnold or F.R. Leavis would recognize as 'culture', those manifestations of art, science and philosophy characteristic of human creativity at its best.[16]

In practice, marked by an ethnocentric evolutionism evident in

Tylor's own work, anthropology has limited itself to study of 'primitive' societies. Some societies, it might be said, 'are cultured' in the humanist sense; other societies 'have cultures' in the anthropological sense. The deployment of anthropology is a mark of culture in the first sense. In 'some societies' there are anthropologists, who study 'other societies'. The situation is complicated, and not without irony. Anthropology studies other societies and is constitutionally sceptical about those societies' interpretations of their own practices – incidentally laying itself open from a radical critique to the charge of ethnocentrism. That scepticism, however, is not permitted to operate on the homelands of anthropology, where 'culture' remains supposedly immune from 'scientific' penetration, the 'anthropological' techniques of sociology, including ideological analysis, being commonly regarded as reductive when exercised on anything more complex than the somewhat 'primitive' habits of the working class.

Put less tendentiously it might be said that anthropology as a discipline is essentially implicated in the colonial encounter out of which it arose.[17] From the founding moment of its American prehistory in Fray Ramón Pané's *Relación*, it has almost always involved written accounts of societies without writing: 'At its core [anthropology] is limited to the disciplines that focus on non-literate man ... archaeology and prehistory ... and ethnography and ethnology.'[18] There can be no *theoretical* justification for this narrowness of focus, so desperately at odds with the universalism elsewhere proclaimed. Such self-limitation is doubtless explained by the discipline's consistent and inevitable involvement with the development of colonial power relationships, which has generally ensured that its focus has been directed outwards from its European and North American bases. Given the paradigmatic status of 'scientific objectivity', especially within recent decades, that self-limitation can also be seen as a bid for 'proper' scientific status.

The ideal, subsumed in Rouse's definition, is the mute subject-matter of archaeology. Next best – moving to ethnography and ethnology – is the non-extant native society fully described by reliable (i.e. western) observers. Also permissible is the extant non-literate society, preferably with a single reliable informant to act as mediator. In all these cases 'native' interpretations are, at

worst, minimal. Little interferes with the clear anthropological
vision of the subject-matter. Writing is kept as much as possible
as the defining characteristic of western culture, the pinnacle of
human achievement, with non-phonetic scripts disparaged, and
non-western scripts, when unavoidably recognized as such, usually seen as beyond the ken of their cultural descendants.
Anthropology has consistently operated this dichotomization:
primitive and civilized, non-literate and literate. It has functioned
to divide the world into two, one part (ours) that can be taken at
its word, the other (not ours) that needs the interpreting voice of
the anthropologist to make it comprehensible (to us).[19]

But perhaps the most interesting term in the 'core' definition of
anthropology is 'prehistory', discussion of which will return us to
the Caribbean. The very notion of prehistory must be regarded as
a self-mutilation entirely of a piece with those already discussed.
Generally speaking it operates a guillotine which severs the non-
literate from history since history is here defined by the presence
of written records. The premiss behind this division is that in
'historical' societies we know what happened because there are
written records that tell us, there is a firm substratum of
incontrovertible 'evidence', while in 'prehistoric' societies there
are no written records and so we need to employ various forms of
expertise to interpret the mute remains that have come down to
us.[20] While writing is undoubtedly a special and generically
distinct kind of evidence, it is not distinguishable in principle
from, say, the lithic remains that archaeology works with: both
are texts that must be read. History is indivisible.

But prehistory is also a moveable feast, of special interest here
because it is always and everywhere ended by the colonial
encounter: the prehistory of the Caribbean ended in 1492; the
prehistory of Peru not until 1530. There is a paradox here,
however, which has always haunted anthropology. The onset of
history produces records: it becomes possible to investigate with a
reassuringly textual basis. Yet the object of the investigation lies
always just the *other* side of that great divide: the prehistoric tribe
before the moment of the colonial encounter, when it was still in
its pure and unadulterated state, entirely different.

What complicates matters is that methodologically that moment of the colonial encounter is indeed crucial, but the crux has
nothing to do with the spurious prehistory/history couplet. The
really important distinction concerns the availability or not of

self-description. This needs a word of explanation. All extant societies are potentially self-descriptive. Most will have narratives in some form (written or oral) that account for their social practices; if not, they can always be asked what they are doing and why. All non-extant literate societies were self-descriptive to the extent that we can read their writing.[21] This does not involve, it should be stressed, taking these self-descriptions as adequate accounts: they are simply further but particularly significant evidence. The significance of the evidence is probably wide-ranging, but its most important role, and certainly the one of most interest here, is its unique ability to answer the question 'who?' – 'who?' being a question that can only properly be addressed to the second person: 'Who are *you*?'; and can only properly be answered in the first person: 'We are ...'. Social anthropology has recently recognized the importance of this kind of statement, and terms it 'ethnic self-ascription'.[22] What matters is not so much the ascription itself, though that can be revealing, but the dimension of the 'we', the perception of where the limits of one's community lie. Methodologically, this distinction is absolute: ethnic self-ascription either is available or not. Certainly in the case of non-literate societies there can be no reading back of self-ascription into pre-encounter evidence, a fact of some relevance in consideration of the native Caribbean.

5

The anthropology of the *Handbook of South American Indians* takes no account of ethnic self-ascription. Naming is taken as self-evident and of no great significance. Nothing is made of the fact that the self-ascribed Yamaná of Tierra del Fuego are called in the ethnographic literature Yahgan, a geographical name bestowed on them by a missionary; or that the self-ascribed Choanik of Chile are now for some forgotten reason called Tehuelche; or that the self-ascribed Che, also in Chile, are now called Araucanian after Ercilla's epic poem *La Araucana* (1568–9), Ercilla having coined the name to refer to the Amerindians of the particular locality of Arauco.[23]

It has probably become obvious by now that there is an extraordinary discrepancy in the anthropological accounts of the native Caribbean. The nomenclature of the *Handbook* – which is still standard – is based on analysis of cultural traits. It may sometimes overlap with a possible self-ascription, but that is never a *raison d'être* for the classification: the sub-Taino of the Bahamian islands were hardly likely to refer to themselves as such. But the historical account given of the area speaks confidently of units ('an intrusive and . . . warlike people', 'by which the *Carib* distinguished themselves')²⁴ clearly acting very like national entities with a sense of common identity and purpose.

Just how misleading anthropological nomenclature can be is illustrated by the case of 'The Ciboney', who merit a section of their own in the *Handbook of South American Indians*. Brief European reports from the time of contact had suggested the existence of non-agricultural and non-Arawakan speaking groups in some coastal areas of Hispaniola and Cuba. There is little documented evidence of their contact with Spanish colonists, although rewards were still being offered for their extermination in the extreme western part of Cuba at the beginning of the seventeenth century. Archaeologists have found and analysed non-ceramic complexes both in these remote coastal areas and underneath ceramic strata in other parts of Hispaniola and Puerto Rico. These have been named for their type-sites.²⁵

Very little is known about the people who occupied these sites, and their culture is defined largely by the absence of traits such as pottery. It is presumed that they were the earliest inhabitants of the Caribbean islands but there is still disagreement as to where they had come from: it is even possible that different groups had migrated from different parts of the mainland. There is no evidence of what any of the groups called themselves, if anything, and no likelihood that the different groups were united by a singular ethnic sense.

The word 'Ciboney' is reported by Las Casas and may have been a disparaging term used by the dominant Arawakan-speaking culture on Hispaniola to refer to one or more of those groups not involved in the agricultural economy: a possible etymology is *siba* (= rock) plus *eyeri* (= man).²⁶ But in 1921 M.R. Harrington, in the interests of anthropological typology, employed the word 'Ciboney' to refer to *all* the non-agricultural groups and pre-ceramic complexes in the Caribbean, thereby foreclosing all the important historical questions through the assumption of a common ethnos ('the Ciboney') that almost certainly never existed.²⁷ To compound matters the materially and politically less complex, but still Arawakan-speaking culture of Jamaica and central Cuba is usually referred to as 'sub-Taino', which is rather like calling the agricultural economy of western Ireland 'sub-English.'[28]

These terminological over-simplications do not just affect the marginal native cultures. In 1955 a retired businessman and amateur archaeologist, Fred Olsen, began a series of digs on the island of Antigua that led him back on a trail to mainland South America, following in reverse direction the development of the Saladoid pottery series (named after a site in the Lower Orinoco) which is commonly associated with the culture of the Island Arawaks. This is an intrinsically valuable archaeological task which, arguably, took Olsen towards one of the heartlands of American history.[29] The problem lies in calling the search *On the Trail of the Arawaks* and in speaking of the Amazonian *origin* of 'the Arawaks' 5000 years ago. Irving Rouse, a professional anthropologist, points this out in his preface to Olsen's book, separating Island-Arawak from Arawak and arguing that neither term should be back-projected into the archaeological record: 'I would have referred to the Saladoid and Barrancoid peoples as "ancestors of the Island-Arawaks", instead of simply calling the two peoples "Arawaks".' He continues:

> This problem can best be approached by an analogy. The present inhabitants of southern Great Britain call themselves 'English', and recognize that their ethnic group, the English people, is the product of a series of migrations from the continent of Europe into the British Isles, beginning with various prehistoric peoples and continuing with the Celts, Angles, Saxons, Vikings, and Normans of protohistoric time. Since the English people is a fusion of all these ethnic groups, one cannot trace that people back further than A.D. 1066, when the Normans, who were the last of the migrants, invaded Britain.[30]

Even leaving aside its rather dubious version of British history, this is not a great help. For a start, 'English' is a self-ascriptive term which has no obvious analogy in the native Caribbean since 'Arawak' – as Rouse is well aware – was a word never used by any Caribbean Amerindians. But in addition the word 'people' can be deeply misleading in that 'people', in the sense of groups of human beings, comes almost inevitably to be confused with 'people' in the familiar modern sense of nations – 'the Germans', 'the French', and therefore 'the Arawaks', or even 'the Saladoid people'. The definite article prescribes an ethnic unit where – in the last two cases – none may have existed.

Some version of 'Carib' was the only ethnic name to appear in Columbus's log-book: he gives no name to the Amerindians he actually meets. 'Arawak' does not appear at all as an ethnic name in the early chronicles. It is first found in 1540 when Fray Gregorio Batela, Bishop of Cartagena, gave his opinion on what should be done to occupy the provinces of Caura, Guiana and the mouth of the Orinoco, and mentions by name the Aruaca Indians (as well as the Caribs). Four or five years later Rodrigo de Navarrete wrote an account of 'the Provinces and Nations of the Aruacos, who inhabit the coast of Tierra-Firme two hundred and more leagues from the island of Margarita'.[31] And it appears as an established ethnic name ('aruacas') in Juan López de Velasco's vast geographical treatise of 1574.[32] According to Daniel Brinton 'aruac' was in fact a contemptuous name meaning 'meal-eaters' (from the importance of manioc to their diet) applied by their neighbours to a group of Indians living between the Corentyn and Pomeroon rivers in Guiana. This group called themselves 'lukkunu' (modern 'lokono') which meant, as so often in these cases, simply 'human beings'.[33] Whatever its origin, 'Arawak' (and its variants) was adopted by the Spaniards and applied to both the self-styled Lokono of the Guianas and to their language; and, as the extent of the related languages came to be appreciated, it was adopted as the family name (Arawakan) of what is now recognized as the most widely spread of all American language families.

The first name given to the language of the Greater Antilles was 'Taino', by Cornelius Rafinesque in 1836.[34] 'Taino' may have meant 'noble' or 'person of importance' in the language spoken in Hispaniola.[35] This name was then adopted by Harrington (in 1921) and Loven (in 1935) to refer to the main culture of these islands, and to their inhabitants.[36] So the term slipped imperceptibly, without anyone taking a conscious decision or showing any awareness of the possible consequences, from the level of linguistics, to that of culture, to that of ethnicity. Meanwhile, however, Brinton had suggested in 1871 that Rafinesque's Taino language had been closely related to the

Arawak language of Guiana. The Taino language was thus placed within the family of Arawakan languages.[37]

So neither Arawak nor Taino were ever, as far as we know, self-ascriptions. We should be clear just what this implies. It does not mean that the natives of the northern Caribbean (or the natives of any particular island) had no self-ascription, or, even without self-ascription, did not consider themselves a community of some sort: it is just that we do not have the one thing (a name used by them) that would count as conclusive evidence.

6

Little has been said so far in this chapter about the term 'Carib' because it has usually seemed – at least to anthropologists – much less of a problem. It was realized in the sixteenth and seventeenth centuries that groups on the mainland called themselves 'Karina' or some version of that name, which was seen as the same word as 'Carib', a perception strengthened by the political links between the different communities.[38] For Europeans the inhabitants of the lesser Antilles *were* Caribs (however little the significance of that verb was thought about) and clearly therefore their language was Carib – a view enshrined in the magnificent dictionaries produced by the French missionary Raymond Breton in the seventeenth century.[39] Modern linguistics did not significantly alter this picture. 'Cariban' ('-an' being the linguistic suffix corresponding to the archaeological '-oid') was adopted as a family name for the related groups of languages that included those spoken by the Karina, amongst them (just) 'Island Carib', a few speakers of which could still be found on Dominica at the beginning of this century. The historically attested hostility between Arawak and Carib could also be supported from the glottochronological record, which posited speakers of a proto-Cariban language spreading out along the South American rivers in much the same way as the proto-Arawakan speakers before them, probably contesting for the best agricultural land.[40] These proto-Cariban speakers were clearly then – so the story went – the ancestors of the Caribs who spilled out on to the islands, presumably exterminating – given their post-1492 absence – the Arawakan-speaking men, and taking their women as wives. It was certainly recorded by all the early witnesses that the women had their own language:

> A peculiar feature of the language of the Lesser Antilles is that Carib was spoken only by the men, while the women spoke Arawak. The reason for this undoubtedly is that the Arawak had been the principal object of Carib raids and that male captives were killed but the women taken as wives. The segregation of the sexes and the slavelike status of these women ... were sufficient to preserve the language differences.[41]

But this account has one significant weakness which should – if its implications are followed – prove quite catastrophic to the whole edifice of early Caribbean history presented in these last paragraphs. And that weakness is that 'Island Carib', the language of the hostile, man-eating, Arawak-hating natives of the Lesser Antilles, is in fact an *Arawakan* language.

How is it, then, that with only one exception all the anthropological linguists that have classified South American languages in the last thirty years have called Island Carib a *Cariban* language, when all specialist studies for at least a hundred years now have concluded that Island Carib is, on the evidence of Breton's dictionary but in contradiction of his title, an *Arawakan* language with a certain number of Carib lexemes?[42]

The problem lies, as we saw in the last section with the word 'Arawak', in terminology overlapping from one discipline to another. 'Carib' is a term used by anthropologists to refer to a widespread ethnolinguistic culture, 'Carib' itself being a self-descriptive term used by many of these groups. These groups then form the core of the widespread language-family of 'Cariban' speakers. For analytic purposes it makes no difference at all what linguists choose to call the languages they study nor, given an equally clear set of procedures, does it matter what anthropologists call the individual groups they set out to classify. But in each case there has grown up haphazardly over the years a conventional nomenclature that overlaps with certain terms used as ethnic self-ascriptions. In the seventeenth and eighteenth centuries the 'Caribbees' of the Lesser Antilles referred to themselves by some version of that name. 'Carib' had been the first ethnic name reported to Europe from the New World. Breton had researched his magnificent Carib/French dictionary on Dominica. The material culture of the island Amerindians was similar to that of the mainland Caribs and there appeared in the seventeenth century to be political ties between the two groups. How then could a group called 'Island Carib' possibly speak anything other than a Cariban language? So once again the Island Carib – here in the shape of their language – proved an uncomfortable anomaly for anthropological discourse, one too unsettling to be confronted.

There never was a separate Cariban language spoken in the Lesser Antilles; the non-Arawakan lexemes were pure Carib, not a related language. The men were, in other words, diglossic rather than bilingual.[43] That purported explanation of the dual language system was in any case self-evidently spurious since segregation of the sexes would ensure that, if there had been two languages, the children would have been brought up speaking the *women*'s language. The Carib lexemes presumably constituted a special jargon, reserved for the men, that might have played a role in the adolescent initiation ceremonies marking the passage from boy to warrior.[44] The presence of the lexemes could be explained by raiding parties from the mainland having settled on the islands; but it is more likely that Kari'na – as that Carib language is now called – was used as a lingua franca for trading and was widely known over the whole area.[45]

So if the Island Carib spoke an Arawakan language, in what sense at all could they be considered 'Carib'? Again care is needed over just how the term is used. Certainly by the sixteenth century the inhabitants of the Lesser Antilles considered themselves as an ethnic unit and called themselves 'Carib'. According to Oviedo, the word at this point meant in the native language 'brave and daring', which perhaps suggests that it had been adopted from Spanish usage as a badge of courage and unity in the war of resistance, since the Spaniards employed it in fear.[46] They may, on the other hand, have called themselves 'Carib' before 1492; but there is no way of knowing. It seems possible that Columbus's *canibal* was the native *kanibna*, meaningful in Arawakan languages but probably not in Cariban.[47] Perhaps therefore 'the Caribs', like 'the Ciboney', was a name endowed on certain alien groups by the Taino, and which might not have corresponded at this stage to any self-perceived ethnicity on the part of those groups. Some of these questions – though ultimately unanswerable – are pursued further in section 9 of this chapter.

7

We have seen how the anthropological stereotypes of Arawak and Carib found their underpinning in European accounts of the native Caribbean and in assumptions about the native languages spoken there. But, although there is no longer any direct ethnographic evidence available from the Caribbean, anthropologists can also point to comparative mainland evidence, where Arawak and Carib sometimes function as ethnic ascriptions in a manner not far removed from the stereotypical picture. The US anthropologist Lee Drummond takes this observation as the starting point for his useful analysis of just what 'being Carib' might signify today in Guyana.[48]

Drummond gives a detailed description of the social structure along the Upper Pomeroon River in Guyana. There are indeed two identifiable types of settlement. One type tends to be close to the Creole villages and schools, and is inhabited by Arawaks; the other tends to be closer to the bush and more self-sufficient, and is inhabited by Caribs. Creole English is the dominant language in both communities, although the indigenous languages may be used in the home. The Arawak claim to be more sophisticated; the Carib are aggressive but shy. The anthropological descriptions are unexceptionable; the interest of Drummond's piece comes when he presses the question: just what does it mean in these circumstances to 'be Arawak' or to 'be Carib'? Where is the *essence* of the distinction between the two communities? He shows quite clearly that it does not come from any rigid social separation: the physical boundary between the two communities is far from sharp. But neither does it come from endogamy: of one hundred births analysed by Drummond for the period 1969–70, nearly half were to couples not perceived as both Arawak or both Carib. In fact it turned out that Randolph, an old man recommended to Drummond by other Caribs as a 'real Carib', was the son of an Arawak father, and that his own son is married to an Arawak woman.

The conclusions Drummond draws are not inherently surprising. Ethnicity is to be viewed as a matter of perception – no doubt a complicated interaction of self-perception and perception by others – rather than of being. There is no way of being *inherently* Carib or Arawak, certainly no genetic pool that guarantees the inheritance of a particular set of characteristics and personality traits. That does not mean to say that the Carib/Arawak distinction is of no significance, but rather that its significance stems from its power as an ideology of tribal identity, no less real in its determination of social and political life in that area.

Particularly interesting though is Drummond's historical perspective. He analyses the Carib/Arawak couplet as primarily a pair of polarized stereotypes which can be traced back to the beginnings of European colonization in the Caribbean:

> The European experience in the Caribbean and the Guianas was ... with one of two kinds of Indians, as different in the colonists' eyes as night and day: the Arawak and the Carib. The Carib were distinguishable as a people by their warlike nature; they, or their ancestors, had pillaged and cannibalized throughout the Lesser Antilles and along the 'Wild Coast' of the Guianas. The Arawak, in contrast, were notable for their 'pacific disposition' .... They submitted to extermination with admirable grace and, where a few survived, settled down peacefully in villages near colonial settlements.[49]

Once established, the stereotype becomes a self-fulfilling prophecy. If the Arawak are perceived as peaceable and likely to settle near a colonial town for the purposes of trade, then any Amerindian settling near a colonial town must 'be an Arawak', QED. And likewise any hostile Amerindian must, by definition, 'be a Carib'.

This is as far as Drummond's own analysis goes. It is not entirely clear just how far back he is prepared to push the notion of stereotype; there is a suggestion in 'the European *experience*', not entirely counteracted by 'in the colonists' eyes', that the origins of the stereotypical couplet are being grounded in a 'real' Carib/Arawak distinction that existed in the fifteenth-century Caribbean. If so, this is an understandable move because surely, one might think, a stereotype cannot simply spring out of nowhere: it must be grounded in some sort of experience, however faulty the perceptions were. This question is closely related to another. In twentieth-century Guyana the ethnic couplet Carib/Arawak is deeply constitutive of Amerindian life, so constitutive that it would be impossible not only for an anthropologist to give an account of Amerindian society but even for Amerindians to make sense of their own lives without using the terms. And yet it could be argued (as Drummond does, implicitly) that the terms themselves are deeply colonialist, predicated upon the norms of white society from which the major ethnic groups of this particular area (Creole, Arawak, Carib) take their difference in a series of negative definitions: Creole from white, Arawak from Creole, Carib from Arawak.[50] If this is true then it demonstrates the quite spectacular success of the process of hegemonization, in which even such a potentially disruptive notion as identity of ethnic origins has been controlled from the centre of political power.[51] But must there not be some point of contact with the distribution of ethnic identities in pre-1492 South America? After all, ethnic identity was not itself a European invention.

These questions return us towards that epistemological boundary constituted by 1492. But surely we do not quite have to run up against that particular brick wall again? Can we not stop just short, within the parameters of European experience rather than ungrounded speculation, in order to ask the more limited question: what was the situation at the moment of contact? What did the ethnic map look like at the time of the first European reports? But this would only be to rephrase the terms of our problem. To begin with, we have already seen in the case of the Caribbean how difficult it is to gather reliable evidence for ethnic ascription, let alone ethnic self-ascription. But, a more radical difficulty, even to speak of 'the moment of contact' is to obscure an important theoretical problem. However fine your pencil, however diplomatic your presence, that line of 'contact' cannot be made to disappear, that observer cannot be posited as invisible and neutral. Strangers can be dealt with in many ways but they cannot be ignored. So no evidence at all is neutral, none can pretend to offer a description of the case before its own arrival. All observed practices may be reactive but we do not even know that, since, because we have by definition nothing to judge them against, there is no criterion for making the distinction between reactive and non-reactive. In a realm of pure knowledge this would be an insuperable problem: ethnography would have to remain an impossible dream. In the world of relative knowledges that we inhabit it is still possible to write about native Caribbean societies as long as one realizes that the object of study is to be redefined as something like 'native Caribbean societies in contact with European colonialism'. This is not just a form of words. It is a necessary shifting of terrain, which opens up a different series of questions, questions not just somehow overlooked on the previous terrain, but structurally invisible.[52] The most important possibility thereby raised is that the ethnic map of the Caribbean area as described (however sketchily) by the early European colonists, was itself the product of that colonial presence. This would imply an interaction, whose strands it would be impossible to separate, between three elements: the ethnic map as it existed just before 1492; the ethnic realignments that may have taken place in response to the European arrival; and the power of European ideology to impose its own 'perception' of that ethnic map on to the Amerindian population. The fact that the first of these three strands is by definition unknowable should not mislead us into thinking that the other two are unproblematically observable. The evidence is far from complete, and not easy to assess.

8

The point of this long digression into historical linguistics and contemporary anthropology is to make it clear that the ethnographic record is considerably less straightforward than might appear to be the case. 'The . . . *Caribes*, a fierce nation of the West Indies, who are recorded to have been *anthropophagi*' (OED) is questionable not just because of the hidden implications of 'who are recorded to have been' – as was suggested in the last chapter – but also because 'the *Caribes*' is a far from self-evident term, implying much more, with regard to ethnic or cultural boundaries, than can feasibly be supported from the evidence. But it was clearly the early Spanish usage that determined the word's subsequent role in European discourse, so it is this stage of the word-history that now needs clarifying.

In the major European languages there is at present a clear

separation in usage between the term cannibalism (and its variants) referring to a particular practice, and the term Carib (and its variants), as substantive and adjective, referring to a member of an ethnographically or linguistically defined group inhabiting parts of north-eastern South America and, formerly, the south-easterly islands of the Caribbean chain. The adoption of non-European words by European languages is an interesting phenomenon. There seems little logic involved in which native Caribbean toponyms gained European currency: Cuba, rather than Columbus's Juana, Jamaica, but not Borinquen which became San Juan de Puerto Rico. Columbus used 'Caniba' to refer to the particular island occupied by the 'canibales' (at that stage unvisited by him) and it survived as a generic name: 'las islas canibales' and later, in English, the Caribbee Islands, the official name throughout the period covered by this book for the islands subsequently called the Windward and Leeward Islands and now generally referred to as the Lesser Antilles. In one sense, then, the 'canibales' were simply those people that inhabited the island called 'Caniba', that name perhaps having no more other 'meaning' than 'France' has in contemporary French. In fact, of course, 'canibales' was never used in the European languages in this relatively neutral way, which is why it is of special interest in this colonial context; nor, equally predictably, was its native meaning – in whatever language – inquired into.[53]

The major slippage, however, was between ethnic name and definitive social behaviour. The classical model acted here as norm. The Anthropophagi were seen as an ethnic group: they lived together in a particular part of the world (though not always the same particular part), and their defining characteristic was that they ate human flesh. Their name – anthro-pophagi – defined them in its Greek transparency, and no further questions needed to be asked. There was no suggestion that they might call themselves by another name or choose, if asked, to highlight other aspects of their social or gastronomic behaviour. These questions were unthinkable within the deeply ethnocentric horizons of classical ethnology/teratology.

The influence of Columbus's *Letter* and, one must assume, of the oral reports of the first voyage that circulated, especially in Seville and its environs, were immediate. Dr Diego Alvarez Chanca, physician of the fleet, wrote the most graphic account of

Columbus's second voyage to the Caribbean in a letter addressed to the Chapter of the city of Seville, probably sent in January 1494. He tells of a ship's boat landing on Guadeloupe, of the native inhabitants of a village running away at the sight of the Spaniards, and of the captain of the boat bringing away (i.e. stealing) a portion of everything he could find:

> he took two parrots, very large and quite different from any we had seen before . . . a great quantity of cotton, both spun and prepared for spinning, and articles of food . . . besides these, he also brought away four or five bones of human arms and legs. On seeing these we suspected that the islands were those of Carib [las de Caribe], which are inhabited by people who eat human flesh.[54]

Obviously in 1493 the word 'caribe/canibal' had no independent or transparent meaning in Spanish. Dr Chanca's letter is probably the first indication that the gloss 'who eat human flesh' would attach itself so persistently to the word that it would, in time, become its meaning in Spanish. The 'evidence', in the Journal at best hearsay, is, if now material, hardly more convincing since burning the flesh off the bones of dead bodies was common mortuary practice throughout the native Caribbean. But the Spaniards were predisposed to be convinced. A few days later one of the parties sent to explore the island disappeared: 'We had already looked upon them as killed and eaten by the people that are called Caribes, for we could not account for their long absence in any other way.'[55] They turned up four days later having got comprehensively lost. Or again, writing about the 'Ciguayos' of northern Hispaniola, with whom some of Columbus's men had had a skirmish towards the end of the first voyage, Peter Martyr says: 'They are fierce and warlike, and it is believed that they descend from the cannibals (canibales), because when they come down from the mountains to the plain to make war on their neighbours they kill some of them and eat them.'[56] So the web of arrogations gradually expands. In Columbus the 'canibales' attack and eat their enemies; in Chanca 'evidence' of anthropophagy is evidence of the presence of 'canibales'; in Peter Martyr the reports of anthropophagy amongst a non-Carib tribe – indeed one that seems to have been under Taino control – mean that they must have 'canibales' as ancestors.[57]

The word's reception into English in the mid-sixteenth century was very similar. Richard Eden's *A Treatise of the New India* (1555), a translation of Sebastian Münster's *Cosmographia*, has as a heading 'Of the people called *Canibales* or *Anthropophagi*, which are accustomed to eate mans fleshe';[58] Othello (1604) speaks of 'the Cannibals, that each other eat' (I.iii.143). As in Spanish the gist of that gloss is unremitting, gradually welding the imputation of anthropophagy to the word 'cannibal' until it really does become its meaning, a process not fully complete in English (on the evidence of the *Oxford English Dictionary*) until 1748 when Anson can write, without gloss, of 'the necessity of turning cannibal'. The endstop of this process comes when it can be asserted as evidence of Carib anthropophagy that 'carib *means* anthropophagous'.

Beyond this lies only the tautology of 'carib means cannibal'. Within the course of these historical steps, though, the general meaning of 'cannibal' as someone who eats human flesh had become separated from 'caribbee' as an ethnic and geographical term, in interesting contrast to Spanish where the term 'canibal' tended to disappear altogether during the sixteenth century, only reappearing in the nineteenth under English and French influence. This might seem to make sense. After all, given Spain's close involvement with the Caribbean in the early sixteenth century, one might expect whichever term prevailed as the ethnic and geographical marker (in this case 'caribe') to become established in the language, while the vaguer and more mythological term was dispersed by the power of empirical experience. Modern attempts to draw an ethnic map of the Caribbean could then be grounded in very early colonial ethnogeography.

Some of the early Spanish examples certainly suggest an ethnic referent. In 1498 Pané, talking of a Tainan invasion myth, has 'Pero ellos pensaron primero que estos habrían de ser los canibales' (But they thought first that these must have been the cannibals), where the definite article appears to be a mark of ethnicity.[59] And in 1503, as the demand for slaves grew acute, Queen Isabella, probably swayed by lurid tales of anthropophagous savages actively propagated by slave traders such as Juan de la Cosa, issued her famous edict authorizing the capture and enslavery of the Canibales, who are clearly envisaged as an ethnos inhabiting certain specified islands ('donde estaba una gente que se dice Canibales').[60]

Obviously at this time, with the word not yet well established in Spanish, the usages fluctuate, and it is not always easy to specify the field of reference implied by any particular example. Gradually, however, as 'caribe' came to replace 'canibal' as the usual form, it becomes clear that ethnicity is no longer connoted by the word. The best evidence for this comes from the fact that its attested antonym, long before Arawak, was the Taino 'guatiao', a word and concept, adopted from native Caribbean social practice, of supreme importance within early colonial discourse. 'Guatiao' is sometimes translated as simply 'friend', but seems to have meant something more like 'compadre', in other words the closest relationship that can be established between two individuals from different communities. Bartolomé de Las Casas, speaking of Juan de Esquivel and the Taino Cotubano has: 'they called one another *guatiao*; this was seen as a close relationship [*parentesco*] and as a bond of perpetual friendship and confederation.'[61] Such a bond usually involved an exchange of names. Chosen from the various ways of dealing with powerful strangers, becoming 'guatiaos' no doubt seemed to the Taino an especially canny way of coping with the potentially dangerous white men. It was swiftly adopted by the Spaniards as being exactly the sort of relationship they wanted with their native hosts, designating those who were prepared – at least initially, but then initially was all that mattered – to give them the necessary support, especially by supplying food.

This usage was officially adopted in the report prepared in 1520 by Rodrigo de Figueroa, who had been asked in 1518 by the new king, Charles V, to investigate just which 'indios' could rightly be called 'caribes' since there had been plentiful evidence, supplied by Las Casas and others, of indiscriminate, and therefore illegal, slaving. Figueroa begins with the southerly Caribbean islands (with certain named exceptions), saying that he must and does declare them 'ser de caribes e gentes bárbaras, enemigos de los cristianos, . . . y tales que comen carne humana', leaving it unclear whether 'caribe' is to be taken as an ethnic name, with what follows (barbarous people, enemies of Christianity, such as eat human flesh) as descriptive of them; or whether 'caribe' is to be understood as itself an adjective *describing* the population, with its meaning glossed by the phrases that follow.[62]

The difficulty is resolved when he moves to the mainland and introduces the term 'guatiao' as the antonym to 'caribe':

going along the coast as far as the gulf of Paria, there is another province which stretches as far as Arruaca, this one being considered as carib [*se tiene por de caribes*]; and beyond this province is Arruaca itself, which I must and do declare as guatiao [*declaro por de guatiaos*] and friends to the Christians.[63]

Each province is declared either 'caribe' or 'guatiao', with the exception of the coast below Unari, which 'at present I declare that I lack the information to determine whether they are carib or guatiao [*si son caribes o guatiaos*]'.[64]

So Figueroa's report is not the careful work of ethnogeography it might appear to be if 'caribe' were read back as the ethnic name it has since become. It is, rather, a work of *realpolitik*, establishing which Amerindians were prepared to accept the Spaniards on the latter's terms, and which were 'hostile', that is to say prepared to defend their territory and way of life.[65] The division was absolute: either 'guatiao' or 'caribe'. Here the adoption of native terms – or what were taken as such – seems to have functioned as a denial of the essential. What the Spanish classification actually revealed was the *response* on the part of the Amerindians to the presence of the Spaniards. The use of Amerindian terms suggested on the contrary that what someone like Figueroa was establishing was precisely an ethnogeography – an empirical reality that was being discovered and, through the adoption of its own names, somehow respected. Nothing could be further from the truth.

So what linguistic morphology is blind to is that while the word 'carib' and its cognates have a continuous history in the European languages from 1493, and a seemingly logical development, it existed at different moments within different linguistic subsystems that, diacritically, gave it different meanings. Even if initially, in the *Journal,* 'canibal' was potentially an ethnographic term, its dominant meaning, by the time the word became established in the Spanish language, was 'those who are hostile and eat human flesh'. If this is indeed the case, then the supposedly unbroken lines and relatively clear terminology of ethnographic history are disrupted and the simplicities of 'Carib' and 'Arawak' shown as concealing a tortuous discursive history deeply implicated in its beginnings with the decimation of the native population of the Caribbean islands and mainland during the first twenty-five years of Spanish presence.

The temptation at this point, having become aware of those discursive complexities, is simply to reverse the colonialist terms and to replace the traditional story with its negative image, a native Caribbean of no divisions and no hostility. But that would be merely another way of falling victim to those colonialist categories, and taking the native Caribbean out of history altogether.[66] Everything that has been said in the last two chapters has urged caution in taking at face value European accounts of what was supposedly the native case at the moment of European contact. This must be true particularly of the accounts of conflict, given the inevitably disruptive presence of the European reporter. What remains, the residue from an ideological analysis of the colonial accounts of the native Caribbean, is *difference*: there was clearly a differential response on the part of the native societies to European presence. Much of this difference can be explained by history: the circumstances did after all change dramatically between late 1492 and, say, mid-1496. This explanation is the one most vigorously obscured by colonialist discourse, as will become clear in the course of the next two chapters. But the differential response must also have been to some extent the result of pre-existing differences within the native Caribbean. Some of this would have been difference in material culture, due perhaps to the chequered migration patterns on to the islands – different groups at different times with different technologies. But there may also have been socio-political difference.

9

During the course of collating the material for the *Handbook of South American Indians* Julian Steward began to recognize the inadequacy of the culture-area typology and suggested a possible reclassification in accordance with patterns 'which integrate the institutions of the sociopolitical unit'.[67] Subsequent analysis by political anthropologists has for the most part used a fairly well-established terminology of band, tribe and state; but it has also adopted – usually under the description 'chiefdom' – the characteristic socio-political formation of the Taino, known originally in Spanish, from the native word, as *cacicazgo*.[68] Although recently extended to analysis of other areas, the features of the chiefdom were originally drawn exclusively from the circum-Caribbean area – circum-Caribbean taken here as a purely geographical term.

The concept of chiefdom offers a political and historical perspective in which to produce a reading of the ethnographic material pertaining to the Caribbean, rather than the usual, determinedly ahistorical, anthropological ideal of the moment of contact snapshot. More concretely, it offers a way of grounding native Caribbean difference without recourse to inappropriate European categories of 'nation', 'war' and 'conquest', and without the need to support that recourse through finding spurious dualisms in the archaeological and linguistic records. Having said that, it should be made clear that what follows is merely a sketch, lacking the detailed backing that it would require to become anything like a full interpretation of the pre-1492 history of the Caribbean.

Baldly stated the key *general* hypothesis in the sketch claims that the origin of the chiefdom is to be explained through coercive incorporation of rival villages following conflict over circumscribed agricultural land. This is Robert Carneiro's account – divested of reference to his particular example of the Andean valleys:

Force, and not enlightened self-interest, is the mechanism by which political evolution has led ... from autonomous villages to the state .... Yet ... while we can identify war as the *mechanism* of state formation, we need also to specify the *conditions* under which it gave rise to the state .... Since autonomous villages are likely to fissure as they grow, as long as land is available for the settlement of splinter communities, these villages undoubtedly split from time to time. Thus, villages tended to increase in number much faster than they grew in size ... until all the readily arable land ... was being farmed .... Even before the land shortage became ... acute ... villages were undoubtedly fighting one another over land .... A village defeated in war ... faced only grim prospects. If it was allowed to remain on its own land, instead of being exterminated or expelled, this concession came only at a price. And the price was political subordination to the victor. This subordination generally entailed at least the payment of a tribute or tax in kind, which the defeated village could only provide by producing more food than it had produced before. But subordination sometimes involved a further loss of autonomy on the part of the defeated village – namely, incorporation into the political unit dominated by the victor. Through the recurrence of warfare of this type, we see arising ... integrated territorial units transcending the village in size and in degree of organization. Political evolution was attaining the level of the chiefdom.[69]

This theory would certainly seem to make sense as far as the establishment of chiefdoms on the Caribbean islands is concerned. The three islands that had chiefdoms at the end of the fifteenth century – Cuba, Hispaniola and Puerto Rico – were those that offered the richest agricultural possibilities, particularly in contrast to the smaller volcanic islands to the south, so there is likely to have been great competition for the land there – and competition would lead to chiefdoms. This change from 'village autonomy' to 'supravillage integration' was, Carneiro argues, 'the really fundamental step', a change in *kind*; anything that might follow, up to the establishment of empires, would be a change in degree.[70] Chiefdoms, then, become a political organization of supreme importance even though they are not themselves states, at least states as classically defined. That step involves a further movement whereby one chiefdom gains control over its neighbours, thus reaching the *third* level of organization: village, region, state.[71]

Interesting from a Marxist point of view is that class distinctions were initiated in the move to chiefdom and therefore, within this terminology, preceded the origin of the state.[72] Carneiro suggests that there was a move directly from a classless society to a society of three classes, since the subordination of neighbouring villages would involve the taking of prisoners to act as servants/slaves by those who had distinguished themselves in the fighting, and to these two classes would be added the intervening third of the original village's non-combatants and less successful fighters. Neither servant nor slave is a very good word for the prisoners since they were probably incorporated relatively quickly into the victorious society, so that there would have been a permeable boundary between the lowest and the 'middle' class.[73] There would clearly be a long period of fluidity in these political and social arrangements but with a constant tendency for the class barriers to become more rigid and for the chief and nobility in particular to become hereditary ranks.

Such a perspective gives a much simpler and in many ways more convincing map of the native Caribbean. If one leaves aside the non-agricultural groups referred to earlier, one can speak in anthropological terms of a single material culture spreading from about twenty centuries ago over the whole of the Caribbean – although it is probably better to consider this in its larger context as geographically *circum*-Caribbean. That culture would vary significantly only according to the determination of environmental factors. The islands may have formed part of an interlocking trade area with Kari'na, a Cariban language, used as a lingua franca on the trade routes. Conflict was endemic in the whole of this area, although it was probably a largely ritualized affair involved with the exchange of women, since the villages are likely to have been endogamous. Conflict presumably intensified under competition for land.[74] So one can reasonably speak of a relatively homogeneous and stable system over a large part of northern South America: there were language differences within the area as a whole (though not significant ones within the Caribbean), but the material culture and the patterns of trade, hostility and marriage showed only *graduated* changes, with no significant cultural boundaries.

The development of chiefdoms altered this position in certain fundamental respects. The economic base was probably not significantly changed, but a socio-political system emerged (with its concomitant ideologies) that divided the Caribbean villages into two: those that were part of a chiefdom and those that were not. The development of chiefdoms disrupted the relatively stable system that had previously existed. For example, what may have been a relatively ordered system of reciprocal exchange of women – even if involving ritual conflict – would have been transformed into the *acquisition* of women by chiefs, both because that was – at one and the same time – a demonstration and perquisite of their prestige, and because a rapid increase in population was the surest way of being able to defend the contested agricultural land. A climate of intense hostility could therefore have been expected, presumably as a transitional phase eventually to be stabilized either by the incorporation of the autonomous villages into existing chiefdoms or, more likely, by the establishment of new chiefdoms and the creation of a balance of power. In time a single native Caribbean state might have been formed.

From this perspective, then, the designation 'Taino' has a certain applicability – though not necessarily ethnic significance – since the emerging upper classes of the chiefdoms had a vested interest in the maintenance of the status quo; but there was clearly considerable jostling still in progress at the time of European contact between the chiefdoms on the larger islands; even if it would tend to be of a different nature from the open hostility between chiefdoms and autonomous villages in the larger islands, and between the chiefdoms of the larger islands and the autonomous villages of the smaller islands. These latter may well have been designated 'Carib' by some or all of the chiefdoms, certainly without there being any self-perceived ethnicity on the part of those designated; and possibly without there being at least initially any perception of common interest at all. The fluidity of the situation in 1492 can probably not be overstressed, but there may have been a pattern to the conflict between chiefdoms and autonomous villages. The chiefdoms would have had larger and more settled villages, made possible by the terrain and fixed by the incipient political structure. They would be more interested in subduing neighbouring autonomous villages or raiding adjacent chiefdoms than organizing long-distance war-parties that might put at risk their internal political order.[75] The autonomous villages on the other hand, while no doubt in some traditional conflict with one another, would recognize that they would have more to gain in raiding the larger and less mobile chiefdoms – who were less likely to retaliate. However, the *size* of these chiefdoms would mean that joint raiding parties would be necessary. There is a double irony here. What was undoubtedly seen by the chiefdoms as the *aggression* of the autonomous villages resulted only from the breakdown of the previous social system – and it was their development into chiefdoms that initiated that breakdown.[76] Meanwhile, the response of the autonomous villages, while no doubt a *reaction* against a new situation they found intolerable, tended, inasmuch as it encouraged joint military operations, to imitate the very process that had brought about the formation of chiefdoms in the first place.

This delicate process was cut short by the arrival of the

Spaniards. By chance their appearance caught the autonomous villages at that moment when they had the maximum amount of military development and flexibility without having yet formed the more rigid socio-political structure that would have made them as vulnerable as it did the chiefdoms of the larger islands – and concomitantly more so the even more stratified societies of Mexico and Peru. The European invasion therefore shattered the socio-political evolution of Caribbean societies, destroying for ever (or, better, taking over and thereby destroying) the established chiefdoms, but moulding the autonomous villages *nolens volens* into a military alliance of tremendous tactical competence and incredible durability – which the European nations had then to fight for nearly 300 years.

10

The last section was a hypothetical sketch to give an idea of what an alternative reading of some of the historical and ethnographic material might look like. But however much credence it might be given, some persistent questions are likely to be considered still unanswered. At the equivalent point in his study of Zande 'cannibalism', Evans-Pritchard, after disposing in magisterial fashion of all the 'evidence' put forward in its support, surrenders meekly with the telling comment 'There's no smoke without fire'.[77] This might hardly be the watchword of the empirical scientist, but the paramount persistent question no doubt remains: were the Caribs – or, as we now have to say, those who for whatever reason came to be called 'Caribs' – really cannibals?

Since the question is unavoidable, it needs a careful response. In that form, of course, it must be refused: given the discursive morphology of the words 'Carib' and 'cannibal' the question is superogatory, the dictionary being proof that the 'Caribs' *are* 'cannibals' – by definition. But the word 'cannibal' must not just be refused: its original deployment itself needs questioning. No other word, except perhaps 'sex', is so fraught with our fears and desires. And yet, while biologists and sociologists have a whole panoply of alternative terms for sex in order to limit the connotations surrounding their references, ethnographers (and dieticians) have only 'anthropophagy', a more neutral word but one little employed. The *Handbook of South American Indians*, for example, refers exclusively (in its index) to 'cannibalism'. Moreover each chapter of the *Handbook* is divided into sections, and the section on 'Culture' is subdivided into 'Subsistence activities; Dwellings; Dress and Adornment; Transportation and Trade; Manufactures; Social and Political Organization; Life Cycle; Warfare; Cannibalism; Esthetic and Recreational Activities; Religion and Shamanism'. Sometimes the discussion of 'cannibalism' is merged into the section on warfare. So even in an anthropological text 'cannibalism' is allowed to retain by implication at least some of what might be considered from a scientific point of view to be its 'popular' connotations of ferocity and violence through its supposed connections with 'warfare'.

But say this argument is accepted; say, in addition, that it is agreed that we are talking not about eating to survive *in extremis*, nor about an occasional mouthful in revenge (both of which can be accepted as rare but not unknown occurrences in many societies), but about a regular practice of eating human flesh, devoid of moralistic or any other overtones. Surely the question would then have to be confronted, if reformulated to read: 'But did the Caribs really, as a matter of custom and practice, eat human flesh?' Then and only then the answer could be given: 'We do not know'; an answer which would further require two different glosses.

There is of course a considerable literature on anthropophagy ranging from the sensationalist to the scientific.[78] But there have only been four sorts of answers given to the question of *why* anthropophagy exists or once existed. The first answer, the one adopted spontaneously by Columbus and rarely questioned during the colonial period, is the explanation through innate characteristics: this has a secular form – 'cannibalism' (never in this answer anthropophagy) as an expression of innate aggression; and a religious form – 'cannibalism' as an expression of innate vice.[79] The second answer, popularized by Hans Staden's narrative of his capture (1557), is the explanation through revenge. This obviously has connections with the aggression thesis but it concentrates on the ritual nature of the torture and consumption of the enemy body in an endless exchange of avenged insults.[80] The third answer again focuses on ritual, but this time the ritual of agricultural societies, which usually has the absorption of familiar bodies (in other words *endo*anthropophagy), perhaps in the form of mortuary ashes, as part of a procedure to guarantee the growth of crops: anthropophagy as 'une façon de penser autant qu'une façon de manger.'[81] This explanation through symbolism is then undercut by the fourth answer, the seemingly materialist assertion that what is involved is nothing more nor less than a necessary consumption of protein.[82]

These arguments have their own fascination and, no doubt, their own symbolic importance within the discipline of anthropology and within western culture generally. What is not clear is that they have any reference to actual social practices at all. In other words, in answering the question 'why?' they have generally neglected to ask the question 'whether?'[83] This, at any rate, is the general thesis advanced in W. Arens's *The Man-Eating Myth* (1979), which argues that there is no reliable evidence for the custom of anthropophagy ever having existed at all. Arens is too careful to claim that anthropophagy has never existed – it is impossible to *disprove* the existence of any practice by direct evidence; but he does cast serious doubt on what is usually taken as proof of anthropophagous practices. The strongest section of the book is devoted to a discussion of *kuru*, the mysterious New Guinea disease, whose investigation of which – including the hypothesis that it was transmitted by anthropophagy – recently gained two US anthropologists a Nobel Prize. Through careful analysis of the extensive literature on *kuru* Arens is able to suggest that anthropophagy was put forward as an explanatory hypothesis for the transmission of the virus for no better reason than that it had always been assumed to be a cultural characteristic of the New Guinea highlanders and was therefore available for matching against, and potentially explaining, their equally characteristic susceptibility to an otherwise mysterious disease. Once put forward, on no solid grounds, the hypothesis could, like any other, find all sorts of circumstantial support until it was on the point of becoming simply taken as fact.

Arens's survey of the general anthropophalogical literature is acute in other respects. He demonstrates how many 'reports' of anthropophagy are in fact repetitions of earlier 'reports' so that the actual sources are relatively scarce. He identifies those symptomatic topoi where cannibals are never quite to be found *in person* or, the one most relevant in this book, where anthropophagy is witnessed in its residue – the remains of the cannibal banquet. And he has pertinent remarks about what could be the heart of the matter – the general European predisposition for finding 'cannibalism' in all non-European parts of the world.

Indeed, simply to answer 'non-proven', even to the reformulated question, is still to acquiesce to the implicit violence of colonialist discourse. The question, to quote one of Pierre Macherey's important, if dense, formulations, is itself the answer to a question that cannot be openly confronted within that discourse.[84] To put it in those terms is to turn the discussion back towards the central theme of this book, the part that notions such as 'cannibalism' have played within the discourse of European colonialism. But before that central theme is resumed some more general speculations will make up a second gloss on the answer.

'Cannibalism' is a topic of endless fascination for our culture. This is easily demonstrated but not so easily explained: there are certainly no sociological investigations of that fascination. One possibility is that the fascination is universal – which would lend credence, one might think, to a psychoanalytical explanation. Freud used the term 'cannibalistic' only in passing, to refer to the oral stage of pregenital sexual organization, though Karl Abraham later distinguished between a pre-ambivalent, primary oral stage, and an ambivalent oral-sadistic stage which is cannibalistic in its desire to incorporate the object.[85] Unfortunately Freud's later speculations in *Totem and Taboo* and *The Future of an Illusion* grounded this psychic ontology in an anthropological phylogeny, giving credence to a supposed 'cannibalistic' stage of human social development, and directing later psychoanalytical investigations towards 'explanations' of the practice of anthropophagy.[86]

Our fascination with 'cannibalism' is certainly ambivalent in a way that ought to be of interest to psychoanalysis. Like incest it marks a forbidden form of behaviour and therefore, predictably, examples of it are deeply intriguing to us. The Andes air crash and its resultant literature supply perhaps the best recent example: there cannot be many people in Europe and America over, say, 25 years of age (in 1986) who would not immediately know what you were referring to if you said 'the Andes air crash'.[87] And yet, despite the objectively horrific circumstances of this and other examples, 'cannibalism' can hardly, it seems, be discussed – or

indeed practised – without laughter. This certainly sets it apart
from incest and from other taboos on the mutilation and
torturing of the human body. It need hardly be said that the
presence of laughter is by no means an indication of triviality. In
the Andean case, laughter was clearly, for the survivors, a
necessary part of the innuring procedure that had to precede the
eating of the flesh of dead companions. *Our* laughter is less easy to
explain. Two forms of that laughter can be distinguished. There
is, on the one hand, a certain bantering tone almost always
adopted in the discussion of 'cannibalism', which in the academic
literature will almost always manifest itself in academics'
favourite form of humour – the pun. Even Mary Douglas, in a
discussion of Pope Paul's 1965 edict about the Eucharist, *Mys-
terium Fidei* – one of the least humorous documents in living
memory – has some modern Catholics finding its arguments
'hard ... to stomach'.[88] On the other hand there is the more
formal category of 'the cannibal joke', beloved of anthropologists.[89] It is not difficult to see the origin of the cannibal joke in
the imperial experience of European countries in the nineteenth
century, and perhaps not difficult to understand it by analogy
with, say, the Irish joke in contemporary British society as a
highly economical way of expressing deep cultural scorn (and
therefore justifying the exercise of political oppression) while
denying even to yourself that the scorn is serious – 'But it's only a
joke'. Freud's work on the psychic mechanisms of this process is
still unequalled, but we are badly in need of a way of understanding even the social mechanisms of origin and transmission of
jokes, let alone the more complex psychocultural processes
involved.[90]

But even if we could understand these processes we would not
necessarily be any closer to understanding the *currency* of cannibal
jokes. Surely they should have reached their apogee at the end of
the nineteenth century during the period when the European
empires were most in need of self-justification? There are a
number of possible answers. Perhaps the most obvious would be
that at the end of the nineteenth century the European empires
felt in no need of self-justification; the cannibal joke therefore
only came into its own during the imperial twilight and after. But
such an explanation would tend to repress unconscious process.
The difficulty here is again a theoretical problem of wide

relevance: the absence of a vocabulary in which to talk about collective subjects. The possibility of writing 'European empires felt' is indicative of how our language has no resistance to endowing collective subjects with inappropriate individual subjectivities. 'Guilt' is a tricky enough concept as it is for psychoanalysis (especially 'unconscious guilt'), without trying to endow a feeling of it to such things as empires, declining or not. A less obvious – and certainly more speculative – answer would attempt to explain our fascination with 'cannibalism' (both horror and laughter) as a late manifestation of the contact between the 'civilized' and the 'primitive'. These are ideological, not historical, categories and as such have a long history, but the very shock of the contact between Europe and America gave the couplet a new lease of life. These days there are few human societies unaffected by the expansion of Europe and its aftermath, yet ideologically the couplet's demise seems capable of almost infinite postponement. There is always at least the rumour of a last 'primitive' society, inevitably cannibalistic, unvisited by camera or notebook and which, when visited, turns out to have renounced cannibalism only recently. Fortunately, just beyond the next hill there is another society, unvisited as yet by anthropologists, and they are still cannibals. Exactly the story Columbus heard nearly 500 years ago. Arens, demonstrating the persistence of this myth, concludes that 'anthropology and anthropophagy ... have had a comfortable and supportive relationship' and that it is possible that 'in their present form one could not exist without the other'.[91] Anthropology is seen, in other words, as merely the institutional manifestation of a more widespread desire for the existence of some touchstone of the absolutely 'other', frequently represented by 'cannibalism'.

Only now, within this particular context, is it possible to undertake the specific task of defining the signified of 'cannibalism', thereby relocating the argument on to the plane of discourse, and reasserting the historical matrix of semantic questions. The point can be made by saying that Arens should, in the quotation in the previous paragraph, have spoken of 'anthropology and *cannibalism*' since what is at issue is not just an idea (of eating human flesh) but rather a particular *manner* of eating human flesh – ferociously – that is denoted in the European languages by the specific term 'cannibalism'. There are weaker forms of this argument such as: ferocious is an important *connotation* of 'cannibalism', or the meaning of a word consists of all its signifieds taken together – and 'bloodthirsty savagery' is listed as a figurative meaning in the *OED*. But the stronger form will be insisted on here: that the meaning of the term 'cannibalism' is 'ferocious consumption of human flesh'. The thrust behind this argument is partly historical: this is the meaning the word *has always had*, even if recent exceptions can be cited. But it results mainly from an insistence that the process of signification never takes place outside specific discursive networks. It is not a question of a discourse employing a particular word whose meaning is already given: *the discourse constitutes signification*. 'Cannibalism' is a term that has no application outside the discourse of European colonialism: it is never available as a 'neutral' word. Confirmation for this argument could be found in the usual absence in discussions of 'cannibalism' of the Christian communion. Even to have 'cannibalism' and 'Christian communion' in the same sentence seems indecorous. Yet of course the Christian communion consists in eating the flesh of man and there should be no difficulty, at least for believers, in calling it an act of cannibalism – if, that is, 'cannibalism' were to be defined simply as the eating of human flesh. The shock of the juxtaposition is salutary, and ought to dispose of any such 'simple' definition; but there are perhaps wider historical implications.

Between the eleventh and the fifteenth centuries there developed what Francis Jennings has called a 'Crusader ideology', a militant Christianity associated with a medieval colonialism that consisted of largely internal expansion, although it also included what in retrospect might be seen as the consolidation of an ideological identity through the testing of Eastern frontiers prior to the adventure of Atlantic exploration.[92] The beginning of the Crusades is conventionally dated from Urban II's address to the council of Clermont-Ferrand (27 November 1095). A symbolic end to that process could be considered Pius II's 1458 identification of Europe with Christendom, an ideal match of the geographic, the political and the religious.[93] Essential to this process – the ideological counterpart of its internal colonialism – was the purging of heretics and pagans from within the body of Christendom: Europe's inner demons, in Norman Cohn's title, hinting at the degree of projection involved in the exercise. An

early marker of this purge would be the first accusation of a
Jewish ritual murder of a Christian (in 1144 at Norwich);[94] the
final acts, of course, the defeat of Granada and the expulsion of the
Jews from Spain in 1492.

Such an account, although abbreviated, is probably not conten-
tious. More speculative would be the suggestion that an important part was played in this process by Innocent III's resolution at
the fourth Lateran Council in 1215 of the long debated nature of
the Eucharistic sacrifice in favour of the most literal interpretation
– the host becoming, upon the priest's words, the actual flesh of
Christ. The partaking of the host was transformed from just one
rite amongst several into the pre-eminent act of communion
whereby Christians could be distinguished from pagans.[95] From
the middle of the thirteenth century to the end of the fifteenth,
Jewish communities were massacred all over Europe and the
massacres frequently followed charges of anthropophagy.[96] The
pattern is important: boundaries of community are often created
by accusing those outside the boundary of the very practice on
which the integrity of that community is founded. This is at one
and the same time both a psychic process – involving repression
and projection – and an ideological process – whereby the success
of the projection confirms the need for the community to defend
itself against the projected threat, thereby closing the circle and
perpetuating it. This is – as the next two chapters will suggest –
the central regulating mechanism of colonial discourse.

More particularly, though, that pattern further specifies the
possible function of 'cannibalism' given the possibility that, as
early as the thirteenth century, 'anthropophagy' was operating as
the 'other' of the still developing concept of 'Europe'. If that idea
can be given any weight, then it would have been extraordinary if
Columbus had *not* returned with tales of man-eating: he may not
have been too sure where he was, but he knew it was not Europe.
So Arens is absolutely right to draw the analogy he does between
witchcraft and 'cannibalism' and to speak of 'the collective mind'
of that era being 'beset by Christian heretics, alien Jews and
American Indians who committed unspeakable crimes involving
the use of human flesh and blood'; but there is no need for him to
speak of 'reasons which can no longer be fully comprehended'.
What was involved was a comprehensive ritual purging of the
body of European Christendom just prior to, and in the first steps

of, the domination of the rest of the world: the forging of a European identity.[97]

So in this perspective, too, 'cannibalism' has nothing to do with social practices at all. The logical step, therefore, is to leave 'anthropophagy' for those who want to talk — for whatever reason — about the eating of human flesh, and reserve 'cannibalism', henceforward cannibalism, as a term meaning, say, 'the image of ferocious consumption of human flesh frequently used to mark the boundary between one community and its others', a term that has gained its entire meaning from within the discourse of European colonialism.

In the native Caribbean context the only interesting question about cannibalism is: could the Taino have used the word 'canibal' with this kind of significance? The importance of this question probably has to lie in its asking, in its implicit recognition that it is a question about ideology, not about dietary practices, since any answer would have to be a gloss on another 'we do not know'. Our ignorance has two areas: whether the *signified* of 'canibal' was 'eater of human flesh' or not; and whether its *reference* was human or mythological. Only 'human eater of human flesh' would allow an affirmative answer.[98]

There is an old argument which sees an analogy between the Caribs and Spaniards as colonists: the Caribs were beginning to colonize the islands but were defeated by the more powerful European colonists against whom they turned their outward thrust, resentful of the Europeans' superior strength. There was never much to be said for this argument at the best of times, so it should not be too surprising if it makes better sense on its head. If there is an analogy to be drawn then it would be between the Spaniards, recent consolidators of the political power and ideological purity of their state, and the Tainos, at the very beginning of the process that might have led them from chiefdom to state. We have little evidence about Taino ideology but it would at least be credible to posit their need for a strong emphasis on ethnic community through clear designation of those who do not belong — the very role anthropophagy was playing for the Europeans at this time. Cannibalism arguably gains a substantial part of its ideological power through its negation of the sacredness of the body *as symbol*. We tend to think of our repulsion as 'natural', an index no doubt of the hold certain symbolizations have for us; but there is nothing unnatural *per se* in eating *human* flesh. It would in fact be more logical to argue against eating flesh altogether, but that argument can only work by reversing the terms and saying that flesh-eating is repulsive *because* natural. The power of the body as symbol may well be universal but there seems little doubt that it really comes into its own when it can inform the analogy with the body *politic*.

It would not be surprising, given that the Taino chiefdoms were still in the early stages of consolidation, if cannibalism formed part of an ethnic ideology concerned with the formation of a Taino identity. And if there is any ground at all to those speculations then the earlier definition of cannibalism can be glossed to the effect that the threat it offers, although figured as the devouring of human flesh, is in fact addressed to the body politic itself.[99] That is the ideological role of cannibalism. If the analogy with Europe can be followed further and the same mechanism of repression and projection posited, we would be left with a series of evolving Taino chiefdoms repressing the conflict at the root of their socio-political structure by projecting on to those outside the structure, those about perhaps to be devoured by it ('incorporated' into it) the violence on which that body politic is inevitably based, the exploitation inseparable from divided societies.[100]

Figure 9 'The Enchanted Island: Before the Cell of Prospero' (1803); engraved from the painting by H. Fuseli. One of the many attempts to represent Caliban's strangeness of form.

3

Prospero and Caliban

O thou mine heir
Of Naples and of Milan, what strange fish
Hath made his meal on thee?
                    (*The Tempest*, II.i.107–9)

1

If Spain's, and therefore Europe's, first contact with America and with the native Caribbean can be dated with satisfyingly dramatic precision, England's own beginning in the New World consisted of a series of stutterings, some of the consequences of which will occupy this chapter and the next. Although the gaining of territory by the European powers in America was in practice purely a matter of opportunism and, where necessary, force, arguments about legality of possession, often turning on the issue of primacy, were still of great importance. Richard Hakluyt, in his unrivalled collection of documents compiled at the end of the sixteenth century, begins his English voyages to America with 'The most ancient Discovery of the West Indies by Madoc the sonne of Owen Gwyneth Prince of North-wales, in the yeere 1170', leaving Columbus – represented of course by his 1488 offer to Henry VII – a distant second.[1] Two thousand two hundred and sixty-one pages of English voyages follow, which, even allowing for Hakluyt's generous definition of 'English', might suggest that England's footing in the New World was firmly established by 1600. This was hardly the case, since the date usually given as marking the first permanent English settlement in America is 1607, the founding of Jamestown. English sailors had, to use

Hakluyt's title, undertaken plenty of 'navigations, voyages, traffiques and discoveries': permanent colonies in America were not visualized until the last quarter of the sixteenth century, with Humphrey Gilbert and Walter Ralegh as the prime movers and John Dee as ideologist, the first man to use the phrase 'The British Empire'. By the end of the 1630s England could be said to have established its American beginning: Virginia was growing tobacco for export on lands expropriated from the Algonquian, and had been joined on the north American mainland by the colonies in Maryland and New England; and against all odds the small islands of the Lesser Antilles, like St Christopher's and Barbados, were beginning to produce significant amounts of sugar – although the real take-off in production was to follow the introduction of black slaves in the early 1640s. But the years on either side of 1600 had been fraught. Several attempts to establish colonies in Newfoundland had been unsuccessful; the first two Virginia colonies had failed, the second, at Roanoke in 1587, simply disappearing off the face of the earth; and Ralegh's Utopian ambitions for Guiana, for many years the main focus of English interest in the New World, had foundered in the fiasco of El Dorado. These failures and successes were obsessively logged in a quite self-conscious effort to create a continuous epic myth of origin for the emerging imperial nation. Samuel Purchas continued Hakluyt's work, collecting together many of the diaries, log-books, letters, anecdotes, maps and histories that could constitute that epic. It is a period of wonderful stories: of Ralegh's discovery of the 'large rich and beautiful' empire of Guiana in 1595; of the loss of the *Olive Branch* in the Caribbee Islands in 1605 and the reappearance of several of its crew in England many years later; of the shipwreck of the *Sea-Venture* in the Bermudas in 1609 and the miraculous survival of its crew and passengers; of the terrible massacre by the Indians of over a third of the English settlers in Virginia in 1622, from which the colony somehow recovered. From this time of disaster and heroism two stories in particular have survived and prospered to such an extent that they have become emblematic of the founding years of English colonialism: Shakespeare's play *The Tempest*, first performed in 1611, where Columbus's 'canibal' makes his anagrammatic appearance, and the story of Pocahontas and John Smith, first told by Smith in 1624, although Pocahontas herself had died on a visit to England eight years earlier. Pocahontas is the subject of the next chapter, Caliban of this, eventually.[2]

2

The Tempest's relationship to the New World is nowadays little disputed, though it must be recognized that the relationship is peripheral, indeed interesting because peripheral. Stoll's dismissal of the claim – 'There is not a word in *The Tempest* about America'[3] – is in one sense perfectly just; it certainly obliges us to clarify the nature of *The Tempest*'s links with this decisive phase of English colonial activity.

Stoll's remark could be made at all because the secondary arguments – in the absence of overt reference – have usually been couched within the terms of a positivist scholarship which has put forward two connected claims: that Shakespeare was acquainted with members of the Virginia Company; and that there are close verbal parallels between parts of *The Tempest* and what have become known as the Bermuda Pamphlets, a series of documents pertaining to the shipwreck of the *Sea-Venture* and the salvation of its crew. Of these pamphlets William Strachey's letter, dated 15 July 1610 and now known as *The True Reportory of the Wracke* is generally reckoned the most likely source for at least the opening scene of *The Tempest*.[4]

The difficulty with these arguments is not so much the quality of the evidence put forward – variable as that might be – but its kind. Shakespeare's biography has its own fascination, but greater knowledge of his life and acquaintance would not inevitably supply us with greater comprehension of the significance of his plays: he could have sailed on the *Sea-Venture* without that making *The Tempest* a play about the New World, so possible acquaintance even with Strachey is, strictly speaking, irrelevant. The 'source' argument has similar weaknesses since there can be no incontrovertible evidence for a 'source'. For one thing, close verbal parallels – even identity of wording – could be explained by a common source, perhaps lost, and there is no way of distinguishing between what stands 'in need of' explanation, and what is simply common coin, part of the language. These difficulties are recognized in the best of the source studies by speaking only of 'probable' and 'possible' sources, a distinction which is to a large degree subjective. So the 'evidence' of source scholarship proves illusory.[5]

Frank Kermode's rather uneasy discussion of these matters in the introduction to the New Arden edition is revealing of the difficulties. When it comes to the story of *The Tempest* Kermode is dismissive of the claims made in favour of Ayrer's *Die Schöne Sidea* or the fourth chapter of Eslava's *Noches de Invierno* or Thomas's *History of Italy* as Shakespeare's sources. Even if Shakespeare could conceivably have known these texts, and there is no evidence that he did, the suggested parallels are, Kermode finds, either too far-fetched, too commonplace, or too irrelevant to be of interest. He is happy enough, though, to accept Ayrer and Eslava as possible analogues of *The Tempest* on the grounds that 'ultimately the source of *The Tempest* is an ancient *motif*, of almost universal occurrence' and therefore there are bound to exist innumerable analogues.[6] The Bermuda Pamphlets are re-cognized as a different kettle of fish, largely, it would seem, on the circumstantial grounds that Shakespeare was more likely to have read them, and on the positivist grounds that only verbal parallels can count as hard evidence. So portions of Strachey's letter are reprinted in an appendix 'and the reader may judge of the verbal parallels for himself'. The assumption behind the recognition of these parallels is that 'Shakespeare has these documents in mind' at the time of writing *The Tempest*. Nevertheless this must clearly remain 'inference' rather than 'fact' and so, while

> the relations of the play to the literature of voyaging remain of the greatest interest and usefulness . . . it is as well to be clear that there is nothing in *The Tempest* fundamental to its structure of ideas which could not have existed had America remained undiscovered.[7]

Kermode's hesitations here tend to show that source criticism, for all its seeming openness to a wider textual realm, operates with such a narrow conception of 'legitimate' comparisons that the importance of the wider intertextual relationships within which *The Tempest* could be viewed is always in the end underplayed.

As a first step out of this morass it must be recognized that source criticism is profoundly misconceived if its ultimate aim is to suggest what was 'in Shakespeare's mind' at the time of writing. All claims based on this premiss are at best circular and at worst totally speculative, given our necessary ignorance of such an inaccessible entity. This, of course, is the 'intentional fallacy' argument, correct as far as it goes, but not to be followed to its anti-historicist cul-de-sac, as in the New Criticism where the internal organization of a literary text becomes the exclusive focus.

The other pincer of the New Critical argument is that even close verbal or narrative parallels are likely to have little relevance to the text as a whole. Kermode takes cognizance of this position in his comments that *Die Schöne Sidea* is too 'naif and buffoonish' to be taken seriously as a source, and that Shakespeare may have known the *History of Italy*, 'but it matters little either way'.[8] It would be difficult to quarrel with these judgements, but it is also important to draw from them the theoretical point that for all its positivist trappings the discussion of sources and analogues is never divorced a priori from an interpretation of the play's significance. Only within a particular reading of the text can other texts be judged as relevant or not.[9]

To counter these antinomies, the moment of production of *The Tempest* needs conceiving within an historical context which is not weighed down by random accumulations of supposed 'sources' or hamstrung by specious speculations concerning 'Shakespeare's mind'. Only then could the colonial implications of the play be properly considered. The critical vocabulary of 'source' and 'analogue' can in fact be replaced from within the body of Shakespearean criticism by the term 'congener' used in James Smith's subtle but little-quoted essay on *The Tempest*.[10] He introduces the term to justify discussion of Eslava's and Strachey's texts as more than mere sources from which, as he puts it, Shakespeare may have taken 'scraps of information'. Congeners can cast light by virtue of their deeper similarities, independently of any putative influence. More recently Charles Frey, in a careful reconsideration of the New World material, rejects the idea of an autotelic text and suggests that the relevant question should concern not what the play's 'sources' were, so much as what 'linguistic and narrative force-field we should bring to the play to disclose its meanings'.[11] The play's discursive milieux can be read, he suggests, without concern for what Shakespeare might or might not have read. The object of study is the common coinage, not a numbered account.

It would be presumptuous to imagine that such a project solved at a stroke any of the abiding problems of textual analysis. 'To disclose its meanings' is a phrase that conceals behind its uneasy plural the suspicion that there might be as many 'meanings' to the text as one chose to bring 'force-fields'. If the meaning is not known in advance, how can the appropriate force-field be chosen? Are these choices not inevitably made by critical readers, and therefore the meanings disclosed theirs rather than the text's? Inasmuch as such pointed questions indicate that a text can never act as guarantor to its own presumed meaning, they cannot be gainsaid: indeed in that sense, as was made clear in the Preface, our histories are inevitably, in Croce's phrase, histories of the present. But it does not follow that critical readings merely *produce* meanings for texts, not least because texts offer constraints and resistances to the readings made of them. Texts will inevitably remain sites of struggle where different and incompatible readings clash.

The method adopted here will be to look at three congeneric texts that tell, in different ways, of 'colonial encounters', the better to specify the links between *The Tempest* and the colonial ventures of the period, thereby contesting some of the deeply ahistorical readings that have been made of this play.

3

As it happens, England's sphere of American interests in 1611 could be defined geographically by the presence of that novel and much-feared natural phenomenon, the hurricane. Like the English, its centre of activity was the Caribbean basin but it could be found as far south as Guiana and as far north as Virginia. Storms were familiar from the Mediterranean and the eastern Atlantic, but hurricanes were different in kind. Not simply more ferocious, their cyclonic form defeated any possible nautical strategy. Sailing ships were absolutely helpless in the grip of a hurricane.[12] Arguably no phenomenon – not even the natives themselves – characterized so well the novelty of the New World for Europeans; and as a result no natural phenomenon was more open to the interpretative skills of the age. Often, of course, the sheer power of the hurricane would evoke man's helplessness in the face of God's will. But there was also the famous hurricane of July 1502 which destroyed the fleet of Columbus's enemy Bobadilla as it sailed away from the harbour of Santo Domingo. Since Columbus had warned Bobadilla of its approach, and since one of only three ships not sunk was carrying Columbus' personal fortune, he was accused of being a magician and of having summoned the hurricane to strike down his enemies.[13]

Novelty in experience is generally perceived in the first place as dangerous – particularly if it tends to sink ships and kill people. Linguistically there are two general strategies available: the novelty can be subsumed under a current signifier in an attempt to domesticate it, or it can be marked as novel – and therefore alien – by being given a new signifier, often one adapted from an alien discourse. The period from 1575 to 1611 was in this sense, in the English language, a period of transition. The Arawakan *hurakan* had readily been adopted into Spanish and had already been used in English by Richard Eden in the forms 'Furacanes' and 'Haurachanas' as early as 1555.[14] The *Oxford English Dictionary* notes five other occurrences prior to 1611: 'Furicanos' in 1587, 'Vracan' in 1588, 'Furicanoes' in 1596, 'Hyrricano' in 1605, and 'Hurricano' in 1606. As with 'cannibal', discussed in the previous chapter, it is impossible to pinpoint the moment when 'hurricane' was adopted into English, but many of these early examples feel the need to gloss the novel word: Hakluyt's 1587 entry, for example, has 'Their stormes . . . the which they call Furicanos'. By 1617 Ralegh could write 'That night . . . a hurlecano fell vppon us' without further explanation, so the word had presumably by then become established, at least in the circles for which Ralegh was writing.

In this transitional period the alien 'hurricane' had to replace its most obvious translation, 'tempest'. In several of the *OED* entries the words are yoked together: for example 'These tempestes of the ayer . . . they call *Furacanes*' (Eden, 1555), and 'Oviedo reporteth of a Huricano or Tempest' (Purchas, 1613). Shakespeare had twice used the word 'hurricane' ('hyrricano' in *King Lear* III.ii.2, and 'hurricano' in *Troilus and Cressida* V.ii.172) so his title *The Tempest* is significantly, rather than just contingently, not *The Hurricane*; and in one of *The Tempest*'s congeners, Strachey's *The True Reportory of the Wracke*, 'tempest' appears consistently despite the quite evident novelty of the meteorological phenomenon that struck the *Sea-Venture*, a possible oddity that will bear further investigation.

In May 1609 five hundred colonists in nine ships set out from

Plymouth for Virginia. On 25 July one of the ships, the *Sea-Venture*, carrying Sir George Somers, the leader of the expedition, and Sir Thomas Gates, who was to be the the new temporary governor of the colony, was separated from the others in a hurricane and driven on to the reefs off the coast of the Bermudas, a small group of uninhabited islands feared for many years by ships that had had to work northward to their latitude, close-hauled to the trade wind, in search of the prevailing westerlies that would take them back across the Atlantic. Consequently the Bermudas were widely referred to as the Islands of the Devil. The other ships reached Virginia and reported the loss, but in fact the crew and passengers of the *Sea-Venture* managed to survive in relative comfort on the Bermudas and built two other ships, the *Patience* and the *Deliverance*, which eventually reached Jamestown in May 1610. In England, news of the loss had been seized upon by critics of the colonial enterprise as a condemnation by Providence, so it was inevitable, when news reached London of the group's survival, that the Virginia Company's officials and supporters would hasten to demonstrate how Providence was in fact on their side. Strachey's account of the storm begins by emphasizing its novelty through the contrast with his Mediterranean experiences:

> Windes and Seas were as mad, as fury and rage could make them; for mine owne part, I had bin in some stormes before, as well upon the coast of Barbary and Algeere, in the Levant, and once more distressfull in the Adriatique gulfe, in a bottome of Candy, so as I may well say. Ego quid sit ater Adriae novi sinus, & quid albus Peccet Iapex. Yet all that I have ever suffered gathered together, might not hold comparison with this.[15]

The terrors of the storm – 'fury added to fury'; the non-stop pumping to keep afloat – 'with tyred bodies, and wasted spirits, three days and foure nights destitute of outward comfort'; the onset of despair – 'it wanted little, but that there had bin a generall determination, to have shut up hatches': all are graphically described the better to heighten the salvation that awaits them.[16] In other words the language of the Bible proved retrospectively capable of comprehending what was only *apparently* a truly novel phenomenon. St Paul's perilous voyage in the Mediterranean had been threatened by what the King James Bible called a 'tempest'

(Acts 27: 18), but one controlled, as Paul knew, by a beneficent deity. Redemption – and the word itself is used by Strachey – was made all the more appropriate an allegorical conclusion to the misadventure by the nature of the islands of the Bermudas. As Strachey puts it:

> such tempests, thunders, and other fearefull objects are seene and heard about them, that they be called commonly, The Devils Ilands, and are feared and avoyded of all sea travellers alive, above any other place in the world. Yet it pleased our mercifull God, to make even this hideous and hated place, both the place of our safetie and meanes of our deliverance.[17]

And, not only did the island turn out not to be fearful, it was, according to another passenger who wrote his own account, 'in truth the richest, healthfullest, and pleasing land . . . and merely natural, as ever man set foot upon'.[18] The conclusion to be drawn from this reading was therefore that God had kept those islands secret from everyone else and protected them by their reputation for tempest and thunder so that they could be bestowed upon the people of England. England was beginning to discover its manifest destiny.

Discursively, it could be said then that the narrative of the *Sea-Venture*'s voyage could be cast within the terms of existing genres: a figural reading of events using mainly biblical terminology proved ideologically satisfactory. To put it in geographical terms, the discourses of the Mediterranean were still adequate for the experience of the Atlantic.

It can well be imagined, but perhaps not proved, that during this transitional phase 'tempest' would tend to be used when the outcome of the narrative could be favourably interpreted, and 'hurricane' when otherwise. If that were the case the transitional phase could be expected to end upon greater acquaintance with the Caribbean islands and their frequent and unpredictable hurricanes. By 1638, the close of the period under consideration in these two chapters, the English had spent fourteen years establishing colonies on some of the smaller Caribbean islands: St Christopher's, Barbados, Nevis, Montserrat and Antigua. Towards the end of that year a pamphlet by John Taylor was published in London entitled 'New and strange News from St *Christophers*, of a tempestuous Spirit, which is called by the

Indians a *Hurri Cano*, which hapneth in many of those Islands of
America, or the *West-Indies*, as it did in August last the 5. 1638'.[19]
John Taylor's news was presumably – although there is no firm
evidence – based on the oral account of a sailor recently returned
from the Caribbee Islands. It is in many ways a naïve text, an early
form of popular journalism, enabling us to see more clearly the
discursive transformations taking place. The title itself gives
various clues. The place occupied in Mediterranean discourse by
the word 'tempest' here needs a considerable circumlocution: 'of a
tempestuous Spirit, which is called by the *Indians* a *Hurri Cano*'.
The biblical discourse is fractured by the irruption of a new and
alien term which is marked as belonging to someone else's
discourse ('called by the *Indians*') and signalled as novel and
strange ('New and strange News'). Why should this have been
necessary? What exactly was no longer adequate about the word
'tempest'?

The obvious answer – and a necessary but not sufficient
explanation – is that by 1638 the English colonists had had
considerably more experience of the devastating nature of hurricanes, which almost every year destroyed houses and crops on at
least one of the islands. But although this extra–discursive
experience was a necessary condition, biblical vocabulary was
only finally displaced because of the discursive difficulty in
allegorizing, except with very unfavourable conclusions, the
destruction of colonists' property. Taylor's pamphlet struggles
with this difficulty.

It opens with the conventional Christian observation, cast in
biblical terms, that God sometimes chooses to punish or restrain
obstinate sinners by terrible events, 'by which meanes *He makes
his wayes to be knowne upon Earth and his saving health among all
Nations*'. The hurricane is God's message, but what does it mean?
The difficulty begins with the last phrase: it is not clear under
what interpretation the devastation wrought by a hurricane could
be said to bring 'saving health' to anyone. The pamphlet
continues:

> And it is to be noted, that where God is least known and
> honoured, there the Devill hath most power and domination.
> But hee that drew light out of darknesse, hath often (and can
> when he wil) draw good out of evill: for through slavery and

bondage many people and Nations that were heathens, and barbarous, have been happily brought to Civility and Christian Liberty.[20]

The argument is considerably less logical than the conjunctions suggest. It becomes clear at some point in the course of those two sentences that the hurricane has been caused by the savagery and barbarity of the native inhabitants, dominated as they are, in the absence of knowledge of God, by the devil. But what is still by no means clear is to whom the 'message' of the hurricane is addressed. Is it to the natives themselves in retribution for their savagery? In which case why is it that the bearers of God's word suffer more severely than the savage natives? Or is it a broad hint to the settlers that the civilizing process should be speeded up? The moment of slippage that enables the text to continue in the face of these difficulties is that movement of 'light out of darknesse'. The gesture is again towards the language of tempest and redemption, the light of salvation that follows the darkness of the storm. But as well as the experience of the colonists suffering from the hurricane (or more properly here 'tempest') and from which 'good' can in the end be expected to come, darkness – the key switchword in all this – is at the same time descriptive of the state of savagery in which the natives live and from which they can be delivered only via a slavery and bondage that will lead them to true liberty. This common seventeenth-century topos of slavery as the necessary stage between savagery and civility is the firm ground that the text's floundering syntax gratefully seizes.[21] After expounding the topos at some length the text eventually circles back to its subject to assert more explicitly the link between barbarity and hurricanes:

> Yet in the latest Dayes of the World all are not civilliz'd; there are yet many Heathens, *Indians*, and barbarous Nations un-converted: as for knowne Examples in *America*, and in divers Islands adjacent, where this *Hurri Cano* is frequent;[22]

So the hurricane now appears to be less a message from God for his chosen people than an attribute of savagery itself. As such it is essentially an alien phenomenon and must be clearly identified by use of the native word. The main interpretative difficulty has thereby been settled: the hurricane is an attribute of native savagery, a fact confirmed by its tendency of attacking precisely what have, in the earlier paragraph, been given as the marks of civility: the building of towns and the practices of tillage and husbandry.

What the explanatory powers of the pamphlet fail to cope with is the information that the Caribs are able to predict when a hurricane is approaching: 'the Indians are so skilfull, that they doe know two or three or foure dayes before hand of the comming of it'.[23] This is clearly just too far from the original premiss of God's messages coming through terrible events, and the text retreats in confusion to the by now much repeated story of the *Sea-Venture*'s deliverance from Bermuda, thereby providing a route back to the comfort of biblical parallels and to the 'strange and fearefull Signes and warnings' that 'are Recorded in our Owne Histories, to have happened in our owne Countrey' and of which Taylor has an account at hand in verse of a 'prodigious Tempest and lamentable Accident at Withycombe, neare *Dartmoores* in *Devonshiere*'.[24] However on St Christopher's itself the logical next step was soon taken and the success of the Caribs' weather forecasts seen as evidence of their counsel with the devil, and therefore grounds for their banishment from the island.[25]

Almost inevitably, Taylor's report of a hurricane in the Caribbee Islands mentions anthropophagy as one of the signs of barbarity, referring in this case to the peoples conquered by Alexander: 'in their Freedomes they did use to kill their aged Parents inhumanely, to eate them with savadge, ravenous, most greedy Gormandizing'.[26] 'Hurricanes' and 'cannibals' in fact have an interesting relationship. Both words came into the European languages via Spanish and were adopted relatively rapidly. Both ultimately displaced words from an established Mediterranean discourse that were clearly thought inadequate to designate phenomena that were alien and hostile to European interests. And as alien and hostile phenomena they tended to be linked through having the same adjectives describe them, a part of that general process whereby the discursive and the economic mirrored one another in the establishment of a central civility (eventually the plantation house) surrounded by a variety of savage phenomena whose individual characteristics were less important than their definition as 'other' than the central civility.

But what is particularly striking about the history of the two words 'hurricane' and 'cannibal' in the European languages is that, having been adopted as new words seemingly to strengthen an ideological discourse, they were both subsequently subject, in almost identical ways, to attempts at what can only be called etymological recuperation. 'Hurricane' still existed in English in a bewildering number of forms until the late seventeenth century. Dr Johnson eventually justified the final form by actually giving it the same etymology as 'hurry', the Gothic *hurra* meaning to move rapidly or violently.[27] But the most interesting of the early English forms, based on an early Spanish variant, is 'furacan' or 'furicano' – a form found as late as 1632 in English. The connotation here is obviously the appropriate one of 'fury/furious'. But by 1726 the Spanish *Diccionario de autoridades* could call the contemporary Spanish 'huracán' – which is phonetically close to the native American form – a corruption of the so-called 'earlier' 'furacán', to which it now gave a Latin root, *ventus furens*: a good example of authority not only erasing its traces but constructing a false trail as well. Similarly, from the 1520s '*canibal*/cannibal' was derived from the Latin *canis* (dog). This derivation, found again in Dr Johnson's dictionary, was current in English until the late nineteenth century. According to Humboldt, Bishop Geraldini of Santo Domingo, who first proposed this etymology, 'recognized in the Cannibals the manners of dogs', although the comparison itself is already implicit in Peter Martyr's first *Decade* where he compares the 'manhuntyng *Canibales*' with lions and tigers.[28] So by the early sixteenth century scientific etymology had supported the evidence of 'empirical observation' that the native cannibals of the West Indies hunted like dogs and treated their victims in the ferocious manner of all predators, tearing them limb from limb in order to consume them. It was clearly only poetic justice that such predators should themselves be the victims of Europe's most ferocious hunting dogs.

4

If the texts of Strachey and Taylor are allowed as benchmarks then *The Tempest* would seem, on almost all possible criteria, closer to the language of *A True Reportory*. The storm in the play is very clearly 'tempest' rather than 'hurricane' in the sense that it is interpretable through the master code of Providence. The relevant trope within the rhetoric of Christian historiography is the *felix culpa*: what seems in the immediate present to be an unmitigated disaster is revealed in the long term to have had its appropriate and necessary place in God's full narrative. The storm that opens the play is only momentarily a natural catastrophe of the kind that Taylor has eventually to designate via an alien discourse: the storm is part of a design and therefore not the disaster it initially appears. Prospero's assurance to Miranda on that score – 'not so much perdition as an hair / Betid to any creature in the vessel' (I.ii.30–1) – echoes that providential biblical paradigm of St Paul's shipwreck on Malta.[29] Subsequently the whole play appears to conform to this pattern. To Miranda's question – 'What foul play had we, that we came from thence? / Or blessed was't we did?' (I.ii.60–1) – Prospero can answer: 'Both, both, my girl' (I.ii.61), the initially foul no longer being so in the long run of Providence, although it will take Alonso five acts to discover this good news. Prospero, it might be said, after beginning the play in distant exile from his rightful dukedom, is finally allowed to live up to his name, rather as The Fortunate Islands of European myth, having been along the way either alien (Islands of the Bermudas) or satanic (The Devils Islands), were finally vindicated in a happy homonym, named for Sir George Somers.[30]

But while a superficial reading of the early parts of Strachey's *True Reportory* might bear witness to the explanatory power of the providential narrative, the letter as a whole reveals some of the strains which that code is under at this period.[31] Providence has already intervened twice, as we saw earlier, saving the ship from sinking and revealing the Bermudas to be happily free of the devilish presence imputed to them. Later in the letter it has even more work to do after Jamestown has actually been abandoned by the desperate colonists. Purchas's marginal note catches the mood: 'The highest pitch & lowest depth of the Colonies miseries scarsly escaping the jawes of devouring desperation'.[32] But before the departing ships could leave the estuary, 'we discovered a long Boate making towards us . . . by which, to our no little joyes, we had intelligence of the honorable my Lord La Warr his arrival'.[33] God did indeed seem to be on their side.

As in *The Tempest*, though, not all the human actors are happy with the plot. In Bermuda there are three separate conspiracies, one of which, led by a Stephen Hopkins, argues on quite sophisticated grounds:

> that it was no breach of honesty, conscience, nor Religion, to decline from the obedience of the Governour, or refuse to goe further, led by his authority (except it so pleased themselves) since the authority ceased when the wracke was committed, and with it, they were all then freed from the government of any man.[34]

Many of the colonists wanted, sensibly enough in the circumstances, to stay where they were rather than go to certain hardship and possible death in Jamestown. There are hints here, perhaps, of Gonzalo's new dispensation ('no name of magistrate;/ . . . /And use of service, none' (II.i.145/7)), and of the conspiracy by the lower orders in *The Tempest*; but there is of course a distinct difference in genre. In *The True Reportory* the conspiracies are real threats to the survival of the company – one man was shot for his recalcitrance; while in *The Tempest* the conspiracy is contained within the comic mode of the sub-plot, although Prospero, strangely, takes it somewhat seriously in a moment to which this chapter will eventually give considerable weight.

The sloth and dissoluteness of the colonists are anything but amusing to Strachey. Arriving in Jamestown:

> we found the Pallisadoes torne downe, the Ports open, the Gates from off the hinges, and emptie houses (which Owners death had taken from them) rent up and burnt, rather then the dwellers would step into the Woods a stones cast off from them, to fetch other fire-wood . . . with many more particularities of their sufferances (brought upon them by their owne disorders the last yeere) then I have heart to expresse.[35]

A True Declaration of Virginia, the official account published in 1610, is even more forthright about their inadequacies:

> every man sharked for his present bootie, but was altogether carelesse of succeeding penurie . . . our mutinous Loyterers would not sow with providence, and therefore they reaped the fruits of too deere bought Repentance . . . . Unto idlenesse,

you may joyne Treasons, wrought by those unhallowed
creatures that forsooke the Colonie, and exposed their desolate
Brethren to extreame miserie.[36]

The list of charges goes on for page after page.

In each text the language of authority plays a key role. *The
True Declaration* bemoans how the violent storm 'separated the
head from the bodie',[37] exiling the Governor on the Bermudas
while the monstrous body wandered headless in Virginia. *The
True Reportory* wonders 'into what a mischiefe and misery had
wee bin given up, had we not had a Governour with his
authority, to have suppressed the same?'[38] Yet unlike *The
Tempest*'s conspirators, who are easily routed and sent off to cool
their ambitions in a cesspit, two of the *Sea-Venture*'s crew avoided
recapture and stayed behind on the Bermudas to become, in later
years, the source of a different account of what had really
happened on the islands, a tale of fundamental disagreements
between the Governor and the Admiral which led to intense
rivalry and bitterness between two quite separate factions, only
hints of which can be found in the story told by Strachey – who
was of course Gates's secretary.[39]

So the Bermuda story, when looked at closely, already tells a
full colonial tale of political intrigue amongst the gentry, of
serious disaffection amongst the lower orders, and of a conspiracy
too deeply rooted to be eradicated: the providential narrative
survives, but we see it here at full stretch even in a writer as skilful
as Strachey. Little wonder that it snapped in the hands of John
Taylor.

5

In many ways Strachey's story – not least because of the strained
attempt to use Providence as a hermeneutic – is reminiscent of a
novel by Defoe, perhaps *The Farther Adventures of Robinson Crusoe*
to which it bears some striking resemblances. Its 'realism' – if the
word be allowed in a loose sense – stands as a useful marker
against which to measure what in conventional terms would be
phrased the 'romance' of *The Tempest*, using that word to indicate
a story whose development and resolution is not seen to depend

upon any attempt to capture a sense of the contingency inherent in a world ungoverned by the rules of art.

For a long time conventional readings of the play worked exclusively within this frame of reference. Generically the play was seen as a pastoral tragicomedy with the themes of nature and art at its centre, fully and confidently Mediterranean, as its title would suggest, a play moving majestically to its reconciliatory climax with hardly a ripple to disturb its surface. Admittedly a numer of different emphases could be encompassed, from the autobiographical *envoi* through the pastoral tale to the full-scale court masque, although Kermode, writing in 1954, rightly deplored the depressing homogeneity of *Tempest* criticism.[40] Nor were these readings necessarily deaf to arguments about the relevance of New World material to *The Tempest*, arguments that had been current since the beginning of the nineteenth century. That material could well find its place within the larger Mediterranean frame as a twelve-year interlude between Prospero's two tenures of the Dukedom (as he sees it) or as part of the field of references to a 'nature' which is subdued by the play's higher 'art', or, in formal terms, as belonging essentially to the sub-plot which echoes in an appropriately minor key the play's major Old World themes. Despite the topography these themes are not, of course, necessarily Italian – in fact in the allegorical readings they are much more likely to be British; but in their concern for legitimacy, civility and humanity, they are quintessentially European. The coping-stone to this critical edifice would then be the play's adherence to the classical unities, underlining its final commitment to the higher order of art.

What underwrote this interpretation was, in the last analysis, always the unquestioned assumption that Prospero was to be identified with the authorial consciousness behind the work, a presence that seemed to guarantee, in a profound and perhaps ultimately religious sense, the deep simplicity of the play. There was impacted here, in this identification, a deeply satisfying condensation of the three terms God, Shakespeare and Prospero, made possible no doubt by the fact that the very idea of Providence is a textual trope rooted in the essentially narrative paradigm of Christianity.[41] In this view Shakespeare's perfect artistry, necessarily demonstrated at its purest in his final work – but which had appropriately been given pride of place in the

Folio, is only comparable to the Christian God's immanent presence in the perfect universe He has created, of which Prospero's invisible and ultimately beneficent control over his world of the island is the dramatic manifestation.

It was a long time before the manifold cracks in this critical edifice were noticed, but over the last quarter century the fabric has shown a distinct tendency to dissolve. Prospero's own 'heroic' qualities have tarnished especially rapidly: his irascibility and manipulativeness have become less tolerable, his treatment of Ariel and Caliban less defensible in an era of decolonization, his psychic anxieties more apparent to well-informed Freudian readings. His newly acquired clay feet have necessarily played havoc with the providential code which had previously franked the generic designation of the play as 'pastoral romance'. The simplicity of the unified Mediterranean reading fractured with the demise of Prospero as its unquestioned transcendental guarantor. What has largely taken its place – especially since George Lamming's pioneering essay of 1960 – is the reading that moves colonialism, and therefore the New World, Atlantic material, to the very centre of the play. The rest of this chapter will explore the links between Prospero's diminished but still imposing 'authority', and the tropes of colonial discourse that are the continuing focus of this volume.[42] Under the pressure of some fine recent criticism and scholarship *The Tempest* has become a much more complex play than it used to be. What will be suggested here is that the key to this complexity lies in gauging the relationship between the Mediterranean and the Atlantic frames of reference within the play, a task made more difficult by the way in which that Atlantic discourse is itself often articulated through a re-inscription of Mediterranean terms.

The topography of the play can stand as an emblem of these complexities, particularly since it has been the subject of such long-standing debate. Predictably, there is a positivist tradition that tries to identify the island setting as Sicily or Malta or Lampedusa or Bermuda. And equally predictably there is an aestheticist tradition which says that the play takes place only in the rarefied latitudes of art and that any attempt to make sense of its geographical references is futile. Both traditions have a kernel of value. *The Tempest* is not a log-book, it need make no particular geographical sense; and to seek to identify the island is to misrecognize the project of the text, to mistake it for a different kind of text altogether. On the other hand, Shakespeare's plays have a wealth of geographical detail, some of it no doubt conventionally symbolic, but some of it not – as in the case, say, of *Othello* where the play's dramatic conflicts are very carefully mapped by the Mediterranean references. *The Tempest's* complexity in this respect can be said to stem from its *dual* topography: the Mediterranean, certainly – Naples, Tunis and Algiers; but also the 'still-vexed Bermoothes'. The latter has been dismissed as simply an exotic touch – distance being presumably immaterial to the immaterial Ariel – but it belongs to a larger pattern of New World terms, including Gonzalo's use of the colonial word 'plantation' – its only occurrence in Shakespeare; the Patagonian god called 'Setebos'; the Algonquian dance seemingly recalled in Ariel's first song; and of course Caliban, metathesis of 'canibal', that first ethnic name noted by Europeans in the New World, and which serves to root those New World references in the Caribbean, that crucible of the early colonial ventures and ground of the historically archetypical meeting of cultures.[43]

Caliban is, according to one recent critic, 'perhaps the most disputed character in the Shakespearean canon':[44] much admired, from Dryden onwards, for the originality of his creation, and yet almost impossible to put convincingly on stage. Morton Luce summed up the exasperation of many critics at 'this supreme puzzle' when he said that:

> if all the suggestions as to Caliban's form and feature and endowments that are thrown out in the play are collected, it will be found that the one half renders the other half impossible.[45]

Caliban is, to give a sample of these descriptions, 'a strange fish!' (II.ii.27); 'Legg'd like a man! and his fins like arms!' (II.ii.34); 'no fish' (II.ii.36); 'some monster of the isle with four legs' (II.ii.66); 'a plain fish' (V.i.266); and a 'mis-shapen knave' (V.i.268). He is also, at different times, a man and not a man according to Miranda's calculations.[46]

Luce's exasperation over Caliban's resistance to visualization reminds him 'of the equally futile attempts to discover his enchanted island',[47] and the parallel is acute, though perhaps less of a dead-end than Luce imagines. The island is the meeting place of the play's topographical dualism, Mediterranean and Atlantic, ground of the mutually incompatible reference systems whose co-presence serves to frustrate any attempt to locate the island on a map. Caliban is similarly the ground of these two discourses. As 'wild man' or 'wodehouse', with an African mother whose pedigree leads back to the *Odyssey*, he is distinctly Mediterranean.[48] And yet, at the same time, he is, as his name suggests, a 'cannibal' as that figure had taken shape in colonial discourse: ugly, devilish, ignorant, gullible and treacherous – according to the Europeans' descriptions of him. Cannibalism itself features only indirectly: Alonso, pondering the fate of his son, asks 'what strange fish / Hath made his meal on thee?' (II.i.108–9), 'a strange fish!' being Trinculo's first description of Caliban (II.ii.27). There is, however, a difference between the two processes. The topographical references are mutually contradictory, but Caliban's characteristics merely overburden him since Atlantic colonial discourse is itself based upon that Herodotean language discussed in the chapter on Columbus's log-book.[49] The play's title page catches this distinction nicely: the mutually contradictory topographies cancel each other out leaving the island 'uninhabited'; Caliban, on the other hand, bears his double inscription: Caliban, savage, deformed, slave – a multiple burden of Atlantic and Mediterranean descriptions.[50] Discursively, it could be said, Caliban is the monster all the characters make him out to be.[51] In a way Caliban, like Frankenstein's monster, carries the secret of his own guilty genesis; not however, like a bourgeois monster, in the pocket of his coat, but rather, like a savage, inscribed upon his body as his physical shape, whose overdetermination baffles the other characters as much as the play's directors. The difficulty in visualizing Caliban cannot be put down to a failure of clarity in the text. Caliban, as a compromise formation, can exist only within discourse: he is fundamentally and essentially beyond the bounds of representation.

Two emblems – one textual, the other geographical – can stand for the relationship between the two frames of reference, Mediterranean and Atlantic. The first is a palimpsest on which there are two texts, an original Mediterranean text with, superimposed upon it, an Atlantic text written entirely in the spaces between the Mediterranean words, the exception being Caliban, who is thereby doubly inscribed, a discursive monster, a compromise formation bearing the imprint of the conflict that has produced him. The second emblem is Leslie Fiedler's when he adapts D.H. Lawrence's terms to talk about the discovery of America as a new magnetic pole compelling a reorientation of traditional axes: the conventional opposition between Europe and Africa, articulated within Mediterranean discourse, is disrupted by the third term of America, an 'other' so radically different that you can no longer bring yourself to respond to its threat by offering it your daughter, however much you imagine it wants you to.[52] So even before considering the fully Atlantic themes of the play – which must centre on the relationship between Prospero and Caliban – there is evidence of a scrambling of traditional reference points within the supposedly familiar terms of the Mediterranean world.

An intrinsic characteristic of *The Tempest* seen as a fully European play was its confident use of classical allusions and analogues, combining, in a manner splendidly congruent with such works as *Arcadia* and *The Faerie Queene*, elements of the pastoral and epic. Behind *The Tempest* stood, in other words, the great Mediterranean epic of Virgil's *Aeneid*, in one reading the ultimate source of the play's causal plot.[53] The difficulties attendant upon such a claim have never revolved around the question of the *presence* of such Virgilian echoes in the play: on the contrary such echoes are, if anything, rather *too* present. In other words, rather than appearing as shadowy outlines beneath the words of the text, satisfactory reminders of generic and ideological continuity, the very question of classical parallels to the dramatic narrative breaks through the surface of the play to become a subject for discussion by the characters, but in a manner so seemingly trivial that many commentators, most notably Pope, have dismissed the passage – near the opening of Act II – as at least impertinent and irrelevant, if not actually an interpolation by irreverent actors:

> *Gonzalo* Methinks our garments are now as fresh as when we
> put them on first in Afric, at the marriage of the King's
> fair daughter Claribel to the King of Tunis.
> *Sebastian* 'Twas a sweet marriage, and we prosper well in our
> return.
> *Adrian* Tunis was never grac'd before with such a paragon to

their Queen.

Gonzalo Not since widow Dido's time.

Antonio Widow! a pox o' that! How came that widow in?
widow Dido!

Sebastian What if he had said 'widower Aeneas' too? Good
Lord, how you take it!

Adrian 'Widow Dido' said you? you make me study of that:
she was of Carthage, not of Tunis.

Gonzalo This Tunis, sir, was Carthage.

Adrian Carthage?

Gonzalo I assure you, Carthage.

Antonio His word is more than the miraculous harp.

Sebastian He hath rais'd the wall, and houses too.

Antonio What impossible matter will he make easy next? . . . .

Gonzalo Sir, we were talking that our garments seem now as
fresh as when we were at Tunis at the marriage of your
daughter, who is now Queen.

Antonio And the rarest that e'er came there.

Sebastian Bate, I beseech you, widow Dido.

Antonio O, widow Dido! ay, widow Dido.

Gonzalo Is not, sir, my doublet as fresh as the first day I wore
it? I mean, in a sort.

Antonio That sort was well fish'd for.

Gonzalo When I wore it at your daughter's marriage?

Alonso You cram these words into mine ears against
The stomach of my sense. Would I had never
Married my daughter there! for, coming thence,
My son is lost, and in my rate, she too,
Who is so far from Italy removed
I ne'er again shall see her . . . .

Sebastian Sir, you may thank yourself for this great loss,
That would not bless our Europe with your daughter,
But rather loose her to an African;

(II.i.66–85, 92–107, 118–22)

Gonzalo plays a key role in this discussion as the character most
eager to tease out the significance of the experiences undergone
by the court party: he is, as it were, both actor and critic, a
combination which allows the play to discuss its own meaning in

an almost Brechtian fashion. He is the scholar who sees a pattern of classical repetition: Claribel, Queen of Tunis, is the new Dido, just as Tunis itself is the new Carthage. The others – especially here the shadowy Adrian, though Antonio and Sebastian soon take up the banter – are the modernists whose world is the new realm of Machiavellian contingency, and to whom such parallels are therefore self-evidently ludicrous. Most critics presume Gonzalo's mistake and pass on, but the matter is more complex than that. 'Tunis was Carthage' is not a self-evidently ridiculous remark since Tunis grew up close to the ruins of Carthage – close enough for those ruins to lie well within the perimeter of the modern city. Arguably the other courtiers' arrogant scepticism – apparently based on little but the presumption of absolute difference between cities with different names, and lacking the historical perspective that might make sense of the relationship between them – betrays far more ignorance than does Gonzalo's assertion of identity. The handful of miles between Carthage and Tunis balances our reading on a knife edge.

Very similarly, the general merriment over Gonzalo's 'widow Dido' is not easy to interpret. Do we see Gonzalo trying to demonstrate his knowledge of Virgil by a casual reference to Dido as paragon Queen, while retaining decorum through invoking her as 'widow' rather than as the lover deserted by Aeneas, a reference better left unspoken so soon after the Tunisian wedding breakfast? Yet if so, the excessive hilarity at the remark would seem to rebound again, since it implies that the others, knowing Dido only in the context of her affair with Aeneas, are ignorant that she was indeed the widow of Sychaeus. The point becomes even stronger if it is remembered that Virgil could imagine the affair at all only by collapsing the 340 years between the fall of Troy and the founding of Carthage, and that Elissa, to give her her Phoenician name, was called Dido in the first place, meaning in Latin *virago*, precisely because of her decision to kill herself rather than marry Iarbas.

Yet if Gonzalo is to some extent vindicated for his remarks in this exchange, his attempts at parallelism backfire disastrously as soon as they are inspected more closely. To recall Carthage is to bring to mind several centuries of punishing wars with Italy, not the happiest of memories when presumably – though this is only implied – Claribel has been a gift to fend off a dangerous new

power in the central Mediterranean. After all Dido, the Carthaginian *virago*, died sooner than marry an *African* king, the fate
that has been imposed upon Claribel to the evident distress of the
whole party, including the father who forced her into the
marriage. Antonio has his own reasons for over-emphasizing the
distance between Naples and Tunis ('Ten leagues beyond man's
life' (II.i.242)), but Alonso also talks of his daughter as 'so far from
Italy removed / I ne'er again shall see her' (II.i.106–7). Since Tunis
is closer to Naples than Milan is, the distance must be predomi-
nantly the cultural one implied in Sebastian's bitter remark that
Ferdinand's presumed demise is the punishment due to Alonso,
'That would not bless our Europe with your daughter, / But
rather loose her to an African' (II.i.119–21), despite her 'loathness'
for the match.

It is perhaps no longer possible – if it ever was – to fully
untangle the skeins of this Mediterranean labyrinth.[54] The
essential point would seem to be that the very boundaries of what
has here been called Mediterranean discourse are no longer
holding firm. The Maghrib, for so long defined within that
discourse in terms of 'moor' and 'barbarian', has gained the power
to shake off the chains that define. Claribel, who haunts the
margins of the play, never present but never forgotten, is a
sacrifice offered to that new power – complementing Othello, the
renegade who proves Europe's weakness by being the only
general strong enough to defend it from its enemies.[55]

The problem is that, once introduced, the parallels and
analogues begin to multiply, breaking down any hierarchy of
comparisons. Aeneas left Carthage for Cumae, which stands in
relation to Naples as Carthage does to Tunis. Carthage (Qart
Hadasht) is Phoenician for 'new city', as is Naples (Neapolis).
There might be suggestions here of the westward course of
empire, the *translatio imperii*, except that all that novelty has
presumably worn thin given the ironic application of the epithet –
'o brave new world' – to the tawdry representatives of the old. So
the Atlantic references by no means stand in obvious counterpoint
or opposition to the Mediterranean register. The 'new' world is
merely one of a series; Gonzalo brings to his ideal plantation some
of the most venerable topoi of classical literature; and, most
disconcerting of all, the new land has an inhabitant who claims
title via the primacy of his mother, an exile from Algiers.

Figure 10 Spanish mastiffs savaging American indians; from Theodore de Bry's *Grands Voyages*. One of the chief ingredients of the Black Legend through which the English distinguished their brand of colonialism from the Spanish. Caliban is hunted by dogs at the end of Act IV of *The Tempest*.

Prospero, having suffered at the hands of a doubling brother who overturned his primacy, finds himself doubled again, this time by a Mediterranean woman who had got there first.[56] Sycorax, the second of the text's three absent women, proves such a posthumous threat to Prospero that she must constantly be vilified. In one of his historical excursuses during the second scene of the play, Prospero presses Sycorax's story on to Ariel: her impregnation by an incubus, her banishment from Algiers, her casting away on the island, the birth of Caliban, her imprisonment of Ariel, her death; a story that Prospero presumably only knows through Ariel in the first place, since he would hardly have heard it in that form from Caliban. Needless to say, Ariel, having spent a dozen years confined in a cloven pine, can hardly be considered an impartial witness in the matter. Once again much is seen to turn on the status of Prospero's words. If he is seen as the very embodiment of authorial consciousness, then to cast doubt on what he says would be out of the question. But in a play where so much of what is crucial has taken place before the curtain rises we are obliged to ask who is telling us what and how they know. Prospero, after all, has good reason to resent the Sycorax he never knew since their respective one-parent families (father–daughter, mother–son) hint at a complementarity that would ruin Prospero's plans for his daugher. The otherwise inevitable concession of Miranda to Caliban is therefore contested discursively: Caliban is 'got by the devil himself' (I.ii.321), 'a born devil, on whose nature / Nurture can never stick' (IV.i.188–9), strenuously distanced from the social world into the satanic and the bestial, despite the grudging admittance of Caliban's humanity in that eminently misreadable double negative:

> Then was this island –
> Save for the son that she did litter here,
> A freckled whelp hag-born – not honour'd with
> A human shape.   (I.ii.281–4)

A statement whose last six words are still quoted on their own as 'evidence' of Caliban's lack of human shape.

Sycorax, like Prospero an exiled magician, is also too close for comfort. She is, of course, a witch with her mischiefs and sorceries, we are told, again by Prospero, while he is a magician with his Art, a distinction much buttressed by critics with their investigations of Neo-Platonic self-discipline, but somewhat undermined by Prospero himself when his role model – as inappropriate as Dido for Claribel – turns out to be Medea, the same Medea canvassed as a prototype for Sycorax:

> I have bedimm'd
> The noontide sun, call'd forth the mutinous winds,
> And 'twixt the green sea and the azur'd vault
> Set roaring war: to the dread rattling thunder
> Have I given fire, and rifted Jove's stout oak
> With his own bolt; the strong-bas'd promontory

Have I made shake, and by the spurs pluck'd up
The pine and cedar: graves at my command
Have wak'd their sleepers, op'd, and let 'em forth
By my so potent Art.   (V.i.41–50)[57]

Kermode gamely makes out a case for only those elements of
Medea's incantation consistent with 'white' magic being taken
over for Prospero, but even he has trouble with 'graves at my
command', the clearest indication that Prospero has taken his role
as 'god o' th' isle' a little too literally for the comfort of religious
orthodoxy.[58]

7

The traditional identification of Prospero with Shakespeare,
though totally spurious, half grasps the crucial point that Prospero, like Shakespeare, is a dramatist and creator of theatrical
effects. The analogies between the play he stages and *The Tempest*
itself are close and important and for long stretches of the middle
three acts the two are almost identical, at least as far as the
audience is concerned, since the outer frame, the play *without* the
play, becomes attenuated. Prospero's play is, at root, a project
whose outcome depends upon his skill at presentation, his
ultimate purpose being to manoeuvre Alonso physically and
psychologically in such a way that the revelation of his son's
seemingly miraculous return from the dead will be so bound up
with Ferdinand's love for Miranda that Alonso will be in no
position to oppose the union that guarantees the security of
Prospero's Milanese dukedom, at least during the remainder of
Prospero's lifetime.

The preparation for that climax involves suspense: the revelation must be delayed until the last possible minute in order to
intensify Alonso's surprise, but also in order to accumulate as
much humiliation as Alonso is thought capable of bearing.
Prospero's plan involves taking at least a substantial bite out of the
cake of revenge as well as keeping it intact so as to bestow a
wholesome forgiveness on the parties who have offended him.[59]
Where Prospero's play differs most from *The Tempest* is that its
audience on stage does not, until the last moment, realize that it is

a play at all. The final scene contains no such surprise for *The Tempest*'s audience: during that scene we simply witness, rather than share, the *anagnorisis* of the court party.

Just how far can Prospero's identification as a playwright be pushed? The minimal argument would presumably be that he simply engineers the initial dispersal of the courtiers and the series of machines and devices, while the characters themselves act absolutely according to their own will and volition, actors who, within certain physical limitations, improvise their own lines and behaviour. This would limit Prospero's role to that of stage-manager. If Prospero were properly playwright, on the other hand, he would have *total* control over the words and deeds of the other characters. This stronger version of the argument can hardly be supported. It would, to begin with, rob the play of any suspense; but there are internal points to be made against it too, such as Antonio's recalcitrance which tends to sour Prospero's last scene and which therefore, if 'playwright', he would presumably have removed.

But seeing Prospero as simply stage-manager underestimates, if not his actual control, then at least the sense we are given of how he wants his play to proceed. In the thwarted attempt on Alonso's life, for example, the court party is put to sleep by Ariel's music, but with Sebastian and Antonio left deliberately awake. That this is no accident is made clear by their comments: '*Seb.*: What a strange drowsiness possesses them! . . . *Ant.*: They fell together all, as by consent' (II.i.194 and 198). Prospero, one might say, gives Antonio and Sebastian the time and the opportunity for conspiracy; they oblige by acting according to type, and are suitably thwarted. Likewise Caliban is, as it were, introduced to Stephano and Trinculo and left to follow the course that Prospero at least foresees, elaborating the conspiracy that Prospero remembers in the strange moment of passion that brings the celebratory masque to such a sudden and confused end. Prospero *remembers*: so the conspiracy is no surprise to him and, even if he has been monitoring its progress off-stage (suggested by IV.i.171), the fact that he has not bothered to immobilize the conspirators indicates that he desires the conspiracy to run its course. Clearly it is an essential element in his play – and 'the minute of their plot / Is almost come' (IV.i.141–2) draws neatly from the registers of both conspiracy and the theatre – yet it is an element that, paradoxically, he almost manages to forget.

Giving full weight to the notion of Prospero's play within the play would also allow the recuperation of at least some earlier *Tempest* criticism, which makes perfect sense if read as referring to Prospero's play alone, rather than to *The Tempest* as a whole. The dramatic structure of *The Tempest* has always looked too straightforward to merit much detailed analysis, yet the five-act division, if accepted as original, appears a somewhat arbitrary arrangement of the play's materials, so much so that Kermode, for one, discerns a 'neo-Terentian' (i.e. four-part) division underpinning the action.[60] In fact when, towards the climax of the *epitasis* – the central complicating movement of the play – Prospero shows what Kermode calls 'apparently unnecessary perturbation . . . at the thought of Caliban', Kermode suggests that this must be explained through 'an oddly pedantic concern for classical structure' causing it 'to force its way through the surface of the play'.[61] Odd indeed, given Shakespeare's supposed life-long disregard of such neo-classical prescriptions.

A better starting point would be the observation that the structure of the play must be dual: *The Tempest* has a structure, perhaps even a four-part one, but so does Prospero's play within the play, which is considerably more formal and highly-wrought than *The Tempest* itself. Generically, in fact, Prospero's play is closest to a court masque of the elaborate Jacobean kind, a fitting form for Prospero to celebrate his reaccession to his rightful dukedom, with its contrast, proper to such ornamental state occasions, between order and disorder, between a stable society subject to a God-like monarch and an anarchic world of brutality and folly. The emphasis of the masque is on device and display, culminating in a spectacular sequence of events: the anti-masque of the disappearing banquet, the magnificent betrothal celebrations, the 'theophany' of Prospero's delayed appearance before his enemies, and the final moment of revelation which discovers Ferdinand and Miranda playing chess.[62] Such a form, in the words of Enid Welsford, 'expresses, not uncertainty, ended by final success or failure, but expectancy crowned by sudden revelation'.[63] Of course only Prospero, the masque presenter and inductor, and Ariel, the assistant producer, are in a position to appreciate the full significance of this spectacle of state since the various 'actors' and 'spectators' on stage are unaware of their participation within Prospero's play. All in all the masque is distinctly Pirandellian. The dramatic analogy could be pressed

further to suggest that the point of Prospero's elaborate deceit is
to confuse Alonso as to the genre of his experiences on the island.
He must – if Prospero's plans are to succeed – believe himself to
be living a 'tragedy' which in the climactic *anagnorisis* turns into a
'comedy', its true status as masque being prudently reserved by
Prospero for later revelation (V.i.303–5). *The Tempest contains*
Prospero's masque but it is in no sense identical to or coterminous
with it, as the dramatic structure reveals. The discovery of
Ferdinand and Miranda is a fine and complex moment: we
witness the amazement of the court party as they recognize
Ferdinand, and we see Prospero's satisfaction at the triumphant
climax of his masque as he also witnesses their amazement. But
the revelation of Ferdinand and Miranda is no peripeteia for us
since we have been privy to all the preparations.

The simplest way of stating the difference between Prospero's
play and *The Tempest* would then be to say that *The Tempest*
stages Prospero's staging of his play: only during the first scene are
we unaware that everything happening on stage is in some sense
under Prospero's control. So as well as watching the enactment of
the masque, we also hear his reasons for staging it, see his
preparation of the theatrical machines that will produce it, witness
him watching that production from the wings, and observe the
constantly changing audience on stage. This audience is probably
the key to the distinction, yet it is a distinction that nearly
disappears from view if we choose – as many critics have done –
to view simply the performance on stage, rather than *that
performance as attended by its audience*. Support for this surmise
comes when, at the height of the betrothal celebrations (the most
spectacular moment of both plays and when we are therefore
most likely to be oblivious to the distinction between them) the
machinery of the masque grinds to a halt. The Nymphs and
Reapers, a moment ago in the middle of a graceful dance, heavily
vanish to a strange, hollow and confused noise, and we are
forcefully reminded of the spectators on stage (at this juncture
Ferdinand and Miranda) by hearing them comment on the
breakdown in transmission: a moment of 'recognition' – that
there is a play within the play – likely to constitute a true
peripeteia for *The Tempest*'s audience. It is Ferdinand who speaks
for the audience: 'This is strange: your father's in some passion /
That works him strongly' (IV.i.143–4), to which Prospero's

immediate response is a clever *tu quoque*: 'You do look, my son, in a mov'd sort, / As if you were dismay'd' (IV.i.146–7), thereby allowing him the 'revels' speech to regain his composure and to assume the guise of military officer ordering his troops ('*Pros*.: We must prepare to meet with Caliban / *Ari*.: Ay, my commander' (IV.i.166–7)). The text strikes a delicate balance here: our surprise at Prospero's disturbance is recent enough for our perspective still to be sufficiently askew from Prospero's to note the ludicrousness of elaborate preparations to deal with a woefully inadequate force who could be immobilized on the spot. On the other hand, our disturbance has been soothed, not to say anaesthetized, along with Ferdinand's, by the most beautiful poetry in the play, as Prospero tries to explain away his disturbance by insisting that the revels are properly concluded, just as everything comes to an end, even life itself – in the context of Prospero's play a brilliant piece of improvisation to cover a necessary change of scene and hustle Ferdinand and Miranda out of the way.

The improvisation is only necessary because of Prospero's sudden remembering of Caliban's conspiracy, the one moment in the play when his plans run less than smoothly. His perturbation has proved understandably perplexing. After all, politically, the conspiracy has no role to play whatsoever: strictly speaking, Alonso and Ferdinand are the objects towards whom Prospero's skill is directed – his ends can still be reached irrespective of Antonio's response, which is of course just as well. The conspirators are supplementary, a sub-plot in Prospero's play, and therefore 'understandably' forgettable in the celebration of his own power which is to precede the final dénouement – 'some vanity of mine Art' (IV.i.41) may be self-deprecatory, but it is none the less true: the celebratory masque is in one sense a vain demonstration of power, purely the 'corollary' that Prospero himself calls it. He is guilty of celebrating before the story is over, and suffers for his presumption. But why is the 'supplementary' conspiracy there in the first place? And why, above all, is 'the strangeness of the disturbance ... strangely insisted on',[64] Prospero being in such a passion that Miranda can say: 'Never till this day / Saw I him touch'd with anger, so distemper'd' (IV.i.144–5)?

Prospero's play is in fact a subtle instrument of revenge and Caliban occupies a crucial role in it, though this is a fact kept hidden from Caliban for as long as possible: he, like the other 'actors', is not aware that he is in a play at all, let alone aware of the nature of his part. What might seem initially odd, though, is that whilst Caliban is the pivot around which the discursive axes of the play turn, and whilst his conspiracy clearly troubles Prospero, *dramatically* its importance appears undermotivated: Caliban is after all a mere slave of Prospero's, powerless against his magic, and incapable of mounting a serious coup. So, if the seemingly trifling sub-plot of Prospero's play causes such distress when its moment comes, it has to be because it is not trifling at all but, on the contrary, the very nub of the matter, representable at all by Prospero only in the 'differently-centred' production staged by his desire.

8

In its own terms Prospero's play is undoubtedly a success: it achieves what he wants it to achieve. Yet in always showing us more than this elaborate masquerade *The Tempest* leaves room for other questions to emerge. The most crucial of these questions concerns the relationship between Prospero's sub-plot and the main plot of his masque. The function of the masque is clear and its procedure, though complicated by the court party's dual role as actors and spectators, easily comprehensible given Prospero's initial premisses. From the perspective of Prospero's main plot the conspiracy is of minor importance. It merely echoes in a lower and more comic key the confusions of the noble Italians, but the two plots are not in any way dramatically interwoven: the courtiers have no glimpse of Caliban until less than a hundred lines before the end of the play, when Prospero ostentatiously completes *his* play by revealing how he has foiled the plot against his life. Of the principals only Prospero, then, is in the position of the ideal spectator able to view the progress of the respective plots. The masque *as a whole* is for his eyes only.

His dramatic construction makes it clear that the conspiracy is to take the subsidiary part in the production: in accordance with neo-classical criteria its action begins later and ends earlier than the main plot. This undoubtedly suits Prospero's purposes and corresponds to his perception of the conventions of the masque, where disorder is well and truly routed. But this is not necessarily our view of the conspiracy.

We are in a position, for example, to see how Prospero's drama is in essence a series of repetitions. The courtiers must repeat Prospero's primary suffering: the distress at sea, the absence of food, and the powerlessness in a hostile environment. Prospero takes pleasure in their suffering and then, when the moment is right, brings the suffering to an end in order to obtain his final purpose. The last move in Prospero's psychological manoeuvring of Alonso is especially acute or, to put it another way, little short of psychopathic, showing Prospero's obsessive observance of the patterns of repetition. Alonso's genuine distress at the supposed loss of his son – the key element in Prospero's plan – has to be matched by Prospero's cruelly factitious grief for 'the like loss . . . for I have lost my daughter . . . in this last tempest' (V.i.143, 147–8, 153), a shrewd blow which associates the two children in Alonso's mind and has him wishing them King and Queen of Naples, just as Prospero desires – thereby, of course, plumbing unwittingly Prospero's cleverly figurative meaning of 'losing' his daughter.

But the repetition does not stop there: it must be completed in the sub-plot by a controlled repetition of the primary trauma. Prospero stages a fantasized version of the original conspiracy with the difference that, this time, he will defeat it.[65] Caliban must re-enact Antonio's usurpation, enabling Prospero to take a part in his own play. But, whereas the other 'actors' have to remain ignorant of the play's fictiveness, Prospero can indeed act – in both senses – in stark contrast to his earlier state of passive unpreparedness. Twelve years ago, 'rapt in secret studies', Prospero had been helpless before Antonio's determination to close the gap between – the words are Prospero's – 'this part he play'd', as acting Duke, and the reality behind the role, 'Absolute Milan' (I.ii.107–9). This time it is Prospero who can 'play the part' of ruler under threat from disloyal subject, this time discover the plot before it comes to fruition, and this time triumph over it. The repetition cancels out the original, the twelve years are as nothing, and Prospero has created for himself a second chance. The pleasures of total revenge can be so easily forsworn because revenge presupposes an original insult and it is Prospero's intent to wipe the very record of that insult from his consciousness: 'Let

us not burthen our remembrance with / A heaviness that's gone'
(V.i.199–200).

The sub-plot, far from being the mere echo of his main plot
that Prospero's dramatic ordering would have us believe, is
therefore the enactment of a repression which takes from
Prospero's consciousness the memory of his usurpation by
Antonio, so that Prospero can resume his position – at least his
fantasized position – as much-loved Duke of Milan, untroubled
by a record of negligence. Alongside the public performance of
the masque runs this private psychodrama, this 'other scene'
whose importance Prospero keeps to himself. The terms of the
settlement make it clear, however, that the victory thereby
achieved is indeed primarily psychic rather than in any meaningful sense political: the price Prospero pays for his restoration is
presumably the eventual envelopment of the Duchy of Milan into
Ferdinand's Neapolitan empire. Prospero mortgages his inheritance for a chance to repress a history of failure. Thus ends the
Mediterranean story.

On this reading Caliban, unbeknown to him, plays the part of
Antonio who, this time, will fail. But, at the same time, Caliban
is, as it were, playing himself, except that 'himself' means the self
that Prospero has cast for him – the treacherous slave. This is a
complication that needs some unpacking. For Prospero, Caliban
is playing the part of Antonio in the remake of his psychodrama,
the new version with the happy ending. For Prospero, Caliban is
an appropriate actor for this part because he is a 'natural'
usurper, this nature only held in check by Prospero's power. This
power is relaxed during the course of the play so that Caliban can
impersonate Antonio – proving to Prospero's satisfaction that his
assessment of Caliban's character is correct. If *The Tempest*'s critics
have conceded that much turns on how you define Caliban,
Prospero has no doubts: he offers Caliban the part of the
treacherous slave with the silent entailment that acceptance – of
what Caliban of course takes as a 'real' opportunity – will be
taken as definition of being. For Prospero this is merely confirmation of what he knows already: Caliban, like Antonio and
Sebastian, only has to act according to character. What is more,
Prospero can in the end only see Caliban as acting according to
character because Caliban does indeed seize upon the part offered
to him and plays it with a gusto only diminished by the fatuity of

his fellow-conspirators. It would be difficult, incidentally, to deny that *The Tempest* here has its finger on what is most essential in the dialectic between colonizer and colonized, offering a parable of that relationship probably never equalled for its compelling logic. So Caliban is, in other words, doubly inscribed in Prospero's play as both himself and a surrogate for Antonio, thereby putting into motion his double burden from the play's title page, Atlantic and Mediterranean.

Yet Caliban's part in *The Tempest* is not coextensive with his part in Prospero's play, since he has appeared in that delayed prologue at the beginning of the second scene which includes, to continue the theatrical language, some preparatory shaping up of Prospero's team, ensuring – via threat and bribe – that Ariel will obey orders, and – via invective and abuse – that Caliban will be in a suitably resentful frame of mind. Prospero's moves are effective, but at the price of allowing us to hear what Ariel and, more to the point, Caliban have to say for themselves. This scene repays close attention.

The confidence of the opening *coup de théatre* has been immediately undermined by the evidently urgent need to hark back to other earlier beginnings. For Prospero, the real beginning of the story is his usurpation twelve years previously by Antonio, the opening scene of a drama which Prospero intends to play out during *The Tempest* as a comedy of restoration. Prospero's exposition might seem to take its place unproblematically as the indispensable prologue to an understanding of the present moment of Act I, no more than a device for conveying essential information. But to see it simply as a neutral account of the play's prehistory would be to ignore the contestation, which follows insistently throughout the rest of that scene, of Prospero's version of true beginnings. In this narration the crucial early days of the relationship between the Europeans and the island's inhabitants are covered by Prospero's laconic 'Here in this island we arriv'd' (I.ii.171). And this is all we would have, were it not for Ariel and Caliban. First Prospero is goaded by Ariel's demands for freedom into recounting at some length how his servitude began, when, at their first contact, Prospero freed him from the cloven pine in which he had earlier been confined by Sycorax. Caliban then offers his compelling and defiant counter to Prospero's single sentence when, in a powerful speech, he recalls the initial mutual trust between them 'When thou cam'st first', with benefits bestowed by each on the other, Prospero making much of Caliban, Caliban showing Prospero 'all the qualities o' th' isle' (I.ii.334–40); a trust broken by Prospero's assumption of the political control made possible by the power of his magic. Caliban, 'Which first was mine own King', now protests that 'here you sty me / In this hard rock, whiles you do keep from me / The rest o' th' island' (I.ii.344–6).

It is remarkable that these contestations of 'true beginnings' have been so commonly occluded by that uncritical willingness to identify Prospero's voice as direct and reliable authorial statement, and therefore to ignore the lengths to which the play goes to dramatize its problems with the proper beginning of its own story. Such identification hears, as it were, only Prospero's play, follows only his stage directions. But although different beginnings are offered by different voices in the play, Prospero has the effective power to impose his construction of events on the others. While Ariel gets a threatening but nevertheless expansive answer, Caliban provokes an entirely different reaction. Prospero's words refuse engagement with Caliban's claim to original sovereignty ('This island's mine, by Sycorax my mother, / Which thou tak' st from me' (I.ii.333–4)); yet Prospero is clearly disconcerted. His sole – somewhat hysterical – response consists of an indirect denial ('Thou most lying slave' (I.ii.346)) and a counter accusation of attempted rape ('thou didst seek to violate / The honour of my child' (I.ii.349–50)), which together foreclose the exchange and are all that Prospero ever has to say about his early days on the island.

Nevertheless, this second scene opens up an important space which the play proceeds to explore. Prospero tells Miranda (and the audience) a story in which the island is merely an interlude, a neutral ground between extirpation and resumption of power. Ariel and Caliban immediately act as reminders that Prospero's is not the only perspective, that the island is not neutral ground for them. So right from the beginning Prospero's narrative is distinguished from the play's: we are made aware that Caliban has his own story and that it does not begin where Prospero's begins. A space is opened, as it were, behind Prospero's narrative, a gap that allows us to see that Prospero's narrative is not simply history, not simply the way things were, but a particular *version*.

In that gap Caliban is at least allowed to begin his story. This account of the opening of *The Tempest* makes the play a paradigmatic text for the writing of this book. Not only – as has often been pointed out – can Prospero and Caliban be seen as archetypes of the colonizer and the colonized, but Prospero is also colonial historian, and such a convincing and ample historian that other histories have to fight their way into the crevices of his official monument.

Of course Prospero's arrival on the island occupied by Caliban and Ariel remains an event as inaccessible to us as the arrival of the first Europeans on the Caribbean islands. In one case we have only Columbus's opaque text. In the other we have three stories: Prospero's two accounts – the brief 'Here in this island we arriv'd' (I.ii.171), and the fuller version he gives to remind Ariel of his place; and Caliban's alternative version, which Prospero denies only with the vague 'Thou most lying slave' (I.ii.346). Speculation about what 'really' happened would be even more futile here in this fictional story than in the earlier chapter, but it is surely significant that Caliban's account of the beginning of the relationship is allowed to stand unchallenged while Prospero responds by charging him with the attempted violation of Miranda. Shakespearean criticism has, as noted earlier, recently grown more sceptical towards Prospero's behaviour and achievements, especially with respect to Caliban.[66] There are various ways of looking at this. Even as master to slave, Prospero speaks and behaves with an excessive vehemence, threatening punishments out of all keeping with the supposed crimes. This has tended to become more of an issue as it has become less easy to see Caliban as some sort of semi-human figure, the 'missing link' of Daniel Wilson's evolutionary fantasies.[67]

It is perhaps less of a strain than it was a hundred years ago to see as genuinely human a figure described in animal terms by Europeans. Much also turns on the attempt at violation. Once upon a time that would have been enough to justify any punishment inflicted on Caliban. Today it is possible for at least one critic – and a religious one at that – to defend Caliban on the grounds that he was simply refusing to accept the European code of ethics.[68] Perhaps more to the point is that Prospero's way of phrasing the insult (he 'lodg'd thee / In mine own cell, till thou didst seek to violate / The honour of my child' (I.ii.348–50)) makes it clear that Caliban's crime is ingratitude towards him, Prospero: violation of Miranda would be a trespass on his property. Prospero's extraordinary possessiveness – at first mention Miranda, Ariel and Caliban are respectively, 'my dear one' (I.ii.17), 'my Ariel' (I.ii.188), and 'my slave' (I.ii.310) – is open to both political and psychoanalytical readings, the two by no means incompatible. Miranda's virginity is an important political card for Prospero, in some ways his only one, and he takes great care – as all commentators note – to make sure that it is not accidentally trumped by Ferdinand's premature ardour. Like many Shakespearean fathers, Prospero needs such political incentives to loosen his grip on his daughter and, even so, he goes through a ludicrous charade in order to gain what David Sundelson calls 'a symbolic victory over [Ferdinand's] confident sexuality'.[69] That is probably as far as the warrant of the play's words themselves permits. Recent psychoanalytical criticism has gone further. Coppélia Kahn reads Prospero's actions as an intricate yet unsuccessful attempt to work through his Oedipal past.[70] Mark Taylor questions whether 'violation' may not be Prospero's interpretation of 'a perfectly honourable action', on the grounds that 'Caliban's pursuance of the normal forms of courtship, with or without Miranda's responding positively to them, would be seen by him, Prospero, as an effort to violate her'. So, 'rather than indict the daughter for disloyalty in choosing a man other than himself, the father castigates the suitor's dishonourable methods – a classic displacement, which allows the father to retain belief in his daughter's loyalty'.[71] These can only be speculations – 'reasonable inferences' Taylor optimistically calls them[72] – but they find their justification in the seemingly consistent way in which the play undercuts Prospero's attempted explanations of the past, the best example being the self-induced tangle he gets into over his wife:

> Pros. Thy father was the Duke of Milan, and
>   A prince of power.
> Mir.   Sir, are not you my father?
> Pros. Thy mother was a piece of virtue, and
>   She said thou wast my daughter; and thy father
>   Was Duke of Milan.   (I.ii.53–8)[73]

In a word, as Freudian readings force us to pay attention to suggestions that there is more to Prospero's accounts of past

events than immediately meets the eye, we are likely in
consequence to look carefully at what alternative versions of
events we do have. It is not that Caliban somehow speaks the
truth that undermines Prospero's false or misleading history: there
is no way in which the status of their respective words could be
thus accented. But Caliban is allowed to articulate a history, it is a
history markedly distinct from Prospero's, and we see Prospero
attacking Caliban for daring to speak it, without himself ever
offering an alternative version of those early days on the island.
Interestingly enough, his inadequate denial of Caliban's charge –
'Thou most lying slave' (I.ii.346) – is repeated three times by Ariel
in the scene where he taunts Caliban (III.ii.40–150) as if to
emphasize that there is no narrative counter to Caliban's arguments: Ariel himself is also accused by Prospero in identical terms
during *their* disagreement over historical matters: 'Thou liest,
malignant thing!' (I.ii.257).

For Caliban the issue is simple: 'I am subject to a tyrant, a
sorcerer, that by his cunning hath cheated me of the island'
(III.ii.40–2): Prospero's power, his magic, has usurped Caliban of
his rights. But the text inflects this usurpation in a particular
direction: Prospero has taken control of Caliban, made him his
slave, and yet 'We cannot miss him' (I.ii.313) – Caliban is
indispensable to Prospero, the usurper depends upon the usurped.
Why should this be if Prospero is so powerful a magician? Why
should he have to depend upon a lowly slave like Caliban? We
need to comprehend more clearly the precise nature of Prospero's
magic.

This does not imply further investigation of Prospero as
Renaissance magus on the way to enlightenment, or subtle
distinctions between black and white magic. A simpler question
needs answering: just how extensive is Prospero's power? In some
ways this overlaps with the discussion of Prospero as playwright:
he has the sort of power that can erect an invisible barrier, that can
inflict physical punishment, and that can take human and animal
form; but he does not have direct power over human thoughts,
words and actions. But one can go beyond this, still on the basis of
the play's own evidence: his magic is only effective within certain
distances since he has depended on 'accident most strange'
(I.ii.178) to bring the court party within his sphere of influence; it
was not effective in Milan or else he could have defended himself
against Antonio; or on the open seas since he and Miranda needed

'Providence divine' (I.ii.159) to come ashore; but *was* effective either immediately upon, or soon after, reaching the island since he freed Ariel from the cloven pine. If Prospero's extraordinary speech of abjuration is to be believed (V.i.33–57) his powers extend to plucking trees out of the ground, and even, as discussed earlier, to wakening the dead. But on the other hand he cannot, or will not, chop wood, make dams to catch fish or do the washing up, all tasks for which Caliban's services are required.[74]

If such a listing seems open to the charge of excessive literalism, that is precisely the point. The text is not concerned with the exact configuration of Prospero's magical powers, but rather with two broad distinctions: Prospero's magic is at his disposal on the island but not off it; it can do anything at all except what is most necessary to survive. In other words there is a precise match with the situation of Europeans in America during the seventeenth century, whose technology (especially of firearms) suddenly *became* magical when introduced into a less technologically developed society, but who were incapable (for a variety of reasons) of feeding themselves. This is a topos that appears with remarkable frequency in the early English colonial narratives, as it had in the Spanish: a group of Europeans who were dependent, in some cases for many years, on food supplied by their native hosts, often willingly, sometimes under duress.

Possible verbal parallels with 'sources' such as Strachey's letter tell us nothing about *The Tempest* as a 'Caribbean' play. But the topos of food is such a staple of Atlantic discourse that congeneric examples can significantly illuminate the materials that the play is here deploying. One final Caribbean story, therefore, will be set alongside *The Tempest*.

9

In April 1605, the *Olive Branch* with some seventy passengers sailed from England to join Leigh's recently established colony in Guiana. According to the account of John Nicholl, one of the adventurers on board, the master seems to have missed his course and, after seventeen weeks at sea, with shortages of food and drink making 'our men's minds very much distracted, which bred amongst us many fearful and dangerous mutinies',[75] they fetched up on the shore of St Lucia, an island still without European settlements:

> And so having been seventeen weeks at sea, instead of our hopeful expectations of attaining to a pleasant, rich and golden Country, and the comfortable company of our friends and Country-men, there as we supposed then resident, we were brought to an Island in the West India somewhat distant from the main, called Santa Lucia, having about twelve degrees of North latitude, inhabited only with a company of most cruel Cannibals, and man-eaters, where we had no sooner anchored, but the Carebyes came in their Periagoes or Boats aboard us with great store of Tobacco, Plantains, Potatoes, Pines, Sugar Canes, and divers other fruits, with Hens, Chickens, Turtles, & Iguanas: for all which we contented and pleased them well. These Carrebyes at their first coming in our sight, did seem most strange and ugly, by reason they are all naked, with long black hair hanging down their shoulders, their bodies all painted with red, and from their ears to their eyes, they do make three strokes with red, which makes them look like devils or Anticke faces, wherein they take a great pride.[76]

The disjunction between the discursive and the experiential could hardly be clearer. 'Cannibal', it should be noted, is no longer the ethnic name, for which 'Carebye' has become established; but the association between the two is so immediate that the text has no problem in speaking, before the moment of actual contact, of 'most cruel Cannibals, and man-eaters'. Even if this description were retrospective, bestowed in the light of Nicholl's perception of their subsequent behaviour, it would still sit uneasily with the welcome supply of food with which the Caribs chose to begin the intercourse with their visitors.[77] The story that follows is in many ways predictable. The English were given a whole village in which to stay, in return for a single hatchet. The master wanted to leave the sick to fend for themselves but the captain disagreed, so the company split, half staying on St Lucia and half leaving on the *Olive Branch*. Those remaining were left a cannon from the ship but the two parties quarrelled and the gun was actually fired *at* the ship, with both sailors and settlers giving different stories to the Caribs, who must have been thoroughly bemused by these strange happenings.

After the departure of the *Olive Branch* relations were good between the Caribs and their guests: large amounts of vegetables, fruit and game were supplied by the Amerindians, and the Europeans made some effort to catch turtles, although they seem to have spent most of their time cutting down trees and building a stockade to defend themselves 'lest the Carrebyes should at any time assault us'.[78] Three events seem to have triggered the deterioration in the relationship. It was discovered that, contrary to instructions, one of the company had sold a sword to a Carib chief: the English captain reclaimed it without compensation. Then, inevitably, the English started asking about gold and got different answers from different Caribs: 'these contrary tales made us suspect some villany'.[79] And finally the Caribs stopped bringing food, so the English started stealing it from their gardens. Eventually the ambush came: the nineteen who survived it barricaded themselves in their stockade and prepared to die of hunger – but the Caribs brought them food:

> Thus for the space of 6 or 7 days, every day fighting for the space of three or four hours, and then our victual began to fail again, which caused us to hold out a Flag of truce: which the Indians perceiving, came in peaceable manner unto us.[80]

This way of fighting clearly had little to do with European ideas of warfare. In the end the English offered to leave behind all their hatchets, knives and beads in return for a canoe and some food. The offer was accepted and the survivors, not without further hardship, reached Venezuela and (some of them) thence Spain and England.

Behind Nicholl's narrative of heroism in the face of cruel cannibals it is possible to reconstruct a story of initial hospitality, increasing suspicion in the face of boorish behaviour, and eventual loss of patience with a hostile drain on the economy that showed little inclination to shift for itself. It seems probable that fear of guns dictated the early diplomacy but it cannot explain the continuing supply of food when there were less than twenty survivors. If the Caribs' main objective had been to kill the English rather than to get them to leave, they would only have had to deny them food. The magic of technology has its limits.

At issue is not the influence of Nicholl's account on *The Tempest* but rather the congruence between, on the one hand, his and numerous other New World narratives, and on the other, the words and actions of the play. Even the most cursory of structural analyses would reveal common features in almost all the early reports: initial native hospitality – especially supply of food; growing misunderstandings; and then violent conflict, perceived by the Europeans as 'treachery'. There seems little doubt that as far as the Amerindians were concerned the turning point was always the realization that their 'guests' had come to stay. The Europeans were blinded to this by their failure to comprehend that what confronted them was an agriculturally based society with claims over the land. Unable to understand the effects of their own behaviour the only narrative that they could construct to make sense of both the hospitality and the violence was a narrative of treachery in which the initial kindness was a ruse to establish trust before the natives' 'natural' violence emerged from behind the mask. The next chapter looks more closely at this syndrome.[81]

For the moment it can serve as the larger context within which to view the limits of Prospero's power and the essential offices that Caliban performs. For such a supposedly 'spiritual' play *The Tempest* has much to say about food. One would perhaps expect such material concerns in the sub-plot where Caliban quickly appreciates – presumably having learned from his earlier visitors – that the way to Stephano's heart is through his stomach: 'I'll show thee the best springs; I'll pluck thee berries; / I'll fish for thee, and get thee wood enough' (II.ii.160–1). But they appear no less insistently elsewhere, particularly in the two masques where, first, Ariel shows his devouring grace that Prospero finds so amusing and, later, the betrothal is somewhat inappropriately presided over by Ceres rather than the banished Venus, as if visions of golden harvests were more suited to the present straitened circumstances than idylls of married bliss. Caliban makes it plain ('I must eat my dinner' (I.ii.332)) that Prospero's most powerful weapon over him is the withholding of food – the food that Caliban is himself responsible for collecting and preparing.[82] Here the master/slave relationship begins to take on, if not exactly a Hegelian reciprocity, then at least a more delicate balance than might at first be apparent. Prospero is dependent upon Caliban's labour for his food supply and general material requirements; Caliban is forced by Prospero's magic to labour in order to be able to eat even a small portion of the food he prepares. We are now, finally, in a position to see that Caliban's second inscription within Prospero's play is exactly parallel to the first in its project of effacement, thereby continuing the dizzy sequence of parallelisms. Just as the first inscription, as an Antonio figure, effaces Prospero's original usurpation by his brother, so this inscription, as revolting slave, effaces both the *original* relationship between Caliban and Prospero, a relationship of host to guest, of Prospero's dependence – which has continued – on Caliban's labour; and the moment of violence, the moment when Prospero used his power to change host/guest into slave/master. Prospero's usurpation of Caliban is effaced by the engineered drama of Caliban's conspiracy against Prospero. The gap in Prospero's narrative is thereby filled: Caliban's 'treacherous' nature is 'proved' beyond dispute, and his continued subjection 'justified'.

Each of Caliban's two inscriptions is, just to complicate matters, disguised as the other. The repetition is not simply a fantasy – because Caliban really is conspiring to murder Prospero; but the conspiracy as enacted cannot genuinely be Caliban's attempt to regain what is rightfully his – because it is so clearly yet another plot against the rightful Duke. For Caliban his double inscription is a double bind. Either he is a slave who can only allege his usurpation, or a conspirator whose failure confirms his treachery; leaving Caliban little option but to 'seek for grace' in an attempt to minimize his suffering, whatever the justice of his claims may have been.

This brings the Atlantic story to a very satisfactory end as far as Prospero is concerned. Bewildering Alonso by means of that ultimate *anagnorisis* into agreeing to Ferdinand and Miranda's marriage was not a significant strain on Prospero's ingenuity: to give his daughter to his enemy's son is apparently a small price to pay for Alonso's recognition of Milan's temporary independence. The recognition afforded him by Caliban is altogether sweeter, since it franks that repression of the colony's early history which we have watched the play enact. Caliban repudiates his claims *of his own volition*. The violence of slavery is abolished at a stroke and Caliban becomes just another feudal retainer whom Prospero can 'acknowledge mine' (V.i.276). This is the wish-fulfilment of the European colonist: his natural superiority voluntarily recognized.[83]

We should now, finally, be in a position to understand the interrupted masque. Formally, the moment of Caliban's conspiracy is merely the working through of the sub-plot to its appointed conclusion. But that moment also triggers the screen behind which Prospero's usurpation of Caliban can be concealed, his proven treachery providing a watertight alibi against any claims of prior sovereignty that might be lodged. To remember Caliban is essential if that alibi is to be constructed, but to remember him is to remember why the alibi is needed in the first place. Prospero's sub-plot is a finely wrought piece, but the displeasure of that memory outweighs, for a moment, the need to put it into action. Hence the sudden perturbation.

This hiccough in the running order of the masque, this seemingly trivial moment over which commentators have fretted, is quite simply the major turning point in the larger play because, as Prospero's anger briefly but dramatically holds the two plays apart, we are able to glimpse the deeper import of that conspiratorial sub-plot, able to realize that, though it is kept to a minor place within Prospero's play, that very staging is the major plot of *The Tempest* itself. The Atlantic material, seemingly at the periphery, proves to be at the centre.

The conclusion to Act IV is the culmination of the dramatic action, a powerful and deeply ambivalent scene in which the conspirators are hunted by dogs and hounds, one of them called Tyrant, another Fury. It is cast, as Prospero's entire sub-plot has been, in the comic mode, further evidence of his commitment to the dramatic adequacy of the Mediterranean tradition, and it has of course proved possible to read the scene in its entirety through that mode.[84] The one question that remains is whether *The Tempest* – allowing us to see Prospero's brilliant deployment of the paraphernalia of comedy – permits any ambiguities to attenuate that scene of farce. There are perhaps two.

The final chastisement of the conspirators is out of all proportion to their powerlessness: they may have plotted murder but their chance of success has been nil from the start. Admittedly the connotations of being hunted by hounds are open to discussion: some, like G. Wilson Knight, will see them as 'impregnated with a sense of healthy, non-brutal, and . . . man-serving virility';[85] others will feel uneasy, if not nauseous, at the sight of dogs hunting men – Las Casas's denunciation of the hunting of Amerindians with dogs had already been translated into English as part of the construction of the 'Black Legend' of Spanish cruelty.[86] They are not of course 'real' hounds; it is, after all, only a joke. But what is considered to be a joke is often as revealing as an action in earnest.

And, finally, Caliban is allowed to make desperate efforts to avoid the comic mode: almost all his words in this scene are warnings to his companions not to be diverted from their purpose, and he alone refuses the tempting finery on the lime-tree, thereby possibly foiling the very last piece in Prospero's jigsaw since he will not *dress* as Antonio – in Milanese clothes – for the culminating moment of the repeated coup. Admittedly the scene is classically ironic since the audience sees, as Caliban cannot, the all-powerful hand of his enemy behind even this opportunity for revenge, but the poignancy of his position should surely sour any possible laughter. Caliban, though defeated, is allowed to retain his dignity in spite of Prospero's best efforts to degrade him.[87]

Figure 11 The 1622 'massacre' of the Virginia settlers; from Theodore de Bry's *Grands Voyages*. The key event for the English narrative of early Virginian history.

4

John Smith and Pocahontas

John Smith stood close beside her as he spoke, with his back to the others in the room. For the first time they really looked at each other. Pocahontas blinked back her tears and she said softly:

'I remember well how my father called you son. I remember that my brothers called you brother. I remember that you called me dear child. Now you say only "Lady Rebecca".'

The tea cup in John Smith's hand trembled ever so slightly.[1]

1

The early history of the English colony of Virginia contains one story – perhaps its most famous – that has tantalizing parallels with *The Tempest*. At the beginning of this century Morton Luce suggested that Shakespeare's account of the relationship between Miranda and Ferdinand might have been affected by the story of how Pocahontas, a young Amerindian 'princess', saved the English colonist John Smith from the wrath of her father by throwing her body over his as he was about to be executed.[2] The dates are certainly interesting. Pocahontas's 'rescue' of John Smith happened in December 1607. John Smith's *A Trve Relation of such occurrences and accidents of noate as hath hapned in Virginia since the first planting of the Collony* was published in London in August 1608. It tells of mounting hostility between the English and the Virginia Algonquian, and of how the Algonquian chief Powhatan sent as emissary his daughter Pocahontas, 'a child of tenne yeares old . . . the only *Nonpariel* of his Country. This hee sent by his most trustie messenger, called *Rawhunt*, as much exceeding in deformitie of person; but of a subtill wit, and crafty vnderstanding.'[3] Miranda is also a 'nonpareil' (III.ii.98) and Rawhunt suggests Caliban in his deformity and craft. But Smith's *A Trve Relation* contains no mention of his 'rescue' by Pocahontas, a story not told in print until 1624, long after Pocahontas's death.[4] The story may have been orally current in London in 1608–9, and Shakespeare may have heard it. It is more likely that Luce was influenced by the way in which the story of John Smith and Pocahontas had been later turned into the first great American romance, and saw parallels where none exist. John Smith has little if anything in common with Ferdinand, and there is no evidence at all of a romance between Smith and Pocahontas – indeed she later married another English colonist, John Rolfe. On the other hand, Miranda and Pocahontas are similar enough for another Shakespearean scholar, Geoffrey Bullough, to call their identity 'a tempting fancy which must be sternly repressed'.[5]

Once again source criticism of this kind proves a misleading guide to the connections between texts: those connections exist, but are not found through imagining a *clef* in early colonial history. As in the last chapter, the significant similarities between contemporary colonial texts concern common tropological and diegetic features of the textual structure, the most important of which, in this particular case, is that, like *The Tempest*, the story of Pocahontas and John Smith tells of an 'original' encounter of which no even passably 'immediate' account exists, a blank space which has not been allowed to remain empty.

2

Historians of the United States have had much to say about the 'American Genesis'. This is the account given by Perry Miller, one of the most respected US historians, of how his intellectual vocation was revealed to him in the 1920s:

> It was given to Edward Gibbon to sit disconsolate amid the ruins of the Capitol at Rome, and to have thrust upon him the 'laborious' work of *The Decline and Fall* while listening to

barefooted friars chanting responses in the former temples of
Jupiter. It was given to me, equally disconsolate on the edge of
a jungle of central Africa, to have thrust upon me the mission
of expounding what I took to be the innermost propulsion of
the United States, while supervising, in that barbaric tropic, the
unloading of drums of case oil flowing out of the inexhaustible
wilderness of America . . . . The vision demanded of me that I
begin at the beginning, not at the beginning of a fall . . . but at
the beginning of a beginning . . . . It seemed obvious that I had
to commence with the Puritan migration. (I recognize, and
herein pay my tribute to, the priority of Virginia, but what I
wanted was a coherence with which I could coherently
begin).[6]

The historical ironies can speak for themselves. What will be
taken here from this rich piece of writing are its obsession with
beginnings and coherence, and the bracketing of Virginia's
guiltily acknowledged chronological 'priority'.

New England has a complex history but it has always been
possible in retrospect to see it as having a coherence denied to
Virginia. That coherence was largely provided by the ideology of
Puritanism, and one of its main planks was the establishment of a
very clear division between civilization and savagery, between
the city on the hill and the alien and unregenerate forces that lay
beyond the pale. Much of the history of the United States, down
to its current defence policies, can be traced back to that image of
righteousness under threat from savagery.[7]

Virginia is doubly incoherent. Its proper 'beginning' is unsatis-
factorily hesitant. The first 'settlers', from Grenville's 1585
expedition, returned home with Drake in 1586, except for fifteen
volunteers who were never seen again. John White's more
substantial 1587 colony had disappeared without trace by 1590.
Even the 1607 settlement was nearly evacuated in June 1610, and
only just survived the 'massacre' of 1622 (see Figure 11). There is
little in Virginia's early history to give a satisfying sense of an
'innermost propulsion' at work. Even worse, perhaps, Virginia
had difficulty maintaining the coherence and integrity that its
name had hopefully suggested, the proper boundary between
'self' and 'other' necessary to any establishment of national
identity. And it is here, in the discussion of integrity and
boundaries, that the story of Pocahontas finds its purchase.[8]

3

The founding but most problematic moment of that story is the 'rescue'. During a reconnaissance mission towards the end of 1607 John Smith was captured by Pamunkey Indians after his two companions had been killed. He was taken by the Pamunkey chief Opechancanough to his brother Powhatan – leader of the confederacy of tidewater Algonquian – at the capital of the region, Werowocomoco.

> At his [John Smith's] entrance before the King [Powhatan], all the people gaue a great shout. The Queene of Appamatuck was appointed to bring him water to wash his hands, and another brought him a bunch of feathers, instead of a Towell to dry them: having feasted him after their best barbarous manner they could, a long consultation was held, but the conclusion was, two great stones were brought before *Powhatan*: then as many as could layd hands on him, dragged him to them, and thereon laid his head, and being ready with their clubs to beate out his brains, *Pocahontas* the Kings dearest daughter, when no entreaty could prevaile, got his head in her arms, and laid her owne upon his to saue him from death.[9]

This is Smith's own account, written in the Caesarian third person and published for the first time in 1624, seventeen years after the incident described. Apart from Pocahontas's intervention the account is much the same as that given in Smith's *Trve Relation* of 1608, which has led to considerable scepticism about the later revelation. It is difficult to see that the question of authenticity could now be settled one way or the other. These days Smith's stock as a historian is probably as high as it ever has been, thanks largely to the work of Bradford Smith and Philip Barbour, but no totally convincing explanation has ever been offered for the rescue's absence from the 1608 account.[10]

The later elements of the story are less controversial in themselves although they have been much elaborated. In 1609 Smith was injured in an accident and returned to England. In April 1613 Pocahontas, now some 18 years old, was kidnapped by an English captain, Samuel Argall, possibly with the idea of using her as a hostage. Instead she was instructed in Christianity, baptized, and married to the colonist John Rolfe. In 1616 Rolfe and Pocahontas (now Lady Rebecca) with their young son Thomas travelled to London where the 'Indian princess' was an object of much interest, being presented to the Royal Family and attending the famous Twelfth Night masque in January 1617. Pocahontas was eventually visited by John Smith, who wrote a fascinatingly elliptical account of their final conversation. Then, preparing to return to Virginia, she fell seriously ill on board ship and died shortly afterwards. As Samuel Purchas put it: 'she came at Gravesend to her end and grave'.[11]

Around this skeletal narrative has grown a vast body of material – novels, poetry, history books, comics, plays, paintings – that constitute what can only be called the myth of Pocahontas.[12] The major feature of this myth is the ideal of cultural harmony through romance. What is lacking in Smith's telling of the story, and what the mythic versions always feel the need to supply, is any elaborated motive for Pocahontas's behaviour. Smith just speaks of her 'compassionate pitiful heart'.[13] The mythic version resorts to the established literary model and posits Pocahontas's instant love for Smith, very much in line with Miranda's 'I might call him / A thing divine; for nothing natural / I ever saw so noble' (I.ii.420–2). The rest of the story then falls into place. Distressed at Smith's sudden return to London Pocahontas marries Rolfe on the rebound, only to have her heart broken when she meets Smith again in London, almost immediately dying of the shock. Smith never married. Inseparable from Pocahontas's love for Smith is her recognition of the superiority of English culture. It is this that leads her to act as mediator between the two communities, to inform the English of an impending Algonquian attack and, finally, to accept English religion and culture as her own. As a recent biographer of Pocahontas puts it, with deep and unconscious condescension:

> Encountering a new culture, she responded with curiosity and concern, and she accepted the potential for change and development within herself. She rose, surely and dramatically, above the ignorance and savagery of her people.[14]

This myth of Pocahontas has its own interest, although strictly speaking it is a product of the early nineteenth-century search for a United States national heritage, while the task here is to understand the story as a colonial beginning in its seventeenth-century context.

4

The first point to make about Pocahontas's crossing of the cultural rift – however that crossing is interpreted – is that it was quite exceptional. The Algonquians were on the whole remarkably slow to perceive the superiority of English culture. And the predecessors Pocahontas did have had tended to set bad examples. Around 1560 a Spanish ship had picked up an Algonquian who was probably Pocahontas's uncle. He was baptized Don Luís de Velasco, educated in Cuba and Spain, and taken back with a group of Jesuits to the York river to establish a mission. His family called him Opechancanough, 'he whose soul is white'. In 1572 he defied his name by organizing and leading the massacre of the Jesuits and the destruction of their mission.[15] Similarly in 1584 Ralegh's expedition to Roanoke brought back to England two Algonquians with the idea that they should learn English and serve as interpreters: one of them immediately defected when taken back to America.

Crossing cultures was a fraught business right the way through the colonial period. Particularly during the early years interpreters were crucial to the survival of colonies like Virginia which depended on barter and sympathy. Many of the colonists obviously had a smattering of Algonquian – Smith, Hariot and Strachey all left word-lists – and there were presumably Algonquian equivalents, but there was no substitute for genuinely bilingual interpreters. The problem was that to know enough Algonquian to ensure accurate and reliable interpretation they had to be so steeped in Algonquian culture that their very identity as Englishmen, and therefore their political reliability, became suspect. They became, as it were, cultural half-breeds inhabiting that dangerous no-man's-land between identifiable cultural positions, and therefore seen as inherently suspicious and potentially dangerous translators who might quite literally be traducers, crossing cultural boundaries only to double-cross their king and country. There was a series of this sort of interpreter in colonial Virginia, usually either released captives or voluntary exchanges, and they were all at one time or another suspected of treachery. One of them – who enters this story at a later stage – was called, ironically, Thomas Savage.

So Pocahontas's successful 'crossing' was exceptional in that it did not lead to her being perceived as occupying a dangerous position – possibly because she was seen as young enough for the formative influences still to be English. But the crossing was even more exceptional in the sense that it was also against the run of play. It had always been clear – though not of course palatable – that captives might end up having considerable sympathy for their captors, to the extent of not wanting to leave them. But there is also evidence of a persistent flow of Englishmen voluntarily leaving the harsh conditions of Jamestown for the Algonquian towns in the surrounding area where, at least before 1622, they were rapidly and unproblematically assimilated.[16] Even the other contestant for the founding myth of the United States, the lost colony of Roanoke, is shadowed by the suspicion that it might simply have gone native, which would be much too incoherent to count as a national beginning. The only surviving mark made by the lost colony of 1587 was the word 'CROATOAN' (the name of the neighbouring Indians) scratched on a tree, without the agreed distress signal of a cross. Historically this seems in part to have *had* to remain a mystery because the obvious explanation, that the settlers simply *became* Croatoans, is too uncomfortable to be seriously contemplated. So the Pocahontas story has gained at least some of its potency from being the one single exception to the rule of cultural crossing in early Virginia, the one possible match between ideological expectations and historical – or at least attested – occurrence. In other words Pocahontas was indeed, as John Smith called her, a 'non-pareil', though not in quite the way he meant.

That one of the motives for that widespread crossing of boundaries was the anticipation of sexual relationships is indicated by Rolfe's strenuous denial of the role of his own carnal desires in his wish to marry Pocahontas, elaborated in the long letter he wrote to Sir Thomas Dale in the early months of 1614.[17] The path to the marriage was discursively convoluted, although there are no recorded objections beyond that of King James who was said to be worried about the propriety of an English commoner marrying an Indian princess. That is a particularly fascinating intersection – between the boundaries of race and class; and Pocahontas – like many similar figures – can in the end assume an ideologically potent mythic status despite her race only because she is an intelligent, pure and, above all, *noble* Indian. Purchas says that she 'still carried her selfe as the Daughter of a King, and was accordingly respected'[18] and there was obviously a period before about 1700 when a high density of blue blood could lighten the skin. In the nineteenth century the eastern seaboard of the United States, seeking a heritage and secure from the violence of the frontier, would look back to its Amerindians for a genuinely native ancestry, as long as it came with something like Pocahontas's acceptable nobility and was well diluted with white genes.[19]

All the same, Rolfe's letter is a classic Puritan document because of the doubts that he himself had to overcome, and those doubts clearly centre on miscegenation. The convolution can only be gauged from a long quotation:

> Lett therefore this my well advised protestacion, which here I make betweene God and my owne Conscience be a sufficient wyttnes, at the dreadfull day of Iudgement (when the secretts of all mens hartes shall be opened) to condemne me herein yf my chiefe intent & purpose be not to stryve with all my power of boddy and mynde in the vndertakinge of soc waighty a matter (noe waye leade soe far foorth as mans weaknes may permytt, with the vnbridled desire of Carnall affection) for the good of the Plantacion, the honour of our Countrye, for the glorye of God, for myne owne salvacion, and for the Convert- inge to the true knowledge of God and Iesus Christ an vnbeleivinge Creature, namely Pohahuntas: To whome my hart and best thoughtes are and have byn a longe tyme soe intangled & inthralled in soe intricate a Laborinth, that I was even awearied to vnwynde my selfe therout. But Almighty God whoe never faileth his that truely invocate his holy name, hathe opened the Gate and ledd me by the hande that I might playnely see and discerne the safest pathes wherein to treade.[20]

The classical reference here needs a Puritan rewriting. Rolfe is Theseus; but Pocahontas as Ariadne, rather than helping, has Rolfe so intangled in her erotic threads that he has to unwind *himself* out of the labyrinth in order to escape the unmentioned Minotaur, that monstruous result of unholy unions which appears paraphrased a few lines later in the words of the Book of Ezra as 'the inconvenyences which maye ... arrise' from the 'mar- rienge of straunge wyves'.[21] Pocahontas's barbarism is freely, even excessively, admitted: 'whose education hath byn rude, her manners barbarous, her generation Cursed, and soe discrepant in all nutriture from my selfe';[22] but one of the strengths of the Bible and its commentaries as a source of authority is that most actions can be justified if you know where to look. Rolfe's marriage to Pocahontas would be politically expedient for the Virginia Company: God therefore shows the safest path. Rolfe refers to Calvin's *Institutions* for the idea that the children of Christians are to be accounted holy 'although they be the yssue but of one parent faithfull';[23] and there is a further and powerful argument implicit in the subtle intertextual strategy whereby Pocahontas is baptized as Rebecca. The relevant passage is, in the Geneva Bible, from chapter 26 of Genesis. Rebecca was barren; Isaac – her husband – entreated the Lord, and his wife conceived twins:

> But the children strove together within her: therefore she said, seeing it is so, why am I thus? wherefore she went to aske the Lord.
> And the Lord said to her, Two nations are in thy wombe, and two maner of people shall be devided out of thy bowels; and the one people shall be mightier then the other, and the elder shall serve the younger.
> Therefore when her time of deliverance was fulfilled, behold twinnes were in her wombe.
> So he that came out the first was red, and hee was al over as rough as a garment, and they called his name Esau.
> And afterward came his brother out, and . . . his name was called Iaakob.
> Now Iaakob sod pottage, and Esau came from the field and was wearie.
> Then Esau sayd to Iaakob, let me eate, I pray thee, of that pottage so red, for I am wearie . . .
> And Iaakob said, Sell me even nowe thy birthright.
> And Esau said, lo, I am almost dead, what is then this birthright to mee?
> Iaakob then said, sweare to me even now. And he sware to him, and solde his birthright to Iaakob.

So much for the mythic version of a single culture. Rebecca will give birth to *two* nations, a red and a white, and the red will despise his birthright and sell it for a mess of pottage. An odd exchange, perhaps, but a legally binding contract about which Jacob need not reproach himself. No text could have sat more comfortably with English desires. The colonists were of course impermeable to the irony that their settlement had only survived its early years through constant infusions of Algonquian pottage.

So, fortified by biblical precedent, the governor allowed the marriage and quickly packed off Rolfe and his new wife to London to demonstrate how successfully the Virginia Company had been purveying Christianity and impressing the high-born natives, who were not – as popularly believed – cruel savages, but in fact gentle and potentially cultured natives who could be relied upon to see the error of their former ways.

London's atmosphere proved so baleful that Rolfe had to take Pocahontas away to the healthier climes of Brentford to rest, and it was there that Smith finally went to see her:

> hearing shee was at *Branford* with diuers of my friends, I went to see her: After a modest salutation, without any word, she turned about, obscured her face, as not seeming well contented; and in that humour her husband, with diuers others, we all left her two or three houres, repenting my selfe to haue writ she could speake *English*. But not long after, she began to talke, and remembred mee well what courtesies shee had done: saying, You did promise *Powhatan* what was yours should bee his, and he the like to you; you called him father being in his land a stranger, and by the same reason so must I doe you: which though I would haue excused, I durst not allow of that title, because she was a Kings daughter; with a well set countenance she said, Were you not afraid to come into my father Countrie, and caused feare in him and all his people (but mee) and feare you here I should call you father; I tell you then I will, and you shall call mee childe, and so I will bee fore euer and euer your Countrieman. They did tell vs alwaies you were dead, and I knew no other till I came to *Plimoth*; yet *Powhatan* did command *Vttamatomakkin* to seeke you, and know the truth, because your Countriemen will lie much.[24]

None of Pocahontas's words have come down to us directly, so we have no immediate access at all to what she might have thought of the strange pattern of events in which she was caught up. Smith is not universally regarded as a reliable witness, and we certainly have no reason to presume that he could recall his conversation verbatim. And yet these words are worth taking a chance on, if only because they so clearly make no sense at all to Smith and yet had so impressed him as a statement of Pocahontas's opinion that he quotes them without further comment. So a case will be argued for the importance of this quotation, but that can be done only by broadening the argument considerably, and drawing together strands from this and earlier chapters.

5

What was the fundamental difference between Algonquian and English cultures? Inasmuch as a large and single answer to this question can be risked, it could be claimed that the native American cultures under discussion here acted according to norms of *reciprocity*; and that the European cultures did not. No more accurate general distinction could be made; but it is obvious at the same time that such a statement raises more questions than it gives answers.

Some of the larger and more difficult questions must be given less attention than they deserve. The classic study of reciprocity is Marcel Mauss's *Essai sur le don* (1925), where it denotes the complex system of exchanges between individuals and villages by means of which undivided (i.e. pre-state) societies function: 'The gift is the primitive way of achieving the peace that in civil society is secured by the State'.[25] Divided societies are, by definition, no longer reciprocal, although the ideology of reciprocity has a long and continuing history. In at least certain subsequent modes of production something that might tentatively be called 'unequal reciprocity' could be seen to operate, for example the complex and unequal, but reciprocal, system of duties and responsibilities between lord and vassal under feudalism. Only under the fetishized social relations of capitalism does reciprocity disappear altogether, however loudly its presence is trumpeted – 'a fair day's work for a fair day's pay'.[26]

Reciprocity itself refers to a series of practices distinctly una-
menable to breakdown into the economic, social, political and
ideological. This is the gist of Mauss's argument:

> In tribal feasts, in ceremonies of rival clans, allied families or
> those that assist at each other's initiation, groups visit each
> other; and with the development of the law of hospitality in
> more advanced societies, the rules of friendship and contract are
> present – along with the gods – to ensure the peace of markets
> and villages; at these times men meet in a curious frame of
> mind with exaggerated fear and an equally exaggerated
> generosity which appear stupid in no one's eyes but our own.
> In these primitive and archaic societies there is no middle path.
> There is either complete trust or mistrust. One lays down one's
> arms, renounces magic and gives everything away, from casual
> hospitality to one's daughter or one's property. It is in such
> conditions that men, despite themselves, learnt to renounce
> what was theirs and made contracts to give and repay.
>   But then they had no choice in the matter. When two
> groups of men meet they may move away or in case of mistrust
> or defiance they may resort to arms; or else they can come to
> terms. Business has always been done with foreigners, although
> these might have been allies . . . . It is by opposing reason to
> emotion and setting up the will for peace against rash follies
> . . . that peoples succeed in substituting alliance, gift and
> commerce for war, isolation and stagnation.[27]

This is probably as accurate a brief account as could be given of
how the native American societies of the extended Caribbean
functioned in the centuries before the arrival of the Europeans. It
is particularly useful for the emphasis placed on the vital
importance, yet constant tentativeness, of that nexus of relationships between selves and others. Without the authority of a state
all intercourse would teeter between alliance and hostility. To
treat with others was the indispensable requirement for life, yet it
entailed a constant risk of death.[28] Mauss's account highlights too
the importance of ritual as a way of attempting to control these
risky encounters. Boundaries, whether physical or social, are
places of danger. Strangers are to be feared. Fear is coped with by
ritual. Hospitality dissolves the category of stranger, resolving it
into either alliance or hostility.[29]

In stateless societies these categories are a matter of constant lived experience: they make up the very fabric of economic, social, political and cultural life. As it happens, the native societies of Virginia and the Caribbean were at least on the brink of forming states: what is usually called the Powhatan confederacy of tidewater Virginia (the 'Tsenacammacah') was probably a chiefdom of the sort discussed at the end of Chapter 2. Though far from a sovereign in Hobbes's sense, Powhatan himself was a powerful enough figure to act as guarantor for internal intercourse. But the confederacy was a recent enough alliance for dealing with strangers still to be a constant source of anxiety.

The native position, whether in the Caribbean or Virginia, was, as far as it can be judged, entirely consistent. Strangers were dealt with hospitably, fed and honoured, until their intentions could be assessed. Transients and traders would be welcomed and, if appropriate, alliances entered into. Settlers, rivals for limited resources, would be sent on their way or killed. European transients and traders benefited greatly from this attitude. The ships carrying the 1607 Virginia colony called in at Dominica, headquarters of the dreaded Caribs, and traded peacefully: and such examples could be multiplied.[30] But settlement was always a different matter. Here again the Virginia enterprise can stand as typical of the deep misunderstanding that existed from the start. Smith writes 'where now is Jamestown, then a thick grove of trees' – civilization out of wilderness; but the growth of trees was in fact secondary, the site an ex-settlement of the Paspahegh that had been left to grow into a hunting ground.[31] Misunderstanding of this kind was rife: the English clearly had as little notion of Amerindian ideas of communal property rights as the Algonquians had of English ideas of private property.

What emerges from Smith's narrative is precisely what the English were blind to – that Powhatan acted in accordance with a set of established social and political practices. It is difficult to judge just how novel the arrival of the three English ships would have been to Powhatan, but the establishment of the fort clearly called for a response. In accordance with the concepts outlined earlier, Smith, the stranger, already perceived by the Algonquian as a figure of some importance within the English ranks (he cleverly passed himself off as a *werowance* or shaman), was put into the limbo of hospitality and fed non-stop for several days, no doubt partly as a softening up process and partly to impress him with the bountifulness of the local produce. With a modicum of exaggeration Smith later remembered this lengthy meal as a six-week fattening up process in readiness for a cannibal feast.[32] At the end of the three days Powhatan and Smith exchanged descriptions of their respective kingdoms:

> I requited his discourse (seeing what pride hee had in his great and spacious Dominions, seeing that all hee knewe were vnder his Territories) in describing to him the territories of Europe, which was subject to our great King whose subject I was, the innumerable multitude of his ships, I gaue him to understand the noyse of Trumpets, and terrible manner of fighting under Captain *Newport* my father . . . . At his greatnesse, he admired: and not a little feared.[33]

'A long consultation' was then held by the chiefs of the confederacy. Powhatan's decision must have been that the English were too dangerous to be alienated: an alliance should be made, perhaps with a view to absorbing them into the confederacy. The appropriate ceremony was prepared. The *pawcoronce* was brought in, Smith laid upon it, and clubs raised above him. At a prearranged signal Pocahontas threw herself upon him and pleaded for his life. Powhatan granted her request. Smith – though he was obviously unaware of it – had passed through an elaborate ritual of mock-execution whereby he allied himself with Powhatan.[34] But what exactly was the nature of the alliance?

The ceremony seems to bear out Mauss's general analysis. 'There is no middle path': at the end of the liminal period of hospitality Smith's identity as stranger would be dissolved. Depending on whether there was 'trust or mistrust' he would be a friend or dead. The Algonquian word for the relationship established has not survived, but the evidence clearly points to what was earlier encountered under the Taino term *guatiao*, the closest relationship that two individuals of different kin could achieve; it could in fact be described as a 'kinning' of strangers. There were probably two major forms: the familiar one of connection through marriage, and – the relevant one here – a form of sponsorship in which a relationship between two individuals was cemented by one of them becoming sponsor to the other's child. It is possible that the Spaniards in the Caribbean were able to make such good use of this relationship because it had a close equivalent in the Mediterranean *compadrazgo* whereby sponsorship at baptism sealed an alliance between sponsor and natural parent (*compadres*) that would often prove stronger than blood-ties.[35] In England – certainly in seventeenth-century Protestant England – the relationship had no equivalent. Religious sponsorship existed, godparent to godchild, but the relationship between godparent and natural parent could not even be named, the ancient term 'godsib' surviving only in the derogatory form of 'gossip'. Although Smith was unable to perceive this formal establishment of *compadrazgo*, the English clearly sensed Pocahontas's special status with respect to their community. Smith was careful, as we have already seen, to present Newport as his 'father', rightly presuming that the kin term would carry greater weight than the merely military title. Soon afterwards an exchange of children took place to facilitate later communication. One of Powhatan's young servants, Namontack, was exchanged with an English boy called Thomas Savage. But the English told Powhatan that the boy's name was Thomas *Newport*, thereby appearing to reciprocate Powhatan's 'gift' of his daughter, an action which may have affected Powhatan's subsequent behaviour since he seems never to have detected the deceit.[36]

This formal, almost political, relationship between Pocahontas and Smith has universally been read as romantic, at least from the beginning of the nineteenth century, Pocahontas's otherwise 'inexplicable' action 'explained' as the spontaneous gesture of an instant love. The reunion at Brentford is therefore a tragic climax, Pocahontas confronting her true love, the man she *should* have married if only she had known he was still alive, a final meeting that would break her heart. To such a reading Pocahontas's words must remain impenetrable, a piece of clotted rhetoric to be rephrased into the more comfortable clichés of romantic fiction, as in the epigraph to this chapter. On any reading Pocahontas's words constitute an extraordinary passage of writing, and nothing is stranger than that Smith should have reported in direct quotation what so obviously meant nothing to him at all, almost as if he recognized, even if only fleetingly, the extent of his ignorance of this woman and her culture and, as a final gesture, perhaps a sort of homage, recorded her alien words in his text, for all the world like a nugget of the strange Algonquian language set amongst the familiar cadences of Jacobean prose.

The sentences are pellucid, their balance the balance of reciprocity: 'You did promise Powhatan what was yours should bee his, and he the like to you; you called hime father being in his land a stranger, and by the same reason so must I doe you'. All that Smith can oppose to that is a demurral based on his inferior rank, which only serves to bring down the full weight of Pocahontas's scorn. Can Smith, who did not fear to be a stranger in her land, be afraid of her calling him father in his own land? She insists on the relationship: she is the 'child' to his 'father', a kinship established at Werowocomoco. The insistence is on a reciprocity of which Smith has no conception at all.

6

This is perhaps as close as we can get to the native world of reciprocity, a tentative and no doubt idealized picture of a society that no longer exists. But the subject here is the European response to that world. So far this chapter has isolated two moments of evident crisis for that response, two moments when the discourse of colonialism proved to be less than a seamless web. Those places in the fabric of that discourse where the stitching is loose snag against the critical reading, enabling the task of unravelling to begin. Stranger, though, are the places where the pattern seems deliberately irregular, where the inevitable discrepancies between words and deeds seem highlighted rather than concealed. This is odd, since ideologies are almost by definition the constitution of what can be counted as 'truth': they might, according to certain sorts of Marxist analysis, be revealed as 'false', or at least as 'constructions', but they are not generally supposed to flaunt their falseness. For example, during the course of Smith's conversation with Powhatan at Werowocomoco:

Hee asked mee the cause of our comming.

I tolde him being in fight with the Spaniards our enemie, beeing overpow[e]red, neare put to retreat, and by extreame weather put to this shore . . . our Pinn[a]sse being leak[i]e, we were inforced to stay and mend her, till Captain *Newport* my father came to conduct vs away.[37]

There is obviously no attempt here on Smith's part to pass his words off as anything other than a tactical lie: they certainly bear no relationship at all to the earlier part of his narrative. The question, it should be stressed, is not about the making of such statements, but about their presence in the 'relations' of early colonial history: it is a matter not of what happened, but of what is recalled and articulated within the connected narrative. In a case of this kind 'truth' is clearly not perceived as having any relevance at all: the discourse is concerned instead to create a particular kind of colonial hero with the ability to escape from difficult situations – something at which Smith, judging at least from his own accounts, was indeed an expert.

It is impossible, then, to discompose such moments by setting an alternative account against them: the tactic must rather be to unsettle the image of the ever-resourceful hero. Smith presents himself as a consummate improviser, master of discourse, turning the thrust of Powhatan's question. But the improvisation proves on closer inspection to be a repetition of words already spoken, by Odysseus, when asked Powhatan's question by Polyphemus:

> But after he had briskly done all his chores and finished, at last he lit the fire, and saw us, and asked us a question: 'Strangers, who are you? From where do you come sailing over the watery ways?' . . . and I said to him: 'We are Achaians coming from Troy, beaten off our true course . . . . Poseidon, Shaker of the Earth, has shattered my vessel. He drove it against the rocks on the outer coast of your country, cracked on a cliff, it is gone, the wind on the sea took it; but I, with these you see, got away from sudden destruction.'[38]

The situations are certainly not dissimilar. Odysseus covets the land of the Cyclops in familiar terms, versions of the topoi of the 'golden age' still in use in the Virginia Company's propaganda:

> For it is not a bad place at all, it could bear all crops in season, and there are meadow lands near the shores of the gray sea, well watered and soft; there could be grapes grown there endlessly, and there is smooth land for plowing, men could reap a full harvest always in season, since there is very rich subsoil. Also

there is an easy harbor, with no need for a hawser nor anchor stones to be thrown ashore nor cables to make fast; one could just run ashore and wait for the time when the sailors' desire stirred them to go and the right winds were blowing.[39]

The Cyclops' only crime seems to be that they keep themselves to themselves: Odysseus implicitly criticizes their lack of civic institutions and their lack of commerce with other islands. But their misanthropy is epitomized by their supposed lack of hospitality. Odysseus goes on shore specifically to test whether they are 'hospitable to strangers',[40] and is not backward at demanding his rights as 'guest' from Polyphemus. And Odysseus's final taunt, flung from the safety of his ship (which had of course not suffered from Poseidon's attentions), is that Polyphemus has been punished for daring 'to eat your own guests in your own house'.[41] Cannibalism, here as elsewhere, seems to have much less to do with dietary practices than with acting as a potent emblem for strangers' failure, for whatever reason, to supply food to their visitors.

As it happens the Virginia enterprise – or at least its intellectuals – was well aware of the precedent. Between 1621 and 1625 George Sandys, treasurer and director of industry at Jamestown, completed his translation of an commentary on Ovid's *Meta-morphoses*. The commentary includes this passage:

Now the *Cyclops* (as formerly said) were a salvage people given to spoyle and robbery; unsociable amongst themselves, and inhumane to strangers: And no marvell; when lawlesse, and subject to no government, the bond of society; which gives to every man his owne, suppressing vice, and advancing vertue, the two maine columnes of a Common-wealth, without which it can have no supportance. Besides man is a political and sociable creature: they therefore are to be numbred among beasts who renounce society, whereby they are destitute of lawes, the ordination of civility. Hence it ensues, that man, in creation the best, when averse to justice, is the worst of all creatures. For injustice, armed with power, is most outragious and bloody. Such *Polyphemus*, who feasts himselfe with the flesh of his guests; more salvage then are the *West-Indians* at this day, who onely eat their enemies, whom they have taken in the warres; whose slighting of death and patient sufferance is remarkable; receiving the deadly blow, without distemper, or appearance of sorrow; their fellowes looking on, and heartily feeding on the meate which is given them; yet know how they are to supply the shambles perhaps the day following . . . . Injustice and cruelty, are ever accompanied with Atheisme and a contempt of the Deity.[42]

This is probably as good a short statement of seventeenth-century political commonplaces as any, illustrating in the process the way in which the familiar Mediterranean topoi of classical literature are used to gauge the novelty of Caribbean savagery. Emanating from Virginia the commentary offers a slight but significant displacement. A comparison with Virginia itself would probably be too fraught: if the English were not 'guests', as they clearly were not, then what were they?; so the Caribs make a safer point of colonial reference for the establishment of native injustice and cruelty — and therefore implicit identification of the Greek and European civilizing ventures. They can even be allowed a certain militaristic virtue in their scorning of death since that virtue is directed at the Spaniards. It would ironically be only a matter of months after Sandys wrote this passage that Tegreman, the Carib chief of the Caribbean island called by the English St Christopher's, asked Thomas Warner about the suspicious-looking loopholes in the wooden fort he had just constructed. Warner told him they were for keeping an eye on the chickens.[43]

The classical parallel, then, is in many ways close, yet, as in *The Tempest*, it tends to haunt Smith's text with its uncanniness rather than bolster it as a welcome precedent. Smith, to draw on an earlier contrast, belongs to the world of Antonio rather than that of Gonzalo; he is, in other words, fully at home within that ideology of individualism so essential to a developing capitalism, which insists that all actions are singular and unrepeatable. Humanist historiography — deeply collusive with that ideology — can say only that Smith at this point in his story was telling a tactical lie, any tone of moral disapproval in that statement merely acting as a screen for the blindness to the larger colonial pattern. Both Odysseus and Smith are involved in a very particular discursive manoeuvre. They present to their inter-rogators miniature narratives that function to close off the larger narrative frames that Polyphemus and Powhatan are seeking to establish. In each case their arrival is presented as the result of a set of accidental circumstances unsusceptible to larger diegetic explanation. Odysseus and Smith refuse to be characters in the narratives that Polyphemus and Powhatan try to construct for them. They are both playing for time.

Pocahontas's last recorded words are, 'because your Countriemen will lie much'. Words that have been read as a sexual reproach speak the language of reciprocal obligation. What baffles Pocahontas more than anything is that the words spoken at Werowocomoco should not be just as valid at Brentford: words are, after all, spoken only to be remembered. But for Smith there are *two* worlds: the world of civility – of Sion Park where the conversation may have taken place, of legal and governmental institutions, of contracts and guarantees, where words are embedded in solid and stable discursive practices; and an alien and hostile world where words, like actions, are improvised in a savage void, having no resonance beyond their immediate effect. Colonialist discourse has no memory – which is only another way of saying it has no narrative – until it provokes the occurrence that it will never forget. So Smith, at Brentford, in 1616, can make no sense of Pocahontas's pellucid words. 'Civility' – European civility – can only guarantee the stability of its own foundations by denying the substantiality of other worlds, other words, other narratives.

7

Whilst Smith's colonial narratives present a picture of our hero on the leading edge of the frontier, that large distinction between civilization and savagery was articulated for the most part by the European ideologists who remained at home, processing the firsthand material from the colonies in the light of classical precedent and canon law. In a sense Francisco de Vitoria reading Cicero in Salamanca improvised no less than John Smith facing Powhatan in Werowocomoco, though Vitoria called what he was doing 'commentary'.

The strategies of colonial discourse were directed in the first place at demonstrating a separation between the desired land and its native inhabitants. Baffled at the complex but effective native system of food production, the English seem to have latched on to the one (minor) facet of behaviour that they thought they recognized – mobility, and argued on that basis an absence of *proper* connection between the land and its first inhabitants.[44] During the planting season the Algonquian would live in their villages. Their agriculture was intensive and productive. After storing the season's produce the entire population would migrate for the climax of the year's hunting, returning home to live off the stored supplies. In times of shortage the villages might break up into smaller groups and live off the land, gathering shellfish and nuts. According to classical slash and burn technique, fields were used intensively for a short period and then allowed a long period of fallow. If necessary villages would be moved to new sites, but even this movement would usually be cyclical. Production was no doubt as precarious as it always is in agricultural societies, but food appears to have been usually plentiful judging from the Algonquian ability to supply the English with a good deal, if not on demand, then at least after their harvests. The widely attested stature and physique of the Amerindians would suggest a good and plentiful diet. Communities lived in clearly marked out territories with an agreed system of property rights, mainly communal although family and individual property rights seem to have existed as well.[45] On one level the English colonists were aware of something of all this. They could, most basically, see seeds planted and food grown on a regular basis. They visited villages, described them in their texts and drew them in their pictures. Yet this settled pattern of living became in the discourse of colonialism an aimless, nomadic wandering that, by extension, left the land empty and virgin.

Francis Jennings has traced the path of the key phrase in this argument. In 1612 the Jesuit missionary Pierre Biard, describing Canadian Amerindians, wrote:

> Thus four thousand Indians at most roam through, rather than occupy, these vast stretches of inland territory and sea-shore. For they are a nomadic people, living in the forests and scattered over wide spaces as is natural for those who live by hunting and fishing only;

'roam rather than occupy' being a translation of Biard's 'non tenentur, sed percurruntur'.[46] In 1625 Samuel Purchas wrote of the Virginia Algonquian:

> so bad people, having little of Humanitie but shape, ignorant of Civilitie, of Arts, of Religion; more brutish then the beasts they hunt, more wild and unmanly then that unmanned wild Countrey which they range rather then inhabite.[47]

And in 1629 in New England John Winthrop assimilated Purchas's point to the legal argument of *vacuum domicilium* by which the Indians had 'natural' but not 'civil' rights over the land because they had not 'subdued' it.[48] To Jennings's evidence could be added two earlier pieces, Robert Johnson's neat condensation of the bestial and nomadic in the patronizing pastoral description of the natives as 'lost and scattered sheep';[49] and Robert Gray's more sophisticated argument:

> Some affirme, and it is likely to be true, that these Sauages have no particular proprietie in any part or parcell of that Countrey, but only a generall residencie there, as wild beasts haue in the forrest, for they range and wander up and downe the Countrey, without any law or government, being led only by their owne lusts and sensualitie, there is no *meum & tuum* amongest them: so that if the whole lands should bee taken from them, there is not a man that can complaine of any particular wrong done unto him.[50]

Both these pieces were written in 1609 as part of a renewed propaganda effort on the part of the Virginia Company at the time of the Gates/Somers expedition. Gray's sentence is particularly dense. The 'generall residencie' looks forward to Winthrop's 'natural' but not 'civil' rights; the nomadic bestiality is neatly linked to the lusts that are their sole guide; and the final point is a brilliant *tour de force* of Lockeian proportions by which native communality becomes the alibi for extirpation on the grounds that no *individual* has been harmed.[51]

Absence of true 'settlement' left the land *virgin*: probably no single word has had to bear so heavy a weight in the construction of American mythology from the moment when, in Samuel Eliot Morison's immortal words, 'the New World gracefully yielded her virginity to the conquering Castilians.'[52] The novelty of America was always perceived in overtly sexual terms. To speak of the 'maidenhead' of Guiana or Virginia was to condense into one potent image the absence of significant native agriculture and the joyful masculine thrust of Elizabethan expansion. But it was one thing for Ralegh to assert that 'Guiana is a countrey that hath yet her maydenhead', and quite another for the ideologists to articulate that image discursively, especially when the representative of English masculine thrust was a Virgin Queen.[53] Chapman, in his celebratory 'De Guiana carmen Epicum' (1596), has Guiana 'whose rich feete are mines of golde, / Whose forehead knockes against the roofe of Starres', standing on tiptoe looking at fair England, 'And every signe of all submission making' towards 'our most sacred Maide'. Faced at this point with the risk of having to specify the relationship between the two, Chapman opts for comprehensive cover: Guiana wants 'To be her sister, and daughter both', Elizabeth will 'in this affaire / Become her father, mother, and her heire'.[54]

In the event Guiana proved a little too Amazonic. The articulation of Virginia showed an increase in rhetorical subtlety. Personification was dispensed with as too unreliable, as was the acceptance of native names. 'Virginia' was not in any sense a pre-existing entity, as Ralegh had imagined Guiana to be, along the lines of Peru, its putative model. 'Virginia' denoted that enormous stretch of coastline from Newfoundland to Florida, and connoted what was assumed to be its pure state: 'Virginia', a virgin land awaiting its English suitors. But even if you have the Virgin Queen bringing fruitfulness to a barbarous yet virgin chaos through the surrogates of her male courtiers, the cosiness of this colonial romance is inevitably disturbed by the unfortunate presence of the other parties who were there beforehand and who could only be seen as, at best, recalcitrant fathers or brothers holding back the love-match, at worst already the husbandry to the 'virgin' land. This then was the classic colonial triangle, memorably rearticulated by Samuel Purchas in his 1625 essay 'Virginia's Verger'.

Winthrop's distinction between 'civil' and 'natural' rights can usefully be read back into 'Virginia's Verger'. Many of Purchas's arguments are pitched at the civil level, concerned with England's rights under the Law of Nations to trade freely and to settle on unpeopled lands. Yet however sophisticated these arguments were, it was quite clear under the Law of Nations that it was not lawful for Christians simply 'to usurpe the goods and lands of Heathens'.[55] Such usurpation could only be justified by infractions of Natural Law. Writing in 1625 Purchas is able to speak confidently of such infractions having taken place:

> But when Virginia was violently ravished by her owne ruder Natives, yea her Virgin cheekes dyed with the bloud of three Colonies . . . the stupid Earth seemes distempered with such bloudy potions and cries that shee is ready to spue out her Inhabitants.[56]

The initial separation of land from inhabitants in the bestowal of the name Virginia pays handsome dividends here. Not only can the 'virgin' land be savagely raped by its own natives (Purchas is referring to the 'massacre' of 1622), but the blood thereby spilt on to its (posterior?) cheeks is that of the English colonies themselves, which are, in the process, identified with the Virginia that has been ravished. The Amerindians become satisfactorily 'unnatural Naturalls',[57] forfeiting any rights they may have had under Natural Law. In other words the 'massacre' has performed a miraculous reversal by which the settlers have become the natural inhabitants – identified with the land – and the original inhabitants have been discursively 'spewed out' by their own territories. The master narrative of Christianity then enables Purchas to complete the romance plot with Virginia, restored to her pristine condition, marrying England – easier to manage now that England has a king – and the Algonquian reduced to sullen and rejected suitors, whose very contact with the soil under their feet is at least trespass, if not a continuous indecent assault. The question of Christian usurpation is once again completely bypassed.

Purchas's symbolic reading of the 1622 'massacre' is instructive in several respects, not least in its attempt to deploy the language of sexuality in a discussion of natural rights over land, Prospero's tactic in his response to Caliban's claim to sovereignty. While, though, in that case, Prospero was the father protecting his daughter's virginity from the native male, here, more strangely, the colonizing power is identified with the 'female' land, the passive victim of native violence, just as Smith, the very masculine hero of *A Trve Relation* is, in his later work, presented as the passive victim of Powhatan, dependent for his survival on the intervention of a young girl.

At the heart of European recourse to the Law of Nations was the grandiose concept of *consortium hominum*, an intellectual version of the reciprocity discussed earlier inasmuch as it posited an ideal of exchange of various kinds as the centre of properly human activity. *Consortium* was the seed of many arguments that would be developed at length between the twelfth and eighteenth centuries; and at its core was what Albertus Magnus called *communicatio*, thereby stressing that it was through language that men came to understand that their common purposes could be achieved only through bonding together in civil society.[58] *Consortium* operates in civil law on two levels: between individuals – where it can be called friendship; and between social units – where it takes the initial form of mutual hospitality, which may develop into stronger links through trading partnership or military alliance. Barbarians, by definition, are incapable of such *communicatio*. Their *complete* lack of language, exemplified in Caliban's supposed gabbling, is a dramatization of their inability to form a community: they are condemned to a life of ceaseless hostility, Hobbes's 'Warre of all against all'. They can therefore be recognized, as in the case of Polyphemus, by their lack of hospitality. Now if it could be argued, Francisco de Vitoria suggested, somewhat circumspectly, that the Amerindians were refusing to 'receive' the Spaniards, thereby closing the channels of human intercourse that the *jus gentium* demanded should be left open, then they would by their actions be defining themselves as barbarians and giving the Spaniards just title for conquest.[59] Interestingly, Vitoria's textual support here comes from the opening book of the *Aeneid*, where an unnatural storm, caused by magical powers, shipwrecks a group of travellers on their way to Italy and casts them up on an unknown shore where they are described as 'driven from Europe and Asia'.[60] A familiar story. They are refused even the hospitality of the sands to mend their ships, and ask 'what manner of men are these? What land is this that allows them / Such barbarous ways?'[61] The text is well chosen because of its irrelevance to the case at hand. The Trojans, unlike the Spaniards, had no choice but to land on the African shore; unlike the Spaniards, the Trojans were treated 'barbarously' through no fault of their own; unlike the Spaniards, they had no intention of staying – in fact it was Dido who tried to persuade them to settle in Carthage, a colonial consummation devoutly to be wished. Odysseus visiting the Cyclops would have been a more appropriate, but dangerously ambiguous text.

The English ideologists argued along much the same lines. Purchas translates classical *consortium* into a more mundane, but powerful argument about trade:

> Non omnia possumus omnes, Nec vero terrae ferre omnes omnia possunt; God in manifold wisedome hath diversified every Countries commodities, so that all are rich, and all poore; not that one should be hungry and another drunken, but that the whole world might be as one body of mankind, each member communicating with other for publike good.[62]

Or, as George Peckham had put it:

> And first for traficke, I say that the Christians may lawfully travaile into those Countries and abide there whom the Savages may not justly impugne and forbidde, in respect of the mutuall society and fellowship betweene man and man prescribed by the Lawe of Nations.
>
> For from the first beginning of the creation of the world and from the renuing of the same after Noes floode, all men have agreed, that no violence shoulde be offered to Ambassadours. That the Sea with his Havens should bee common. That such as should fortune to be taken in warre, should be servauntes or slaves. And that Straungers sholde not be dryven away from the place or Countrey whereunto they doo come.[63]

Already in 1610 the Virginia Company's *A True Declaration* was putting forward as one of its panoply of justifications for the lawful presence of the English in Virginia the violation by the natives of 'the lawe of nations'; because

> they . . . used our Ambassadors as Ammon did the servants of David: If in him it were a just cause to warre against the Ammonites, it is lawfull, in us, to secure our selves, against the infidels;[64]

an analogy also used by Purchas fifteen years later.[65]

The difficulty with this sort of argument was the number of witnesses attesting to the hospitable and friendly behaviour of the natives, at least in the initial exchanges. What therefore came into focus was their supposed inconstancy, their failure to be either friendly (submissive) or hostile, but rather both, depending on the circumstances, a pattern of behaviour the English interpreted as *treachery*.[66] The complex interplay between expectation and experience is nicely caught in Gabriel Archer's comment: 'They are naturally given to trechery, howbeit we could not finde it in our travell up the river, but rather a most kind and loving people.'[67] The attribution was soon a commonplace. Already by 1612 they were 'a daily daring treacherous people';[68] in 1618 the Jamestown Assembly pronounced them 'a most treacherous people'.[69] An essence was being named that would function to explain the change in native behaviour: if they were initially friendly and later hostile then, so the logic goes, their friendship must have been faked,[70] and therefore their nature, the one underlying constant, must be treacherous. Just why they should have gone to so much trouble to keep the English colonists alive, only later to attack them so murderously, was mysterious but less problematic than the contradictory, unthinkable coupling of genuine friendliness and genuine hostility; and, of course, infinitely preferable to investigating the possible effects of the English colonists themselves upon native behaviour. Alexander Brown's puzzlement catches the tenor perfectly:

> All accounts agree that for some reason the Indians did daily relieve them for some weeks with corn and flesh. The supplies brought from England had been nearly exhausted; the colonists had been too sick to attend to their gardens properly, and this act of the Indians was regarded as a divine providence at that time .... What was the real motive for the kindly acts of the Indians may not be certainly known; but it probably boded the little colony a future harm.[71]

Such partial interpretation does not take long to become accepted description. Kermode's note to Caliban's 'I'll show thee every fertile inch o' th' island' (II.ii.148) remarks in a matter-of-fact way: 'The colonists were frequently received with this kindness, though treachery might follow', as if this were simply a 'fact' whose relevance to *The Tempest* we might want to consider, without seeing that to speak of 'treachery' is already to interpret, from the position of colonizing power, through a purported 'description'.

From the native point of view, of course, their own behaviour was perfectly comprehensible and absolutely consistent. Reception of visitors was friendly, hospitality was ample, trade was welcomed; but a line was drawn when it became apparent that the visitors were here to stay. Amerindian attitudes were therefore dependent on English behaviour. There is no reason to imagine that the Algonquians found this behaviour easy to fathom, particularly given some of the incidents already referred to, although counting the number of ships that arrived at Jamestown would provide an obvious rule of thumb. Three stages might be imagined. An initial one of curiosity, bewilderment, fear and sympathy that ended, probably to their relief, with the apparent abandonment of the colony in June 1610; only for the immediate arrival of De La Warr to mark the beginning of a second stage of growing suspicion as the English, under a new set of instructions from London, began to act more aggressively.[72] The third and decisive stage began in 1619 with the new system of land grants which, coupled with the growing success of the tobacco crop, led to an influx of settlers and an unprecedented demand for land.[73] At that point the colonists became invaders to be repelled at all costs. This pattern of perception would have been subject to a number of complicating factors, amongst them the internal politics of the Powhatan confederacy, usually, and perhaps accurately, interpreted as a conflict between the weak and vacillating Powhatan and his more decisive brother, the militant Opechancanough. But there is little doubt that the main complicating factor, from the Amerindian point of view, was the strange behaviour of their visitors. Even if we pass charitably over the ingratitude, the threats, and the wanton violence, putting them down to the pressure on individual colonists in a new and dangerous land, and look instead at colonial *policy* as it was articulated in London, it is easy enough to imagine the confusion that must have been felt by the Algonquian.

It is difficult to give brief indications of this policy which obviously altered in the light of colonial experience. But take this early paragraph from a set of 'Inducements to the lykinge of the voyadge intended to that parte of America which lyethe betwene 34. and 36. degree', written by the elder Richard Hakluyt in 1584, well before permanent settlement was achieved by the English on the American mainland:

> Yf we fynde any kinges readye to defende their Tirratoryes by warre and the Countrye populous desieringe to expell us that seeke but juste and lawfull Traffique, then by reason the Ryvers be lardge and deepe and we lordes of navigacion, and they without shippinge, we armed and they naked, and at continuall warres one with another, we maye by the ayde of those Ryvars joyne with this kinge here or with that kinge there at our pleasure and soe with a fewe men be revenged of any wronge offered by them and consequentlie maye yf we will conquere fortefye and plante in soyles moste sweete, most pleasaunte, moste fertill and strounge. And in the ende to bringe them all in subjection or scyvillitie for yt is well knowen they have bynne contented to submytte them selves and all that which they possesse to suche as hathe defended them againste there Enemyes speciallie againste the canibales.[74]

In some ways this quotation epitomizes the initial difficulty that colonial ideology faced: how to get from the beginning of the first sentence (defence of territory by occupants) to its end (plantation in sweet soils). The rhetoric of these pieces should by now be becoming familiar. The grammatical structure is one of compelling logic: 'Yf ... then ... we maye ... and soe ... and consequentlie ...'; the argument itself tortuous and self-contradictory, and thereby revelatory of the underlying issues. The route from conditional expulsion to future plantation involves some subtle moves. The object of the initial desired expulsion is defined as 'us that seeke but juste and lawful Traffique', people carrying out legitimate commercial activities. But a sentence that seemed to begin in the realm of international law passes quickly into a discussion of military strategy. The assertion of technological superiority is conventional (though 'armed' and 'naked' an interesting opposition), the statement of the *realpolitik* enabled by such technological superiority startling in its clarity: 'we maye ... joyne with this kinge here or with that kinge there at our pleasure'. The consequence of this 'pleasure' is the immediate gratification of conquest, fortification, and plantation in sweet and fertile soils. Clearly the benefits to be gained from the revenge of any 'wrong' are so desirable that offence must be courted. What the sentence inscribes (and in this it is typical of colonial ideology as a whole) is the impossibility of any transgression on the part of the colonial power: there can be no paragraph considering the possibility of kings ready to trade yet prepared to defend their territory from invasion. Ideology exiles the unthinkable.

The strain that Hakluyt's sentence has to go through to reach its desired end is salved by what follows. Violence, however justified, should not after all be necessary since it is 'well knowen' that they submit themselves and their property to those who have defended them against their enemies. 'Well knowen' seems to amount to a report given by David Ingram, one of the sailors marooned by John Hawkins on the American mainland after the disaster of San Juan de Ulloa, who claimed to have walked from the Gulf of Mexico to Cape Breton, and who tells of how the savages of the mainland are pursued and devoured by cannibals.[75] Our friends the cannibals have been offstage for a while now but reappear, as always, at a critical moment, here, the final word in Hakluyt's paragraph, as a guarantee that aggression is *elsewhere*, that those who do violence against the savages are not, definitely not, the English themselves, who are on the contrary friends and protectors.[76] At their pleasure of course.

Hakluyt was tactician as well as strategist. The early expeditions were advised to disguise their intentions carefully: food must be obtained from the natives, he says, before they realize that permanent settlement is intended.[77] Courtesy and 'friendly signes' are therefore the first order of the day.[78] Once a foothold has been established a different tack is necessary: the immediate neighbours, now suspicious of their 'visitors' and therefore dangerous, must be weakened through alliances between the colonists and *distant* Indians. The instructions given to Sir Thomas Gates (1609) are in this respect explicit:

> If you make friendship with any of these nations, as you must doe, choose to doe it with those that are farthest from you and enemies unto those amonge whom you dwell.[79]

The pattern that emerges from these various threads is remarkably consistent. The colonists made four central claims about the native Americans in justification for their dispossession: that the natives were not properly 'settled'; that the land was not cultivated; that the natives behaved in a duplicitous and treacherous fashion; and that they cruelly broke the universal rules of hospitality. These claims were not only false, they were a systematic reversal of the actual state of affairs, since the native Americans were fully settled, farmed the land intensively, acted hospitably until provoked beyond endurance, and behaved in what, even at this distance and without sympathetic evidence, appears as a relatively consistent and comprehensible manner. But even more to the point is that the claims were a systematic projection of *European* behaviour on to native Americans.[80] In those early years it tended to be the Europeans who were not 'settled', living from plunder and barter; it was the Europeans who proved incapable of feeding themselves from the fertile soil; it was the Europeans whose duplicity and cunning kept their colonies alive by manipulating the trust of their hosts; and eventually by betraying it.

The Tempest is so crucial for this period because it is the only text which deals – in however oblique a manner – with the key relationship between superior technology and the inability to produce food. What in recent years a more attentive (or perhaps *differently* attentive) reading of the seventeenth-century sources has shown is that the colonists' irrational response to that discrepancy can only be explained in psychological terms: after all to *burn* cornfields when you are starving, rather than stealing the corn, is to court the charge of psychosis. It is one of the strengths of Edmund Morgan's great book on colonial Virginia that he is prepared to tackle this problem:

> If you were a colonist, you knew that your technology was superior to the Indians'. You knew that you were civilized, and they were savages. It was evident in your firearms, your clothing, your housing, your government, your religion. The Indians were supposed to be overcome with admiration and to join you in extracting riches from the country. But your superior technology had proved insufficient to extract anything. The Indians, keeping to themselves, laughed at your superior methods and lived from the land more abundantly and with less labor than you did. They even furnished you with the

food that you somehow did not get around to growing enough of yourselves. To be thus condescended to by heathen savages was intolerable. And when your own people started deserting in order to live with them, it was too much. If it came to that, the whole enterprise of Virginia would be over. So you killed the Indians, tortured them, burned their villages, burned their cornfields. It proved your superiority in spite of your failures. And you gave similar treatment to any of your own people who succumbed to the savage way of life. But you still did not grow much corn. That was not what you had come to Virginia for.[81]

This terse summary was speakable only as its repetition in the ricefields of Vietnam brought the original to light. What it reveals so clearly is the massive, almost self-destructive effort needed to create the self-image of the technologically superior.[82] The discursive webs woven in and around these events in Virginia in the early seventeenth century to produce its 'history' constitute at the same time a massive effort of repression whereby the violent dispossession of the native Americans is rewritten as a crusade against the unregenerate savage, the guilt of conquest being transferred from usurper to usurped: as from Prospero to Caliban.[83]

8

Although the fully-fledged Pocahontas myth belongs to the nineteenth century, some of the story's implications were glimpsed by its contemporaries. It is difficult to judge exactly what effect the marriage between Rolfe and Pocahontas had on the relationship between the English and the Algonquian in Virginia, but it certainly symbolized a period of uneasy truce. If Gates's instructions marked the beginning of English consolidation on the Virginian mainland it was only the rapid increase in demand for land to grow tobacco after 1619 that made it clear beyond shadow of doubt that the English intended not just to stay, which might have been tolerable, but actually to expand their toehold on the continent.

So in the winter of 1616–17 that saw Rolfe and Pocahontas in London the decisive moves had yet to be made. The colony's future was still not secure: the Company's internal politics were convoluted, its propaganda not always successful, its assets almost exhausted, its recruiting record poor.[84] John Rolfe's *A True Relation of the State of Virginia*, written during his stay in London, was an attempt, probably prompted by a disaffected section of the Company, to suggest that the colony's problems stemmed from past mismanagement and that Virginia itself offered wonderful opportunities still, especially in the light of the peace that existed with the Amerindians.[85]

Pocahontas, now Rebecca, is a fitting image for the prospect of such future co-operation given her appreciation of her proper place in the order of things. Her baptism, her new name, her grasp of English, all mark her ritual passage into the fold of civility. An engraving was made of her wearing English clothes and, in the oil painting copied from the engraving, she even begins to lose her Amerindian features. The comprehensiveness of this process, coupled with the evident delight at her royal carriage and 'great demonstration of her Christian sinceritie',[86] conveys a certain anxiety, as if the friends of the Virginia enterprise were determined to leave nothing to chance. Appropriately then, Pocahontas's virtual canonization is seen to have its discursive consequences because lodged in Purchas's text is the only other member of the large Algonquian party to interest the English, Uttamatamakin (also called Tomocomo), husband of Pocahontas's sister:

> With this Savage I have often conversed at my good friends Master Doctor Goldstone, where he was a frequent guest; and where I have both seen him sing and dance his diabolicall measures, and heard him discourse of his Countrey and Religion, Sir Tho. Dales man being the Interpretour ... a blasphemer of what he knew not, and preferring his God to ours, because he taught them ... to weare their Devill-lock at the left eare; hee acquainted mee with the manner of that his appearance, and beleeved that his Okee or Devil had taught them their husbandry, & ... Tomocomo was as wise in computation of his sailing, reckoning each night ... as another day. Hee is said also to have set up with notches on a stick the numbers of men, being sent to see and signifie the truth of the multitudes reported to his Master. But his arithmetike soone failed, and wonder did no lesse amaze him at the sight of so

much Corne and Trees in his comming from Plimmoth to London, the Virginians imagining that defect thereof had brought us thither.[87]

So yet again we find the two figures, 'guatiao' and 'canibal', but now walking the streets of London and even visiting its drawing rooms. And, if the 'guatiao' has become almost indistinguishable from an English lady, the 'canibal', in dialectical consequence, remains threateningly unregenerate in manners, beliefs, dress and, perhaps most important of all, hair style.[88] Purchas is threatened enough by this determined 'otherness' to need to comfort himself with some heavy sarcasm at the Algonquian's expense, although we can but sympathize with Tomocomo's amazement at the sight of 'so much corne': what a stupid native indeed to believe that English demands for food in Virginia were something to do with them not having enough of their own back home.

In the Rotunda of the Capitol in Washington there is a series of paintings illustrating the pre-history of the United States. Virginia is represented by Pocahontas, but the picture, by John Chapman, shows neither the famous 'rescue' nor her marriage with John Rolfe. Instead it depicts Pocahontas's baptism, shrewdly choosing the moment when European ritual symbolized her rejection of her own culture and her incorporation into the ranks of the saved (see Figure 12). Lurking in the shadows at the side of the picture is a sullen figure with shaved head and single lock clearly visible. The official publication brought out to celebrate the painting's placement identifies him:

> while her uncle, the sullen, cunning, yet daring Opechankanough, shrunk back, and probably even then brooded over the deep laid plan of massacre which he so fearfully executed years after.[89]

This is the final resolution of the colonial triangle, a splitting of the problematic third term, a severance of niece and uncle, available female and hostile male, 'good' Indian and 'bad' Indian, which leaves Pocahontas to be mythologized and Opechancanough to lead a last desperate effort to extirpate the English from Virginia and, in 1646, at nearly one hundred years of age, to be shot in the back by an English soldier.

Figure 12 'The Baptism of Pocahontas' (1840); a painting by J.G. Chapman which hangs in the Rotunda of the Capitol, Washington, DC.

Once again the 'massacre' displays its retrospective importance to any event that preceded it: only the 'massacre' could allow Virginian history to begin at all. That is not to say that such a history has 1622 as its starting point, but rather that the period between 1607 and 1622 could not satisfactorily be narrativized until the 1622 'massacre' provided the authoritative organizing principle that would reduce the earlier chaos to the order of syntagmatic coherence. From this perspective the absence of Smith's 'rescue' from his earlier account can be better understood. In 1608 such an event would have been, in the strict psychoanalytical sense of the word, a trauma for Smith, an event impossible at the time to incorporate fully into a significant context or narrative. So *The Trve Relation* represses all mention of the incident, not risking opening in the prospective Virginian narrative a traumatic breach that no trope could close. After 1622 the 'rescue' becomes comprehensible: it can be articulated into a narrative in which Pocahontas has an increasingly central role to play as evidence that Algonquian recognition of the values of European culture could have provided the basis for a harmonious relationship, had not the inherent viciousness of her uncle destroyed all hope of peaceful co-operation. Within such an overarching narrative Smith's own position as the great white hero having to be rescued by an adolescent girl becomes acceptable for the first time since he is thereby retroactively identified with the colony itself, the innocent 'virgin' victim of the native aggression only postponed in 1607 through Pocahontas's gesture, to return a hundredfold fifteen years later.

The 'massacre' provided what had proved to be most necessary for the colony to survive: a huge infringement of Natural Law which left its victims free to pursue any course they wanted, unregenerate savagery having forfeited all its rights, civil and natural. The zealousness with which the English ideologists drew the consequences of the 'massacre' indicates something of the relief that was mixed with the horror at the news. Edward Waterhouse, who wrote the most detailed account, finds an appropriate image:

> our hands which before were tied with gentlenesse and fair vsage are now set at liberty by the treacherous violence of the Sauages: not vntying the Knot, but cutting it.[90]

The Gordian difficulties of coexistence could now be set aside by the 'justified' establishment of an aggressive pale, an armed frontier finally built in 1634 between the headwaters of the James and York rivers and behind which the English would develop their pastoral economy and grow large amounts of tobacco. Bolstered by the memory of the treacherous massacre, that frontier would expand as and when it could, the rights of those thereby displaced no longer an issue. This chapter can end with Waterhouse's ferocious version of Virginia's future, not without its parallels to the ending of Act IV of *The Tempest*:

> the way of conquering them is much more easie then of ciuilizing them by faire meanes, for they are a rude, barbarous, and naked people, scattered in small companies, which are helps to Victorie, but hinderances to Ciuilitie: Besides that, a conquest may be of many, and at once; but civilitie is in particular, and slow, the effect of long time, and great industry. Moreouer, victorie of them may bee gained many waies; by force, by surprize, by famine in burning their Corne, by destroying and burning their Boats, Canoes, and Houses, by breaking their fishing Weares by assailing them in their huntings, whereby they get the greatest part of their sustenance in Winter, by pursuing and chasing them with our horses, and blood Hounds to draw after them, and Mastiues to teare them, which take this naked, tanned, deformed Sauages, for no other then wild beasts, and are so firece and fell vpon them, that they feare them worse then their old Deuil which they worship, supposing them to be a new and worse kinde of Deuils then their owne.[91]

Figure 13 'Rescue of the Spaniard', from an 1885 edition of *Robinson Crusoe*. Almost all illustrated editions choose to depict this key moment. The Spaniard 'was an European and had cloaths on', and is clearly a second Crusoe. Friday, his features obscured by his borrowed clothes, massacres the 'naked' Caribs. The foregrounded skull functions as a *memento anthropophagi* – a reminder of why such battles have to be fought.

5

Robinson Crusoe and Friday

[L]ike Christofer he bears
in speech mnemonic as a missionary's
    the Word to savages,
its shape an earthen, water-bearing vessel's
    whose sprinkling alters us
into good Fridays who recite His praise,
    parroting our master's
style and voice, we make his language ours,
    converted cannibals
we learn with him to eat the flesh of Christ.[1]

1

When I was come down the hill to the shore, as I said above,
being the S.W. point of the island, I was perfectly confounded
and amazed; nor is it possible for me to express the horror of
my mind, at seeing the shore spread with skulls, hands, feet,
and other bones of humane bodies; and particularly I observed
a place where there had been a fire made, and a circle dug in the
earth, like a cockpit, where it is supposed the savage wretches
had sat down to their inhumane feastings upon the bodies of
their fellow-creatures.[2]

Nothing conveys the flavour of cannibalism better than the
graphic depiction of its aftermath, the scattered limbs and
scorched bones that horrify Robinson Crusoe exactly as they
had Dr Chanca some 200 years previously on a slightly more

northerly Caribbee island.[3] This cannibal residue is Crusoe's first 'evidence' of a savage presence on his island, one moment in that long and suspenseful section of the novel leading up to the paradigmatic colonial encounter, that key scene of colonial literature where the recently rescued Caribbean Amerindian, soon to be named Friday, places his head beneath the foot of a bewildered European.

Crusoe's island is situated by the text in the estuary of the Orinoco, within sight of Trinidad; and the Amerindians that feature in the book, including Friday, are all referred to as Caribs.[4] Yet, oddly, despite this degree of geographical specificity, *Robinson Crusoe* is not usually seen as in any significant sense 'a Caribbean book'. It is 'a Puritan fable', the first true work of 'realism', the novel of 'economic individualism' or, most popularly, the story quite simply of a man on an island – the location of that island being of, at best, subsidiary importance. This chapter will try to return *Robinson Crusoe* to the Caribbean.

2

Most recent criticism of *Robinson Crusoe* has taken as its reference point Ian Watt's influential 1957 book *The Rise of the Novel*, subtitled 'Studies in Defoe, Richardson and Fielding'.[5] In this book Watt argued for *Robinson Crusoe*'s crucial place in the history of the novel on three grounds: as the pre-eminent novel of the 'individualism' that characterizes modern realistic fiction; as fulfilling more generally the criteria of what he called 'formal realism'; and as demonstrating, in Crusoe's wanderings, 'the dynamic tendency of capitalism itself, whose aim is never merely to maintain the status quo, but to transform it incessantly'.[6] The main line of dissent to Watt's arguments has come from what has been called 'the rediscovery of a pervasive spiritual motif' in the novel which, against Watt's *marxisant* understanding of Defoe's 'purely formal adherence' to religious values, emphasizes the importance of the cycles of sin and regeneration that underlie the surface realism of *Robinson Crusoe*, seeing it therefore as a deeply religious book, a Puritan fable of spiritual life.[7]

But the true import of the 'religious' reading lies in its attempted solution to critical difficulties about the coherence of

Defoe's text. Within Ian Watt's trio of rising novelists both Defoe and Fielding occupy somewhat anomalous positions, leaving Richardson as the only representative of the 'mature' novel of realism.[8] Watt's objection to Fielding's novels is that his authorial interventions and classical plots 'tend to compromise the narrative's general air of literal authenticity by suggesting the manipulated sequences of literature rather than the ordinary processes of life'.[9] Defoe's novels on the contrary 'embody all the elements of formal realism',[10] but to an almost embarrassing degree. They suggest so successfully the 'texture of daily experience'[11] that they threaten to cease being literature at all. Plot is at the centre of both anomalies. Nothing is more characteristic of literary narrative than plot – it is the manifestation of the crafted work; yet nothing is more destructive than plot, as a sign of artifice, of that semblance, intrinsic to formal realism, that the novel is 'an authentic account of the actual experiences of individuals'.[12] The logic of formal realism would take certain 'novels' outside Watt's notion of literature altogether: *Journal of the Plague Year* has caused notorious difficulties for precisely this reason. Watt refuses that logic by balancing Defoe against Fielding with Richardson as the pivot who squares the circle, 'dealing with . . . the problem . . . of plot . . . which Defoe had left unsolved'.[13] The criterion by which Richardson is judged to have 'resolved the main formal problems which still confronted the novel' is that he had created 'a literary structure in which narrative mode, plot, characters, and moral theme were organized into a *unified whole*'.[14] Coherence proves to be the ultimate standard. This is not an uninteresting way of approaching *Clarissa*, although it has to be noted that Richardson's manner of 'dealing with' the problem of plot was to embed it in such a detailed evocation of the processes of everyday life that it never had a chance to become a flagrant example of literary artifice – not a model that many novelists have chosen to follow.

The modern realist novel, as understood by Watt, can usefully be defined by its absolute incompatibility with any notion of Providence. Nothing defines Providence more clearly than its reliance on plot: Providence is history with a plot, authored by God. On the surface, Watt's position would seem confirmed by the analogy: the novel is, in Lukács's famous phrase, 'the epic of a world that has been abandoned by God',[15] a thoroughly *secular* form, its secularity secured by the aversion of formal realism to the 'literary' machinery of plot. But Watt is reluctant to go that far: the appearances of 'literature' have to be saved by the reintroduction of plot, which is, in effect, nothing less than the reintroduction of a providential authority into the world of the fiction.

Even *Clarissa*, Watt's prime exhibit, falls victim to this antinomy. While the epistolary form seems to offer a perfect semblance of an 'authentic' writing, one produced entirely by the fictional characters themselves, Richardson was horrified to find that it enabled readers to draw their *own* conclusions – by, for example, sympathizing with Lovelace and finding Clarissa priggish, an outcome Richardson attempted to block in later editions of *Clarissa* by adding explanatory and didactic footnotes, in other words by reintroducing into the seamless and seemingly unauthored text the providential voice of the Author.[16]

For Watt, then, Defoe's novels, however crucial to the thesis of formal realism, remain 'immature' examples, flawed by their lack of anything more than the most episodic of plots. *Robinson Crusoe*, important enough to stand at the head of Watt's studies of individual novels, is, in the last analysis, shunted off into a category of 'works singular and original', representative of nothing other than itself,[17] a realistic but episodic novel, lacking 'intrinsic coherence' – that touchstone of bourgeois aesthetics. The perception of the spiritual pattern, revealing *Robinson Crusoe* as a formally sophisticated and coherent narrative, has therefore been welcomed by the literary academy as sidestepping Watt's implied criticism of *Robinson Crusoe* and affirming the true 'literary' value of such a seminal work.

The textual analogy used by the 'spiritual' reading is that of the Puritan journal, an immediate and transparent recording of everyday experience – a 'writing to the moment' in Richardson's phrase – which would on retrospective reading reveal to the keeper of the journal providential patterns not obvious in the crowded sensations of the lived moment.[18] So, the argument goes, *Robinson Crusoe* mimes the texture of daily experience so accurately that only the most careful of rereadings will perceive the underlying spiritual pattern that gives the narrative its true significance.

Without doubt *Robinson Crusoe* is studded with religious

references and symbols which arguably form part of a larger pattern. What, nevertheless, remains at issue is the meaning of this pattern of religious references given that no authorial voice, whether as overt commentator or 'implied author', is present to endorse them. *Robinson Crusoe* may well have the structure of a redemption narrative but, within the fiction, the structure of *Robinson Crusoe* is given by Crusoe himself; it is an aspect of his autobiographical strategy, the way he chooses to compose his life story and, as such, has no *authoritative* status beyond the reach of the usual interpretative procedures. Indeed on several occasions Crusoe himself discusses the possible providential significance of particular episodes. When such delicate questions of interpretation are themselves turned into the very matter of fiction Providence can in no way be said to provide a privileged masterplot to the narrative.

The 'spiritual' reading of *Robinson Crusoe* attempts – unsuccessfully – to remedy the scandal of the secular text whose interpretation is not guided by any authorial voice, but which has been published as the character's own story, 'Written by Himself', an assertion, as Watt rightly saw, of the primacy of individual experience as defiant in its own – fictional – way as Descartes' *cogito ergo sum*.[19]

3

A different, and perhaps more productive way of framing the critical disagreement between the 'economic' and 'spiritual' readings of *Robinson Crusoe* is to see them as constructing two different Defoes. Against Watt's 'modern' Defoe – Defoe/Richardson/Fielding – is set a seventeenth-century Defoe – Milton/Bunyan/Defoe. Against Watt's assertion that Defoe was the 'complacent apologist of nascent industrial capitalism' is set the conservative economic theorist bitterly opposed to the unregulated financial dealings of the new exchange.[20] Despite the notorious problems of authorship and changing political allegiance – let alone questions of intentional fallacy when it comes to reading the novels – there are important issues here that need careful following since they relate, in the last analysis, to colonial matters.

Ian Watt's argument about 'the dynamic tendency of capitalism' being manifest in Crusoe's career has been usefully modified by Stephen Hymer, who sees that career as illustrating Marx's analysis of the origins of the capitalist economy in the period of primitive accumulation.[21] Hymer can therefore contrast the story of Crusoe's accumulation of capital in the Africa trade and later on his Brazilian plantation – the looting of the non-European world – with what Marx, in ironic reference to the conventional view, called 'the rosy dawn of the era of capitalist production'.[22] Hymer's model, it is true, is thoroughly mimetic: what *Robinson Crusoe* gives us is a picture of 'the actual facts of what happens in the international economy'.[23] But his analysis has the great merit of not ignoring the island episode. In response to Watt's reading of the novel one critic pointed out that 'No one in his senses would choose the story of a man cast alone on an uninhabited island to illustrate a theory which only applies to the exchange of goods and services'.[24] But according to Hymer:

> In many ways [Crusoe's] solitary sojourn represents the alienation suffered by all under capitalism.... There is no real paradox in this. To capitalism belong both the production of the most highly developed social relations in history and the production of the solitary individual.[25]

This is a good dialectical point. Unfortunately Hymer's way of putting it strains the mimetic model to its logical terminus where the novel becomes a secular allegory ('it seems to me that Defoe ... is presenting an allegory about the life of all men in capitalist society'),[26] a conscious and coherent analysis therefore dependent upon a particularly knowledgeable subject ('Defoe (1659–1731) was particularly well placed to observe and understand the essence of the rising bourgeoisie and the secrets of its origins').[27] There are two things wrong with this. The demand for such coherence endows texts with a spurious or at least a premature unity. And, while it offers the usual assessment of Defoe's 'position' with respect to economic matters, such a view is seriously oversimplified, especially when it comes to reading *Robinson Crusoe*.

At least three strands in Defoe's economic writing need distinguishing: Defoe as the complete ideologist of trade – the constant baseline to his economic thought; Defoe as the propagandist for the age of projecting; and Defoe as the scourge of the stock-jobbers. The crux of the critical disagreements has tended to rest on the relationship between these last two strands. On the one hand there is the contrast made between Defoe's projecting spirit as the embodiment of the 'New Age' of capitalism over and against the conservative politics of nostalgia represented by Swift, Pope and Bolingbroke. On the other hand, Defoe's commitment to established mercantile practices is contrasted to his condemnation of contemporary stock-jobbing.[28]

In part the confusion has stemmed from the ambiguity of the important term 'projector'. Defoe's famous *Essay on Projects* (1697) is largely a paean to the projecting spirit, but it is often considered that by the early 1720s projecting had been irreparably tainted by the South Sea Bubble fiasco or even – more relevantly since it pre-dates *Robinson Crusoe* – by the failure of the Darien project in 1699, that ill-fated attempt at a Scottish colony on the isthmus where Central and South America join. But, although the Darien scheme had been launched by his close friend William Paterson, there is no evidence that Defoe's commitment to his own pet project of a South Sea trading area based on a new English colony in South America with an entrepôt on the Pacific coast – clearly akin to the Darien idea – was in the least reduced: his plans remain remarkably consistent from the 1690s through to 1727, well after the bursting of the Bubble.[29]

Of the variants to Defoe's scheme the two 1719 versions are most relevant to *Robinson Crusoe*, by date, but also because they couple the idea of a southern trade with a reactivation of Ralegh's plans to exploit the gold of Guiana, the territory that lies just beyond Crusoe's island.[30] The importance of Ralegh's project to the study of Defoe is that it enables us, following Defoe's own lead, to separate the notion of projecting from the stock-jobbing which had become its inevitable implication following the debacle of 1720. The suggestion, then, is that an important thread in Defoe's patchwork economic ideology harked back to the golden age of Elizabethan privateering. The Caribbean, of course, had been a projectors' sea from the time of Columbus onwards. In England Drake's stupendously successful 1585 voyage to the Caribbean initiated a whole series of similar projects, of which Ralegh's Guiana expedition was probably the most ambitious and the most ill-fated adventure (though that title might also go to Cromwell's 'Western Design').[31] None of these, though, had quite the lasting hold on the imagination of seventeenth- and eighteenth-century English writers as the shipwreck of the *Sea-Venture* on the Bermudas, which had snatched spectacular success from the jaws of tragedy in the tradition of the best adventurers, and provided one of the most consistent reference points for the remaining years of the English presence in the Caribbean.

The great Caribbean 'adventure' of Defoe's lifetime was William Phips's 1687 'voyage to the wreck', lacking perhaps the aura of Drake and Ralegh, but still an extraordinary scheme – to locate the wreck of the Spanish treasure ship *Nuestra Señora de la Concepción* sunk off the coast of Hispaniola – which produced a return of forty-seven-fold on investment. The total revenue of nearly a quarter of a million pounds sterling of bullion is sometimes seen as having provided the foundation for that period of financial experimentation which produced the Bank of England and the modern system of public credit.[32]

'Treasure' and 'adventure' are closely associated, though the relationship is inevitably complex for any world-view influenced by Puritan ideas. Around Ralegh's 'Guiana' certainly hovered the spell of El Dorado, but from the evidence of, say, *A New Voyage Round the World*, Defoe was immune to, or at least cautious towards, the prospect of easy riches of that kind.[33] Probably more relevant was the relative proximity of Ralegh's Guiana to the new sources of Brazilian gold recently discovered by Paulista adventurers in Minas Gerais, which were important enough to England, at a time when the East India Company was draining the country of bullion, for Defoe to defend the Methuen Treaty of 1703 through which England was given complete freedom to trade with Brazil and therefore access to a regular supply of gold.[34] In other words, Guiana's 'treasure' might need to be worked for in a satisfactorily Puritan manner.

As with 'projector' the meanings of 'adventurer' need careful unpacking since the word conceals a contrast that, at least since Defoe's time, has carried considerable ideological weight. In one form or another the term has had a continuous existence from the twelfth century to the present day to refer to certain kinds of investor, originally 'merchant adventurer' – anyone investing in overseas trade – more recently 'adventure capitalist', the asset stripper who occupies in contemporary populist demonology the place of the early eighteenth-century stock-jobber. Yet the

interest of the word obviously lies in its overlap of the financial
and the colonial, the worlds of *Lloyd's List* and John Buchan, the
common element being risk. It might be said that the 'pure'
adventure story, which has to take place outside metropolitan
Europe and preferably in as remote an area as possible, reached its
apogee as the tentacles of European colonialism were at their
greatest reach in the late nineteenth century.[35] The larger the
degree of *financial* involvement in the non-European world, the
more determinedly *non*-financial European adventure stories
became. Captain Mayne Reid's novels are perhaps the 'purest'
examples, telling tales of discovery, of buried treasure, of battles
against nature or vicious savages. There is certainly no such purity
about Robinson Crusoe's 'strange surprizing adventures', but
neither is he merely an adventure capitalist. The Elizabethans here
offer an important precedent. Drake and Ralegh could be said to
have held in heroic suspension the (for us) twin meanings of
'adventure'. They risked their capital *and their bodies* in search of
quick and high returns: their investment was personal as well as
financial, as opposed to the joint-stock holder whose 'risks' were
purely vicarious. In the *Essay on Projects* the despised 'meer
projector' leaves the poor 'Adventurer' to carry the can; the
'Honest Projector' combines the roles of projector and adventurer, putting his own project into execution.[36]

Connotation is difficult to gauge and not even constant at any
one period. What evidence we do have, however, suggests that
'adventures' were both officially and popularly regarded in a
favourable light during the Elizabethan period, as both benefiting
the national economy and singeing the king of Spain's beard.
Popular suspicion of the financial experiments that followed the
1688 settlement would have tarred 'adventurer' with the same
brush as 'projector' when it came to the stock-market, and in
foreign trade 'adventurers' would be subject to the disapproval of
the large monopolies – and therefore perhaps fascinating to
everyone else – because of their disregard of the new trade
regulations. Braudel, for example, quotes an official report of
1699 which refers to 'interlopers and adventurers', but in a
seemingly favourable way – perhaps an early hint of the paradox
involved in a capitalist empire claiming to adhere to an ideology
of personal freedom.[37]

In a way, then, Defoe holds the history of the word 'adventure' together for us. By looking back beyond the great merchant companies to the age of Ralegh, Defoe could endow Robinson Crusoe with something of the heroism of the adventurer who risked life and limb as well as capital, therefore, adventitiously, providing a link between the Elizabethan era and the true age of adventure in the second half of the nineteenth century – an age which, through Ballantyne, Marryat and many others, sought the purity of adventure precisely through rewriting the story of *Robinson Crusoe*. For Crusoe, it needs stressing in conclusion, 'adventure' is replete with what, for us, has come to be its two separate meanings. When he speaks of 'my first adventure' (p. 39) he means, inseparably, his dangerous voyage to Guinea and his £40 investment in 'toy's and trifles' to sell to the natives for gold dust. This £40 comes from his father, or possibly his mother, but they never receive a return on their investment.[38]

4

Crusoe's concern with accounting is legendary, so the details of his financial career can be easily mapped. Under the direction of the 'honest and plain-dealing' captain (p. 39) he spends his £40 on trinkets and toys which he exchanges for £300 of gold dust. £200 is left with the captain's widow and the rest, converted again into trading goods, lost when the ship is captured by Turkish pirates. Due to the 'generous treatment' of the Portuguese captain who eventually rescues him (p. 55), Crusoe ends up in Bahia – at the southernmost point of the extended Caribbean (and not far from the gold-bearing area of Minas Gerais) – with 220 pieces of eight, payment for his 'possessions', all of them – boat, guns, slave – stolen from his master in Sallee. He learns sugar planting, buys land and sends for half of his English capital, which arrives in useful goods which he sells to great advantage in order to buy a negro slave and a European servant (p. 58). After thirty years of careful management by others in Robinson Crusoe's absence, Crusoe finds himself, as well as owner of a Caribbean island, 'master . . . of above 5,000 *l.* sterling in money, and . . . an estate . . . in the Brasils, of above a thousand pounds a year' (p. 280), plus, if he has not already included it, the money he brings off the island from the wrecks:

£36 from his ship (p. 75), 1100 pieces of eight, six doubloons of gold, and some small bars of gold from the Spanish ship (p. 197).

But there is a danger here of not seeing the historical wood for the economic trees. Too great an emphasis on the financial detail of Crusoe's career can obscure the important way in which, however sketchily, the early chapters of the book recapitulate the European 'history of discovery': the first tentative voyages down the West African coast, the entanglement with Islam, the crossing of the Atlantic, even the movement of Brazilian expertise to the Caribbean which was essential to the early economies of the English and French islands. This certainly does not mean that Crusoe is in any unproblematic sense an 'embodiment' of European colonialism – that would only make the book another kind of mimetic allegory. It points, if anything, in the opposite direction. Crusoe's colonial career can in fact be divided between the rather bathetically secondary, dependent on the goodwill of a series of benevolent Portuguese, and the heroically, but rather ridiculously, primary. Five days south of Sallee he is speaking of the wild animals never having heard a gun before (p. 47); and twelve days further south, near the point Crusoe is heading for precisely because it is the crossroads of the colonial trade routes ('I know that all the ships from Europe, which sailed either to the coast or Guiney, or to Brasil, or to the East-Indies, made this cape or those islands' (p. 50)), he shoots a leopard to the 'astonishment' and 'admiration' of the 'poor' negroes, who are properly grateful for this manifestation of European technology (pp. 51–2), a rehearsal for Crusoe's more important demonstration of fire-power in front of an equally 'amazed' Friday (p. 213). But Crusoe is most strikingly primary in his island interlude, reliving one of the original Caribbean adventures – Somers and Gates on the Bermudas perhaps, or even Columbus himself on Hispaniola, but in any case a European in a part of the world that has supposedly never seen a white man. Appropriately enough its introduction is to hear what Crusoe believes 'the first gun that had been fired there since the creation of the world' (p. 72).[39]

Those who take Defoe's 'realism' for granted do not often get as far as the Caribbean, so the relevant historical points need making firmly. The only uninhabited islands in the (extended) Caribbean were the unapproachable Bermudas – and they became a favourite reference point for that very reason. John Parry has written that the only uninhabited land in America tended to be uninhabitable:[40] the Amerindians would certainly not have ignored Crusoe's remarkably fertile island unless they had been driven off by the European competition for Caribbean land which was in full swing by 1659. But in *Robinson Crusoe* the Caribs use the island only for periodic picnics, and other Europeans make only a belated appearance, leaving Crusoe to live out alone his repetition of colonial beginnings.

This is said not to indict *Robinson Crusoe* for not being realistic enough, or for not fulfilling its realist promise, but rather to suggest that the realistic *detail* of the text obscures elements of the narrative that, if the above description is accurate, would have to be called mythic, in the sense that they have demonstrably less to do with the historic world of the mid-seventeenth-century Caribbean than they do with the primary stuff of colonialist ideology – the European hero's lonely first steps into the void of savagery, 'those uninhabited lands', in the unforgettable words of Lattimore's doubtless apocryphal parson, 'where only the heathens dwell'.[41]

The island episode of *Robinson Crusoe* is mythic in the same way as *The Tempest*: it provides a simplifying crucible in which complexities can be reduced to their essential components. Such a formulation would probably gain assent, but the simplification of the episode needs careful, if seemingly paradoxical, glossing. It has of course been seen as simplifying in the sense of being the reduction to a logical starting-point through the resolutive method pioneered by Galileo and applied to political societies by Hobbes and, in a rather different way, by Locke and Rousseau; a method which enables the analyst to recompose the initial complexity of lived experience through a process of imaginative recombination of the relevant simples.[42] This view has Robinson Crusoe on the island, according to two of its variants, as the initial unit of a market economy interacting, when need arises, with similar producers; and as natural man, existing in a pre-social world before combining with others to form a 'society'. Neither of these analyses of the simplification of the island episode has proved convincing. The reasons have been spelled out by Marx and Watt amongst others,[43] but amount basically to two points: the lack of interest shown by the text in the compositive leg of the analysis which, for political and economic analysts, takes methodological precedence; and the 'impurity' of Robinson Crusoe as a simple, so graphically illustrated by the various trips to the wreck, but equally importantly represented by what Christopher Hill calls Crusoe's 'mental furniture',[44] the ideological and cultural presuppositions he inevitably carries with him to the island.

A further reason for rejecting such facile versions of the relationship between the fictional and the politico-economic discourses of the eighteenth century is the latter's indifference, as scientific fables, to the topographical and historical contexts whose very importance to *Robinson Crusoe* this chapter is trying to demonstrate. But two caveats need immediately adding to this statement. Despite the purely hypothetical status of the fables of origin in Hobbes, Locke and Rousseau, it should be remembered that they all in fact seek empirical support for their hypotheses in the contemporary state of America and, in Rousseau's case, refer specifically to the Caribs.[45] Conversely, despite the importance of *Robinson Crusoe*'s topography, there is a sense in which the island episode is, so to speak, a retreat from chronology and from geography into a moment that can in certain respects be called 'Utopian', though again some precision needs adding to this term.

The episode certainly has the mythic qualities of an original encounter between civilization and savagery, and is Utopian therefore in the sense that the specific characteristics of the historical Caribbean in the middle of the seventeenth century are stripped away to highlight the purity of the experience. And the island setting, as in many Utopias, facilitates the isolation necessary for such paradigmatic fables to develop. Then again, Crusoe's island shares some of the paradisaical elements of certain Utopias, especially that tradition of what might be called 'colonial Utopias', those which stand outside the mainstream of the Utopian tradition both by being primarily a sought ideal and only secondarily discursive, and by being constantly anti-authoritarian in impetus. The model for this tradition comes from the *Odyssey*: the Lotus-Eaters of Book IX whose food makes Odysseus's sailors lose the desire to return home. The first Caribbean example is probably the community established by Roldán in the south of Hispaniola in flagrant challenge to Columbus's authority; the most relevant that outlined by Stephen Hopkins in challenge to Somers after the shipwreck of the *Sea-*

Venture, and imperfectly practised by those who remained behind on the Bermudas; the two most resonant, the famous pirate commonwealth of Madagascar and, right at the end of the period covered by this book, that established, or at least held up as a potent ideal, by Fletcher Christian, in revolt from Captain Bligh's attempt to solve the problem of what to feed the Caribbean slaves.[46] *Robinson Crusoe*'s relationship with this tradition is by no means straightforward. More's pun on eutopia is especially problematic given Crusoe's anxiety and despair, but it should not be forgotten that Crusoe's island has the kind of tropical fertility that rewards labour, even if it does not make it unnecessary. In addition, the social dimension of the colonial Utopias is, strangely enough, present: both in Crusoe's benevolent despotism – which, amongst other things, is an insistence that the social relations proper to Europe will not apply on *his* island; and in the language he uses to talk about his property.

But the primary dimension of the narrative's parabolic simplicity is found in Crusoe's solitude on the island, and it is here, surely, in its analysis of the novel's 'radical individualism' that Watt's account stands uncontradicted. The particular significance of the use of the autobiographical memoir as an assertion of the primacy of individual experience by both Descartes and Defoe offers a comparison worth pursuing. The *Discourse on Method* tells a story similar in many respects to *Robinson Crusoe*: a story of travel and adventure cast in autobiographical form which culminates in a period of absolute solitude in which the protagonist is completely isolated from the world in which he lives. This is Descartes' account:

> it is exactly eight years since this wish made me decide to leave all those places where I had acquaintances, and to withdraw here to a country where the long duration of the war has established such discipline that the armies maintained there seem to serve only to ensure that the fruits of peace are enjoyed with the maximum of security; and where, in the midst of a great crowd of busy people, more concerned with their own business than curious about that of others, without lacking any of the conveniences offered by the most populous cities, I have been able to live as solitary and withdrawn as I would in the most remote of deserts.[47]

Descartes' solitude is very much an act of will, Crusoe's seemingly an involuntary exile from the world – although the island episode could also be seen as the logical culmination to a process of voluntary isolation that began with Crusoe's rejection of his father at the very beginning of the book, a denial of the past every bit as symbolic as Descartes' abandonment of the study of letters.[48] Their spheres are clearly different, consciously at least, but Crusoe and Descartes both set out to become very precisely self-made men: involved in a long quest for the composition of the self.

The differences may still seem striking. After all, Descartes arrives through a rigorous process of courageous self-examination at the certainty of a subjectivity that can ground knowledge; Crusoe tries, for the most part unsuccessfully, to compose himself in the face of dreadful anxieties. At best, surely, Descartes is the pure theorist of the self, operating in a world untrammelled by practical considerations; Crusoe an embodiment of the practical man of the world who operates entirely in a realm of trial and error. The differences should not be minimalized, but it has at least to be clear that behind the bland assurance of Descartes' prose lies a maelstrom of narrative and syntactical complexities that severely compromise the purity of that 'I'; and that, despite the 'pure' philosophical tradition stemming from his work, De-scartes' own concern was to establish:

a practical philosophy ... by which, knowing the power and the effects of fire, water, air, the stars, the heavens and all the other bodies which surround us ... we might put them in the same way to all the uses for which they are appropriate, and thereby make ourselves, as it were, masters and possessors of nature;[49]

– an enterprise entirely congruent with Crusoe's career and outlook.

5

An earlier focus was the dramatic contestation of 'proper beginnings' that occupies much of the second scene of *The*

Tempest. Despite the date of its composition, *Robinson Crusoe* is equally concerned with that mythic 'beginning' moment of the colonial encounter although, read against *The Tempest* as a model, it can be seen to have a *dual* colonial beginning, Crusoe's first days alone on the island being separated from his first meeting with Friday, whereas Prospero had met Caliban on his arrival on the island. Despite the supposed plainness, even negligence, of Defoe's style, the first beginning moment is presented with quite labyrinthine complexity.

An opening, and seemingly uncomplicated, description is given in its expected narrative place in the course of Crusoe's autobiography:

> After I had solaced my mind with the comfortable part of my condition, I began to look round me to see what kind of place I was in, and what was next to be done, and I soon found my comforts abate, and that in a word I had a dreadful deliverance; for I was wet, had no clothes to shift me, nor any thing either to eat or drink or comfort me, neither did I see any prospect before me, but that of perishing with hunger, or being devoured by wild beasts; and that which was particularly afflicting to me was that I had no weapon either to hunt and kill any creature for my sustenance, or to defend my self against any other creature that might desire to kill me for theirs. In a word, I had nothing about me but a knife, a tobacco-pipe, and a little tobacco in a box; this was all my provision, and this threw me into terrible agonies of mind, that for a while I run about like a mad-man. Night coming upon me, I began with a heavy heart to consider what would be my lot if there were any ravenous beasts in that country, seeing at night they always come abroad for their prey.
>
> All the remedy that offered to my thoughts at that time was to get up into a thick bushy tree like a firr, but thorny, which grew near me, and where I resolved to sit all night, and consider the next day what death I should dye, for as yet I saw no prospect of life; I walked about a furlong from the shore, to see if I could find any fresh water to drink, which I did, to my great joy; and having drank and put a little tobacco in my mouth to prevent hunger, I went to the tree, and getting up into it, endeavoured to place my self so, as that if I should sleep

I might not fall; and having cut me a short stick, like a truncheon, for my defence, I took up my lodging, and having been excessively fatigued, I fell fast asleep and slept as comfortably as, I believe, few could have done in my condition, and found my self the most refreshed with it that I think I ever was on such an occasion. (pp. 66–7)

Not surprisingly that first experience of the island stays with Crusoe, and he is reminded of it many years later when he sympathetically observes the despair of the prisoners being cast away by the English mutineers:

This put me in mind of the first time when I came on shore, and began to look about me; how I gave my self over for lost; how wildly I looked round me; what dreadful apprehensions I had; and how I lodged in the tree all night for fear of being devoured by wild beasts. (p. 250)

What complicates matters is that by this later stage of the story we have already had two additional accounts of the moment of trauma. Crusoe, it will be remembered, spends some two weeks making twelve trips to the wreck and then at least another three weeks building his initial fortification and sorting out his domestic arrangements. Only then does he have the time to turn to such secondary matters as writing:

And now it was when I began to keep a journal of every days employment, for indeed at first I was in too much hurry, and not only hurry as to labour, but in too much discomposure of mind, and my journal would ha' been full of many dull things. For example, I must have said thus: 'Sept. the 30th. After I got to shore and had escaped drowning, instead of being thankful to God for my deliverance, having first vomited with the great quantity of salt water which was gotten into my stomach, and recovering my self a little, I ran about the shore, wringing my hand and beating my head and face, exclaiming at my misery, and crying out, I was undone, undone, till tyred and faint I was forced to lye down on the ground to repose, but durst not sleep for fear of being devoured.' (p. 86)

It is not clear whether this is an *example* of the dull things that Crusoe would have written had he started his journal immedi-

ately, or whether this is what he would have written had he not
been in 'too much discomposure of mind' to write at all. More
worryingly: is one to presume that it would only have been the
discomposure that would have made him mention the vomiting,
edited from the other accounts, and would have caused him to
end the entry sleepless on the ground rather than snug in the tree?
Something odd certainly seems to be happening. Either, the
suggestion would appear to be, a composed mind would know
what to edit from its account; or there are inexplicable discrepancies between Crusoe's different accounts: not just, in fact,
between the narrative present account (pp. 66–7) and the narrative present reconstruction of what he would have said (p. 86),
but also between both of these and what immediately follows,
which is the journal entry itself:

> SEPTEMBER 30, 1659. I, poor miserable Robinson Crusoe, being
> shipwrecked, during a dreadful storm, in the offing, came on
> shore on this dismal unfortunate island, which I called the
> Island of Despair, all the rest of the ship's company being
> drowned, and my self almost dead.
>
> All the rest of that day I spent in afflicting my self at the
> dismal circumstances I was brought to, viz. I had neither food,
> house, clothes, weapon, or place to fly to, and in despair of any
> relief, saw nothing but death before me, either that I should be
> devoured by wild beasts, murthered by savages, or starved to
> death for want of food. At the approach of night, I slept in a
> tree for fear of wild creatures, but slept soundly tho' it rained all
> night. (p. 87)

Since Crusoe has just given us the journal entry he would have
written for September 30th had he then been writing a journal,
the only possible status for this passage is as a retrospective entry
written when the journal was really started some four or five
weeks later. Despite the presumed composure of early November
this entry is not noticeably different in manner or dullness from
the hypothetical account, except that it is bereft of some of the
detail about how he afflicted himself. It confirms the tree-sleeping,
but adds the new detail that 'it rained all night', something it is
difficult to imagine Crusoe knowing since he 'slept soundly'
(p. 87) and woke to find 'the weather clear' (p. 67).
    It would be too easy to put these discrepancies down to Defoe's

carelessness. *Robinson Crusoe* does not have to be turned into *Tristram Shandy* to see the text grappling here with some of the complexities involved in 'writing to the moment'.[50] Two points need emphasis. The first is that this radical textual disturbance occurs in the description of Crusoe's beginning on the island, a moment no doubt of acute personal trauma for Crusoe, but at the same time a moment resonant with legal and ideological implications for colonialist discourse: it is always this beginning moment that the discourse hesitates over. Secondly, although Crusoe presents his 'discomposure' as of short duration, an assessment that the view of Crusoe as rational man would second, the textual evidence gives no support to this view, offering in place of the discomposed hypothetical version an account *purporting* to have been written at the time but which we know from what we have just been told could not have been written until at the very least four weeks later. It is not a question of catching Crusoe out in his discrepancies, but rather of highlighting the desperate difficulties the text has in composing Crusoe's self, an activity, as the word indicates, every bit as much scriptive as it is psychological.

Danger to self threatens Crusoe from, as it were, both directions. His protection against the devouring cannibals is to build a byzantine fortress of monumental solidity in which he can hide as in the womb – the outer layer is a shrubbery entered through a narrow winding passage. But the completion of the fortress is followed by an earthquake which brings the fear of being 'swallowed up alive' (p. 98). Homer Brown in probably right in seeing these two fears as essentially one – 'basically fears of engulfment'[51] – yet there is one small but important distinction made, interestingly enough, by Crusoe himself:

> The fear of being swallowed up alive made me that I never slept in quiet, and yet the apprehensions of lying abroad without any fence was almost equal to it. (p. 98).

But his words are misleading: the fear of sleeping in the open, far from being 'almost equal' to the fear of being swallowed alive, was clearly greater, since Crusoe *never* sleeps 'abroad without any fence' and never abandons his castle despite the danger from earthquakes. Even before the appearance of the footprint, the ungrounded fear of cannibals always outweights his *actual* experiences, however frightening these experiences might be at the moment they occur. This is even more apparent with the various escapes from drowning, none of the effects of which lasts more than a few days. It is not easy to know what to make of this distinction. Being eaten no doubt has little in general to re-commend it, but seas and earthquakes certainly devour as effectively as cannibals, and the 'three of their hats, one cap, and two shoes that were not fellows' (p. 66) prefigure the equally heterogeneous collection of limbs he later finds on the same shore (p. 172). Yet the clothing perhaps also hints at a significant difference in that it is but a metonym for Crusoe's dead companions whose bodies, though 'devoured', are whole. In other words what is to be feared from cannibal devouring is dispersal of corporeal integrity. Although Crusoe never mentions it as an issue, such dispersal would be a particular threat to a Christian at a time when the resurrection of the body at the Last Judgement was taken literally. But even powerful considerations such as this cannot explain the extent and persistence of Crusoe's fear, which proves to be psychotic inasmuch as it constantly disavows all contradictory evidence.

This is a point of some importance for the overall argument of this book, which affirms the existence of such a psychosis at the heart of European perceptions of Amerindian culture in the Caribbean. Crusoe's immunity to the evidence presented – the last failing one would expect of a character so often seen as representative of common-sense English empiricism – is therefore a miniature of the larger picture the present book paints. The issue is not Crusoe's *initial* fear of the cannibals, understandable enough given the views prevailing in the seventeenth century; it is rather his unswerving adherence to this fear despite the evidence that confronts him. Two key episodes are juxtaposed in Defoe's text. At an advanced stage in Crusoe's relationship with Friday – Friday now speaks fluent, if broken, English and is trusted enough to have been initiated into the mysteries of gunpowder and bullet – Crusoe shows Friday the ruins of his ship's boat and is told in response that Friday has seen such a boat before:

> Friday described the boat to me well enough; but brought me better to understand him, when he added with some warmth, 'We save the white mans from drown'. Then I presently asked him if there was any white mans, as he called them, in the

boat. 'Yes', he said, 'the boat full white mans'. I asked him
how many; he told upon his fingers seventeen. I asked him then
what become of them; he told me, 'They live, they dwell at
my nation' . . .

Upon this, I enquired of him more critically what was
become of them. He assured me they lived still there; that
they had been there about four years; that the savages let them
alone, and gave them victuals to live. I asked him how it came
to pass they did not kill them and eat them. He said 'No, they
make brother with them'; that is, as I understood him, a truce:
and then he added, 'They no eat mans but when makes the war
fight'; that is to say, they never eat any men but such as come
to fight with them, and are taken in battle. (p. 224)

It hardly needs saying that Friday's words, produced in an English
fiction, are not comparable with even such complexly mediated
statements as Pocahontas's Brentford discourse. And yet, in a
manner not dissimilar to Caliban's contestation of Prospero's
assumptions, Defoe here has Friday offer an alternative version of
Carib social practices which stands in stark contrast to Crusoe's
lurid vision of unalloyed ferocity. The Caribs, according to
Friday, do eat human flesh but only the flesh of those that offer
aggression: it seems that something like the Law of Nations
operates in the native Caribbean. Moreover the Spaniards,
unharmed, were fed and 'made brother with', an example of the
operation of the laws of hospitality – with its echo of the *guatiao*
system – that makes Crusoe's plans to massacre those who had
offered him no violence look decidedly unethical. It is difficult to
read this episode as other than a rather subtle critique of the hollow
pretensions to 'civilized' behaviour of the European colonists in
the Caribbean.

Even more striking, then, that this episode should be immediately followed by another in which, the weather being serene,
Friday discovers that he can see his homeland:

I observed an extraordinary sense of pleasure appeared in his
face, and his eyes sparkled, and his countenance discovered a
strange eagerness, as if he had a mind to be in his own country
again; and this observation of mine put a great many thoughts
into me, which made me at first not so easy about my new man
Friday as I was before; and I made no doubt but that if Friday

could get back to his own nation again, he would not only forget all his religion, but all his obligation to me; and would be forward enough to give his countrymen an account of me, and come back perhaps with a hundred or two of them, and make a feast upon me, at which he might be as merry as he used to be with those of his enemies, when they were taken in war. (p. 225)

This is a very dense passage, but the main point is clear: Crusoe's fear of being devoured by cannibals is immune to the quite specific evidence as to Carib practice just provided by Friday. In any case one needs a substantially inflated notion of the self to imagine that 'a hundred or two' cannibals could 'make a feast' of one body. It is at such moments that Crusoe seems to have lost touch with reality altogether.

The conclusions to be drawn from this analysis might initially seem at odds with the general drift of my argument because Crusoe's disavowal suggests that the island episode should be read as less a 'realistic' account of English colonialism in the Caribbean than a parable of the anxiety surrounding the kind of 'composition of the self' performed so emblematically by Descartes.[52] The threat from the cannibals would then be read not as the promulgation of a pseudo-ethnographic or even overtly ideological vision of the native inhabitants of the Caribbean, but rather as a graphic image of the *decomposition* of the self that is the price of failure. Crusoe's fear would be the reverse of Descartes' 'first good' which relies, it should be remembered, 'on the disposition of the organs': the 'tremulous private body' of the new bourgeois regime haunted by the image of the violent dispersal of its violently composed body politic.[53] However there are two reasons why such a reading is not in fact at odds with my general drift. First, to *set* such a parable in the Caribbean is itself, even though (or of course because) not a direct comment, still the contribution of a significant strand to the ideological construction of that geographical area within European discourse. And secondly, as will be shown shortly, Crusoe's composed self, tempered in a crucible every bit as intense as Descartes' stove, is ready for action. The parable of the self, remote from social and political concerns as it may seem, has very decisive social and political *effects*.

These effects can be spelled out by looking more closely at the process of Crusoe's self-composition. Schematically it could be said that the initial composition of that self lasts the twelve months that he has a good supply of ink: a year's journal provides him with enough material to check for providential repetitions, and by this time he has established his home (extended self) and his routine (chronological self). Within this year the key event is clearly the ague and the 'terrible dream' that occasions Crusoe's conversion.

There are four moments in the book when this composed self is severely shaken. The first comes after Crusoe's abortive attempt to sail round the island, which has again opened up the prospect of death, this time from starvation. Exhausted, Crusoe reaches his 'country house' and falls asleep, only to be woken by somebody calling his name. The voice belongs to his parrot, but 'it was a good while before I could compose myself' (p. 152). The feared 'other' turns out this time to be merely a repetition of his own voice, as the parrot, that token of the New World, speaks its unique lines, being the only creature, human or animal, to utter Robinson Crusoe's name in the whole book – except that, of course, since self-made men can have no fathers, the parrot calls him Robin rather than Robinson.

The second disconcerting moment is that central incident of the book, the discovery of the footprint. Driven 'out of my self' (p. 162), Crusoe's immediate reaction is to hide in his castle for three days and nights. He is eventually comforted by the thought that what he had seen might be a print of his own foot, so that the feared 'other' could again turn out to be another version of the self. Unfortunately the print is larger and in a place where Crusoe is sure he had never trodden. His reaction now is:

> to throw down my enclosures and turn all my tame cattle wild into the woods, that the enemy might not find them, and then frequent the island in prospect of the same, or the like booty; then to the simple thing of digging up my two corn fields, that they might not find such a grain there, and still be prompted to frequent the island; then to demolish my bower and tent, that they might not see any vestages of habitation, and be prompted to look farther, in order to find out the persons inhabiting. (p. 167)[54]

Just three pages earlier he had been racking his brains how to avoid the terrible possibility that the savages would 'find my enclosure, destroy all my corn, carry away all my flock of tame goats' (p. 164). To conceal the self and to destroy the self turn out to be identical manoeuvres. In such circumstances just how can self and other be distinguished at all?

Hardly has Crusoe recovered from the shock of the footprint when he stumbles across the horrific remains of the cannibal feast. This time his discomposure has two stages. First:

> my stomach grew sick, and I was just at the point of fainting, when nature discharged the disorder from my stomach, and having vomited with an uncommon violence, I was a little relieved. (p. 172)

He walks away:

> and then recovering my self, I looked up with the utmost affection of my soul, and with a flood of tears in my eyes, gave God thanks that had cast my first lot in a part of the world where I was distinguished from such dreadful creatures as these. (p. 172)

So that paradigmatic manifestation of cannibalism finally allows Crusoe to clearly distinguish himself from others. He finally knows who he is; although only after the vomiting symbolically voids him, producing that impossible 'pure' body, alimentarily chaste. Horrific as it may be, tangibility is in inverse proportion to anxiety: after the initial shock Crusoe is content that 'if I did not discover my self to them' (p. 173) he would be safe and sound. As the text conjures up the 'reality' of cannibalism, so the tentative ego is strengthened in its knowledge of itself. It may not be too sure what it is, but it knows it is not a cannibal. It is at this moment that Crusoe becomes the fully-fledged colonial adventurer, self-composed, ready for action.

But action involves entry into a social world, interrelationships with other human beings, and this move is always, for Crusoe, fraught with difficulties. Within the fictional world this is hardly surprising, although Crusoe's actions are sometimes, even given the circumstances, quite remarkable. But the larger political questions concerning the Caribbean are raised in direct fashion by Crusoe himself, enabling us again to read these individual difficulties as socially and politically resonant.

In his imagination Crusoe alternates, wildly, between the two extreme points on the scale of international relations: he dreams of various elaborate contrivances for killing as many of the cannibals as possible, and then decides it would be both morally right and more prudent to leave them entirely alone unless they attacked him first. In the course of these latter meditations Crusoe constructs a classic Montaignesque argument comparing Carib and Christian practices in war:

When I had considered this a little, it followed necessarily that I was certainly in the wrong in it, that these people were not murtherers in the sense that I had before condemned them in my thoughts; any more than those Christians were murtherers who often put to death the prisoners taken in battle; or more frequently, upon many occasions, put whole troops of men to the sword, without giving quarter, though they threw down their arms and submitted. (pp. 177–8)[55]

The point is almost *too* well made. On this criterion Carib practice is indeed little different from Christian; which helps Crusoe decide on his policy of non-intervention, but also throws the whole ideological basis of European colonialism into doubt. Crusoe, with all the nonchalance of a man crossing to the other side of a minefield without even noticing the warning signs, now makes exactly the right move. Some Christians can indeed be called savage murderers: the Spaniards. The ready-made rhetoric of the Black Legend enables Crusoe to reach the safe plateau of righteous indignation, well clear of the slippery slopes of anthropological speculation:

To fall upon them ... would justify the conduct of the Spaniards in all their barbarities practised in America, where they destroyed millions of these people, who, however they were idolaters and barbarians, and had several bloody and barbarous rites in their customs, such as sacrificing human bodies to their idols, were yet, as to the Spaniards, very innocent people; and that the rooting them out of the country is spoken of with the utmost abhorrence and detestation by even the Spaniards themselves at this time, and by all other Christian nations of Europe, as a meer butchery, a bloody and unnatural piece of cruelty, unjustifiable either to God or man; and such, as for which the very name of a Spaniard is reckoned to be frightful and terrible to all people of humanity, or of Christian compassion. (p. 178)

As James Maddox acutely points out, the Spaniards are here discursively produced as a buffer zone between Crusoe (that is to say the English) and the cannibals, rather as Crusoe constructed an intermediate zone between the two walls of his fortification: some breaches can take place without all being lost. So both the hard-to-defend barriers that separate Crusoe from others and European from Carib can be managed: the Spaniards are allowed to be like Crusoe – only not as efficient; and they are chosen to bear the brunt of the undeniable similarities between European and Carib. Crusoe has fed himself – the Spaniards are fed by the Caribs; Crusoe teaches Friday English – the Spaniards learn the Carib language. Cannibalism – admittedly at a moment when being devoured is not such an imminent threat – is *favourably* contrasted by Crusoe with falling into the hands of the Inquisition (p. 243). Earlier, after witnessing the aftermath of a shipwreck on the coast of the island, Crusoe has imagined that the survivors:

> were all gone off to sea in their boat, and being hurry'd away by the current that I had formerly been in, were carry'd out into the great ocean, where there was nothing but misery and perishing; and that perhaps they might by this time think of starving, and of being in a condition to eat one another. (p. 192)

The frontier between civilization and savagery is threatened by such speculations; but the later discovery that the sailors were only Spaniards saves the appearances.[56]

6

The long-awaited arrival of the cannibals some two-thirds of the way through *Robinson Crusoe* heralds the climactic moments of the book; indeed the description of the battle between, on the one side, Crusoe and Friday, and on the other, twenty-one cannibals, is in many ways the climax of the particular discourse of colonialism being investigated here.

The moment is important for a number of reasons. It marks the second stage of 'beginning', the true colonial encounter when the complex matter of the European/native relationship must be negotiated. It is the moment when the parable of the self comes somewhere near resolution. And, more mundanely but no less important, it is the moment when *Robinson Crusoe* comes into its own as an adventure story in the now conventional sense of the word. Most crucially, these three things are simultaneous, constituting a moment of intense narrative excitement which, without the need for excursus, inscribes matters both colonial and metaphysical.

At the level of adventure a quite straightfoward account of the episode could point to the increase in tension which begins with Crusoe's discovery of the footprint and builds up through his various schemes for dealing with the cannibals, along with his doubts about the morality of killing them, to the moment of greatest excitement when Crusoe rescues Friday; the culmination coming with the final massacre undertaken to rescue the European prisoner and a native who turns out to be Friday's father.

This adventure story is interwoven with the metaphysical level in some obvious ways. The period between the discovery of the footprint and the arrival of the cannibals is the period of greatest anxiety for Crusoe, the period in which, one might say, his notion of self is most under threat; the period which turns to almost unbearable intensity the screw of the paradox that what makes solitude so frightening is that you might not be alone, until, in the firing of the gun, you reach that other paradox that the fear of being eaten is dependent on the *absence* of the cannibals. Their presence dispels Crusoe's anxiety and ends the parable of the self: he has composed his self, as the best adventurers always do, under pressure. The parabolic nature of the whole episode, it could in any case be argued, is signalled right from the beginning in the determinedly unrealistic presence of the single, isolated footprint in the middle of the beach, more like a pure trace of the idea of otherness than the actual track of another human being.

In some respects the colonial aspect of this part of the story is identical with the adventure aspect. On this reading Crusoe's acquisition of Friday is, quite literally, 'peradventure' – the chance result of his confrontation with the dreaded cannibals, and Friday's gratitude towards Crusoe for saving his life is altogether proper. Generically this is the realist reading, inadequate but ideologically useful because it obscures the crux of the colonial question.

The appearance of Friday is obviously important for readings of *Robinson Crusoe* such as Stephen Hymer's, which can see in the Crusoe/Friday relationship an adumbration of capital and labour and, more particularly, a parallel to the 'actual procedures of colonization used in the last two hundred years.'[57] There is a lot to be said in favour of this reading, which traces the stages from Crusoe's naming of Friday, through his teaching Friday English, placing him – in a small-scale version of plantation architecture – in the intermediate position between outer and inner stockade, teaching him Christianity, and finally initiating him into the use of firearms.[58] But the problem remains the same as before: mimetic readings such as this simply reduce the text to another kind of allegory. A more productive contextualization would come from pursuing the comparison with *The Tempest*. As a cannibal, Friday's initial connections would seem to be with his anagrammatic cousin Caliban, but the circumstances of his enrolment into Crusoe's service are remarkably similar to those surrounding Prospero's recruitment of Ariel: crucially, both are dependent on the spontaneous gratitude which results from the liberation of the captive party. The differences between Ariel and Friday are also instructive. Friday, though phenomenally quick about the house and woods, does not have Ariel's supernatural powers; but that may on balance be an advantage for Crusoe. After all, Ariel, freed from imprisonment, is clearly reluctant, after a suitable period of showing his gratitude, to exchange one captivity for another, and Prospero has to depend on a rather volatile mixture of threats and promises to keep him up to the mark. It is not entirely clear whether Prospero's magic would have been sufficient to bring Ariel back from, for example, the 'still-vex'd Bermoothes', had he decided to stay put. A thoroughly socialized Friday has the advantage of being a good deal more dependable.

A closer reading of the episode itself is also revealing. To begin with, Crusoe's actions were not as peradventure as they might have seemed. He presents himself, it is true, in the classic pose of the improvisatory adventurer – 'so I resolved to put my self upon the watch, to see them when they came on shore, and leave the rest to the event, taking such measures as the opportunity should present, let be what would be' (p. 203) – but the appropriate plan has already been revealed to Crusoe by, of all things, a dream that he had had some eighteen months previously:

> I dreamed that as I was going out in the morning as usual from my castle, I saw upon the shore two canoes and eleven savages coming to land, and that they brought with them another savage, who they were going to kill, in order to eat him; when on a sudden, the savage that they were going to kill, jumpt away, and ran for his life; and I thought, in my sleep, that he came running into my little thick grove before my fortific- ation, to hide himself; and that I seeing him alone, and not perceiving that the other sought him that way, showed my self to him, and smiling upon him, encouraged him; and that he kneeled down to me, seeming to pray me to assist him; upon which I shewed my ladder, made him go up, and carry'd him into my cave, and he became my servant; and that as soon as I had gotten this man, I said to my self, 'Now I may certainly venture to the main land; for this fellow will serve me as a pilot, and will tell me what to do, and whether to go for provisions; and whether not to go for fear of being devoured, what places to venture into, and what to escape.' (p. 202)

There are several odd features to this dream, but nothing is so odd as its occurrence in the text in the first place. Crusoe's earlier dream (pp. 102–3) had been suitably religious, dense with the symbolism of storm, cloud, fire and spears. He had read it as a providential threat; we could take it physiologically as a result of his ague, psychologically as an indication of his general depres- sion, and even psychoanalytically as a manifestation of his repressed guilt over disobeying his father. In other words the first dream occupies a perfectly comprehensible place in the narrative. But whereas this earlier dream follows with some logic from Crusoe's antecedent state of mind, the second dream, although the result of a similar agitation, is marked by Crusoe himself as disjunctive from its context. The immediate cause of Crusoe's agitation is his reflection on how he had been 'so near the obtaining what I so earnestly longed for, viz. some-body to speak to, and learn some knowledge from of the place where I was'

(p. 202), a reflection brought about by the solitary corpse he finds washed onshore from the wreck of the Spanish ship. The dream is then introduced in this way:

> When this had agitated my thoughts for two hours or more, with such violence, that it set my very blood into a ferment, and my pulse beat as high as if I had been in a feaver, meerly with the extraordinary fervour of my mind about it; nature, as if I had been fatigued and exhausted with the very thought of it, threw me into a sound sleep; one would have thought I should have dreamed of it, but I did not, nor of anything relating to it; but I dreamed that ... (p. 202)

Crusoe wakes to the dejection of finding that his escape was only a dream and, almost as an afterthought, he takes from the dream the lesson that capturing a savage would be the best way to escape. He makes no attempt to incorporate the dream into the surrounding fabric of his narrative by, for example, reading it as a providential prophecy.

There is no doubt that the presence of the dream, eighteen months but no more than a couple of pages before the arrival of the cannibal party, does strange things to the texture of the fictional 'realism'. As Watt pointed out, classical plots are alien to formal realism because they are not new: 'the impression of fidelity to human experience'[59] can only come from 'the novel' – a novelty which *Robinson Crusoe* announces on its title page: 'The Life and *Surprizing* Adventures'. Readers can hardly be totally surprised by Crusoe's adventure with the cannibals when they have just read a rehearsal for it in Crusoe's dream. To complicate matters, the dream also brings to an end a long section in which Crusoe is recounting how, like a drowning man, he 'run over the whole history of my life in miniature, or by abridgement, as I may call it' (p. 200): in other words another of those complex moments of replication – like the episode of the start of the journal – where the narrative seems to fold over on to itself in a way disturbingly unlike any realistic transcription of the empirically real.[60] In one sense, then, the dream acts, rather like the solitary footprint, as an outcrop against the grain of any straightforwardly mimetic reading of the cannibal episode. But what other kind of reading *could* make sense of it?

It was noted earlier, in discussing Hymer's analysis of the way the Crusoe/Friday relationship parallels the 'actual procedures of colonization', that the last stage in those procedures is Crusoe's initiation of Friday into the use of firearms, a lesson that repays its investment when Crusoe and Friday stand shoulder to shoulder shooting and killing the cannibal hordes. This initiation, though, is a final step that, historically, was never taken, the reason being – and this completes the unravelling of the mimetic reading of the episode – that slavery was never founded on the gratitude of the slave. Friday of course is never *called* a slave; but that absence is merely a symptom of the constant process of denial and renegotiation by which the text attempts to redraw the colonial encounter.

The Caribbean Amerindians were enslaved – though not often by the English – but it is not difficult to see in Crusoe's relationship with Friday a veiled and disavowed reference to the more pressing issue of black slavery. Crusoe's description of Friday is an almost classic case of negation: 'His hair was long and black, not curled like wool . . . . The colour of his skin was not quite black . . . his nose small, not flat like the negroes' (pp. 208–9).

Friday is certainly a slave inasmuch as he has no will of his own; and Crusoe, unwilling as he may be ever to call Friday 'slave', has no qualms about adopting the other half of the dialectic – 'I likewise taught him to say Master, and then let him know, that was to be my name' (p. 209). Yet within the fiction the term 'slave' can be avoided because Friday's servitude is voluntary, not forced:

> At last he lays his head flat upon the ground, close to my foot, and sets my other foot upon his head, as he had done before; and after this, made all the signs to me of subjection, servitude, and submission imaginable, to let me know how he would serve me as long as he lived. (p. 209)

The problem with slavery is that slaves are dangerous because forced to labour against their will; the danger is removed if their 'enslavement' is voluntary and therefore not slavery at all. Defoe, it could be said, has gone one better than Locke's thesis that a person who forfeits his own life through an act that deserves death may justly have that death delayed and be required to give service to whom he has forfeited his life, and be done no injury by it.[61]

However, forfeiture, just or not, is no guarantee that the slavery will not need enforcing by violence and therefore the master protecting from the threat of reciprocal violence; while the same paragraph of the *Second Treatise* denies the possibility of 'voluntary enslavement' on the classic liberal grounds that you cannot sign away your own fundamental rights. The circumstances of Friday's recruitment are a brilliant negotiation of these twin difficulties. His life is forfeited through Crusoe's intervention to save him, in keeping with Locke's justification of enslavement. But then – in a novel move – Defoe has Friday offer lifelong subjection, or so at least Crusoe imagines in his confident interpretation of the semiotics of Carib gesture. In Lockeian terms this move is theoretically invalid since Friday has no life to give, but its practical effects are incalculably beneficial to Crusoe since Friday's 'subjection' – his self-interpellation as a subject with no will – removes any need for force. By way of consolidation Crusoe, in a subtle move, avoids what might otherwise have seemed the obvious first step at the beginning of any normal social encounter – asking the name of the escaped prisoner. Instead, by naming him Friday – and remember the importance of Pocahontas's baptism as Rebecca – Crusoe underlines to him that his previous life has been forfeited, providing a weekly mnemonic to remind him who was responsible for giving him that second life.

Crusoe has dreamt a dream of wish-fulfilment. He thinks it is a dream of escape and is disappointed:

> I waked with this thought, and was under such inexpressible impressions of joy at the prospect of my escape in my dream, that the disappointments which I felt upon coming to my self and finding it was no more than a dream, were equally extravagant the other way, and threw me into a very great dejection of spirit. (pp. 202–3)

But the dream comes true and the escape that he himself, rather than the dream narrative, had built in ('I said to myself, "Now I may certainly venture ... "') does not materialize as a direct result: Friday fulfils none of the six roles imagined by Crusoe in his dream. This is because – it might be said – the dream was not the fulfilment of Crusoe's wish to escape, but rather the fulfilment of Europe's wish to secure its Caribbean colonies against the danger of rebellion. Friday's gratitude was the fulfilment of that dream. But it was only a dream.

Friday's gratitude proves, however, to be the breakthrough in Crusoe's establishment of social relationships. The Spaniard saved from the barbecue 'let me know by all the signs he could possibly make, how much he was in my debt for his deliverance' (p. 235); and Friday's father likewise 'looked up in my face with all the tokens of gratitude and thankfulness that could appear in any countenance' (p. 239). This is just what Crusoe wants to see. He proves, though, to be no sentimentalist. Addressing the Spaniard:

> I told him with freedom, I feared mostly their treachery and ill usage of me, if I put my life in their hands; for that gratitude was no inherent virtue in the nature of man; nor did men always square their dealings by the obligations they had received, so much as they did by the advantages they expected (p. 243)

– a resolutely Hobbesian view that contrasts starkly with the constant benevolence with which Crusoe is treated by others. The Spaniard, like Friday, has to convert the unguaranteed coin of his gratitude into the ringing currency of an unconditional sworn fealty – backed with a written contract (p. 244). Crusoe is determined to be an absolute sovereign, which is to be in society but not of it.[62]

The final incident in the transitional period of Crusoe's socialization emphasizes his dependence on the gratitude of others. When the English party arrive in the longboat – three prisoners and eight armed men – Crusoe never gives a moment's thought as to who the respective groups might be; whether, for example, the three prisoners might be murderers about to be cast away or executed on the captain's orders. He says with absolute assurance:

> I fitted my self up for a battle, as before; though with more caution, knowing I had to do with another kind of enemy than I had at first. (pp. 251–2)

Poised to attack those whom he unhesitatingly identifies as the 'villains' Crusoe takes time to ascertain from the prisoner he aims to free that the ship 'should be wholly directed and commanded by me in every thing; and if the ship was not recovered, he would live and dye with me in what part of the world soever I would send him' (p. 253), and to lay down his own numbered conditions. Only as absolute despot will Crusoe's composed self enter the social world.

7

Generically *Robinson Crusoe* can be called a colonial romance. The indispensable theoretical point to be made in this context is that generic criticism can be fully historical rather than rigidly essentialist. To call *Robinson Crusoe* a romance is not to suggest that it 'belongs' to such a genre, but rather that it shares some of the features characteristic of that genre. Two quotations from Fredric Jameson's important essay on the topic can help:

> In its emergent, strong form a genre is essentially a socio-symbolic message, or in other terms, that form is immanently and intrinsically an ideology in its own right. When such forms are reappropriated and refashioned in quite different social and cultural contexts, this message persists and must be functionally reckoned into the new form.[63]

Jameson also makes the point that:

> properly used, genre theory must always in one way or another project a model of the coexistence or tension between several generic modes or strands: and with this methodological axiom the typologizing abuses of traditional genre criticism are definitely laid to rest.[64]

'Coexistence or tension' is not quite precise enough: there must be a generic *structure*. 'The puritan mode' is a recognizable but subsidiary generic feature of *Robinson Crusoe*, and the analyses of the two previous sections have showed that the book's 'realism' and its 'novel-ty', though important, are not structurally dominant features either. To call *Robinson Crusoe* a romance is to argue that its romance features are its structurally controlling elements.[65]

This is part of the opening to Northrop Frye's section on romance in the third essay from the *Anatomy of Criticism*:

The romance is nearest of all literary forms to the wish-fulfilment dream .... In every age the ruling social or intellectual class tends to project its ideals in some form of romance, where the virtuous heroes and beautiful heroines represent the ideals and the villains the threats to their ascendancy .... The perenially child-like quality of romance is marked by its extraordinarily persistent nostalgia, its search for some kind of imaginative golden age in time or space.[66]

Robinson Crusoe might not 'fit' Frye's definition in any very obvious manner; nevertheless, his account is pertinent and, suitably refashioned, each of these three descriptions pertains to Defoe's novel in significant ways.

'Where the virtuous heroes and beautiful heroines represent the ideals and the villains the threats to their ascendancy.' The second half of this sentence could read as an epitaph for the Caribs. The simplicity of that division into heroes and villains is, though, an *achieved* simplicity which must, as in the case of the tidewater Algonquian, split the savage other to provide an alibi for unleashing the destructive power of colonial weaponry. Friday's gratitude is the first stage in that conversion, but the process is only completed through his education. This begins with Crusoe and Friday's return to the place where Friday's would-be devourers have been buried, Friday 'making signs to me that we should dig them up again and eat them' (p. 209); and ends with Friday, now trusted with European weapons, being told, in an important symbolic moment, 'do exactly as you see me do' (p. 234). In other words *Robinson Crusoe* is repeating the move basic to European colonial discourse – making the distinction between *guatiao* and *canibal* – but in a changed set of circumstances. By 1719 it was clear that the friendliness of the *guatiaos* had not prevented their extinction – a regrettable crime which could be conveniently laid at the door of Spain (and Crusoe, as we saw earlier, adds his piece to the commonplace English denunciation). So all the remaining Amerindians of the area are now cannibalistic. Something of the gentle Taino/ferocious Carib division remains in the hostility between Friday's nation and their enemies, but that division cannot be ethnographically named ('I asked him the name of the several nations of his sort of people;

but could get no other name than Caribs' (p. 217)) so has to be fictionally produced.

The first step is to wean Friday off human flesh. Defoe's ideas of Carib diet belong to the bizarrer end of the spectrum sketched in Chapter 2. By 'cannibal' he seems to understand that Friday will eat nothing but human flesh: Crusoe certainly operates on the principle that 'in order to bring Friday off from his horrid way of feeding, and from the relish of a cannibal's stomach, I ought to let him taste other flesh' (p. 213). He does this by setting up a barbecue ('This Friday admired very much' (p. 215)) and roasting a kid, the taste of which instantly cures Friday of his hankering for human meat. This episode gives a clear enough indication of the state of deprivation in which the Caribs are seen as living: so depraved and stupid are they that it has never occurred to them to taste the flesh of the animals living on these islands.[67] Friday is then taught to beat and sift corn, and eventually promises that, if he went back to his own country, he would 'tell them to eat corn-bread, cattle flesh, milk, no eat man again' (p. 226). It is not clear, given Friday's ignorance about other foods, just what kind of 'victuals' were given to the shipwrecked Spaniards.

Another essential feature in Friday's education is navigation. Crusoe determines to build a large canoe, consults Friday as to the fittest type of wood, but rejects the Carib method of burning out the trunk by fire in favour of hacking it out with metal tools. He then builds a mast, sail and rudder, the sight of which leaves Friday standing 'like one astonished and amazed' (p. 229). 'With a little use' Friday 'became an expert sailor' except that 'as to the compass, I could make him understand very little' (pp. 229–30).[68]

Defoe was a novelist and not an ethnographer, and there is little point in looking for an accurate depiction of Carib life and culture in *Robinson Crusoe*. What is surprising, though, is that Defoe should have centred the two key episodes in Friday's education on precisely the two aspects of Carib technology, the barbecue and the canoe, that Europe learned from the Caribbean, both 'barbecue' and 'canoe' being Carib (or strictly speaking Island Arawak) words.[69] The 'ignorance' of the savage Caribs is *produced by* the text of *Robinson Crusoe*, which enacts a denial of those very aspects of Carib culture from which Europe had learned.

Friday becomes the most famous Carib in literature the better to enable all the others to become – at the end of the process described here – absolutely defined by their cannibalism upon the body of Europeans: Crusoe's hesitations as to his violence against barbarians are ended by his recognition that one of the prisoners 'was an European, and had cloaths on' (p. 223). The cannibals instantly degenerate, in that paradigmatic moment for all future colonial adventure stories, from a moral problem of some importance to merely a mass of 'dreadful wretches' (p. 234), fodder for the devastating power of European weaponry; accounted for by Crusoe's guns before being accounted for by his chillingly detailed reckoning:

> 3 killed at our first shot from the tree.
> 2 killed at the next shot.
> 2 killed by Friday in the boat.
> 2 killed by ditto, of those at first wounded.
> 1 killed by ditto, in the wood.
> 3 killed by the Spaniard.
> 4 killed, being found dropped here and there of their wounds, or killed by Friday in his chase of them.
> <u>4</u> escaped in the boat, whereof one wounded if not dead.
> 21 in all. (p. 237)

The romance form is useful to the colonial enterprise precisely because it *reduces* (in another sense of that key word) a potentially embarrassing cultural complexity to the simplicity of the essential romance terminology: heroes and villains.

Heroes but no heroines. Despite the centrality of the love-theme to the earlier forms of the romance genre – late classical, medieval, and bourgeois – the masculinist ethos of European colonialism is probably explanation enough of *Robinson Crusoe*'s lack of women, a lack common to many later colonial adventure stories, and certainly not filled – if anything deepened – by Crusoe's eventual marriage and widowerhood in the course of a single sentence (p. 298). But there are still points to be made – however tentatively – about the route taken by the discharge of that sexual current so important in other forms of romance.

First, there is the extent to which the true romance in *Robinson Crusoe* is between Crusoe and Friday. They live in domestic bliss:

> the conversation which employed the hours between Friday and I was such as made the three years which we lived there together perfectly and compleatly happy, if any such thing as compleat happiness can be formed in a sublunary state. (p. 222)

Crusoe's description of Friday is certainly tinged with erotic delight, though this is not easy to separate from a master's joy in a well-proportioned and healthy slave. But perhaps most striking is Crusoe's response to Friday's pleasure in seeing his home in the distance. Crusoe is distressed by Friday's sparkling eyes and extraordinary sense of pleasure (see the passage quoted on p. 195) and moves swiftly and illogically to the conclusion that he will be made a feast of by Friday's returning countrymen. Crusoe quite openly calls his feeling jealousy:

> While my jealousy of him lasted, you may be sure I was every day pumping him to see if he would discover any of the new thoughts, which I suspected were in him; but I found every thing he said was so honest and so innocent, that I could find nothing to nourish my suspicion . . . nor did he in the least perceive that I was uneasie, and therefore I could not suspect him of deceit. (p. 225)

These are the actions and language of an Othello or, more appropriately perhaps, of Prospero towards Miranda, jealous of any suitor: Crusoe often calls Friday his child. At the very least the language of sexual or paternal jealousy can be said to carry and inflect the sentiments of a slave-owner worrying about the loyalty of his slave.

But of more consequence to the general argument being pursued here is the extraordinary sequence of benefactors that Crusoe relies on. This is a romance feature because, just as the plot of the love romance depends in the last instance upon the absolute spiritual fidelity of the separated loved ones as the tie that binds together what would otherwise threaten to become a heterogeneous set of episodes, so the plot of *Robinson Crusoe* depends upon a generalized spirit of benevolence throughout the commercial world. This benevolence is at one and the same time a *narrative* device which holds together the many disparate strands of

Crusoe's commercial activity, and an aspect of that ideologeme of 'wish-fulfilment' identified by Frye as central to the romance form.

Various characters embody this single actant of 'the benefactor': the 'honest and plain-dealing' captain who helps Crusoe with his first adventure (p. 39); this captain's widow, whose 'unspotted integrity' (p. 296) is often relied on by Crusoe; the 'charitable' Portuguese captain who rescues Crusoe off the African coast, and whose 'generous treatment . . . I can never enough remember' (p. 55) and who is eventually responsible for the transportation of Crusoe's capital from England to Brazil and of his profits in goods from Bahia to Lisbon; English merchants who transmit the earlier order; a London merchant 'who represented it effectually' (p. 57) to the widow and invests the £100 in suitable goods; the 'good honest man' (p. 55) who teaches him the secrets of the *ingenio*; his estate's trustees, their heirs, and the prior of St Augustine, all of whom act with scrupulous honesty during the twenty-nine years of silence after Crusoe leaves Brazil, and of whose actions Crusoe announces: 'Never anything was more honourable than the proceedings upon this procuration' (p. 278).[70]

The simplification effected by the romance structure is another facet of *Robinson Crusoe*'s 'Utopianism'. To go further and, in line with Frye's third point, inflect this Utopianism as 'nostalgic' might seem perverse, since it would not merely take issue – as has already been done – with the nomination of Defoe as spokesman for the new economic order, but actually ally Defoe with those – Pope, Swift, Bolingbroke – usually seen as occupying precisely the *opposite* ideological positions to Defoe. Yet in one respect at least to speak of such a concurrence would not be ridiculous, for on the island Crusoe organizes his domestic economy in a manner largely congruent with the ideals put forward in Pope's *Epistles*.[71] Once his basic needs have been catered for, Crusoe begins to 'improve his estate'. He adds 'my Country-House' to 'my Sea-Coast House'; extends his cultivated fields; and embarks on an enclosure to corral his goats. Particularly impressive is what might be called Crusoe's moral economy. Although he is, as it were, *nouveau riche*, he avoids – not, admittedly, that he has much choice – the temptations of luxury and display, and achieves an admirable degree of self-reliance which is all the more impressive for being dependent on his learning from scratch the bare essentials of the simple life – like making bread. Crusoe's life is, in a word, unalienated, and he thereby achieves something like 'peace of mind' – especially when the ideal feudal relationship has relieved him of the worst of his labour. *Crusoe est beatus vir.*[72]

This is an important dimension of *Robinson Crusoe*, one moment in the dialectic between the two parts of the book – the frame narrative and the island episode. It is, though, a moment hedged with potential ironies. There seems to be more than a suggestion of comedy in the proprietorial language Crusoe uses to describe his modest abodes: a hint, perhaps, of the delusions of grandeur entertained by a lonely man with many lonely years to fill. And while it is true – as Pat Rogers notes – that Crusoe 'conceals the Bounds'[73] of his main property by surrounding it with a thick grove that eventually becomes an impassable wood, this is no longer the action of a *beatus vir* but of an obsessive recluse quite deliberately removing any trace of human presence from the landscape – not quite what Pope had in mind in the *Epistle to Burlington*. Eighteenth-century country houses, though no longer 'castles' ('for so I think I called it ever after this' (p. 162)), certainly had to be strong enough to repel attack from revolting peasants, but they were also there for display – and nothing could be more alien to Crusoe's requirements.

The most potent of these ironies, though, is that the happy man only maintains his happiness through staying still, which implies a continuing meaningful contact with a single place and a philosophical stillness at the centre of political and social and sexual demands; while Crusoe's fearful enforced immobility on the island fulfils the first only at the cost of offering a parody of the second, and ends with his rejection of both possible stable points, the island and the plantation, at the behest of that 'something fatal' (p. 27) which propels Crusoe ever onwards.

8

Robinson Crusoe is a relentlessly 'modern' man, breaking the feudal and patriarchal ties that would bind him to a law career in York in favour of the dangerous 'opening' on to the sea offered by Hull – just as he later throws away the chance of settlement in Brazil. Nothing defines Crusoe better than this relentless mobility, although he can only ever offer banalities by way of explanation: 'ill fate' and 'evil influence' (pp. 37–8), 'my inclination to go abroad' (p. 298). The novel never closes this impetus – as it could easily have done if it were a question of a psychological trait, through weariness or even death – suggesting that Crusoe's constant mobility is an ideological given, an answer to the question that could never be formulated by colonial discourse for itself, the question posed to John Smith by Powhatan, but which *Robinson Crusoe* ensures that Friday is in no position to ask.

But the modern bourgeois subject cannot be expected to arrive full-grown like Pallas Athene from the head of Zeus. If Descartes in his *Discourse on Method* offers one fully self-conscious new subjectivity, Crusoe represents a rather different notion of radical individualism, one which staggers backwards into the future, lacking in self-understanding, full of guilt, self-contradictory, fearful, violent: the modernity of European consciousness shipwrecked in the Caribbean, that very archipelago of its subversion.[74]

In one respect at least the *Discourse* is the more deeply Utopian of the two parables. In the fifth section Descartes speaks of how:

> in order to put all these new truths in a less crude light and to be able to say more freely what I think about them, without being obliged to accept or refute what are accepted opinions among the philosophers and theologians, I resolved to leave all these people to their disputes, and to speak only of what would happen in a new world, if God were now to create, somewhere in imaginary space, enough matter to compose it ... and afterwards did no more than to lend his usual preserving action to nature, and let her act according to his established laws.[75]

His intention was undoubtedly to avoid open conflict with the ecclesiastical authorities, but Descartes' 'espaces imaginaires' also serve to empty the world of social relationships. Bodies exist in Descartes' world to be kept healthy; the only community envisaged is a community of scientists.[76]

One way of speaking of the complexity of *Robinson Crusoe* would be to say that it is such a fraught text because, despite its dwelling in the imaginary spaces of fiction, it does not, like the *Discourse*, finally refuse engagement with the level of the social: it confronts the inevitable anxiety commensurate with stripping the new subjectivity of all existing relationships (the parrot's 'Robin' is here the symptomatic moment) and then posing the question of 'the other'. James Joyce, writing in 1912 from, as it were, the other end of that new subjectivity and with the advantage afforded by the perspective of a line taken on England from the axis Dublin/Trieste, had no hesitation in seeing *Robinson Crusoe* as prophetic of empire:

> The true symbol of the British conquest is in Robinson Crusoe
> .... The whole Anglo-Saxon spirit is in Crusoe; the manly independence and the unconscious cruelty; the persistence; the slow yet efficient intelligence; the sexual apathy; the practical, well-balanced, religiousness; the calculating taciturnity.[77]

'Symbol' and 'prophetic' are dangerous words in a critical vocabulary but they can be defended here because both symbolism and prophecy are used retrospectively. The suggestion is not that Defoe has spoken in such orotund tones, but that now, with the advantage of those 200 years, we can see Crusoe as the 'prototype' (Joyce's word) of the British colonist. That is to say, the new subjectivity is simultaneously an individual and a national consciousness, both forged in the smithy of a Caribbean that is – as of course the Caribbean still is to England – both parabolic and historical at the same time. Concomitantly, the social relationships involved are simultaneously personal and international.

There are three kinds of social relationship that Crusoe becomes involved in, all of them rather unusual. At one end of the scale of social exchange is Columbus's relationship with the cannibals in which their devouring attentions meet the response of his rifle – the just war. The establishment of this socially simple, if morally and technologically complex, relationship takes so long because of its imbrication with the development of a non-violent subordinate relationship. The just war can commence only when the ranks of the cannibals have been split to provide a candidate for salvation and subjection. 'Gratitude' proves such a successful solution to this pressing question that Crusoe adopts it as his model for all social relationships, at least while he is on the island. He then cashes the proffered gratitude in the form of the various services his subjects can perform for him.

Crusoe becomes in a word more and more like Prospero, exercising a rigorous control over his miniature world, mastering his trauma through repetition. He even, like Prospero, manages to be both stage-manager and actor, appearing in the guise of a governor's man in order to surround the figure of the 'governor' with the powerful aura of absence. The mutineers, like the court party in *The Tempest*, are condemned to repeat the governor's tribulations – although in this case they could by no means be said to have caused those tribulations. They tell one another that they have landed on an 'inchanted island', they fear they will all be devoured, they run about wringing their hands in despair, they sit down and then walk about again (p. 263). It seems only appropriate that one of them should be called Robinson (p. 264).[78]

Crusoe constructs himself as a sovereign, monarch, and patriarch. His relationships with his subjects are properly contractual, entered into on their part through an appropriately Hobbesian fear, but guaranteed in the absence of 'the sword' by their gratitude for such almost magical deliverance from danger. By exchanging their natural rights for a guaranteed security they make themselves, in the traditional analogy, children to Crusoe's father, a relationship articulated most clearly with respect to Friday: the Europeans, it might be said, remain 'brothers' when faced with the cannibals, who are not members of the family. The single most important difference between Crusoe's dream of rescuing a cannibal prisoner and his actual rescue of Friday is that in the dream the servant will 'tell me what to do' (p. 202), he will be a father into whose arms Crusoe can entrust himself, while, in the event, Crusoe, more active than in his dream, takes on the mantle of father from the start; there can be no question of Friday calling the tune: he simply follows Crusoe's lead: 'his very affections were ty'd to me, like those of a child to a father' (pp. 211–2).

Maddox, although he does not discuss this example, sees a general pattern through the book of Crusoe's progress 'from helpless and sinful son to all-powerful father . . . from submission to domination'.[79] The previous discussion would seem to support that reading, but only at the cost of ignoring one of the text's most constant features – the unswerving beneficence of the father figures who assist Crusoe so regularly. Within *Robinson Crusoe*'s pattern of social relationships 'beneficence' can immediately be seen as occupying an aberrant position. 'Just war' and 'subordination' are social exchanges of a kind. They are wheels that need plenty of oil to get them moving, but once the cannibals have overstepped the mark by threatening to eat a European, and once Crusoe has gauged the intensity of the gratitude that results from being the agent of such salvation, both turn smoothly to advance the narrative. But the beneficence which so assists Crusoe is unmotivated from within the fiction: it has explanation in neither the attributed psychology of the characters involved nor in the actions of the narrative. No exchange can be completed because Crusoe has nothing to offer his benefactors: after all, beneficence is utterly at odds with the completely Hobbesian realm of his operations in which all exchanges are strictly governed by either force or calculated self-interest.

The benefactors constitute a narrative function: they are in essence mere manifestations of that single actant, the benefactor. Such a description is not reductive, because it exhausts their resonance in the text. But it is less easy to say what function that role plays. Within the overall structure of *Robinson Crusoe*, marked by its division between narrative frame and island episode, the benefactor clearly belongs to the frame narrative: on the island Crusoe reverses roles and becomes, in his own terms, a 'benefactor' to others. Yet such a structural allocation of that textual feature would be misleading in the sense that, within the fictional *time* of the narrative, the benefactors continue playing their parts even during the years of Crusoe's island exile. In fact their role during those years is especially crucial since it involves not isolated examples of honesty or beneficence, but a continuous and accumulative concern for the well-being of Crusoe's Brazilian plantation.

This beneficence is obviously romance wish-fulfilment operating in the economic realm: the actions of the benefactors enable Crusoe to become a rich man. But, coterminously, beneficence functions as the agent of narrative coherence, as, in a word, the plot. It plays, that is to say, the function of chastity in the paradigmatic romance. Only the virtue of the lovers, or at least the heroine, can hold together the disparate series of adventures that the romance protagonists endure; reunited at the end of the story their tribulations are given significance and coherence by the part of themselves that has been kept pure until the final embrace. *Robinson Crusoe* can therefore be described as an economic romance with beneficence playing the providential part of chastity, enabling Crusoe, at the end of the book, to make retrospective sense of a life that would otherwise have been purely episodic; enabling him, that is, to become a biographer rather than merely a diarist.

By far the most important aspect of this enablement is the bringing together of the two seemingly independent parts of Crusoe's life. Several pages ago it was noted that there are four moments when Crusoe's composed self is shaken, and three of the incidents were examined – the parrot, the footprint, and the remains of the cannibal feast. The fourth occurs at the moment of suture of the two halves of the narrative structure. Crusoe, now in Lisbon, receives from Bahia a large packet of papers containing accounts of his affairs and, by the same fleet, large amounts of sugar, tobacco and gold:

> I might well say, now indeed, that the latter end of Job was better than the beginning. It is impossible to express here the flutterings of my very heart, when I looked over these letters, and especially when I found all my wealth about me; for as the Brasil ships come all in fleets, the same ships which brought my letters brought my goods; and the effects were safe in the river before the letters came to my hand. In a word, I turned pale, and grew sick; and had not the old man run and fetched me a cordial, I believe the sudden surprize of joy had overset nature, and I had dy'd upon the spot.
>
> Nay after that, I continued very ill, and was so some hours, 'till a physician being sent for, and something of the real cause of my illness being known, he ordered me to be let blood; after which I had relief, and grew well; but I verily believe, if it had not been eased by a vent given in that manner to the spirits, I should have dy'd.
>
> I was now master, all on a sudden, of above 5,000l. sterling in money, and had an estate, as I might well call it, in the Brasils, of above a thousand pounds a years, as sure as an estate of lands in England: and in a word, I was in a condition which I scarce knew how to understand, or how to compose my self for the enjoyment of it. (pp. 279–80)

There are various ways of looking at this moment. Not least, of course, it marks the discovery of the secret of capital itself, that it accumulates in magical independence from the labour of its owner. But structurally this suture of the two parts of Crusoe's life, the two parts of the narrative, is a moment of recognition, one which confirms that the mode of *Robinson Crusoe* is that of comedy. Strangely, the suture does not hold. Crusoe does not settle down, whether in Brazil or England, to tie up the loose ends of his story as might have been expected, and the episodic reasserts itself at the expense of the plot, to such an extent in fact that the book ends with a strong suggestion of further episodes, which did indeed materialize within a few months. It is no doubt possible to explain the last pages of *Robinson Crusoe* in terms of the *essentially* episodic nature of Defoe's writing, its 'immaturity' when judged against the more formally accomplished novels of Richardson and Fielding; but there are other, more interesting, interpretations. Maddox, for example, who reads Crusoe's story – not altogether incompatibly with the reading offered here – as one of growing mastery over his surroundings, sees Crusoe as reaching the pinnacle of his power when he watches the English mutineers replaying his own story before his very eyes. So:

> Crusoe's narrative problem is one that may be endemic to autobiography as a form. He discovers a myth within his own experience – a myth of mastery of both self and world – but his life goes on after the myth has been fully expressed. As a result, the ending of the story is the least successful part of it: some things are simply left unfinished on the island, and back in Europe, his story degenerates into episodic randomness.[80]

This is well-argued but still ultimately dependent on the mimetic fallacy. 'What is left over' may be a problem intrinsic to the autobiographical form but it is hardly one that *necessarily* imposes itself on fictional autobiographers – Jane Eyre and many others could bear witness to that.

The comparison with *The Tempest* may again be useful. It was mentioned earlier that *Robinson Crusoe* separates out two moments that are coterminous in *The Tempest*: the European arrival on the island and the recruitment to service of a native. Here, perhaps appropriately, this structure is reversed. What was discussed in Chapter 3 as the false and true *anagnorises* – the revelation of Miranda to Alonso, and the vexation of Prospero at the sudden remembrance of Caliban's conspiracy – seem in *Robinson Crusoe* to be brought together. Crusoe is given the demonstration – essential to romance – of that which was thought to have been lost. Yet his reaction, though springing from joy, is a discomposition not unlike Prospero's perturbation, which – somewhat ironically – brings him nearer death than the dreaded cannibals managed. Relief – and again the irony seems startling – comes from the letting of blood, precisely what Crusoe had spent the previous fifteen years or so since the discovery of the footprint trying to avoid.

What the comparison with Prospero's perturbation suggests is that the suture – although it seemingly fulfils all the generic requirements – does not in fact accomplish its purpose. There are hints of other textual dynamics at play. In the packet of documents Crusoe receives from Brazil:

> There was a letter of my partner's, congratulating me very affectionately upon my being alive, giving me an account how the estate was improved, and what it produced a year, with a particular of the number of squares or acres that it contained; how planted, how many slaves there were upon it; and making two and twenty crosses for blessings, told me that he had said so many *Ave Marias* to thank the blessed Virgin that I was alive; inviting me very passionately to come over and take possession of my own. (p. 279)

Nothing in this analysis of *Robinson Crusoe* has given credence to the myth of Defoe as a careless writer and, in any case, he clearly paid scrupulous attention to financial details in his novels; so it is strange indeed that Crusoe should receive a letter from his 'partner', since his earlier account of his Brazilian affairs made it very clear that he had no partner. Even without making much of the conventional language of romance in the letter ('inviting me very passionately to come over and take possession of my own') this ghostly 'partner' is, if not Crusoe's double, then at least the part of himself left behind before the fateful voyage of 1659. The bloodletting is the necessary and much-delayed final act in Crusoe's self-composition because at this moment he regains his full self after thirty years, a traumatic event for his body and spirits. This is indeed an apposite end to the romance of bourgeois individualism – and a further explanation of Crusoe's aphanisis: the hero swoons when, after thirty years apart, he is finally reunited – with himself.

But this dramatic suture cannot *resolve* the novel any more than the conventional marriage of romance can settle the political questions that form the unconscious of its projected ideals. In the end the suture heals only a self-imposed rift which was, all along, a displacement of the major questions confronted by the text. The discretion between the two parts of the narrative structure and between the divided selves of Robinson Crusoe is a technique for negotiating the unspeakable – and eventually uncloseable – gap between the violence of slavery and the notion of a moral economy. The imperial production of *Robinson Crusoe* as a boys' adventure in the nineteenth century inevitably foregrounds the colonial alibi – the man alone, on a desert island, constructing a simple and moral economy which becomes the basis of a commonwealth presided over by a benevolent sovereign. The colonial reading must reassert that the book's tremendous effort to reconstruct that economy fills up the narrative space in which, in that other place, silently, Crusoe's other self, his ghostly 'partner', is developing those plantations built on the violently-extracted labour-power of slaves which will provide the capital to displace that moral economy with a less volatile mode of production. Crusoe, so sated with his sudden transfusion of the profits produced from the blood of thirty years' slavery that he needs letting, is on reflection an appropriately sanguinary emblem of such exploitation.

Only by such literal excess can the ultimate colonial question – the question that asks by what right land is taken away from those living on it, the question that asks, in other words, why there is a need for a rift to exist between moral economy and productive economy, justice and violence, labour and capital – remain unposed, if ultimately 'answered' by the configurations that make up Robinson Crusoe's 'strange and surprizing' adventures.

Figure 14 'Un Anglais de la Barbade vend sa Maitresse'; an engraving by Jean-Marie Moreau le Jeune for G.-F.-T. Raynal's *Histoire des deux Indes* (1780). Yarico frozen in the moment of her betrayal by the calculating Englishman.

6

Inkle and Yarico

Quod genus hoc hominum? quaeve hunc tam barbara
   morem
Permittit patria?

(*Aeneid* I. 539–40)[1]

1

The last major challenge to European hegemony in the islands of
the Caribbean came in the thirty years at the end of the eighteenth
century. To some extent this challenge formed part of the
revolutionary ferment that saw the independence of Haiti, but
native resistance also had, as was earlier seen, its own history and
its own specific forms of struggle.

   By 1760 the intermittent war between the native inhabitants of
the Caribbean and the European colonizing powers was clearly
entering its last phase.[2] The high culture of the Tainos on the
north-westerly islands had been quickly destroyed in the sixteenth
century; it seems likely that pockets of native culture remained,
especially in the Cuban interior, but there was little further
fighting. The Bahamian Lucayans had been pressed into slavery
and soon destroyed. On the more mountainous islands to the
south-east, military resistance had been more feasible, and from
1624 the native Caribs had fought a skilful defensive war against
European encroachment, but force of numbers, superior weaponry and European diseases had slowly taken their toll. Before
the end of the seventeenth century the Caribs had been obliged to
sign a treaty with the British and French by which they
renounced any claim to the majority of their islands in return for
possession in perpetuity of Dominica and St Vincent, at that

moment the least desirable islands from the European point of view.[3] This treaty was clearly – again from the European point of view – a dead letter by the time of the Treaty of Paris (1763) when Dominica and St Vincent, along with Tobago and Grenada, all fairly sparsely settled by the French, were turned over to England.[4] The possibilities for plantation agriculture were severely limited by Dominica's mountainous terrain, and the small Carib population coexisted, if uneasily, with the moderate influx of English settlers in the 1760s and 1770s.

The case of St Vincent was rather different. The land was in general more suitable for plantation agriculture, especially the windward side of the island; but the Carib population was much larger and much less fragmented than that of Dominica. An additional complicating factor was the existence of two separate Carib groups, the so-called 'Yellow' or 'Red' Caribs, who lived on the leeward side of the island, and the Black Caribs, who lived mainly on the windward side. The Black Caribs were so called because of intermarriage with escaped or shipwrecked black slaves over a number of decades, the group remaining culturally and linguistically Carib. But it may also have been the case that the relative ethnic 'purity' of the 'Yellow' Caribs was due in the first instance to the existence of a division within the Vincentian Caribs between those willing to accommodate themselves to the European settlers and those determined to fight for complete sovereignty over at least part of the island. An agreement between the French and the Black Caribs drawn up in 1700 had guaranteed the windward half of St Vincent to the Black Caribs (see Figure 15, p. 243) and in 1763 there were no European settlements north-east of that dividing line.[5] Since, however, all the desirable land lay to the east, the English commissioners appointed to sell off the gains of the Seven Years War to private planters inevitably faced a conflict with those who did not recognize the commissioners' right to dispose of their lands, a conflict that resulted in the two Carib Wars of 1772–3 and 1795–6.

2

The previous chapter discussed *Robinson Crusoe* as a mythic version of the contact between Englishmen and native Caribbeans but, as if sharp dichotomization of the savage into docile Friday and fierce cannibal had exhausted all the options, no literary work that has achieved significance dealt with the subsequent, and final, period of English/Carib relationships. Yet a story does exist, often retold in the latter part of the eighteenth century, which seems to stand in a fraught and highly mediated relationship with the final extirpation of the island Caribs from the Caribbean.

The story of Inkle and Yarico was one of the most often repeated and most popular narratives of the eighteenth century, called by David Brion Davis a 'great folk epic.'[6] In his definitive study Lawrence Price lists forty-five separate versions in three languages (English, French and German), some of which – like Steele's version in *The Spectator*, Chamfort's *La Jeune Indienne*, and Gellert's *Inkle und Yarico* – also exist in numerous contemporary translations into most European languages.[7] In 1766 Goethe announced his intention of writing a play on the theme; and in 1792 Mary Wollstonecraft wrote of how to 'make an Inkle' of a child with no further explanation necessary.[8] Yet after about 1810 the flood suddenly dried, and Inkle and Yarico were quickly and almost completely forgotten.

The story itself can be reduced to the four moments common to almost all its versions. Inkle, an Englishman, is shipwrecked and separated from his companions; he is succoured by a native girl, Yarico, who falls in love with him and for whom he professes love; they are rescued by an English ship; and they arrive in Barbados where Inkle sells Yarico into slavery. There are no full novelistic treatments of the theme but there are prose sketches, 'historical' narratives, poems (some in the form of epistles from Yarico to Inkle, and even some replies from Inkle), plays, ballets, pantomimes and musicals.[9]

Like the story of Pocahontas, with which it has much in common, the beginnings of the narrative are difficult to ascertain. One often accepted beginning is Richard Ligon's 1657 *A True and Exact History of the Island of Barbados*, probably the single most valuable source for the history of the English Caribbean islands in the seventeenth century. However, from the point of view of literary history the most influential of the early versions is usually said to be that of Richard Steele, recounted in No. 11 of *The Spectator* on Tuesday, 13 March 1711.

In 1734 'The Story of Inkle and Yarico. From the 11th. Spectator' appeared in verse in the *London Magazine*, and by 1738 three more anonymous poems had appeared in London, all based on Steele, and two of them in the form of epistles addressed by Yarico to Inkle. By 1754 there had appeared the first play, the first French poem, and the first German poem, later much reprinted and translated. After 1754 no more than a year or two passed without an addition to the Inkle and Yarico corpus in English, French or German until 1802. Yet after 1802 (and excluding a handful of translations) there were no new versions in England at all; and on the Continent merely a French pantomime in 1807 and a German musical in 1808.[10]

One of the general difficulties with psychoanalytical analysis when transferred away from the parameters of an individual's consciousness and its associative hinterland, is in locating within an 'autonomous' narrative signs of the process of unconscious production. 'Inkle and Yarico', the product of no single authorial consciousness but rather a story that English (and European) society chose persistently, over a period of seventy years, to tell itself, has the advantage of providing a narrative that changes over time so that it is possible, at least in theory, to produce a time-length equivalent to that revealed in analysis, laying bare something of the story's political aetiology.

3

The conventional location for the story of Inkle and Yarico is within the 'literature of sentiment', often seen as one of the characteristic European literary forms of the century between the English Restoration and the French Revolution.[11] The constituent vocabulary of sentimentalism includes such key words as 'sentimental', 'sensibility', 'humanity' and 'benevolence', all of which were used with increasing frequency and intensity in this period, and at least one of which, 'sentimental' itself, does not exist in English until this time – probably around 1740. These linguistic changes reflect and codify the increased value given to 'natural feelings', a valuation as apparent in the philosophy of Shaftesbury and Hutcheson as in the Latitudinarian movement within the Church, and perhaps best exemplified by Rousseau's paragraphs on 'the inner impulse of compassion'.[12]

The great theme of sentimental literature is sexual love and one of its great topoi is the frustration of that love. Inkle and Yarico are therefore contextually related to the better known pairs of Antony and Cleopatra (Dryden's), Oronooko and Imoinda, Abelard and Eloisa, Clarissa and Lovelace, Julie and Saint-Preux, Paul and Virginie and, right at the end of the period but appearing for the first time in literary form, Pocahontas and John Smith.[13]

These contexts can be narrowed down in two ways. Frustrated love often led to the isolated figure, the deserted or bereaved lover, usually – as with Yarico – the woman: Pope's Eloisa, Marianne Alcoforado of the *Lettres d'une religieuse portugaise*, Dryden's Dido.[14] And – again as with Yarico – the purity of true love would often be the product of a 'natural' society destroyed by some form of European corruption, calculation or double-dealing. Here Yarico is closest to Pocahontas but also, in a strange but significant way, to Dido, who was also betrayed by a 'European' with his mind on other things.

Native America supplied much of the material for this litera-ture of sentiment, from Dryden's heroic dramas such as *The Indian Queen* (1663–4), through Marmontel's *Les Incas* (1777), to poems like Wordsworth's 'Complaint of a Forsaken Indian Woman' (1798) and Southey's 'Song of the Chikkasah Widow' (1799); with the anti-Spanish theme often prominent, as in Joseph Warton's 'The Dying Indian' (1758) or Edward Jerningham's 'The Fall of Mexico' (1775) or Sheridan's *Pizarro* (1799), one of the many translations of Kotzebue's *Die Spanier in Peru* (1795).[15]

But in many ways a more powerful tributary to the torrent of sentimentalism was the stream of largely French, documentary, historical and philosophical treatises. The latter part of the century saw the influence of Bougainville's and Cook's accounts of the South Sea islanders along with Diderot's famous *Supplément*, as the primitivistic ideal, once exclusive to America and the classical civilizations, was extended to the newly discovered South Pacific and even to Africa itself, long subject to a quite different descriptive vocabulary.[16] Sentimental sympathy began to flow out along the arteries of European commerce in search of its victims. In the earlier period, however, the key texts still focused on America, and three of them – du Tertre's history of the French-speaking Antilles, Rousseau's discourse on inequality, and Raynal's *Histoire des deux Indes* – had significant things to say about the Caribbean.[17] Du Tertre who, after Raymond Breton, lived longest and closest to the Caribs of the islands, left a detailed and in many ways eulogistic account of their idyllic way of life:

> Now as I have shown that the air of the torrid zone is the purest, healthiest and most temperate of all atmospheres, and that the earth there is a little Paradise, always green and washed by the sweetest waters of the world: it is appropriate to show in this treatise that the Savages of these islands are the most content, the happiest, the least vicious, the most sociable, the least deformed, and the least afflicted by disease in the whole world. For they are just as nature produced them, that is to say living in great and natural simplicity: they are all equal, almost without knowledge of any sort of superiority or servitude . . . . No one is richer or poorer than his companion, and they all limit their desires to what is useful and necessary to them, scorning all superfluities . . . . [T]hey are of good build, well-proportioned, large and powerful, so energetic and healthy that it is common to see amongst them old men of a hundred or a hundred and twenty . . . who have hardly any white hair, their foreheads marked by hardly a wrinkle.[18]

The topics of the 'golden age' survive almost unaltered, embedded in and constitutive of a discourse which, if not ethnographic in the full sense, clearly passes as a description of observed behaviour. And to du Tertre might be appended Labat's comment, which makes very cogently the political point so pungently explicit in Montaigne's famous essay on the cannibals:

> There is not a nation on earth more jealous of their independency than the Charaibes. They are impatient under the least infringement of it; and when, at any time, they are witnesses to the respect and deference which the natives of Europe observe towards their superiors, they despise us as abject slaves; wondering how any man can be so base as to crouch before his equal.[19]

Rousseau, drawing on du Tertre for his essay on the origins of inequality, then promulgated the notion that the Caribs were the closest surviving example of a people living in 'savagery' – in Rousseau's very precise sense of that word:

Of all existing peoples, the Caribs have least departed from the state of nature, and it is they who are most peaceful in their sex lives and least subject to jealousy, even though they live in a hot climate, which always seems to make these passions more active.

Therefore, on the central analogy of species to individual life, the Carib were living in the true youth of the world.[20] This sentimental image of the Carib, even though philosophical rather than ethnographic, was to provide a powerful fund of rhetoric to deploy against the planters' determination to seek a military solution to the Carib occupancy of lands suitable for plantation agriculture on St Vincent. The vocabulary of sentiment was therefore to make its way into the political debate of the period. One of the particular techniques of the *Histoire des deux Indes* in the course of its mordant assessment of European greed was to focus on representative stories such as that of the Amerindian on Hispaniola who refused a deathbed baptism on the grounds that if heaven was full of Spaniards he would rather be in hell. Inkle and Yarico – retold from Steele – was such a story and Jean-Marie Moreau le Jeune's engraving (Figure 14) captures that moment of unbearable poignancy as Yarico is sold into slavery by her erstwhile lover.[21] The powerful critique of slavery and the slave-trade mounted by Raynal ensured that Inkle and Yarico would from then on be seen as an illustration of the evils of slavery, however irrelevant that reading might be to the import of the story as told by Ligon or Steele.[22]

A further tributary to the stream of eighteenth-century senti-ment was provided by the continuing visits to England of Americans, Africans and, later, Tahitians. Pocahontas and her entourage had been scrutinized to see whether savage nobility had civilized manners. A century later the emphasis tended to be on the satirical light such visits could be made to cast on European institutions, or on the tremor of compassion felt by the European spectator on witnessing the travails of natural sensibilities in such an alien and hostile environment. The first official embassy of Amerindian political leaders to England was the visit of the four Iroquois sachems in April and May 1710.[23] The sachems became familiar figures and both Addison and Steele used them in the manner of Montesquieu.[24] Steele's interest in Inkle and Yarico may even have been sparked by this visit.[25] In fact the beginning of the Inkle and Yarico cult in 1734 coincided with the next important Amerindian visitor, the Creek Tomochichi; and there were other state visits by three Cherokees in 1762 and Joseph Brant, grandson to the King of the Maquas in 1776 – just as Omai, the Tahitian who had been the sensation of London for two years, was leaving.[26]

In many ways though, the most revealing of the foreign visitors was William Ansah Sesarakoo, called 'the Prince of Annamobee'. As the London magazines of the time told the story, Sesarakoo was the son of a Moorish king on the African coast. The king had been so impressed with the polite behaviour of an English trader that he had entrusted his son to the trader to be brought to England and educated in the European manner. This the captain agreed to do, but then basely sold the prince and his companion into slavery on a Caribbean island, a lack of scruple that exactly parallels that shown by the slave captain in Aphra Behn's *Oronooko*, and by Thomas Inkle. After the death of this captain his officers related the affair to the English government who paid for the release of the prince and his friend and brought them to England where they were put under the care of the Earl of Halifax, first commissioner of trade and plantations. They were introduced to the King and received into English society. The particular occasion of the articles in the press was their visit in February 1749 to Covent Garden to see a performance – of *Oronooko*. As *The Gentleman's Magazine* of February 1749 reports:

> The seeing persons of their own colour on the stage, apparently in the same distress from which they had been so lately delivered, the tender interview between *Imoinda* and *Oronooko*, who was betrayed by the treachery of a captain, his account of his sufferings, and the repeated abuse of his placability and confidence, strongly affected them with that generous grief which pure nature always feels, and art had not yet taught them to suppress; the young prince was so far overcome, that he was obliged to return at the end of the fourth act. His companion remained, but wept the whole time; a circumstance which affected the audience yet more than the play, and doubled the tears which were shed for *Oronooko* and *Imoinda*.[27]

Rarely can the tears of compassion have been more delicious.

What the magazines do not mention is that Sesarakoo was the son, not of a king, but of John Corrente, one of the most powerful black slave traders on the Gold Coast, who was following a well-established tradition in sending his son to England to be educated; so that the efforts of the government, far from being motivated by compassion, were a desperate attempt to regain the goodwill of a key figure in the slave trade, at a time when the French were trying to establish themselves in that part of Africa.[28]

4

So the sentimental context of 'Inkle and Yarico' is already deeply coloured by native American and often specifically Caribbean references. Within the innumerable versions of the story itself the crucial intertextual relationship, at least in the first instance, is that between Ligon and Steele. This is Ligon's account:

> We had an Indian woman, a slave in the house, who was of excellent shape and colour, for it was a pure bright bay; small brests, with the nipls of a porphyrie colour, this woman would not be woo'd by any means to weare Cloaths. Shee chanc't to be with Child, by a Christian servant, and lodging in the Indian house, amongst other women of her own Country, where the Christian servants, both men and women came; and being very great, and that her time was come to be delivered, loath to fall in labour before the men, walk'd down to a Wood, in which was a Pond of water, and there by the side of the Pond, brought her selfe a bed; and presently washing her Child in some of the water of the Pond, lap't it up in such rags, as she had begg'd of the Christians; and in three hours time came home, with her Childe in her armes, a lusty Boy, frolick and lively.
>
> This Indian dwelling neer the Sea-coast, upon the Main, an English ship put in to a Bay, and sent some of her men a shoar, to try what victualls or water they could finde, for in some distresse they were: But the Indians perceiving them to go up so far into the Country, as they were sure they could not make a safe retreat, intercepted them in their return, and fell upon them, chasing them into a Wood, and being dispersed there,

some were taken, and some kill'd: but a young man amongst them stragling from the rest, was met by this Indian Maid, who upon the first sight fell in love with him, and hid him close from her Countrymen (the Indians) in a Cave, and there fed him, till they could safely go down to the shoar, where the ship lay at anchor, expecting the return of their friends. But at last, seeing them upon the shoar, sent the long-Boat for them, took them aboard, and brought them away. But the youth, when he came ashoar in the Barbadoes, forgot the kindnesse of the poor maid, that had ventured her life for his safety, and sold her for a slave, who was as free born as he: And so poor *Yarico* for her love, lost her liberty.[29]

Fifty-four years later Richard Steele wrote in *The Spectator* of a conversation 'upon the old Topick, of Constancy in Love.' Arietta, stung by the general aspersions cast upon women, responds in this way:

when we consider this Question between the Sexes, which has been either a Point of Dispute or Raillery ever since there were Men and Women, let us take Facts from plain People, and from such as have not either Ambition or Capacity to embellish their Narrations with any Beauties of Imagination. I was the other Day amusing my self with *Ligon*'s Account of *Barbadoes*; and, in Answer to your well-wrought Tale, I will give you (as it dwells upon my Memory) out of that honest Traveller, in his fifty fifth Page, the History of *Inkle* and *Yarico*.

Mr. *Thomas Inkle* of *London*, aged 20 Years, embarked in the *Downs* on the good ship called the *Achilles*, bound for the *West-Indies*, on the 16th of *June* 1647, in order to improve his Fortune by Trade and Merchandize. Our Adventurer was the third Son of an eminent Citizen, who had taken particular Care to instill into his Mind an early Love of Gain, by making him a perfect Master of Numbers, and consequently giving him a quick View of Loss and Advantage, and preventing the natural Impulses of his Passions, by Prepossession towards his Interests. With a Mind thus turned, young *Inkle* had a Person every way agreeable, a ruddy Vigour in his Countenance, Strength in his Limbs, with Ringlets of fair Hair loosely flowing on his Shoulders. It happened, in the Course of the Voyage, that the *Achilles*, in some Distress, put into a Creek on the Main of

America, in Search of Provisions: The Youth, who is the Hero of my Story, among others, went ashore on this Occasion. From their first Landing they were observed by a Party of *Indians*, who hid themselves in the Woods for that Purpose. The *English* unadvisedly marched a great distance from the Shore into the Country, and were intercepted by the Natives, who slew the greatest Number of them. Our Adventurer escaped among others, by flying into a Forest. Upon his coming into a remote and pathless part of the Wood, he threw himself, tired and breathless, on a little Hillock, when an *Indian* Maid rushed from a Thicket behind him: After the first Surprize, they appeared mutually agreeable to each other. If the *European* was highly Charmed with the Limbs, Features, and wild Graces of the Naked *American*; the *American* was no less taken with the Dress, Complexion and Shape of an *European*, covered from Head to Foot. The *Indian* grew immediately enamoured of him, and consequently sollicitous for his Preservation: She therefore conveyed him to a Cave, where she gave him a Delicious Repast of Fruits, and led him to a Stream to slake his Thirst. In the midst of these good Offices, she would sometimes play with his Hair, and delight in the Opposition of its Colour, to that of her Fingers: Then open his Bosome, then laugh at him for covering it. She was, it seems, a Person of Distinction, for she every day came to him in a different Dress, of the most beautiful Shells, Bugles and Bredes. She likewise brought him a great many Spoils, which her other Lovers had presented to her; so that his Cave was richly adorned with all the spotted Skins of Beasts, and most Party-coloured Feathers of Fowls, which that World afforded. To make his Confinement more tolerable, she would carry him in the Dusk of the Evening, or by the favour of Moon-light, to unfrequented Groves and Solitudes, and show him where to lye down in Safety, and sleep amidst the Falls of Waters, and Melody of Nightingales. Her Part was to watch and hold him in her Arms, for fear of her Country-men, and wake him on Occasions to consult his Safety. In this manner did the Lovers pass away their Time, till they had learn'd a Language of their own, in which the Voyager communicated to his Mistress, how happy he should be to have her in his Country, where she should be Cloathed in such Silks as his Wastecoat was made of, without such Fears and Alarms as they were there Tormented with. In this tender Correspondence these Lovers lived for several Months, when *Yarico*, instructed by her Lover, discovered a Vessel on the Coast, to which she made Signals, and in the Night, with the utmost Joy and Satisfaction accompanied him to a Ships-Crew of his Country-Men, bound for *Barbadoes*. When a Vessel from the Main arrives in that Island, it seems the Planters come down to the Shoar, where there is an immediate Market of the *Indians* and other Slaves, as with us of Horses and Oxen.

To be short, Mr *Thomas Inkle*, now coming into *English* Territories, began seriously to reflect upon his loss of Time, and to weigh with himself how many Days Interest of his Mony he had lost during his Stay with *Yarico*. This Thought made the Young Man very pensive, and careful what Account he should be able to give his Friends of his Voyage. Upon which Considerations, the prudent and frugal young Man sold *Yarico* to a *Barbadian Merchant*; notwithstanding that the poor Girl, to incline him to commiserate her Condition, told him that she was with Child by him: But he only made use of that Information, to rise in his Demands upon the Purchaser.

I was so touch'd with this Story, (which I think should be always a Counterpart to the *Ephesian* Matron) that I left the Room with Tears in my Eyes; which a Woman of *Arietta*'s good sense, did, I am sure, take for greater Applause, than any Compliments I could make her.[30]

The vast majority of the later examples draw explicitly on Steele: Steele's piece refers to, and gains its authority as an historical example from Ligon. The rhetoric is by no means simple since Steele is not necessarily making the same point as he is having Arietta make; but both of them are dependent on the historicity of the story which is vouchsafed by the reference to Ligon, the historian who actually visited Barbados and is therefore seen as an appropriate guarantor of the story.

Ligon's first paragraph can no doubt be said in some sense to describe the historical Yarico, inasmuch as Ligon is giving an eyewitness account of an Amerindian slave in the house in Barbados where he was residing. Within Ligon's text the paragraph is partly an account of the domestic arrangements in

Barbados – he has just said there are not many Indians but that they tend to be better cooks than the blacks; partly a chance to add to his collection of native breasts, of which he was a tireless admirer; and partly, it would seem, an occasion to wonder at the strange self-sufficiency of savage life. This last note, the dominant one, is by no means sentimental in the manner of the eighteenth-century versions: its ambivalence and prosaicness guarantee that. There is an element of civilized distaste for these savage arrangements, more than counteracted by an undertow of admiration for the modesty ('loath to fall in labour before the men') self-sufficiency ('brought her selfe a bed'), and matter-of-factness ('and in three hours came home, with her Childe in her armes') of Yarico's behaviour, all of which produce, with the minimum of fuss, 'a lusty Boy, frolick and lively'. An impressive cameo of an Amerindian slave woman coping.

The somewhat uneasy conjunction between the two paragraphs probably marks a change of narrative procedure in part concealed by the continuous use of the past tense. The events of the first paragraph have been witnessed by Ligon in the present of 1647: in 1657 he reports them in the past tense. But the events of the second paragraph have been reported *to* him in 1647, and not, one might be sure, by Yarico herself. This is important not principally because it casts doubt on the veracity of the story itself – which of course it does: who after all could have known the details except Yarico and the Englishman involved, who would presumably not have exposed his own ingratitude? – but rather because it inflects that paragraph in Ligon as generically distinct from the surrounding text. The paragraph tells a story, in many ways a paradigmatic and mythic story, that is connected, through no clear narrative sequence, with this particular Amerindian woman. It is an interesting and peculiar way to have become a slave, and therefore worthy of a 200-word paragraph; but any tendency to pathos is defused in advance by the image of the lusty child Yarico produced with another man. She might be unfortunate, but she is clearly a survivor.

As if in recognition of the generic autonomy of Ligon's second paragraph Steele's version draws from it exclusively, allowing him to freeze the forsaken woman in the sentimental tableau of her abandonment, firmly removed from the possibly complicating facts of her later 'history'. Whereas in Ligon there is at least a sense of a dialectic between an oft-repeated story and a lived reality with which that story may or may not be connected, in Steele the story is entirely at the service of 'the spectator': Steele's tears prove that he is, despite his name, a man of sensibility.

Steele expands Ligon's spare narrative. The Englishman is named for the first time as Inkle, with a character sketch to establish that his 'Interests' reign over his 'Passions'. The details of the voyage are filled in by confusing Inkle with Ligon, who himself sailed for the West Indies on 16 June 1647 in the ship *Achilles*. But the greatest expansion in Steele's version comes with the 250 or so words he uses to replace Ligon's laconic account of the time Inkle and Yarico spent together alone. Ligon has Yarico fall in love instantly with the Englishman but then simply 'hid him close from her Countrymen ... in a Cave, and there fed him, till they could go down to the shoar'. Steele lengthens these hours of hospitality into a pastoral idyll lasting several months. This no doubt gives dramatic emphasis to the abruptness with which Inkle later disposes of Yarico; but it also allows Steele to introduce the details of a courtship that owes more to the rituals of Berkeley Square than it does to the north coast of South America, especially since Inkle is lulled to sleep by the melody of nightingales. However, two developments are crucial. Yarico is, in *The Spectator*, 'a Person of Distinction', the mark of such distinction being that she visits Inkle every day in a different dress, quite an achievement for somebody earlier described as a 'naked American'. As a person of distinction Yarico can, like the princely Oronooko and the noble Pocahontas, evoke aristocratic sympathy. And then – in perhaps the most interesting move of all – Steele transfers Yarico's chronologically later pregnancy from Ligon's first paragraph to the moment of arrival on the quayside at Barbados. Yarico, in a desperate attempt to have Inkle commiserate with her, reveals that she is carrying his child; only for Inkle to respond by raising her price, thereby effectively selling his own child into slavery.

These two developments were adopted in most of the versions that began to proliferate in the 1730s, both of Steele's additions increasing the quotient of pathos in the story. But the greater the pathos the more vague the geography and ethnography. In the later versions it is not always a *thoroughly* Caribbean story: it always ends in Barbados, but the first part might sometimes take place on the coast of Africa. Yarico is therefore as often black as Amerindian, or in one poem actually black and Amerindian simultaneously.[31] This geographical vagueness seems connected to a developing ideological inflection to the character of Inkle. In Steele it is only after the rescue that Inkle begins 'to reflect upon his loss of Time, and to weigh with himself how many Days Interest of his Mony he had lost during his Stay with Yarico': his passion and gratitude are genuine enough, it is just that they are eventually outweighed by more important considerations. But in the 1734 poem Inkle is a deceiver from the start, a 'stranger to virtue' behind his 'face and shape divine', who, though impressed by Yarico's 'just symmetry of shape', uses his flaxen hair and honeyed words to help himself out of a difficult spot. So the decision to sell her implies no change of heart and the poem ends with the other Barbadian merchants 'all the prudent youth admire / That could, so young, a trading soul acquire'. Concomitantly, the poem has earlier spelled out the fate of Inkle's companions:

> By winds, or waves, or the decrees of heaven,
> His bark upon a barbarous coast was driven;
> Possest by men who thirst for human blood,
> Who live in caves, or thickets of the wood:
> Untaught to plant (yet corn and fruits abound,
> And fragrant flowers enamel all the ground.)
> Distrest, he landed on this fatal shore,
> With some companions, which were soon no more;
> The savage race their trembling flesh devour,
> Off'ring oblations to th'infernal power.
> Dreadfully suppliant, human limbs they tore,
> (Accursed rites!) and quaft their streaming gore.

It has taken just two textual moves for Ligon's episode in a Caribbean guerrilla war to become the generalized and satanic cannibalism of savage natives. (However much the noble savage, Yarico, caught between the devil of cannibalism and the deep blue sea of the trading soul, is less of a 'savage' than a transposition of the difficult position of the English aristocracy, caught between the savagery of the lower orders and the growing threat from the merchant classes.)[32] The characteristic sentimental move is to universalize: obtrusive circumstantial detail is minimized or removed altogether. The emphasis therefore comes to fall on the climax to the story – the moment of the sale, an emphasis that made 'Inkle and Yarico' so amenable to the anti-slavery movement.

The changes to 'Inkle and Yarico' are analogous to, and illuminated by, those that happened to Aphra Behn's novel *Oronooko*. Published in 1688 *Oronooko* is in many ways a classically sentimental story, telling of the melodramatic love affair between its eponymous hero and the beautiful Imoinda. The immediate parallels are with *Othello*, given the noble black Oronooko's military prowess and his winning of the heart of a senior's daughter in the teeth of parental opposition – here Oronooko's grandfather, who summons Imoinda to his harem. In Mrs Behn's story Imoinda is also black and the two of them suffer with melodramatic frequency from the bad faith of English traders and slave-owners, ending up on a plantation in Surinam – though never, it appears, actually forced to labour. Oronooko leads a failed slave rebellion, kills Imoinda with his own hand, but is saved from suicide by the planters who castrate, disembowel and quarter him.

Like some of the versions of 'Inkle and Yarico' *Oronooko* would seem to use the difference of the protagonist as a mark of nobility to stand in contrast to the unscrupulous lack of honour of the English traders: the politics here would again seem basically domestic, particularly if Oronooko himself can, as has been suggested, be read as the betrayed Charles II, his kingdom turned over to the Dutch, as Surinam had been in 1667.[33] There is clearly no condemnation of the slave trade as such and Oronooko, far from being a representative African, is distinguished in every possible way from his fellow-countrymen, even in his physical appearance:

> He was pretty tall, but of a shape the most exact that can be fancy'd: The most famous statuary cou'd not form the figure of a man more admirably turn'd from head to foot. His face was not of that rusty black which most of that nation are, but of perfect ebony,or polished jett. His nose was rising and *Roman*, instead of *African* and flat. His mouth the finest shaped that could be seen; far from those great turn'd lips, which are so natural to the rest of the negroes. The whole proportion and air

of his face was so nobly and exactly form'd, that bating his colour, there could be nothing in nature more beautiful, agreeable and handsome. There was no one grace wanting, that bears the standard of true beauty. His hair came down to his shoulders, by the aids of art, which was by pulling it out with a quill, and keeping it comb'd; of which he took particular care.[34]

Aphra Behn's *Oronooko* is close in some respects to Ligon's version of the Yarico story. Both are based on earlier visits to the Caribbean (Behn in 1663–4; Ligon in 1647–50), and derive at least part of their authority from presenting themselves as first-hand accounts: Mrs Behn has talked to all the leading actors in her story, including Oronooko himself. Almost inevitably Mrs Behn's historical claims have been challenged, but they seem to have stood up remarkably well, at least as far as the Surinam episode is concerned.[35] Oronooko's retrospective account of the Coromantee court is a different matter, reading very much like a story from the *Thousand and One Nights* or, indeed, from a Restoration drama: but then so did Ligon's second paragraph about Yarico's provenance.

In some ways the oddest detail, never explained in the novel, is Oronooko's name. It is not clear what kind of irony or parallel is implied by the arrival just down the coast from the mouth of the Orinoco (spelt 'Oronooko' in English until the nineteenth century) of an African bearing such an evocatively American name. The oddness is compounded by the opening pages of the novel which set out, with greater determination than narrative motivation, to give an account of the native Amerindians, which turns out to be a particularly pure piece of primitivism ending on a note of *realpolitik*:

we find it absolutely necessary to caress 'em as friends, and not to treat 'em as slaves, nor dare we do other, their numbers so far surpassing ours in that continent.[36]

Southerne's dramatic version of *Oronooko* (1695) and its further adaptation to later sensibilities in 1759 by Hawkesworth were among the most popular plays in eighteenth-century England but, like Colman's *Inkle and Yarico* (1787), coarsened and simplified their narrative original. By the 1770s *Oronooko* had been mobilized so successfully by the anti-slavery movement for it never – despite its huge popularity – to be performed in Liverpool.

5

The debate in England over the First Black Carib War of 1772–3 was influenced by the prevailing ethos of sentimentality.[37] The West Indian interest was quite clear. The Treaty of Paris had given England control of the last remaining land in the Caribbean suitable for sugar plantations. The best land of all was on St Vincent, but unfortunately on the windward half of the island occupied by the large Black Carib community in line with a treaty made with the French in 1700 (see Figure 15).[38] The English government was clearly never disposed to take this treaty seriously. General Monckton's reward for his services during the Seven Years War was a grant of 4000 acres on the Carib side of the dividing line. The commissioners, under William Young, the first baronet, reported that 'very small and detached spots only are here and there cleared and settled by them, whilst large tracts through which they are scattered remained in wood, useless and unoccupied', remaining therefore in what the Council and Assembly later refer to, almost inevitably, as 'a state of nature'.[39] Young himself elsewhere mentions, by way of justification, Carib neglect of 'the obligation to cultivate', linking the English campaign against the Caribs to that long tradition of misrecognition of the forms and practices of native Amerindian agriculture.[40] For support he refers to the legist Emerich de Vattel, who had recently expressed the opinion that those people 'who having fertile countries, disdain to cultivate the earth ... deserve to be exterminated as savage and pernicious beasts'. The establishment of European colonies in North America was therefore found to be 'extremely lawful': 'The people of those vast countries rather over-ran than inhabited them'.[41]

The commissioners decided to make an accurate survey of all 'disputed' areas – that is to say the areas that the settlers had their eyes on – and to build roads that would facilitate such a survey, not to mention any 'pacification' that might prove necessary. The Caribs reacted in traditional style, electing a warchief, Joseph Chatoyer, for the period of the conflict, and beginning a

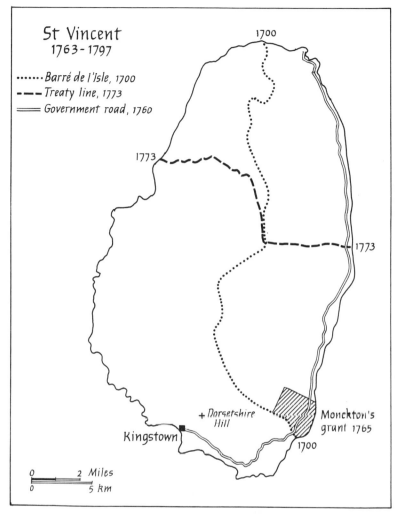

St Vincent
1763-1797

········ Barré de l'Isle, 1700
− − − Treaty line, 1773
══ Government road, 1760

1700

1773

1773

+ Dorsetshire
Hill

Kingstown

Monckton's
grant 1765

1700

0 ──── 2 Miles
0 ──── 5 km

Figure 15 St Vincent 1700–73; showing the two significant divisions of the island between Europeans and Black Caribs.

campaign of harassment against the surveyors and road-builders. The success of this campaign can probably be gauged accurately from the tone of Young's description of the Black Caribs in his report dated April 1767:

They are . . . an idle, ignorant, and savage people, subject to no law or discipline, and scarcely acknowledging subordination to any chief: they speak a jargon of their own, which, added to an extreme jealousy of their liberty, a distrust of those they converse with, and a little affected cunning, make it very difficult to discourse or reason with them concerning their situation, and the arrangements necessary to be taken with respect to them. They go for the most part naked.[42]

The commissioners were losing their patience. The Treasury authorized continuation of the survey and financial compensation to the Caribs for land they agreed to sell, but the surveyors, even with military assistance, failed to make progress. In April 1769 a detachment of forty soldiers was cut off 16 miles within Carib territory and released only after the English had promised to 'give up all immediate pretensions to interfere with their country and never again attempt to make roads of communication through it'.[43] Later in the year four Carib canoes, probably on a trading run to St Lucia, were sunk by a British sloop, and eighty Caribs left to drown.[44] In 1771 a further meeting between the commissioners and the Caribs resulted only in Chatoyer restating his determination to defend Carib sovereignty.[45] The commissioners' report (16 October 1771), giving an account of the meeting, hints at a more radical solution to the problem:

> We conceive it impossible that so small an island can long continue divided between a civilized people and savages, who are bound by no ties of law or religion: and who, from their situation among woods, are even exempted from fear of punishment.[46]

The settlers tried the legalistic approach, suggesting that the eastern half of the island constituted a dangerous *imperium in imperio*:

> that the suffering such a separate Empire as these Indians claim within your Majesty's Dominions is not only incompatible with the safety of your Subjects, but highly derogatory from the Honor and Dignity of the British Crown, that Lenity and every humane Expedient to bring them to a reasonable Subjection has long been tried without success; that with Nature's incapable of Gratitude or Sentiment, the mild hand of Benevolence evidently looses its effect.[47]

The sentimental matrix is recognized as providing the relevant vocabulary but judged inappropriate in this case.

In a separate report Richard Maitland, the island agent, spoke openly of removing the Caribs from the island altogether, broaching a forced removal back to Africa.[48] This suggestion was full of ironies. If anyone was native to St Vincent it was certainly not the English, so they were hardly in a moral position to remove anyone else. None of the Black Caribs had ever seen Africa: inasmuch as they were Carib they had been settled in the Caribbean for several centuries, in so far as they could be considered African they were hardly themselves responsible for being in the West Indies in the first place.

It had, though, always suited the settlers to portray the Black Caribs as usurpers of a legitimate Carib heritage and therefore not legally entitled to their land. This was a line strongly pushed by William Young in a further and telling instalment in the series of 'beginnings', this time the story of the beginnings of the Black Caribs:

> The Negroes, or Black Charaibs (as they have been termed of late years), are descendants from the cargo of an African slave ship, bound from the Bite of Benin to Barbadoes, and wrecked, about the year 1675, on the coast of Bequia, a small island about two leagues to the south of St Vincent's.
>
> The Charaibs, accustomed to fish in the narrow channel, soon discovered these Negroes, and finding them in great distress for provisions, and particularly for water, with which Bequia was ill supplied, they had little difficulty in inveigling them into their canoes, and transporting them across the narrow channel to St Vincent's, where they made slaves of them, and set them to work. These Negroes were of a warlike Moco tribe from Africa, and soon proved restive and indocile servants to the less robust natives of the western ocean.

He tells of an attempted Carib massacre of the blacks, which occasioned a sudden insurrection and escape to the mountains of the north-east. Combining there with other runaways and refugees from justice the shipwrecked Africans

> formed a nation, now known by the name of Black Charaibs; a title themselves arrogated, when entering into contest with their ancient masters.

The savage, with the name and title, thinks he inherits the qualities, the right, and the property, of those whom he may pretend to supersede: hence he assimilates himself by name and manners, as it were to make out his identity, and confirm the succession. Thus these Negroes not only assumed the national appellation of Charaibs, but individually their Indian names; and they adopted many of their customs: they flattened the forehead of their infant children in the Indian manner: they buried their dead in the attitude of sitting, and according to Indian rites: and killing the men they took in war, they carried off and cohabited with the women.[49]

Young's narrative performs the colonial disavowal in a manner very similar to Robinson Crusoe's, or for that matter Purchas's telling of the romance of Virginia. In each case an earlier moment of supposed usurpation is projected to act as a screen for the *present* usurpation which can thereby be presented as a rectification of others' crimes. This time it is the 'true' Caribs who have been dispossessed, the Black Caribs who are the usurpers. To dispossess the dispossessers is merely natural justice. Like all colonialist versions of beginnings this is a mythic story and a familiar one: shipwreck, hospitality, ingratitude. Other evidence can counter its claim to historicity,[50] but equally important is the way in which the narrative can manipulate the elements of that familiar paradigm – which is after all the story again of Inkle and Yarico – to cast an unfavourable light on the enemy of the British settlers. Most striking is the absolute reversal that has taken place in the depiction of the Caribs. Only recently a byword for inhospitable savagery they are turned by Young's account into 'the less robust natives of the western ocean', innocent and pacific victims of black usurpation, an uncanny repetition, down to the linguistic borrowing, of the supposed relationship, three centuries earlier, of Carib to Arawak. Needless to say there was no concomitant intention on the British part to restore these 'usurped' lands to their 'rightful' Carib owners.[51]

The planters' interest in London finally prevailed on the government to take military action, and on 18 April 1772 Lord Hillsborough, the Secretary of State, sent a secret dispatch mobilizing all the military and naval forces in the islands, as well as two regiments from North America. The idea was still to terrify the Black Caribs into accepting a treaty that would give them reserved land in a part of the island not required for sugar growing. However, attempted resistance would lead to 'effectual Measures for the Reduction of them' and their forced removal to 'some unfrequented Part of the Coast of Africa or some desert Island adjacent thereto'.[52] The Carib reaction was that they would not yield any part of their lands, 'which lands were transmitted to them from their ancestors and in defence of which they would die'.[53] Young, summarizing these events, has the 'patient forbearance' of the British government worn down by the 'contumacy' of the Caribs until the war of 1772 became necessary.[54] In fact, despite constant provocation, the Caribs seem to have defended their territory from frequent British incursions with the very minimum of force.

When Hillsborough's secret instructions became public knowledge they provoked a good deal of debate inside and outside Parliament. Two letters are of particular interest. On 10 October 1772 Granville Sharp wrote to the Earl of Dartmouth, Hillsborough's successor. The opening sentence strikes a sentimental note: 'A truly conscientious man is seldom to be met with in this corrupt age'. In the long and eloquent letter Sharp moves from the difficulty of the undertaking through reasons of climate and enemy stubbornness to its injustice. He reviews the French cession of the island to England, arguing that the lands of the Caribs could not have been included 'because the French could have no right to cede what did not belong to them'; invokes '*laws of nations*, and the unalterable principles of *natural justice*', hopes that '*the credit of our nation* may not openly be stained by the horrid crimes of *unjust oppression*, robbery and premeditated murder'; and ends with a pointed threat to Dartmouth as an aid to his conscience:

> good and evil can never change places, and . . . *we must not do evil that good may come.*
>
> These are the *first* and most *fundamental principles of Government*: so that statesmen and politicians, who thus venture to dispense with them, ought to be reminded, that such measures not only accumulate a national, but a *personal* guilt, which they must one day *personally* answer for, when they shall be compelled to attend, with common robbers and murderers, expecting an eternal doom; for the nature of their crimes is essentially the same, and God is no respecter of persons.

Sharp offered to elaborate his arguments in private and was invited to a long interview with Dartmouth the following day.[55]

The attack on the government was continued several weeks later by a pseudonymous letter to Dartmouth published in *The Scots Magazine*, which attacked what it called 'an uncommon scene of cruelty carrying on in the island of St Vincent, against the innocent, natural inhabitants' in the name of civil liberty. 'Probus' also outlined the history of the island, whose legal division now made it disgraceful that Hillsborough should have listened to the planters' petition 'to extirpate all the black native free inhabitants'. He continued:

> Resistance might well be expected, and now intelligence is received, that British troops are employed to put these people to the sword, under the specious pretext of destroying insurgents. This is the British Government reviving the Spanish cruelties at the conquest of Mexico, to gratify avaricious merchants, landholders, and venal commissioners.

He concluded by calling for a parliamentary inquiry unless the expedition was suspended.[56]

A parliamentary debate followed on 9 December, with speakers condemning 'hostilities against a defenceless, innocent and inoffensive people', suggesting that 'they are fighting for liberty, and every English heart must applaud them'. In consequence of a motion, the relevant documents – *Papers relative to the expedition against the Caribbs, and the sale of land in St Vincent*'s – were laid before the House on 23 December; and further criticism of the expedition was voiced in a debate on 10 February 1773.[57]

By this time, however, hostilities were almost at an end. The government had received news dated October 1772 that Carib resistance was 'serious and formidable' and that the military campaign was making little progress. The initial hostilities had turned the Black Caribs into 'most cruel and unforgiving enemies' and Governor Leybourne reported that: 'I very much fear their Reduction, will be a work of time, for they possess a Country very inaccessible, and seem to have a knowledge how to avail themselves of this Advantage'.[58] Urgent dispatches were sent in December to the army commander instructing him to sue for a treaty, which was negotiated in March 1773. The Black Caribs were left in full possession of their lands except for 2000

acres that were ceded to the settlers – but which were partly
resettled by the Black Caribs two years later; and a strip 3 chains
wide around the coast (see Figure 15). In return they pledged
allegiance to the British Crown and its laws, promised to return
runaway slaves, and to allow the construction of roads. The
settlers had gained no significant portion of desired land.[59]

6

The anonymous 1736 'Yarico to Inkle, an Epistle' was reprinted
nine times before the end of the century. The first edition carried
a three line epigraph from Dryden which was replaced in the 1792
Marblehead edition by Ilioneus's poignant questions from the first
book of the *Aeneid*:

> Quod genus hoc hominum? quaeve hunc tam barbara morem
> Permittit patria?   (*Aeneid* I.539–40)
> [What manner of men are these? What land is this that allows
> them such barbarous ways?][60]

– an epigraph that points up the parallels between the stories of
Inkle and Yarico and Dido and Aeneas. These can briefly be
recalled. The Trojans and English are both shipwrecked in a
storm off a hostile coast; Aeneas and Inkle are both separated from
the other sailors and passengers; in both cases an amorous
relationship develops between the traveller and an hospitable
'princess' of the country; in both cases their sexual union is
consummated in a cave, heralding a period of bliss which is
brought to an end when the traveller moves on, deserting the
woman he had loved – or perhaps deceived.[61]
    As with the examples from earlier chapters the significance of
these classical parallels is by no means easy to construe and is
complicated by the already somewhat problematic place of the
Carthaginian episode within the *Aeneid*. The gist of the narrative
is banal enough to obviate the need for explanation through
allusion but, underpinning the more specific parallels, is a sub-text
concerning the great colonial theme of hospitality, which provides the socially symbolic meaning enacted by the story of Inkle
and Yarico. As with that of the Cyclops episode in Chapter 3 the
reading here needs to be double. The story of Dido will help with

the reading of Inkle and Yarico, but will itself need a reciprocal reading to restore its political dimension. In both cases what stands in need of clarification is the political unconscious of a love-story.

It has been a continual source of difficulty to critics of the *Aeneid* that its hero, founder of the Rome that Virgil is celebrating, should be responsible for the death of such a sympathetic character as Dido while, as the *Oxford Companion to Classical Literature* puts it, 'Aeneas goes shabbily away scot-free'.[62] The contemporary sources concerning Dido were too confused for the explanation to be that Virgil had little choice in his presentation of the episode, and so the conventional reading has tended to set destiny against passion: Aeneas, reminded of his duty, tears himself away from his true love; Dido, heartbroken, dies by her own hand; and we, following St Augustine's lead, are left to weep for her. Dido is therefore – as she was re-presented by Dryden in 1697 – a sentimental heroine along the lines of Euripides' Medea and Catullus's Ariadne, deserted by their lovers.

Richard Monti has read the episode rather differently, stressing as a key term the word 'dextera' (right hand) which features prominently in Dido's recriminatory speech to Aeneas:

> Unfaithful man, did you think you could do such a dreadful
> thing
> And keep it dark? yes, skulk from my land without one
> word?
> Our love, the vows you made me [*data dextera*] – do these not
> give you pause . . . ?
>
> . . .
>
> By these tears, by the hand you gave me [*dextramque tuam*] –
> They are all I have left, today, in my misery – I implore you,
> And by our union of hearts, by our marriage hardly begun,
> If I have ever helped you at all, if anything
> About me pleased you, be sad for our our broken home,
> forgo
> Your purpose, I beg you, unless it's too late for prayers of
> mine.[63]   (IV.304–31)

According to the 'sentimental' reading 'dextera' should refer to the hand of betrothal that featured in *Medea*: Dido would then be the betrayed woman berating her lover. Certain commentators, and Monti quotes Richard Heinze in this respect, have taken this line and 'explained' a textual difficulty through inadequate motivation of an adapted source:

> Since it is true that there is nothing in the text before this point which tells of the clasping of right hands in a pledge of marriage, the conclusion to which Heinze's reader is drawn is that Virgil in an excess of zeal surpasses this borrowing from Euripides without making the necessary adjustments in the narrative.[64]

But, as with Kermode's similar reading of Prospero's interrupted masque, a supposedly 'textual' problem proves to be the location of an ideological crux of some importance.[65]

Monti shows, in considerable detail, that both in Virgil and in the literature of the republic generally 'dextera' is usually a political term. Given the intensely personal nature of Roman political alliances this by no means dispenses with the centrality of sexual passion to the relationship between Dido and Aeneas, but it does suggest a more complex story than that of enamoured heroine deserted by duty-bound hero.[66] The lead followed by Monti is that given in Arthur Pease's 1935 commentary on Book IV where he suggests that 'dextera' implies 'a pledge of hospitality or friendship rather than one of troth'.[67]

This suggestion is confirmed by an analysis of the key scene of the first meeting between Dido and the Trojans. Inevitably this meeting has many superficial similarities with the colonial encounters studied in this book, and in particular with the Inkle and Yarico story, although its narrative development is very different. The sub-text of the early exchanges concerns barbarism. Ilioneus, spokesman for the Trojans in the temporary absence of Aeneas, is determined to avoid the charge of piracy. He is aware that Dido, 'who, under God, have founded a new city', is the guardian of civic values; the Trojans, strange and unexpected arrivals from the sea, must appear alien to urban order and therefore need to assert, as it were, their own civilized pedigree:

> We are not come as pirates to waste your Libyan homes
> With the sword, and carry down their plunder to the beaches.
> (I.527–8)

They are city-dwellers themselves, forced to leave their home and on their way to Italy: in other words legitimate travellers. In fact Ilioneus's indignation turns the tables. As victims of the storm they are deserving of a hospitality they have not yet received:

> What manner of men are these? What land is this that allows them
> Such barbarous ways? They bar us even from the sanctuary of the sands.   (I.539–41)

It turns out, of course, that Dido's city is an oasis of civilization in the desert of barbarity which is the coast of Africa. Like Yarico and, to some extent, Pocahontas, she is able to offer a refuge from the prevailing dangers. There is in this the same sense of betrayal that underlies Yarico and Pocahontas's receptivity – as Iarbas later makes clear when he refers contemptuously to Dido as:

> That woman who, wandering within our frontiers, paid to establish
> Her insignificant township, permitted by us to plough up
> A piece of the coast and be queen of it.   (IV.211–3)

But Dido, and here the ironies multiply, is herself a refugee from what can only be described as the barbarism of the city in the form of her murderous brother-in-law Pygmalion. And, in a startling reversal of the incipient colonial situation of Book IX of the *Odyssey*, Dido – while Ilioneus, like a good guest, stresses the shortness of the Trojans' intended stay – offers an equal share in her kingdom:

> vultis et his mecum pariter considere regnis?
> urbem quam statuo, vestra est
>
> (I.572–3)

or as Dryden pointedly, if somewhat loosely, has it: 'My Wealth, my City, and my self are yours',[68] an offer, as Aeneas's warm response suggests, unequalled in the annals of civilized consortium. The final toast, called for by the queen, clarifies the nature of the preceding exchanges:

> Jupiter – yours, they say, are the laws of hospitality –
> Grant this be a happy day for the Carthaginians and those
> Who come from Troy, a day that our children will remember!
>
> (I.731–3)

The hospitium offers not only a temporary refuge but a permanent home, a colonial dream come true; which is something of an
embarrassment for someone too concerned with his destiny as
supposed *founder* of a city to worry – yet – about colonial
conquests.

In this reading Dido's despairing appeal – 'nec te noster amor,
nec te data dextera quondam' (IV.307) – does not consist simply
of a repeated plea to love and lovers' vows; but of a double-
voiced plea: to love and to the political ties established by
hospitality. It is not easy to keep them apart – after all, the climax
of Dido's hospitality is the offer of her body – but the political
inflection needs highlighting, given the tendency to submerge it
in the tears of a purely sentimental recrimination. Aeneas is fully
aware of the political ties that bind him. Conventionally Dido is
seen as the victim of self-deception – she wants Aeneas to stay so
she convinces herself that he will – while Aeneas is merely torn
between duty and love. Psychological hypotheses would be
particularly inappropriate in this case but it should be pointed out
that Dido's convictions are not self-induced: Aeneas *acts as if* he is
staying, adopting Carthaginian dress and superintending new
building work in the city (IV.260–3). So, appropriately, his
response to Dido addresses the political argument and has to
accept its merit:

> ego te, quae plurima fando
> enumerare vales, numquam, Regina, negabo
> promeritam   (IV.333–5)
>   [I'll never pretend
> You have not been good to me, deserving of everything
> You can claim]

Love is not irrelevant, but the real conflict is between two
pressing but incompatible political demands.

This excursus into the *Aeneid* suggests that the pathos of the
deserted heroine motif may, even in the classical archetypes,
obscure the fully political issue of hospitality which, as was argued
at length in Chapter 4, is central to colonialist practices and to
their management in European discourses; and in the light of this
reading of its classical intertext 'Inkle and Yarico' can be properly
seen as a concessionary narrative. Like the story of Pocahontas it
goes some way towards recognizing a native point of view and

offering a critique of European behaviour, but it can only do this by not addressing the central issue. In this sense the narrative is classically Freudian, a compromise that is made possible by displacement.

So far the argument of this chapter has been manifest in its structure. 'History' – the story of the British wars against the Black Caribs in St Vincent, and 'Literature' – the various versions of the story of Inkle and Yarico – have had to occupy alternate sections, placed parallel to one another but rarely meeting or showing any sign of cross-reference. Such parallels as do exist – like that between the structure of the 'Inkle and Yarico' story and the story told by Young of Black Carib origins – have to be excavated from a long way below the textual surface. An argument could certainly be made that this separation of spheres can be 'explained by' – in the sense that it is part of – the historical conjuncture. The last half of the eighteenth century was, according to any reading, a period of crisis for British colonialism, so it is hardly surprising that the final and in some ways half-hearted effort to complete the European extirpation of the population of the native Caribbean should not have had a contemporary *Robinson Crusoe* to embody its ideology. If anything – and this would count as a further 'explanation' – 'Inkle and Yarico' would seem, in its sentimentality and its critique of English calculation, to belong to the emergent ideology for which Granville Sharp was such an eloquent spokesman. 1772, the year of Sharp's letter, also saw a hostile official inquiry into the affairs of the East India Company in the aftermath of its disastrous attempts to administer Bengal, and the judgement in the famous case of James Somerset, both important propaganda victories for the movement of radical libertarianism which was soon to be rendered ineffective on account of the ideological polarization produced by the revolutionary events in France and Haiti in the early 1790s.[69]

This is all true enough. But, as is always the case with the Freudian model, the more successful the displacement the more difficult it becomes to trace the connections between the aetiology of the repression and the formation of a *particular* set of symptoms. For cultural critics, however, as for Freud, the 'perfect' displacement is a theoretical impossibility: there must be a link, however tenuous, in the discursive nexus, that will cathect the two sets of texts, literary and historical. If not, their juxtaposition would be arbitrary. Given the imaginative geography of *The Tempest* and *Robinson Crusoe* it is almost predictable that the point of referential contact between 'Inkle and Yarico' and the Black Caribs turns out to be North Africa. The intertextual connections between Inkle and Yarico and Aeneas and Dido, brought to the textual surface by the Marblehead epigraph, have already been explored. Directly alongside this and finally bringing the parallel lines together should be set William Young's memorandum to Lord Hillsborough, dated 28 July 1772, suggesting that the dominant white feeling in St Vincent at that moment with respect to the Caribs was 'Delenda est cartago'.[70] This Latin tag was supposedly spoken by Cato as the conclusion he had been forced to reach after a visit to a resurgent Carthage. In Plutarch's version the threat is distinctly aimed at Rome's masculinity:

> it is said that Cato contrived to drop a Libyan fig in the Senate, as he shook out the folds of his toga, and then, as the senators admired its size and beauty, said that the country where it grew was only three days' sail from Rome.[71]

The fig is usually read as a potent sign of the proximity of a potential enemy, but it could equally – in the colonial sub-text – be seen as an indication of a source of particularly good figs. So the historical resonances of the memorandum are rich, with Young proposing himself, consciously or not, as a Cato whose personal experience, dramatically symbolized by the fig he shakes from his toga, is in danger of being ignored by metropolitan complacency and, in the Carib case, sentimentality. The brute reality of the planters' desire to destroy the native inhabitants of the island is only utterable in the pure register of classical quotation.

7

As with the similar story of Pocahontas the provenance of the 'Inkle and Yarico' theme has been a subject of dispute. Lawrence Price's *Inkle and Yarico Album*, the most thorough study of the narrative, begins with Ligon; but Gilbert Chinard – and, following Chinard, Wylie Sypher – trace the origin of the story to Jean Mocquet, who sailed with Razilly to Brazil in 1604 and who was later to hold the office of 'Garde du Cabinet des Singularitez du Roy aux Tuileries'. In his *Voyages*, first published in French in 1616, and translated into English by Nathaniel Pullen in 1696,[72] Mocquet's ship meets an English vessel near Cumaná:

> Our Trumpeter shewed me their Pilot, and told me, that he some years before being in an English Vessel, as they were upon the Coasts of the West-Indies, towards St John de Love (the first place of the *Indies* to go to *Mexico*, where the Spaniards are, then their Sworn Enemies) a great Storm overtook them, which cast them upon the Coast, where they were all lost, except this Pilot, who saved himself by Swimming to Land, carrying with him a little Sea-Compass, and went thus wandring about to return by Land to the *Newfound* Countries: Upon that, he had found an Indian-Woman, of whom he was Enamoured, making her fine Promises by Signs, that he would Marry her; which she believed, and conducted him through these Desarts; where she shewed him the Fruit and Roots good to Eat, and served him for an Interpreter amongst the Indians, which he found, she telling them that it was her Husband. After having been thus 2 or 3 years continually wandering about, and that for above 800 Leagues, without any other Comfort but this Woman; At last they arrived at the New-foundland, guiding himself by his Compass: They had a Child together; and found there an English Ship a Fishing: He was very glad to see himself escaped from so many Dangers, and gave these English an account of all his Adventures: They took him on Board their Vessel to make him good cheer; but being ashamed to take along with him this Indian-Woman thus Naked, he left her on Land, without regarding her cry more: But she seeing herself thus forsaken by him, whom she had so dearly Loved, and for whose sake she had abandoned her Country and Friends, and had so well guided and accompanied him through such places, where he would, without her, have been dead a thousand times. After having made some Lamentation, full of Rage and Anger, she took her Child, and tearing it into two pieces, she cast the one half towards him into the Sea, as if she would say, that belonged to him, and was his part

of it; and the other she carried away with her, returning back to the Mercy of Fortune, and full of Mourning and Discontent.

The Seamen who took this Pilot into their Boat, seeing this horrible and cruel Spectacle, asked him, why he had left this woman; but he pretended she was a Savage, and that he did not now heed her; which was an extreme Ingratitude and Wickedness in him: Hearing this, I could not look upon him, but always with Horrour and great Detestation.[73]

Chinard and Sypher talk unproblematically about Yarico making her first appearance in this passage, but some care is needed in establishing the relationship between Mocquet and Ligon. After Ligon all versions of the story are openly intertextual: they refer back either to Ligon himself or to Steele – and therefore by implication to Ligon – as authoritative sources. Ligon is the earth through which the narrative current is grounded in history. Ligon, reporting his meeting with Yarico and the tale associated with her, is a self-conscious originator of a story: intertextual reference to Mocquet is ruled out on principle. As was the case in the earlier discussion of *The Tempest* and its 'sources', the least interesting question – in any case unanswerable – is whether the earlier text was known to the later writer. The undoubted relationship between Mocquet's story and Ligon's is dependent not upon Ligon's possible access to Mocquet's text but on internal similarities.

These similarities are suggestive in a variety of ways. The repetition of the presentational mode – a story told by a third party to the author about a figure who is silent – suggests that we are dealing with a particular narrative genre, a specialized version of 'the anecdote' with a precise axial arrangement whereby the silent figure is established by the third party's report as a subject of fascination, whether of horror or of pity.

Like Ligon's, Mocquet's story has the rough edges and circumstantiality of a true anecdote before it is polished into a literary essay, yet even these edges are identifiable as colonial topoi. The extraordinary 800-league journey recalls Ingram's probably fictional walk up the eastern seaboard; and the compass reappears, again here almost as much a totem of European identity as an instrument for direction-finding. But most remarkable of all is the presence of the child, the living symbol – as Steele and others later realized – of a potential harmony between European and native American, so callously deserted by the English pilot and so savagely destroyed by the Amerindian woman in unconscious parody of the judgement of Solomon, and, for that matter, of Dido's lament that she had not even conceived a 'little Aeneas' to remind her of him (*Aeneid* IV.327–30).

The severed child is too terrible and potent an image for the more refined sensibilities of the eighteenth century. It certainly gives Mocquet's story an awesome power, but also a deep ambivalence since the pilot's ingratitude is overshadowed by his lover's action, which is so unthinkable a violation of the purity of the mother/child couplet, sacred within Christian Europe, that it is difficult to know how to read it at all. It could signify the deep and recalcitrant savagery of the natives; it could be a terrible index of the pilot's ingratitude. But it would seem in the end so awful, in something like the full sense of that word, that it transcends any moral judgements that a reader might want to pass.

What is common, however, to this whole series of stories is that the home territory of the native woman is not the destination of the European ship. The topos that signifies this is normally a shipwreck: Inkle (and his pilot forerunner) are here in the good company of Aeneas, Prospero and Robinson Crusoe in being cast against their will on to a native shore, the best possible excuse for being there, as Odysseus and John Smith proved by pretending that they had suffered the same fate. So there are always two locations involved in the story. In Mocquet they are a Caribbean coast and 'terres neufs' to the north; in Ligon, Steele and others the first is sometimes a Caribbean coast and sometimes an African, but the second is always Barbados. This is where the concessionary nature of the story becomes apparent. Inkle, rescued and succoured and loved, clearly infringes the laws of hospitality by selling Yarico into slavery; but this is, after all, an individual case and no threat is offered to the home territory of the victim. In fact – and this is again a constant from Ligon's version onwards – the Inkle figure is the sole survivor of the violence offered to Europeans by the inhospitable natives. The three key moves are all therefore repetitions of the *Aeneid*: the initial violence complained about by Ilioneus; the Trojan's absence of interest in Carthage; and Aeneas's ingratitude towards Dido. The *Aeneid* is a welcome reference point because, blameworthy as Aeneas's actions may be, they are interpretable as an unfortunate clash between passion and duty and therefore only an infringement of the laws of hospitality, rather than the complete overturning of such laws through the extirpation of the native population. The introduction of Ilioneus's words as epigraph to the 1792 edition of the 1736 'Yarico to Inkle' poem is, therefore, carefully ambivalent, referring equally to Inkle's 'barbaric' action and to the English ship's inhospitable reception on the Caribbean coast, the two breaches tending, the implication would seem to be, to cancel each other out. The insistence on Barbados is to be explained by the fact that, alone of the English sugar islands, it had no native population at the time of the English settlement.[74] It is a relatively 'pure' space in which the scene of the betrayal can take place, another screen or alibi for the extirpation going on elsewhere, a trope entirely congruent with the rift in the structure of *Robinson Crusoe*. The sentimentalizing 'anti-slavery' versions that move the first scene of 'Inkle and Yarico' to the African coast are only consolidating the tendency already inherent in the story to obviate all mention of English settlement of Carib lands.

Strangely the pure space of 'Barbados' nearly mimes in its phonemes the barbarianism which must still be located outside, on the savage islands. The 1738 'Story of Inkle and Yarico' – the one that has Yarico as Negro virgin and Indian maid in different stanzas of the poem – has opposite the title page a list of errata which corrects 'Yarrico' to 'Yarico' throughout, and the 'Cannibals' who dwell on the 'barbarous coast' to 'Canibals'; but which fails to note the revenge of the unconscious in printing 'the *Barbadian* coast' as 'the *Barbarian* coast'.[75]

8

Despite the 1773 treaty the Vincentian planters were determined that Carthage was to be destroyed. Sugar plantations were established in piecemeal fashion by the settlers on Carib lands, and successfully defended. During the governorship of the 'unfortunate' Valentine Morris the Caribs assisted a French take-over of the island, but this brought the incursions into Carib territory to only a temporary halt.[76]

Over the next ten years relationships between the settlers and

the Black Caribs seem to have improved, at least if contemporary
evidence is taken into account. In 1789 the Methodist missionary
Thomas Coke wrote to John Wesley of his favourable impression
of the Caribs:

> I feel myself much attached to these poor savages. The sweet
> simplicity and cheerfulness they manifested on every side, soon
> wore off every unfavourable impression my mind had imbibed
> from the accounts I had received of their cruelties. Cruelties
> originating probably with ourselves rather than with them.[77]

This could be merely the language of sentiment, but the hard-
headed William Young was also favourably impressed by the
demeanour of the Carib leaders when he visited his estates on St
Vincent during the winter of 1791–2.[78]

The retrospective accounts inevitably tell a different story.
Coke's later *History of the West Indies* contains an anxious
rewriting of his letter:

> The simplicity and cheerfulness which, in the midst of cautious
> suspicions, were manifested by the Charaibees towards us,
> soone grew into an attachment which totally banished our
> fears. The unfavourable impressions which we had received
> from a recital of their cruelties soon wore away; their artless
> address gained the ascendancy over previous report, and half
> taught us to believe that they had been wronged by misrepre-
> sentation and prejudice. But artless addresses sometimes pro-
> ceed from excess of artifice and fraud; and the civil history of
> this island stands as a convincing testimony, that no people ever
> practised duplicity with greater impurity than this people. The
> savages of America, we learn from these circumstances, may be
> destitute of the finesse of modern Europe, without being either
> ignorant of deception, or always guided by virtue.[79]

And Charles Shephard, whose history 'is respectfully inscribed
... to the survivors of the Carib War', gives full rein to the
planters' version of events:

> A variety of excesses had been committed by the Caribs against
> the English during the time the Island was under the French
> government, who prudently restrained the sanguinary disposi-
> tion of their allies, nevertheless their behavior on all occasions,

betrayed their deep rooted enmity and aversion, and
occasioned at first a correspondent degree of caution and
prudence on the part of the Colonists; but from the evacuation
of the Island by the French, to the commencement of the
Revolution in France, the treacherous Caribs, having lost their
avowed protectors, put on the smoothest political exterior, and
as early as they could with a good grace, professed themselves
enraptured admirers of the mild and benevolent Constitution
of Great Britain. And strange as it may appear, notwithstanding past events, they were as successful in imposing on the
credulous Inhabitants, as they had been in the former war; and
the Planters with all the zeal peculiar to self interest, wished to
engage their friendship by every means within their reach.[80]

Not for the first time in this sketch of colonial encounters the
story has a familiar ring to it, and the ring – as Shephard half
admits ('strange as it may appear') – is decidedly hollow. Yet
again we are expected to believe that what he elsewhere calls 'this
doubly savage race'[81] – that is to say black and Carib – had so
successfully coated their intrinsic nature with 'the smoothest
political exterior' that the poor credulous planters, wanting so
much to believe the professions of friendship, had allowed
themselves to be taken in. The same planters who had earlier
made it very clear, 'with all the zeal peculiar to self interest', that
they desired the British government to extirpate the Black Caribs
from the island, turn out in Shephard's account to have been
gullible Yaricos easily conned by the 'treacherous Caribs' with
their Inkle-like wiles. Once again the process of reversal is almost
perfect.

Yet for the British the Second Carib War was doubly
determined. Apart from Chatoyer's imitation of Opechancanough with his 'treachery' carefully planned over twenty-
three years, there was also the war against revolutionary France
which brought to a head many of the internal problems of West
Indian security. For some years previously the British forces had
been engaged in several other conflicts apart from that with the
Black Caribs. The longest-running of these was with the Jamaican
maroons, opponents inherited from Spain in 1655, and who,
under their leaders Nanny and Cudjoe, had already in the earlier
part of the eighteenth century inflicted punishing wars on British

troops. Open warfare had not occurred since 1760, but the
maroon communities were seen as at best an unwelcome example
of black independence, at worst an actual provocation to unrest
amongst the slaves. The land-rush following the Treaty of Paris
led to further conflicts, both with French farmers (on Dominica,
Grenada and St Vincent), with established maroons (on Dominica), and with new slave revolts (especially on Tobago). The lines
between these different groups are not easy to draw, as the very
name Black Carib itself suggests: all island maroon groups
probably had some kind of contact with or input from the
remaining Amerindian communities; the boundary between slave
and maroon was permeable – in at least one direction; the white
French often collaborated with any anti-British group; and most
of the previously French islands had a free, black, francophone
section.[82] In addition some co-operation was likely between at
least neighbouring islands and, after the revolutions in France and
St Domingue, this contact was actively fostered by French *agents
provocateurs*, leading the English planters to proclaim the existence
of a wide-ranging and dangerous conspiracy to overthrow
civilization. The repression that followed was probably more
directly responsible for the slave, maroon and Carib uprisings
than was the revolutionary rhetoric. The legendary Victor
Hugues took most of the blame:

> This infamous revolutionary zealot, bloated with the inhuman,
> and wide wasting principles of the democratic system, no
> sooner saw himself in a condition of not only maintaining
> his new conquests, but also of extending them, than he
> endeavoured to convert his hopes into certainty by embroiling
> every Colony in his neighbourhood, and rendering them the
> theatre of internal war.[83]

In 1793 Britain declared open war against revolutionary France
with the Caribbean as a major theatre, the rapid capture of all the
French islands leading to a series of prolonged guerrilla wars. This
was a pattern in which the Second Carib War of 1795 would,
from the British point of view, find a further 'explanation',
starting as it did just a week after Hugues had addressed a
proclamation to the Caribs calling on them to break the chains
imposed by the hands of the tyrannical British.[84] The intra-
European conflict had no doubt given the Black Caribs their

opportunity, but the war was caused – as a Shephard again goes some way to admitting – by settler infringements of the 1773 treaty. The conflict was also – in a historical perspective that both sides may have been aware of – the last battle in a Caribbean war that had lasted almost exactly three centuries.[85]

Within days of the uprising the Carib war-chief Chatoyer had been killed in personal combat with a Major Leith in the battle for the strategically important heights of Dorsetshire Hill, just north of Kingstown. Overcoming this loss, the Caribs – aided by French smallholders and some slaves – fought a skilful campaign against numerically overwhelming opponents. No less than six times the island was effectively saved for the British by the opportune arrival of reinforcements, once on board the appropriately named HMS *Scipio*.

The decisive move, however, was the arrival in the West Indies of General Sir Ralph Abercromby's expeditionary force of 17,000 men which was split between St Lucia, Grenada and St Vincent. Abercromby almost immediately won a major victory in June 1796, but the Black Caribs refused to surrender and, now devoid of allies, fought on until persuaded by some of their leaders that surrender and deportation were preferable to the alternative of inevitable extinction. Five thousand Black Caribs surrendered in October 1796 and after four months on the small island of Balliceaux were transported to the island of Roatan, off the coast of Honduras. On St Vincent fighting continued intermittently until 1805. In a final cynical gesture *all* Carib lands – including those of the indigenous Caribs who had formed such a touching contrast to Black Carib rapacity in earlier propaganda – were declared forfeit to the Crown.

Afterword

The nut-brown warrior has left the scene,
And dim the traces where his step has been,
Hunted from every spot he called his own,
The Charib perished, and his race is gone.[1]

After enormous initial difficulties the Black Carib community
survived and prospered in Central America, where the Island
Carib language is still spoken. And against all odds – and in spite
of Chapman's touching elegy – the 'Yellow' Caribs maintained
a presence both on St Vincent and on mountainous Dominica,
where reserved land was set aside for them in 1903, and where as
recently as 1930 brief 'disturbances' – still referred to as the
'Carib War' – brought about the visit of a government official
and the publication of his report by HMSO in London.[2]

The ideology of savagery forged in the crucible of the
Caribbean proved usefully adaptable to the new political circumstances of modern Europe. One early use of the word 'cannibalism' – generalizing the practice away from the Caribbean –
occurs in Edmund Burke's 1796 *Letters on a Regicide Peace* where
he gives full rein to the rhetoric of gothic horror with which the
ruling classes have ever since depicted all attempts on their
power.[3] Events in the Caribbean during the 1790s provided a
touchstone for European political discourse well into the
nineteenth century, often in conjunction with this vocabulary of
the gothic. In 1824 Frankenstein's monster – which arguably owes
something in the first place to Bryan Edwards's account of the
rising in St Domingue – was invoked by Canning in an anti-
abolitionist speech; while seven years later, in response to the

Lyons silk riots that Marx would refer to as marking the beginning of class conflict in France, Saint-Marc Girardin wrote:

> Let us not dissimulate; reticence and evasion will get us nowhere. The uprising at Lyons has brought to light a grave secret, the civil strife that is taking place in society between the possessing class and the class that does not possess .... If you take any industrial town and find out the relative number of manufacturers and workers, you will be frightened by the disproportion: every factory owner lives in his factory like a colonial planter in the middle of his slaves, one against a hundred; and the uprising at Lyons is to be compared with the insurrection at Saint-Domingue.[4]

Physically and psychologically this is Robinson Crusoe in his fort, the discourse of colonialism providing the terms with which class conflict can be articulated. This makes it appropriate to end by recalling the words of some final native Caribbeans, the Tupis questioned at Rouen in 1562 by Montaigne:

> Some demanded their advise, and would needs know of them what things of note and admirable they had observed amongst us .... They said ... 'they had perceived, there were men amongst us full gorged with all sortes of commodities, and others which hunger-starved, and bare with need and povertie, begged at their gates: and found it strange, these moyties so needy could endure such an injustice, and that they tooke not the others by the throte, or set fire on their houses'.[5]

Notes

The procedure for references adopted in these notes is as follows: within each chapter the first reference to a text is given in full (with the exception of some primary text when the full reference is reserved for Section A of the Bibliography), and subsequent references are to author or to author and abbreviated title.

Introduction

1 Quoted by Lewis Hanke, *Aristotle and the American Indians*, Bloomington, 1959, p. 8. The Bishop had just presented to the Queen, Antonio de Nebrija's *Gramática*, the first grammar of a modern European language, and had been asked by the Queen 'What is it for?'.

2 Although not addressed to colonial discourse in general, the best introduction to the topic is still the Introduction to Edward Said's *Orientalism*, London, 1978, pp. 1–28.

3 Immanuel Wallerstein, *The Modern World-System II: Mercantilism and the Consolidation of the European World-Economy 1600–1750*, New York, 1974, p. 103.

4 The reference is to a three-way debate about the relationship between 'history' and 'theory' whose central arguments can be found in four books: Barry Hindess and Paul Hirst, *Pre-Capitalist Modes of Production*, London, 1975; E.P. Thompson, *The Poverty of Theory and Other Essays*, London, 1978; Perry Anderson, *Arguments within English Marxism*, London, 1980; and Paul Hirst, *Marxism and Historical Writing*, London, 1985. All presuppose the work of Louis Althusser, especially *For Marx*, trans. Ben Brewster, London, 1970; *Lenin and Philosophy*, trans. Ben Brewster, London, 1971; and (with Etienne Balibar), *Reading Capital*, trans. Ben Brewster, London, 1977.

5 Michel Foucault, *Power/Knowledge: Selected Interviews and Other Writings 1972–1977*, ed. Colin Gordon, Brighton, 1980, p. 118.

6 This was the lengthy document required in Spanish law to be read to the Indians by a notary before hostilities could be commenced.

Captains muttered its theological phrases into their beards on the edge of sleeping Indian settlements, or even a league away before starting the formal attack, and at times some leather-lunged Spanish notary hurled its sonorous phrases after the Indians as they fled into the mountains . . . . Ship captains would sometimes have the document read from the deck as they approached an island. (Lewis Hanke, *The Spanish Struggle for Justice in the Conquest of America*, Philadelphia, 1949, p. 34)

7 In conventional anthropological terms the cultures of the native Caribbean were pre-historic in the sense that they had no writing; but such a notion needs careful handling. To divide cultures by the presence or absence of writing is to risk establishing a false division between the transparent and the opaque: writing is not an unproblematic guide, and needs interpreting with as much care as archaeological evidence. It is also not self-evident just what should count as writing: see Jacques Derrida's reading of Claude Lévi-Strauss's 'The writing lesson' (*Of Grammatology*, trans. Gayatri Chakravorty Spivak, Baltimore, 1976, pp. 101–40; and cf. Gordon Brotherston, 'Towards a grammatology of America: Lévi-Strauss, Derrida and the native New World text', in *Europe and Its Others*, ed. Francis Barker, Peter Hulme, Margaret Iversen, and Diana Loxley, Colchester, 1985, vol. II, pp. 61–77). The Caribbean 'documents' would therefore include both the ubiquitous petroglyphs that are mostly undeciphered, and the stone and wooden carvings whose symbolism remains opaque to us.

8 Van der Straet's original drawing for the engraving has the word 'AMERICA' coming from Vespucci's mouth (see Clare Le Corbeiller, 'Miss America and her sisters; Personification of the four parts of the world', *Bulletin of the Metropolitan Museum of Art*, n.s. XIX, 1961, p. 211). The naming was implemented by the geographers of St Die at the beginning of the sixteenth century: see Martin Waldseemüller, *The Cosmographiae Introductio* (1507), ed. C.G. Herbermann, New York, 1907. And cf., for an interesting psychoanalytic reading, W.G. Niederland, 'The naming of America', in *The Unconscious Today: Essays in Honor of Max Schur*, ed. M. Kanzer, New York, 1971, pp. 459–72. Van der Straet's engraving is also discussed in Michel de Certeau, *L'écriture de l'histoire*, Paris, 1975, pp. 7–23.

9 R.G. Collingwood, *The Idea of History*, Oxford, 1946, p. 237.

10 Fredric Jameson, *The Political Unconscious: Narrative as a Socially Symbolic Act*, London, 1981, pp. 19–20.

11 Louis Althusser and Etienne Balibar, *Reading Capital*; and Pierre Macherey, *A Theory of Literary Production*, trans. Geoffrey Wall, London, 1978.

1   Columbus and the cannibals

1 Gabriel García Márquez, *The Autumn of the Patriarch*, trans. Gregory Rabassa, London, 1977, pp. 35–6.

2 On form-history see the *Oxford English Dictionary*, Compact edition, London, 1979, p. vii.

3 The quotations are from Louis-André Vigneras's revised version of Cecil Jane's translation of Columbus's *Diario (The Journal of Christopher Columbus*, London, 1960), slightly amended in places. References to this text take the form of *J* plus page number, and follow the quotation. Where the language is especially important the original will either follow, as here, or be incorporated parenthetically. Carlos Sanz's edition (*Diario de Colón*, Madrid, 1962) which includes a facsimile of Las Casas's manuscript has been used: references are to both edition and facsimile, and brief, unreferenced quotations can easily be traced through their date. On rare occasions the Spanish has been altered where Sanz has appeared to misread the manuscript. Columbus's *Letter*, a short retrospective account of his first voyage, will be important at the end of this chapter. It is included in Vigneras's edition of the *Journal*. For the Spanish, and other translations, see Christopher Columbus, *La carta de Colón anunciando la llegada a las Indias*, ed. Carlos Sanz, Madrid, 1958. For some of the arguments concerning the status of the *Journal*, see the two articles by Emiliano Jos, 'El libro del primer viaje. Algunas ediciones recientes', *Revista de Indias*, X, 1950, pp. 719–51, and 'El Diario de Colón: su fondamental autenticidad', *Studi Colombiani*, II, 1952, pp. 77–99; and Samuel Eliot Morison, 'Texts and translations of the Journal of Columbus's first voyage', *Hispanic American Historical Review*, XIX, 1939, pp. 235–61.

4 Columbus, *Diario de Colón*, fol. 26v.

5 Leonardo Olschki, 'What Columbus saw on landing in the West Indies', *Proceedings of the American Philosophical Society*, LXXXIV, 1941, p. 649.

6 Columbus, *Diario de Colón*, fol. 26v.

7 'Khan' is the established spelling in English but it is important that in Marco Polo and Mandeville it is always written 'Can' or 'Caan' (for its relevance see p. 22). Strictly speaking Cathay was simply the province where the Khan had his capital – as Columbus knew from Marco Polo; but it is the richest geographical signifier. For Columbus's idea of Chinese geography see Figure 5. In some ways the city of Quinsay and the port of Zaiton (both in the province of Mangi – controlled by the Grand Khan) are more important than Cathay itself to Columbus. Quinsay was, according to Marco Polo,

the Khan's treasury, Zaiton his most important port and trading centre for all Eastern products (*The Travels of Marco Polo*, trans. R. Latham, London, 1958, pp. 221 and 237–8).

8 Columbus knew the 1483 Latin edition of Marco Polo's book (*Divisament dou Monde*), printed in Gouda and bound together with Mandeville's *Travels* (Carlos Sanz, *El gran secreto de la carta de Colón*, Madrid, 1959, p. 55). Most of the key terms of the discourse are in Toscanelli's important correspondence with Columbus (in Christopher Columbus, *Journals and Other Documents on the Life and Voyages of Christopher Columbus*, ed. and trans. S.E. Morison, New York, 1963, pp. 11–17). From classical times onwards Europe had entertained a whole host of notions about the East. What is called here Oriental discourse is rather more specific: a series of ideas about the civilization of China, mostly classical in origin, existing in fragmented form during the Middle Ages, but welded into a discourse only by the *Divisament dou Monde* (*c.*1300). The discourse is then disseminated by the various editions and translations of the *Divisament*, its terms given weight and currency by the authority of an eye witness, Marco Polo being the earth that grounds the discourse in the real. The existence of the discourse is only fully understandable in its institutional and ideological context: see pp. 34–9. For an overview of European conceptions of China, see Raymond Dawson. *The Chinese Chameleon: An Analysis of European Conceptions of Chinese Civilization*, London, 1967.

9 'Herodotus' needs to be taken as a shorthand term to emphasize its status as a purely contingent beginning, since the discourse of savagery was clearly an oral phenomenon: the Homeric texts provide, as one would expect, some interesting sites for this discourse. But 'Herodotus' rather than 'Homer' because Herodotus is either the acknowledged authority or the unacknowledged source for the discourse's various topoi as they journey through a variety of Hellenic and Latin texts into the Middle Ages and early vernacular literature. This journey can be traced in: R. Wittkower, 'Marvels of the East: A study in the history of monsters', *Journal of the Warburg and Courtauld Institutes*, V, 1942, pp. 159–97; the early chapters of Margaret T. Hodgen, *Early Anthropology in the Sixteenth and Seventeenth Centuries*, Philadelphia, 1964; and J.B. Friedman, *The Monstrous Races in Medieval Art and Thought*, Cambridge, Mass., 1981, who speaks of the 'Plinian races'. The advantage of reference to Herodotus (or Pliny) is that it stresses the discursive nature of these phenomena, purely 'other' to the thus confirmed humanity of the Greco-Roman and later Christian world. The long process of abstraction and epitomization reached its conclusion (whether pinnacle or decadence) in the *Imago Mundi* of Pierre d'Ailly (*c.*1410,

trans. E.F. Keever, Wilmington, NC, 1948), the *Historia rerum unique gestarum* of Aeneas Sylvius (*c*.1410), and the book of 'Sir John Mandeville' (*c*.1355, *Mandeville's Travels*, ed. M. Letts, 2 vols, London, 1953). The three monstrous races which are of most importance in the *Journal*, and which will reappear in various forms in the pages below, are first mentioned in Homer (Amazons, *Iliad*, 3.189, 6.186) and Herodotus (Anthropophagi, IV, 128; Cynocephali, IV, 191; Amazons, IV, 110–17).

10 See Leonardo Olschki's brave but futile attempt to sift 'fact' from 'fiction', 'observation' from 'story'; to extract some pure Marco Polo from the words of the romancer Rustichello (*Marco Polo's Asia*, trans. John A. Scott, Berkeley, 1960). Until recently it was common practice to deride the Middle Ages for being unable to distinguish Marco Polo from Mandeville. Modern scholarship is less certain: see, for example, Dorothy Metlitzki, *The Matter of Araby in Medieval England*, New Haven, 1977.

11 According to Carlos Sanz, 'gold' is the most used word in the *Journal* with more than 140 appearances (*Diario de Colón*, p. xix).

12 See Peter Hulme, 'Columbus and the cannibals: A study of the reports of anthropophagy in the Journal of Christopher Columbus', *Ibero-Amerikanisches Archiv*, N.F., IV, 1978, p. 128.

13 Olschki says that 'it can be taken for granted that this enticing picture corresponds rather with popular ideas of Oriental wealth and luxury prevailing in Mediterranean tales, than with the imagination of the simple West Indian natives' ('What Columbus saw', p. 656). This is in accord with the gist of my argument, though it should not be forgotten that the gold-clad natives of the mainland would, as it happens, correspond quite closely with European ideas of Oriental wealth: see for example Warwick Bray, *The Gold of El Dorado*, London, 1978 and André Emmerich, *Sweat of the Sun and Tears of the Moon: Gold and Silver in Pre-Columbian Art*, New York, 1977, chapters VII–XIII. The emphasis of my argument tends therefore to fall on the *shift* in terminology.

14 Carl Ortwin Sauer, *The Early Spanish Main*, London, 1966, p. 22.

15 Marginal note in *Diario de Colón*, fol. 19r.

16 Samuel Eliot Morison, *Admiral of the Ocean Sea: A Life of Christopher Columbus*, Boston, 1942, p. 257.

17 Morison, pp. 258–9. See also his 'Columbus and Polaris', *American Neptune*, I, 1941, pp. 1–20 and 123–37.

18 A point made by Björn Landström, *Columbus*, London, 1967, p. 79.

19 Cf. Pierre Macherey's notion of the structural incompleteness of a text, its fundamental 'absence' or 'silence':

> [It] is the juxtaposition and conflict of several meanings which . . . shapes the work: this conflict is not resolved or absorbed, but

simply displayed. Thus the work cannot speak of the more or less complex opposition which structures it; though it is its expression and embodiment. In its every particle, the work *manifests*, uncovers, what it cannot say. This silence gives it life. (*A Theory of Literary Production*, trans. Geoffrey Wall, London, 1978, p. 84)

For 'ideologeme' see P.N. Medvedev/M.M. Bakhtin, *The Formal Method in Literary Scholarship: A Critical Introduction to Sociological Poetics*, trans. Albert J. Wehrle, Baltimore, 1978, pp. 21–5.

20 It is sometimes assumed that the brothers Vivaldi were attempting to circumnavigate Africa, but see Florentino Pérez Embid, *Los descubrimientos en el atlántico y la rivalidad castellano-portuguesa hasta el tratado de Tordesillas*, Seville, 1948, pp. 52–7.

21 C.M. Cipolla, *Guns, Sails and Empires*, New York, 1965, p. 137; Ruth Pike, *Enterprise and Adventure: The Genoese in Seville and the Opening of the New World*, Ithaca, 1966, p. 99 and *passim*; and J.N. Ball, *Merchants and Merchandise in Western Europe 1500–1630*, London, 1977, p. 18. Toscanelli, although Florentine, belonged to a family involved in the spice trade (V. Teitelboim, *El amanecer del capitalismo y la conquista de América*, Buenos Aires, 1963, pp. 82–3).

22 The history of precious metals in medieval and early modern Europe is a complex subject. Spain and Ireland had supplied Rome with much of its gold, most of which had ended up in the Far East, but European mines produced little in the fourteenth and fifteenth centuries. The trade with the East had always run a deficit. Gold came from black Africa by trade but Europe had never found a way of controlling its sources – and would not do so until the nineteenth century. Portugal diverted some of this trade to the coast but, because of *its* trade with the East, little of that gold entered the European economic system. A crisis was eventually averted by the arrival of gold and silver from America, which Castile could not prevent circulating into Europe; and by technical improvements that allowed the working of hitherto inaccessible seams of European silver, especially in Germany. Cf. C.T. Smith, *An Historical Geography of Western Europe Before 1800*, Harlow, 1969; J.F. Healy, *Mining and Metallurgy in the Greek and Roman World*, London, 1978; E.W. Bovill, *The Golden Trade of the Moors*, Oxford, 1978; F. Braudel, 'Monnaies et civilisations. De l'or du Soudan à l'argent d'Amérique', *Annales ESC*, I, 1946, pp. 9–26; and M. Bloch, 'The problem of gold in the Middle Ages', in his *Land and Work in Medieval Europe*, trans. J.E. Anderson, London, 1967, pp. 186–231.

23 Vasco da Gama (whose ships carried cloth and mounted twenty guns between them) headed what John Parry has called 'not . . . a voyage of discovery, but an armed commercial embassy' (*The Age of*

Reconnaissance: Discovery, Exploration and Settlement, 1450–1650, London, 1973, p. 179).

24 See Ferdinand Columbus, *The Life of the Admiral Christopher Columbus by his Son Ferdinand*, trans. B. Keen, New Brunswick, 1959, p. 51. On this Castilian pattern see: Pérez Embid, *Los descubrimientos en el atlántico*; Charles Verlinden, *The Beginnings of Modern Colonization*, trans. Yvonne Freccero, Ithaca, 1970; and Mario de Góngora, *Studies in the Colonial History of Spanish America*, Cambridge, 1975, pp. 1–32.

25 See Felipe Fernández-Armesto, *Ferdinand and Isabella*, London, 1975, pp. 155–63; and P.E. Russell, 'El descubrimiento de las Canarias y el debate medieval acerca de los derechos de los príncipes y pueblos paganos', *Revista de Historia Canaria*, XXXVI, 1978, pp. 10–32.

26 See Pike, *Enterprise and Adventure*, pp. 103–4.

27 Quoted from Columbus, *Journals and Other Documents*, p. 27.

28 Henri Vignaud, *Histoire critique de la grande enterprise de Christophe Colombe*, 2 vols, Paris, 1911; and *The Columbian Tradition on the Discovery of America*, Oxford, 1920; Cecil Jane, 'The objective of Columbus', in *Selected Documents Illustrating the Four Voyages of Columbus*, ed. C. Jane, 2 vols, London, 1930, I, pp. xiii–cxii. Morison's rebuttal of these points is unconvincing (*Admiral of the Ocean Sea*, pp. 106–7).

29 Henri Vignaud, *Toscanelli and Columbus: The Letter and Chart of Toscanelli on the Route to the Indies by way of the West*, London, 1902; Cecil Jane, 'The question of the literacy of Columbus in 1492', *Hispanic American Historical Review*, X, 1930, pp. 500–16. Columbus scholarship is a fertile ground for that peculiar academic blindness whereby an interesting but indefensible hypothesis is followed to its logically necessary but increasingly lunatic conclusions. Columbus, so the argument goes, was not seeking Cathay, *therefore* the correspondence with Toscanelli must be spurious and the text of the *Journal* corrupt.

30 The formula of the capitulations is based on Portuguese agreements concerning voyages of Atlantic discovery in the period from 1460 to 1490. The wording is close to that of the agreement concluded with Columbus's immediate predecessor, the Fleming Ferdinand van Olmen (Verlinden, *The Beginnings of Modern Colonization*, p. 189).

31 My reading of the discursive and ideological conflict is compatible with John Elliott's perceptive characterization of Columbus as the legatee of conflicting traditions:

> Like a commander in the *Reconquista* he had made a private contract with the Crown for very considerable rights over the new lands that he was to win for it. But Columbus himself did not

belong to the tradition of the *Reconquista*. As a Genoese, settled in Portugal and then in southern Spain, he was a representative of the Mediterranean commercial tradition, which had begun to attract Castilians during the later Middle Ages. His purpose was to discover and exploit the riches of the East in association with a State which had conferred its protection upon him. For this enterprise he could draw upon the experience acquired by Castile in its commercial ventures and its colonization of the Canaries. But unfortunately for Columbus, Castile's mercantile tradition was not yet sufficiently well established to challenge its military tradition with any hope of success. While he saw his task essentially in terms of the establishment of trading bases and commercial outposts, most Castilians were accustomed to ideas of a continuing military advance, the sharing-out of new lands, the distribution of booty and the conversion of infidels. Inevitably the two opposing traditions – that of the merchant and that of the warrior – came into violent conflict, and in that conflict Columbus himself was defeated and broken. (John H. Elliott, *Imperial Spain 1469–1716*, London, 1969, pp. 61–2)

See also H.B. Johnson, ed., *From Reconquest to Empire: The Iberian Background to Latin American History*, New York, 1970, pp. 4–28. There is a conventionally Marxist reading of this conflict, stated intelligently if somewhat metaphysically by Victoria Teitelboim, in which Columbus is 'una dolorosa figura de transición' failing to harmonize 'la fuerza innovadora que emergía del alma de la época y le impelía a descubrir, y el caparazón escolástico aun vigente' (*El amanecer del capitalismo*, p. 88). The conflict can also be encoded in Braudel's terminology as a conflict between Mediterranean and Atlantic worlds (or, as he himself rather startlingly puts it, Mediterranean and *European* worlds: Fernand Braudel, *The Mediterranean and the Mediterranean World in the Age of Philip II*, trans. Sian Reynolds, 2 vols, London, 1978, I, p. 224). Castile's sea power was located in Atlantic ports on the northern and southern coasts of Spain; Aragon's by now weakening commercial empire, mortgaged to Genoese bankers, was thoroughly Mediterranean. The Catholic monarchy – Isabella of Castille, Ferdinand of Aragon – embodied the attempt to hold these terms together. Even Seville itself could be seen from its geographical position as almost a compromise formation. But, tellingly, the Indies belonged to Castile alone, a decision that can perhaps be seen as an analogue (in the absence of a vocabulary that would point to any closer relationship) to the victory in the *Journal* of the discourse of savage gold. Pérez Embid has an excellent discussion of the Castilian incorporation of the Indies (*Los descubrimientos en el atlántico*, pp. 251–300).

32　See Las Casas's marginal comments (*Diario de Colón*, fol. 55r. and v.):
　　'no eran caribes ni los hubo en la Española jamás', and 'Estos debían
　　ser de los que llaman ciguayos, que todos traían los cabellos así muy
　　largos'.
33　See Christopher Columbus, *La carta de Colón*, ed. Carlos Sanz.
34　See Aby B. Kleinbaum, *The War Against the Amazons*, New York,
　　1983, p. 104.
35　This is an oversimplification in that most of the early editions of the
　　Letter have 'Charis', a form that did not survive. So strictly speaking
　　the form 'Carib' or 'canibal' was spread via Peter Martyr's letters to
　　Italy and Vespucci's famous 'Mundus novus' letter of 1503–4. See
　　Peter Martyr (Pedro Mártir de Anglería), *Epistolario*, trans, J. López
　　de Toro, Madrid, 1953; and Amerigo Vespucci, *El nuevo mundo.*
　　Cartas relativas a sus viajes y descubrimientos. Textos en italiano, español,
　　e inglés, Buenos Aires, 1951.

2　Caribs and Arawaks

1　E.F. Im Thurn, 'On the races of the West Indies', *Journal of the Royal*
　　Anthropological Institute of Great Britain and Ireland, XVI, 1887, p. 190.
2　Detailed references to much of this material will follow in the notes
　　to this and subsequent chapters, so only the principal works will be
　　mentioned here. The very first European ethnographic study of
　　America, completed in Hispaniola in 1498, is Fray Ramón Pané,
　　Relación acerca de las antigüedades de los indios, ed. J.J. Arrom, Mexico
　　City, 1974. Other works whose authors had first-hand knowledge of
　　the Caribbean in the early fifteenth century include Bartolomé de
　　Las Casas, *Historia de las Indias*, ed. A. Millares Carlo, 3 vols, Mexico
　　City, 1951; and Gonzalo Fernández de Oviedo, *Historia general y*
　　natural de las Indias, ed. J. Pérez de Tudela, 5 vols, Madrid, 1959.
　　Outstanding amongst the accounts of the seventeenth- and
　　eighteenth-century missionaries are Raymond Breton, *Dictionaire*
　　Caraibe-François (1665), 2 vols, Leipzig, 1892; and Jean-Baptiste du
　　Tertre, *Histoire générale des Antilles habitées par les Français*, 4 vols,
　　Paris, 1667–71. The recent development of Caribbean archaeology
　　can be plotted through the nine volumes of the *Proceedings of the*
　　International Congress for the Study of the Pre-Columbian Cultures of the
　　Caribbean (1963–83), most recently the ninth volume, ed. Louis
　　Allaire and Francine-M. Mayer, Montreal, 1983. Succinct accounts
　　can be found in Irving Rouse and J.M. Cruxent, 'Early man in the
　　West Indies', in *New World Archaeology*, comp. Ezra B.W. Zubrow,
　　Margaret C. Fritz, and John M. Fritz, San Francisco, 1974,
　　pp. 71–84; and Irving Rouse and Louis Allaire, 'Caribbean', in

Chronologies in New World Archaeology, ed. R.E. Taylor and C.E. Meigham, New York, 1978, pp. 432–81. The standard anthropological accounts of 'The Arawak' and 'The Carib' (by Irving Rouse) are still those contained in the *Handbook of South American Indians*, ed. Julian Steward, 6 vols, Washington, 1946–50, vol. IV. Important recent work, much of it by Caribbean scholars, would include: Jalil Sued Badillo, *Los caribes, realidad o fábula*, Río Piedras, 1978; José Juan Arrom, *Mitología y artes prehispánicas de las Antillas*, Mexico City, 1975; Douglas Taylor, *Languages of the West Indies*, Baltimore, 1977; and Bernardo Vega, *Los cacicazgos de la Hispaniola*, Santo Domingo, 1980. An excellent brief summary is Mary Helms, 'The Indians of the Caribbean and the Circum-Caribbean at the end of the fifteenth century', in *The Cambridge History of Latin America. Volume One: Colonial Latin America*, ed. Leslie Bethell, Cambridge, 1984, pp. 37–57.

3 In other words 'Arawak' and 'Carib' conforming, as in fact they do, to what Boas and Lovejoy call primitivism and anti-primitivism (*A Documentary History of Primitivism and Related Ideas in Antiquity*, Baltimore, 1935).

4 J.H. Parry and P.M. Sherlock, *A Short History of the West Indies*, London, 1956, pp. 1–3.

5 George Brizan, *Grenada Island of Conflict: From Amerindians to People's Revolution 1498–1979*, London, 1984, p. xv.

6 Irving Rouse, in *Handbook of South American Indians*, IV, pp. 496, 547, 549.

7 'Truculent' is a key colonialist adjective carried straight over from Mediterranean discourse where it is already associated with anthropophagy: one section of the Hereford Mappa Mundi carries the inscription 'Hic sunt homines truculenti nimis, humanis carnibus vescentes, cruorem potantes, filii Caini maledicti' (W.L. Bevan and H.W. Phillott, *Mediaeval Geography. An Essay in Illustration of the Hereford Mappa Mundi*, London, 1873, pp. 50–1).

8 On the population of Hispaniola, which they estimate as eight million in 1492, see S.F. Cook and W. Borah, *Essays in Population History: Mexico and the Caribbean*, Berkeley, 1971, pp. 376–411; in 1518 the number was calculated at 11,000, most of whom were killed by smallpox in the early months of 1519 (Carl Sauer, *The Early Spanish Main*, Berkeley, 1969, pp. 202–3). For a general account of the native resistance see Josefina Oliva de Coll, *La resistencia indígena ante la conquista*, Mexico, 1974. On Enriquillo's elevation see Doris Sommer, *One Master For Another: Populism as Rhetoric in the Dominican Novel*, New York, 1985, chapter 2.

9 See Rouse, *Handbook*, IV, p. 529; and Vega, *Los cacicazgos de la*

Hispaniola, pp. 49–64, who manages to conclude that the Ciguayos of Las Flechas really were Caribs.

10 K. Oberg, 'Types of social structure among the lowland tribes of South and Central America' (1955), in *Peoples and Cultures of Native South America*, ed. D.R. Gross, Garden City, NY, 1973, p. 189.

11 P. Kirchhoff, 'Mesoamerica', *Acta Americana*, I, no. 1, 1943, pp. 92–107.

12 Well demonstrated by Irving Rouse, 'The Circum-Caribbean theory, an archaeological test', *American Anthropologist*, LV, 1953, pp. 188–200, and 'Archaeology in lowland South America and the Caribbean, 1935–60', *American Antiquity*, XXVII, 1961–2, pp. 56–62.

13 Edward Tylor, *Primitive Culture*, 2 vols, London, 1871, I, pp. 13–14. The claim is made by A.L. Kroeber and Clyde Kluckhohn, *Culture: A Critical Review of Concepts and Definitions*, Cambridge, Mass., 1952.

14 R.L. Beals, H. Hoijer and A.R. Beals, *An Introduction to Anthropology*, London, 1977, p. 29.

15 As Raymond Williams points out (*Keywords: A Vocabulary of Culture and Society*, London, 1976, p. 79) Herder's decisive innovation was to speak of 'cultures' in the plural. Despite the claims made for Tylor, George Stocking notes that such a plural only appears with regularity in the anthropological literature in the work of Franz Boas's students around 1910 (*Race, Culture, and Evolution: Essays in the History of Anthropology*, Chicago, 1982, p. 203).

16 The list is from J.M. Cooper, 'Culture diffusion and culture areas in southern South America', *Proceedings of the Twenty-First International Congress of Americanists*, 2nd part, Göteberg, 1925, p. 409. Cooper's work was one of the immediate influences on the *Handbook*'s typology, though the culture-area concept has its origin as a heuristic device for classifying the ethnographic collections at the American Museum of Natural History [*sic*], with Otis T. Mason in 1895 apparently the first to use the term: see Marvin Harris, *The Rise of Anthropological Theory: A History of Theories of Cultures*, London, 1969, p. 374; and James L. Newman, 'The culture area concept in anthropology', *Journal of Geography*, LXX, 1971, pp. 8–15. On the interesting links between Tylor and Arnold, see Stocking's essay, 'Matthew Arnold, E.B. Tylor, and the uses of invention', in *Race, Culture, and Evolution*, pp. 69–90.

17 For an excellent series of analyses of this implication, see *Anthropology and the Colonial Encounter*, ed. Talal Asad, London, 1973.

18 Irving Rouse, *Introduction to Prehistory: A Systematic Approach*, New York, 1972, p. 16.

19 For a devastating critique of the notion of the 'primitive', see Francis
    L. Hsu, 'Rethinking the concept "primitive"', *Current Anthropology*,
    V, 1964, pp. 169–78.
        The shift to a 'modern' anthropology is neatly marked by Claude
    Lévi-Strauss's 1954 change in the title of his lecture course at the
    Ecole Practique des Hautes Etudes, replacing 'Religions des peuples
    non-civilisés' with 'Religions comparées des peuples sans écriture'.
    The standard modern work on script (I.J. Gelb, *A Study of Writing*,
    Chicago, 1963) sees the alphabet as the definitive 'invention'. On
    these points see Gordon Brotherston, 'Towards a grammatology of
    America: Lévi-Strauss, Derrida, and the native New World text', in
    Europe and Its Others, ed. Francis Barker, Peter Hulme, Margaret
    Iversen, and Diana Loxley, 2 vols, Colchester, 1985, II, pp. 61–77.
        My critique of the premises of anthropology is aimed at a
    paradigm perhaps no longer as dominant within the discipline as it
    once was, although there is little sign when it comes to the native
    Caribbean of the influence of the more positive developments
    represented by, say, the work of Stanley Diamond or Marshall
    Sahlins.

20   Prehistory differs from history in the absence of contemporary
        written records. As a consequence it is excluded absolutely from
        access to the individual as a historical agent; its purview is at best
        restricted to the individuality of human groups, nations, peoples
        or races and to their reactions to economic and geographical
        conditions.

    This was written in 1933 – somewhat ironically, given its implicit
    definition of history – by the Marxist V. Gordon Childe (*Ency-
    clopaedia of the Social Sciences*, New York, 1933, vol. XII, p. 316). The
    Oxford English Dictionary's first entry for 'prehistory' is from Tylor's
    Primitive Culture (1871), though 'prehistoric' goes back to 1851. The
    principle of the distinction between history and prehistory is rejected
    by Joseph Greenberg in one of the articles on 'History' in the new
    International Encyclopedia of the Social Sciences (New York, 1968, vol.
    VI, p. 449), which no longer has an entry for 'Prehistory'.
21 Here it *is* writing rather than any other sort of text which is at issue
    because in this context only a discursive text can give a description of
    a practice. One exception might be certain very graphic forms of
    pictorial representation.
22 Theories of ethnicity have largely developed in response to 'minority
    cultures' in the USA: see for example the useful collection of essays
    Ethnicity: Theory and Experience, ed. N. Glazer and D.P. Moynihan,
    Cambridge, Mass., 1963. More relevant here is the work done within

the context of the later phases of European colonialism: see for example *Ethnic Groups and Boundaries: The Social Organization of Culture Differences*, ed. F. Barth, Bergen, 1969.

23 *Handbook*, I, p. 82; I, p. 129; II, p. 690.

24 Parry and Sherlock, quoted on p. 48; and Rouse, *Handbook*, IV. p. 496.

25 *Handbook*, IV, pp. 497–505.

26 Las Casas, *Historia de las Indias*, III, p. 507; *Handbook*, IV, p. 503.

27 M.R. Harrington, *Cuba before Columbus*, New York, 1921.

28 *Handbook*, IV, p. 521.

29 Fred Olsen, *On the Trail of the Arawaks*, Norman, Oklahoma, 1974. Olsen's trail certainly takes him back towards one of the origins, or perhaps *the* origin of agriculture in America, where the *llanos* of central Venezuela border the forests along the galleries on the banks of the Orinoco. This is the heterodox tradition which has its beginning in the work of Carl Ortwin Sauer (*Agricultural Origins and Dispersals*, New York, 1952). It may be that the very success of root-crop agriculture in the flood plain of the central Amazon led to an increase in population and the beginnings of the migrations that were to populate the Caribbean islands with agricultural communities. See the important work in this area by Donald Lathrap: *The Upper Amazon*, London, 1970; 'The antiquity and importance of long-distance trade relations in the moist tropics of pre-Columbian South America', *World Archaeology*, V, 1973, pp. 170–86, and 'Our Father the Cayman, our Mother the Gourd: Spinden revisited, or a unitary model for the emergence of agriculture in the New World', in *Origins of Agriculture*, ed. Charles A. Reed, The Hague, 1977, pp. 713–51.

30 Irving Rouse, 'On the meaning of the term "Arawak"', in Olsen, p. xvi.

31 Rouse, in Olsen, p. xv; and James Rodway, 'Some Spanish accounts of Guiana', *Timehri*, n.s. IX, 1895, pp. 1–20.

32 J. López de Velasco, *Geografía y descripción universal de las Indias* (1574), Madrid, 1894.

33 D.G. Brinton, 'The Arawack language of Guiana in its linguistic and ethnological relations', *Transactions of the American Philosophical Society*, XIV, 1871, p. 427.

34 C.S. Rafinesque, *The American Nations; or, Outlines of their General History, Ancient and Modern*, Philadelphia, 1836.

35 C.H. de Goeje, 'Nouvel examen des langues des Antilles', *Journal de la Société des Américanistes*, n.s. XXXI, 1939, p. 9. Perea and Perea (*Glosario etimológico Taino-Español*, Mayaguez, 1941, entry on *nitaynos*, p. 50) define them as a kind of sub-cacique, and quote Peter

Martyr to the effect that their speciality was knowledge of the provincial frontiers: he calls them 'cosmógrafos no ineptos de su patria'. José Juan Arrom quotes from Dr Chanca and Peter Martyr where the natives of Hispaniola seemed to apply the term to themselves, Chanca saying that it meant 'good', Martyr that it meant 'noble, that is to say not cannibal' (*Mitología*, p. 147). They may in these instances have been using it as a class term to convey their own importance.

36 M.R. Harrington, *Cuba Before Columbus*, New York, 1921; S. Loven, *Origins of the Tainan Culture, West Indies*, Göteberg, 1935.

37 Brinton, 'The Arawack language'. Taino is one of three sub-sub-groups within one of two sub-groups within the group of Northern Arawakan within the Arawakan family. So little is known about some of these languages (especially Taino) that classification is very difficult. 'Northern' is, to begin with, an admission of failure: a convenient geographical designation because not enough is known to support a genealogical argument. See Douglas Taylor, 'Languages and ghost languages of the West Indies', *International Journal of Linguistics*, XXII, 1956, pp. 180–4, and 'The place of Island Carib within the Arawakan family', *International Journal of Linguistics*, XXIV, 1958, pp. 155–6. For a slightly different classification see G.K. Noble, *Proto-Arawakan and its Descendants*, Bloomington, 1965.

38 Marc de Civrieux, *Los caribes y la conquista de la Guayana española*, Caracas, 1976, pp. 5–6.

39 Raymond Breton, *Dictionaire Caraibe-François* (1665), 2 vols, Leipzig, 1892.

40 See M. Durbin, 'A survey of the Carib language family', in *Carib-speaking Indians: Culture, Society and Language*, ed. E.B. Basso, Tucson, 1977, pp. 23–38.

41 J.H. Steward and L.C. Faron, *Native Peoples of South America*, New York, 1959, p. 322.

42 Those classifications are: J.A. Mason, 'The languages of South America', in *Handbook of South American Indians*, VI, pp. 157–318; N.A. McQuown, 'The indigenous languages of Latin America', *American Anthropologist*, LVII, 1955, pp. 501–70; J.H. Greenberg, 'The general classification of Central and South American languages', in *Men and Cultures: Selected Papers of the Fifth International Congress of Anthropological and Ethnological Sciences*, Philadelphia, 1960, pp. 791–4; and C. Loukotka, *Classification of South American Indian Languages*, ed. J. Wilbert, Los Angeles, 1968. The one exception is C.F. and F.M. Voegelin, 'Languages of the world: Native America, fascicle two', *Anthropological Linguistics*, VII, no. 7, October 1965. Cf. A.P. Sorensen jun., 'South American Indian

linguistics at the turn of the seventies', in *Peoples and Cultures of Native South America*, pp. 312–41. For accounts of the specialist studies of Island Carib see Douglas Taylor: 'The place of Island Carib'; and his *Languages of the West Indies*, chapter 1.

43 Taylor, *Languages of the West Indies*, p. 98.

44 'Les vieux ont un baragouin, lors qu'ils prennent quelque dessein de guerre, que les jeunnes n'entendent point' (Père de la Borde, *Relation des caraibes*, in R.P. Louis Hennepin, *Voyage ou nouvelle découverte d'un très-grand Pais, dans l'Amérique*, Amsterdam, 1712, p. 602).

45 See Sued Badillo, *Los caribes*, pp. 108–9.

46 'Caribes, que en lengua de los indios quiere decir bravos e osados' (Oviedo, *Historia general*, I, p. 34).

47 Taylor, *Languages of the West Indies*, p. 25. *Kanibna may have been connected with the word for bitter manioc.

48 Lee Drummond, 'On being Carib', in *Carib-speaking Indians*, pp. 76–88.

49 Drummond, p. 78.

50 Drummond, p. 87.

51 This should not be thought to imply that because the terms of ethnic identity are in some sense controlled they are therefore inauthentic and so unavailable as the basis for political organization: the point is that the terms should be fought over and given a different content.

52 Althusser's terminology seems to me essential here: see 'From Capital to Marx's philosophy', in Louis Althusser and Etienne Balibar, *Reading Capital*, London, 1975, pp. 11–70, especially pp. 24–8.

53 On the European history of the word 'carib/cannibal', see W.S. Trumbull, 'Cannibal', *Notes and Queries*, Series V, IV, 28 August 1875, pp. 171–2; and Pedro Henríquez Ureña, 'Caribe', in *Para la historia de los indigenismos*, Buenos Aires, 1938, pp. 95–102; and cf. Douglas Taylor, 'Carib, Caliban, Cannibal', *International Journal of American Linguistics*, XXIV, 1958, pp. 156–7.

54 In Christopher Columbus, *Four Voyages to the New World: Letters and Selected Documents*, bi-lingual edition, ed. R.H. Major, New York, 1961, pp. 24–5.

55 Columbus, *Four Voyages*, p. 27.

56 Peter Martyr, *Décadas del nuevo mundo*, trans. A. Millares Carlo, 2 vols, Mexico City, 1964, I, pp. 159–60.

57 The cementing of the link between 'carib' and 'man-eating' was enormously accelerated by the illustrations to the early broadsheets and books concerning the New World, most of which depicted graphic scenes of anthropophagy: for an excellent study see Ricardo Alegría, *Las primeras representaciones gráficas del indio americano 1493–1523*, San Juan, 1978; and, more generally, the early chapters of

the equally excellent Hugh Honour, *The New Golden Land: European Images of America from the Discovery to the Present Time*, New York, 1975. Cf. Figure 7 at the beginning of this chapter.

58 In *The First Three English Books on America*, ed. Edward Arber, Birmingham, 1885, p. 29.

59 Pané, *Relación*, p. 58, and see Arrom's note, p. 79.

60 'Provisión para poder cautivar a los Canibales rebeldes', in *Colección de los viajes y descubrimientos, que hicieron por mar los españoles desde fines del siglo XV*, ed. M. Fernández de Navarrete, 5 vols, Madrid, 1825–37, II, p. 415. On Juan de la Cosa, see Louis-André Vigneras, *The Discovery of South America and the Andalusian Voyages*, Chicago, 1976, p. 119.

61 *Historia de Indias*, II, iv, p. 234. Cf. the entry in Perea and Perea: 'Guatiao – La dicción era de uso muy frecuente en los días de la Conquista y pasó enseguida al lenguaje oficial y curialesco. Tiene un sentido individual cuando se refiere a dos conocidos que en señal de mutua confianza cambian sus nombres' (pp. 67–8). Cf. Oviedo, *Historia general*, I, p. 90.

62 Rodrigo de Figueroa, 'Información hecha por el licenciado Rodrigo de Figueroa', in *Colección de documentos ineditos*, 42 vols, Madrid, 1864–84, I, p. 380.

63 Figueroa, p. 381.

64 Figueroa, p. 382.

65 'Guatiao' was used 'para designar a los indios de paz en contraposición a los indios de guerra, o sea, los caribes, y en tal virtud el término vino a tener alcance jurídico y político' (Perea and Perea, p. 68). And cf. Henríquez Ureña, 'Caribe', p. 96.

66 For example: 'no había dos razas en las Antillas, sino una sola de costumbres pacíficas y dulces' (J.I. de Armas, *La fábula de los caribes*, Havana, 1884; quoted by Sued Badillo, *Los caribes*, p. 3).

67 'The native populations of South America', *Handbook*, V. p. 672.

68 The word 'chiefdom' was apparently first used by Oberg (see note 7). The best discussions of the term are: Robert Carneiro, 'The chiefdom: Precursor of the state', in *The Transition to Statehood in the New World*, ed. G. Jones and R. Kautz, Cambridge, 1981, pp. 37–79; and Karl H. Schwerin, 'The anthropological antecedents: caciques, cacicazgos, and caciquismo', in *The Caciques: Oligarchical Politics and the System of Caciquismo in the Luso-Hispanic World*, ed. Robert Kern, Albuquerque, 1973, pp. 5–17. More general discussions would include: Elman Service, *Primitive Social Organization*, New York, 1962; and Morton Fried, *The Evolution of Political Society*, New York, 1967.

69 Robert Carneiro, 'A theory of the origin of the state', *Science*, 169, 1970, pp. 734–5. Carneiro originally contrasts this process as

exemplified by the Andean valleys with the situation in Amazonia where new settlements could simply multiply because of the absence of environmental circumscription (p. 735). But he later in the same piece – and rather confusingly – amends this account by distinguishing between the high quality *varzea* and the less productive hinterlands. This 'amounted almost to a kind of circumscription' (p. 736), although the possibility of riverine (and later maritime) population movement would presumably have delayed the process of chiefdom formation. This account seems compatible with Lathrap's (see note 23).

70 Carneiro, 'A theory of the origin of the state', p. 736. Carneiro's argument clearly has implications for the long-running debate about the population size of Hispaniola in 1492: see his 'From autonomous villages to the state, a numerical estimation', in *Population Growth: Anthropological Implications*, ed. Brian Spooner, Cambridge, Mass., 1972, pp. 65–77. Cf. note 8.

71 This is Carneiro's most recent hypothesis ('The chiefdom', p. 69). There were three levels of organization on at least parts of Hispaniola, usually referred to as village, district and province; and the provincial chiefs seemed to have exercised the three powers that Carneiro judges necessary to speak of state organization – to draft, to tax, and to enforce law – so perhaps we should speak of Hispaniola's states. There is some evidence too that Agueybana could exercise those powers over the whole of Puerto Rico. The Cuban chiefdoms were probably at an earlier stage of development. Rouse's account is still standard ('The Arawak', in *Handbook*, IV, pp. 507–46) though it should be supplemented by Bernardo Vega, *Los cacicazgos de la Hispaniola*, and Jalil Sued Badillo, *Los caribes*. For a relevant comparison see Mary W. Helms, *Ancient Panama: Chiefs in Search of Power*, Austin, 1976.

72 As will be apparent this brief analysis of native Caribbean political structures has been approached from an empirical point of view, and at some point would need articulating with the often very abstract discussions of modes of production in pre-capitalist societies.

Briefly, I would argue that Marx was, quite correctly, only concerned with four modes of production: 1) *primitive communism*; 2) *class societies in general*; of which 3) *capitalism* was a particular and unique example because of its universalizing tendency – so unique in fact that all other examples of 2) were only considered (and perhaps, at least while we live under capitalism, *can* only be considered) in their differences from it; and 4) *communism*.

In fact Carneiro's point about 'the really fundamental step' (see p. 75) could be strengthened by a further, perfectly justified, simplification to non-divided and divided societies (cf. Lawrence

Krader, 'The origin of the state among the nomads of Asia', in *Pastoral Production and Society/Production pastorale et société*, Cambridge and Paris, 1979, pp. 222–3). Relevant here are Paul Hirst, 'The uniqueness of the West', in *Marxism and Historical Writing*, London, 1985; and Eric Wolf, *Europe and the People Without History*, Berkeley, 1982, pp. 73–100.

73 The taking of prisoners predated the emergence of chiefdoms but they would then have served the community as a whole rather than, as in this new situation, working to provide food for an emerging 'nobility' whose time would increasingly be taken in political administration. In the Caribbean chiefdoms this lowest class was known as the 'naborias' (Rouse, 'The Arawak', p. 530), a term adopted by the Spanish colonists to refer to their house servants (I.A. Wright, *The Early History of Cuba*, New York, 1916, pp. 42–8).

74 Although 'warfare' is probably an inevitable term, it must be understood how different native 'warfare' was from the European version which proved so devastating. Derrida's critique of Lévi-Strauss ('The violence of the letter', in *Of Grammatology*, trans. Gayatri Chakravorky Spivak, Baltimore, 1976, pp. 101–40) is deeply flawed by his implicit equation of Amerindian 'violence' with its European form. See in this regard Pierre Clastres, *Society Against the State*, trans. Robert Hurley, Oxford, 1977.

75 See Mary W. Helms, 'Succession to high office in pre-Columbian Circum-Caribbean chiefdoms', *Man*, n.s. XV, 1980, p. 728.

76 There is a parallel here with that archetypal relationship between European 'civilization' and the 'barbarism' of the steppes. Lattimore's account is exemplary:

> not only the frontier between civilization and barbarism, but the barbarian societies themselves, were in large measure created by the growth and the geographical spread of the great ancient civilizations. It is proper to speak of the barbarians as 'primitive' only in that remote time when no civilization yet existed, and when the forbears of the civilized peoples were also primitive. From the moment that civilization began to evolve it began also to spread, seeking more land in which to establish the practices of civilization; in taking up more land, it recruited into civilization some of the people who had held that land, and displaced others, and the effect on those who were displaced was that they had diverged from whatever had been their own line of evolution out of the primitive state; they modified their economic practices and experimented with new kinds of social cohesion and political organization, and new ways of fighting. Civilization itself created its own barbarian plague; the barbarian terror that harried the

northern frontiers of civilization did not erupt from a distant, dark and bloody ground that had nothing to do with civilization; it was an activity of peoples who were the kind of people they were because their whole evolution had been in contact with, and had been molded by, the advance of civilization. (Owen Lattimore, *Studies in Frontier History*, London, 1962, pp. 504–5)

It is perhaps a fairly distant parallel, but the *process* is the same: a complex course of events initiated by internal change is misread by that internally changing society as the arbitrary aggression of 'naturally' savage hordes. European experience of this process may therefore have predisposed them to a parallel misreading of the Caribbean situation.

77 E.E. Evans-Pritchard, 'Zande cannibalism' (1960), collected in his *The Position of Women in Primitive Societies and Other Essays in Social Anthropology*, London, 1965, p. 153.

78 At the sensationalist end of this range are Gary Hogg, *Cannibalism and Human Sacrifice*, New York, 1966; and Reay Tannahill, *Flesh and Blood: A History of the Cannibal Complex*, New York, 1975. E. Sagan, (*Human Aggression, Cannibalism, and Cultural Form*, New York, 1974) has a full-scale Freudian interpretation. Some of the more interesting historical and anthropological works, with particular reference to America, are: E. Volhard, *Kannibalismus*, Stuttgart, 1949, with excellent bibliography; M. Acosta Saignes, *Estudios de etnología antigua de Venezuela*, Asunción, 1964; Paul Shankman, 'Le Roti et le bouilli: Lévi-Strauss's theory of cannibalism', *American Anthropologist*, LXXI, 1969, pp. 54–69; and J.G. Blanco Villalta, *Ritos canibales en América*, Buenos Aires, 1970. Probably the most valuable recent volume has been the collection of essays *Destins du cannibalisme* (*Nouvelle Revue de Psychoanalyse*, 6, 1972). The cultural materialist interpretation of Aztec human sacrifice as a massive state food programme has recently made anthropophagy the centre of an interesting and extremely bitter polemic: see: Marvin Harris, *Cannibals and Kings: The Origins of Cultures*, New York, 1977; Michael Harner, 'The ecological basis for Aztec sacrifice', *American Ethnologist*, 4, 1977, pp. 117–35; Bernard R. Ortiz de Montellano, 'Aztec cannibalism: An ecological necessity?', *Science*, 200, 1978, pp. 611–17; and Barbara J. Price, 'Demystification, enriddlement, and Aztec cannibalism: A materialist rejoinder to Harner', *American Ethnologist*, 5, 1978, pp. 98–115. Cf. Daniel Gross, 'Protein capture and cultural development in the Amazon Basin', *American Anthropologist*, LXXVII, 1975, pp. 526–49; and S. Beckerman, 'The abundance of protein in Amazonia', *American Anthropologist*, LXXXI, 1979, pp. 533–60.

79 At the end of the last century a Colombian scholar set matters straight:

> No era por hambre, ni por venganza, ni por odio, por lo que se devoraban entre si; era por vicio. Era aquella una pasión diabólica que de ellos se había apoderado, un apetito satánico que los llevaba a la destrucción de los unos a los otros . . . . No podremos disculparlos diciendo que los arrastraba el instinto: el instinto repugna a hacer semejante cosa. Solo el Demonio podía sugerirles la idea de servir en sus festines la carne del hombre. (E. Restrepo Tirado, *Estudios sobre los aborígines de Colombia*, Bogotá, 1892, p. 123)

> This Satanic appetite had, as one might imagine, a devastating effect on the population: 'No exageramos al decir que un cincuenta por ciento de los indios que desaparecieron despues de la conquista, fueron víctimas del insaciable apetito de sus enemigos de raza cobre' (pp. 129–30).

80 Hans Staden, *The True Story of his Captivity*, ed. and trans. Malcolm Letts, London, 1928.

81 See the references in note 78 to Volhard, Acosta Saignes, Blanco Villalta; and various of the essays in *Destins du cannibalisme*, especially that by Marcel Detienne, 'Entre bêtes et dieux', pp. 231–46. The quotation is from Jean Pouillon's introduction to *Destins*, p. 19.

82 See the references to cultural materialism in note 78.

83 There is a tradition of denial, which argues that cannibalism does not exist because no human being could possibly ever eat human flesh: L.L. Domínguez (*The Conquest of the River Plate*, London, 1891, p. xxxviii) refuses to believe it 'for the honour of human nature'. The properly sceptical tradition would begin with Alexander von Humboldt's brilliant account, *Personal Narrative of Travels to the Equinoctial Regions of America*, trans. T. Ross, 3 vols, London, 1852, III, pp. 78–87, 413–15; and include J.C. Salas, *Los indios caribes: Estudio sobre el mito de la antropofagía*, Barcelona, 1921; E. de Gandía, *Historia crítica de los mitos de la conquista americana*, Buenos Aires, 1929; F. Carneiro, 'A Antropofagia entre os indios do Brasil', *Acta Americana*, V, 1947, pp. 159–84; Richard B. Moore, *Caribs, 'Cannibals', and Human Relations*, New York, 1972; Peter Hulme, 'Columbus and the cannibals', *Ibero-Amerikanisches Archiv*, N.F., IV, 1978, pp. 115–39; Jalil Sued Badillo, *Los caribes, realidad o fábula*, Río Piedras, 1978; W. Arens, *The Man-Eating Myth: Anthropology and Anthropophagy*, Oxford, 1979; and Anthony Pagden, *The Fall of Natural Man: The American Indian and the Origins of Comparative Ethnology*, Cambridge, 1982, pp. 80–7.

84 Pierre Macherey, *A Theory of Literary Production*, trans. Geoffrey Wall, London, 1978, pp. 8–11.

85 Sigmund Freud, 'Three essays on sexuality' (1905), in *On Sexuality*, Penguin Freud Library, vol. 7, Harmondsworth, 1977, pp. 116–17; Karl Abraham, 'A short study of the development of the libido', in his *Selected Papers*, London, 1927, pp. 442–53.

86 Sigmund Freud, *Totem and Taboo* (1913), London, 1985, pp. 82, 141–2; *The Future of an Illusion* (1927), in *Civilization, Society and Religion*, Penguin Freud Library, vol. 12, Harmondsworth, 1985, pp. 189–90; cf. Sagan, *Human Aggression*. Even *Destins du cannibalisme* is founded on the premiss that it is logical for psychoanalysts dissatisfied with the notion of 'incorporation' to look for help from anthropologists. The papers are interesting *despite* this premiss. The psychoanalytical line that needs pursuing is that represented by Octave Mannoni, *Prospero and Caliban: The Psychology of Colonization*, trans. Pamela Powesland, New York, 1964; Frantz Fanon, *Black Skin, White Masks*, trans. Charles Lam Markmann, New York, 1967; and Homi Bhabha's two essays 'Difference, discrimination and the discourse of colonialism', in *The Politics of Theory*, ed. F. Barker, Peter Hulme, Margaret Iversen, and Diana Loxley, Colchester, 1983, pp. 194–211, and 'Of mimicry and man: The ambivalence of colonial discourse', *October*, 28, 1984, pp. 125–38.

87 See Piers Paul Read, *Alive: The History of the Andes Survivors*, London, 1974.

88 Mary Douglas, *Natural Symbols: Explorations in Cosmology*, London, 1973, p. 69. Or take this *tour de force*, the opening paragraph of an article about Lévi-Strauss:

> Long before academics were devouring each other, people around the world were using their stomachs as cemeteries. But with colonialism the practice of cannibalism waned, and the subject matter passed from the mouths of those who had partaken to the hands of the scholars seeking food for thought. (Shankman (see note 78) p. 64)

89 For example, Rodney Needham's excellent and scholarly review of Arens's book – which a *TLS* sub-editor entitled 'Chewing on the cannibals' – ends in the required bantering tone, and tells the joke about the Uruguayan rugby player, his flying nerve now recovered, being offered the menu by an air hostess and waving it away, saying he would rather see the passenger list. But Needham is acute enough to demand that social anthropology should account 'for the mordant force of this macabre little joke' (*Times Literary Supplement*, 25 December 1980, p. 76).

90 Sigmund Freud, *Jokes and their Relation to the Unconscious* (1905), London, 1966. See also Jeffrey Mehlman, 'How to read Freud on jokes: The critic as *Schädchen*', *New Literary History*, VI, 1975, pp. 439–61; and Mary Douglas, 'Social control of cognition: Factors in joke perception', *Man*, n.s. III, 1968, pp. 361–7.

91 Arens, *The Man-Eating Myth*, p. 161. Cf. Stanley Diamond's parallel argument in *In Search of the Primitive: A Critique of Civilization*, New York, 1976.

92 'Doctrine that had originated to sanctify conquest of the Holy Lands expanded to justify conquest of the world' (Francis Jennings, *The Invasion of America: Colonialism and the Cant of Conquest*, New York, 1976, p. 4). This expansion is traced in James Muldoon's superb study, *Popes, Lawyers and Infidels: The Church and the Non-Christian World 1250–1550*, Liverpool, 1979. In this context a good study of the Crusades is A.S. Atiya, *Crusade, Commerce and Culture*, London, 1962.

93 See Denys Hay, *Europe: The Emergence of an Idea*, Edinburgh, 1968, p. 84. As Norman Daniel says: '[The] moral identity of Europe was preserved by a fiercely determined orthodoxy which wanted nothing to do with any least deviation in the whole field of religion, and . . . religion itself became the expression of that same sense of identity' (*The Arabs and Mediaeval Europe*, London, 1975, p. 303). Other useful historical studies of the period are: Charles Verlinden, *The Beginnings of Modern Colonization*, trans. Yvonne Freccero, Ithaca, 1970; Pierre Chaunu, *European Expansion in the Middle Ages*, trans. Katherine Bertram, Amsterdam, 1979; and Immanuel Wallerstein, *The Modern World-System: Capitalist Agriculture and the Origins of the European World-Economy in the Seventeenth Century*, New York, 1974, chapter 1, 'Medieval prelude'. The ideological background to colonial expansion is superbly drawn in the early chapters of Ronald Sanders, *Lost Tribes and Promised Lands: The Origins of American Racism*, New York, 1978. See also Leon Poliakov, *The Aryan Myth: A History of Racist and Nationalist Ideas in Europe*, trans. E. Howard, London, 1974.

94 See Leon Poliakov, *The History of Anti-Semitism*, trans. Richard Howard, 3 vols, New York, 1974–5, I, p. 58.

95 See Darwell Stone, *A History of the Doctrine of the Holy Eucharist*, 2 vols, London, 1909, I, p. 313. It was also at this Council that Innocent III ordered that Jews, prostitutes and lepers be marked by a special sign on their clothing (Poliakov, *The History of Anti-Semitism*, I, pp. 64–5); and see John Bossy, 'Enemies of the human race', in his *Christianity in the West 1400–1700*, Oxford, 1985, pp. 76–88.

96 Cohn's study of this period, *Europe's Inner Demons*, London, 1976, is parallel to Arens in its iconoclastic scepticism towards sources of 'evidence' before often naïvely accepted at face value. There are overlaps between the two areas. The 'Thyestean feast' – involving anthropophagy and multiple sexual perversions – of which originally Christians were accused (Cohn, p. 8), became a recurrent topos within both anti-semitism and colonial discourse through to its last desperate throws. Hogg (*Cannibalism and Human Sacrifice*, p. 206) refers to the cannibalistic initiation rites of the Mau Mau 'accompanied by sexual orgies and perversions involving many animals .... These orgies are so disgusting that the authenticated reports on them are not available for general study'.

97 It is this identity, subsequently redefined as 'the West', that gives retrospective content to my use of 'our' – as in 'our fascination' (see p. 81). Arens comes close to making this point in his discussion of how accounts of *European* anthropophagy have been treated with differential scepticism (Arens, p. 21). On this point see also Anthony Pagden, 'Cannibalismo e contagio', *Quaderni storici*, L, 1982, pp. 147–64.

98 Sued Badillo argues for 'mythological eater of human flesh' (*Los caribes*, p. 68).

99 I have deliberately said little about other cultures attributing anthropophagy to Europeans because of the epistemological difficulties variously noted, but the evidence would seem to allow for its use as a figure for the destruction of native social systems by European presence. It is almost impossible to assess the effect of anthropological interrogation. These points are both beautifully illustrated in Jean Monod's account of his expedition to the Piaroa: 'Un riche cannibale', *Les Temps Modernes*, XXVI, 1971, pp. 1061–120.

100 Cf. Carneiro, quoted on p. 75: 'But the subordination sometimes . . . involved incorporation into the political unit dominated by the victor'.

3   *Prospero and Caliban*

1 Richard Hakluyt, *The Principal Navigations, Voyages, Traffiques, & Discoveries of the English Nation* (1598–1600), 12 vols, Glasgow, 1903–5, VII, pp. 133–5. On the Madoc story, see Gwyn A. Williams, *Madoc: The Making of a Myth*, London, 1979.

2 The best general work for this period is Kenneth Andrews, *Trade, Plunder, and Settlement: Maritime Enterprise and the Genesis of the British*

Empire 1480–1630, Cambridge, 1984. Samuel Purchas's collection is *Purchas His Pilgrimes* (1625), 20 vols, Glasgow, 1905–7.

3 Quoted by Frank Kermode, 'Introduction' to the Arden edition of *The Tempest* (1611), London, 1958, p. xxvi, n.3. All references to the play are to this edition.

4 See Kermode, pp. xxv–xxxiv, for a summary of the relevant literature.

5 The best of the source studies is Geoffrey Bullough, *Narrative and Dramatic Sources of Shakespeare*, 8 vols, London, 1975, VIII, pp. 237–340. Even the one 'undisputed' source for *The Tempest* (Kermode, p. xxxiv), Florio's translation of Montaigne's essay, 'Of the caniballes', is disputed learnedly by Margaret Hodgen on the ground of a possible common source ('Montaigne and Shakespeare again', *Huntington Library Quarterly*, XXIII, 1959–60, pp. 213–27). The *reductio ad absurdum* of source-hunting is Henri Grégoire's conclusion that the ultimate source of *The Tempest*, unfortunately now lost, was a 'historical Bulgaro-Byzantino-Serb romance (presumably written in Italian)' ('The Bulgarian origins of *The Tempest*', *Studies in Philology*, XXXVII, 1940, pp. 236–56).

6 Kermode, p. lxiii.

7 Kermode, pp. xxv–xxviii.

8 Kermode, pp. lxiv and lxx.

9 Some of these theoretical questions are interestingly pursued in Terry Eagleton, Tony Bennett, Noel King, Ian Hunter, Peter Hulme, Catherine Belsey, and John Frow, 'The "text in itself": A symposium', *Southern Review*, XVII, 1984, pp. 115–46.

10 James Smith, 'The Tempest', in his *Shakespearian and Other Essays*, ed. E.M. Wilson, Cambridge, 1974, pp. 159–261.

11 Charles Frey, '*The Tempest* and the New World', *Shakespeare Quarterly*, 30, 1979, p. 33. Behind this position stands the work of Michel Foucault, especially in this respect, 'What is an author?', in *Textual Strategies: Perspectives in Post-Structuralist Criticism*, ed. J.V. Harari, London, 1979, pp. 141–60. Cf. Francis Barker and Peter Hulme, 'Nymphs and reapers heavily vanish: The discursive contexts of *The Tempest*', in *Alternative Shakespeares*, ed. John Drakakis, London, 1985, pp. 191–205.

12 See I.R. Tannehill, *Hurricanes: Their Nature and History*, Princeton, 1950; and Fernando Ortiz, *El huracán: su mitología y sus símbolos*, Mexico City, 1947. The latter is a comprehensive study of the importance of hurricanes in Native American cultures of this area.

13 See S.E. Morison, *Admiral of the Ocean Sea: A Life of Christopher Columbus*, Boston, 1942, p. 590.

14 For the debate as to the origin of the word *hurakan*, Mayan or

Arawakan, see: J. Corominas, *Diccionario crítico etimológico de la lengua castellana*, Madrid, 1954 (entry for 'huracán'); Eva Hunt, *The Transformation of the Hummingbird: Cultural Roots of a Zinacantecan Mythical Poem*, Ithaca, 1977, p. 242 and note; and Douglas Taylor, 'Spanish *huracán* and its congeners', *International Journal of Linguistics*, XXII, 1956, pp. 275–6.

15 William Strachey, 'A True Reportory of the Wracke' (1610), in Purchas, XIX, pp. 5–72. Strachey's letter was not published until its inclusion in Purchas's collection.

16 Strachey, pp. 7, 10 and 13.

17 Strachey, pp. 13–14.

18 Sylvester Jourdain, 'A discovery of the Bermudas', in *A Voyage to Virginia in 1609*, ed. L.B. Wright, Charlottesville, 1964, p. 109.

19 This pamphlet was entered on the Stationers' Registers on 4 December 1638 as being by John Taylor. It was bought by William Clarke, secretary to General Monck, on 10 January 1638 (i.e. 1639), and left by his son George Clarke to the Library of Worcester College, Oxford in 1736. Quotations are from a photocopy of this pamphlet, with kind permission of the Provost and Fellows of Worcester College, Oxford. The only other known copy is in the Huntington Library (STC no. 21558). The only reprint is in the rare C.H. Wilkinson (ed.), *Two Tracts*, Oxford, 1946.

20 Taylor, *New and strange News from St. Christophers*, London, 1638, p. 2.

21 Purchas had made use of this topos in a marginal comment on Strachey's letter:

> Can a leopard change his spots? Can a Savage be civil? were wee our selves made and not borne civill in our Progenitors dayes? and were not Caesar's Britaines as brutish as Virginians? The Roamane swords were best teachers of civilitie to this and other Countries neere us. (in Strachey, p. 62)

Cf. J.H. Elliott, *The Old World and the New, 1492–1650*, Cambridge, 1970, chapter 2. The English had already used the argument to justify the colonization of Ireland: see Nicholas P. Canny, 'The ideology of English colonization: From Ireland to America', *William and Mary Quarterly*, n.s. XXX, 1973, pp. 575–98.

22 Taylor, pp. 3–4.

23 Taylor, p. 5.

24 Taylor, p. 12.

25 See 'Concerning Hurricanes and their Prognosticks – & Observations of my owne Experience thereupon', Egerton MS. 2395/619–24 (British Library). As a result of the removal of the Caribs from St

Christopher's the planters had to send to Dominica for their weather forecasts.

26 Taylor, pp. 2–3. This is the Freudian version. More common was the eating of children (Aristotle, *Nicomachean Ethics*, VII, v. 2; echoed in *King Lear*: 'The barbarous Scythian / Or he that makes his generation messes to gorge his appetite' (I.i.118–20)).

27 The earlier forms tend to favour 'cano' as an ending, according to the *OED* on the grounds that Spanish words were frequently assumed to end in -o, but perhaps because that other violent manifestation of nature was already well established in English as 'volcano'. That '-cane' became frequent after 1650 might suggest the influence of 'sugar cane', which was what hurricanes were by then chiefly destroying.

28 Peter Martyr, in *The First Three Books on America*, ed. Edward Arber, London, 1885, p. 66.

29 'For there shall not an hair fall from the head of any of you' (*Acts* 27: 34).

30 Cf. the celebratory poems, especially Andrew Marvell's 'Bermudas' (1654).

31 For the decline of that master-code during the period under consideration, see Herschel Baker, *The Wars of Truth*, London, 1952.

32 Strachey, p. 54.

33 Strachey, p. 54

34 Strachey, pp. 30–1.

35 Strachey, pp. 44–5.

36 Quoted in Strachey, pp. 67–8.

37 Quoted in Strachey, p. 67.

38 Strachey, p. 32.

39 See the account by Nathaniel Butler, who was Governor of Bermuda in 1619 and knew one of the 'conspirators', Christopher Carter: published, not under his name, as *The Historye of the Bermudaes or Summer Islands*, ed. J.H. Lefroy, London, 1882, p. 14. Cf. Jean Kennedy, *Isle of Devils: Bermuda under the Somers Island Company, 1609–1685*, London, 1971; and H.C. Wilkinson, *The Adventurers of Bermuda*, London, 1958. Rivalry between seamen and landmen opens *The Tempest*, immediately raising the issue of authority in circumstances outside the usual bounds of civility. See also note 73.

40 'It cannot be hoped that we shall for long be content to go on saying the same things about the play' (Kermode, p. lxxxvii).

41 See Eric Auerbach's classic essay '"Figura"', in his *Scenes from the Drama of European Literature*, Gloucester, Mass., 1973, pp. 11–78.

42 Lamming's essay, 'A monster, a child, a slave', is in his *The Pleasures*

of Exile, London, 1984, pp. 95–117. Smith's essay (see note 10) predates Lamming's in composition but was not published until after his death, in 1974. The colonial implications of the play have also been significantly developed in the following works: Octave Mannoni, *Prospero and Caliban: The Psychology of Colonization*, trans. Pamela Powesland, New York, 1964; Philip Brockbank, '*The Tempest*: Conventions of Art and Empire', in *Later Shakespeare*, ed. J.R. Brown and B. Harris, London, 1966, pp. 183–201; D.G. James, *The Dream of Prospero*, Oxford, 1967; Leo Marx, 'Shakespeare's American fable', in his *The Machine in the Garden*, New York, 1970, pp. 34–72; Roberto Fernández Retamar, *Caliban: Apuntes sobre la cultura en nuestra América*, Mexico City, 1971; Leslie Fiedler, 'The New World savage as stranger: or "Tis new to thee"', in his *The Stranger in Shakespeare*, London, 1973, pp. 199–253; Stephen Greenblatt, 'Learning to curse: Aspects of linguistic colonialism in the seventeenth century', in *First Images of America*, ed. F. Chiappelli, 2 vols, Los Angeles, 1976, I, pp. 561–80; Bruce Erlich, 'Shakespeare's colonial metaphor: On the social function of theatre in *The Tempest*', *Science and Society*, 41, 1977, pp. 43–65; Lori Leininger, 'Cracking the code of *The Tempest*', *Bucknell Review*, 25, 1979, pp. 121–31; and Paul Brown, ' "This thing of darkness I acknowledge mine": *The Tempest* and the discourse of colonialism', in *Political Shakespeare: New Essays in Cultural Materialism*, ed. Jonathan Dollimore and Alan Sinfield, Manchester, 1985, pp. 48–71. Brown's is the closest in general orientation to the reading of the play offered here, and I am indebted to it at a number of points.

Other recent critical work that I refer to or draw on includes: Howard Felperin, *Shakespearean Romance*, Princeton, 1972; Harry Berger jun., 'Miraculous harp: A reading of Shakespeare's *Tempest*', *Shakespeare Studies*, V, 1969, pp. 253–83; Terence Hawkes, *Shakespeare's Talking Animals: Language and Drama in Society*, London, 1973; George Slover, 'Magic, mystery, and make-believe: An analogical reading of *The Tempest*', *Shakespeare Studies*, XI, 1978, pp. 175–206; Jan Kott, 'La tempête ou la répétition', *Tel Quel*, 70, 1977, pp. 136–62; Coppélia Kahn, 'The providential tempest and the Shakespearean family', in *Representing Shakespeare: New Psychoanalytical Essays*, ed. Murray M. Schwartz and Coppélia Kahn, Baltimore, 1980, pp. 217–43; David Sundelson, 'So rare a wonder'd father: Prospero's *Tempest*', in *Representing Shakespeare*, pp. 33–53; Mark Taylor, *Shakespeare's Darker Purpose: A Question of Incest*, New York, 1982; and Stephen Orgel, 'Prospero's wife', *Representations*, 8, 1984, pp. 1–13.

43 Kott's article (see previous note) is an excellent study of this dual

topography. On 'plantation', see Howard Mumford Jones, *O Strange New World! American Culture: The Formative Years*, New York, 1963, p. 164; on Setebos, see Frey, pp. 29–31; on the Algonquian dance, see Rachel Kelsey, 'Indian Dances in *The Tempest*', *Journal of English and German Philology*, XIII, 1914, pp. 98–103.

44 Sister Corona Sharp, 'Caliban: The primitive man's evolution', *Shakespeare Studies*, XIV, 1981, p. 267.

45 Morton Luce, 'Introduction', to *The Tempest*, London, 1938, pp. xxxii and xxxv.

46 Miranda's opinion changes between I.ii.148 and III.i.51–2. There are many descriptions *of* Caliban but no Caliban that is perceptually available to us outside the descriptions. This is no doubt true of all literary characters and constitutes a staple technique of writing, but it is rare for the descriptions to be so divergent that they hardly have any common ground at all. Something similar happens in the obviously congruent case of Othello. Gaines and Lofaro's attempt to answer the question 'What did Caliban look like?' suffers from taking the descriptions literally and trying to make sense of them (*Mississippi Folklore Register*, X, 1976, pp. 175–86). The descriptions inevitably tell us more about the poverty of European attempts to understand the non-European than they do about the 'reality' of Caliban. This applies equally to Prospero's later attempts to deny Caliban's full humanity by suggesting he is half-devil (see p. 114). Cf. Terence Hawkes, 'Swisser-Swatter: Making a man of English letters', in *Alternative Shakespeares*, ed. J. Drakakis, London, 1985, pp. 26–46.

47 Luce, p. xxxv.

48 See Kermode, pp. xxxix–xl. For the wild man, see R. Bernheimer, *Wild Men in the Middle Ages*, Cambridge, Mass., 1952. The Spenserian precedent (*The Faerie Queene*, IV.vii.5) is explored in J. MacPeek, 'The genesis of Caliban', *Philological Quarterly*, XXV, 1946, pp. 377–81.

49 See p. 270n.9.

50 No single word can better evoke the imposition of Mediterranean discourse on the New World than 'slave'. In English 'savage' had, by the early seventeenth century, become a key colonial term, quite often used by Shakespeare, but not at all, for example, by the translators of the King James Bible (1611); for an interesting discussion of the word, see Francis Jennings, *The Invasion of America: Indians, Colonialism, and the Cant of Conquest*, Chicago, 1976, pp. 72–8.

51 The word 'monster' and its cognates appears thirty-seven times in the play, almost always in connection with Caliban.

52 See Fiedler, p. 203.

53 See J.M. Nosworthy, 'The narrative sources of *The Tempest*', *Review of English Studies*, XXIV, 1948, pp. 281–4.

54 For a good discussion of the problems, even if his conclusions are not very exciting, see D.D. Carnicelli, 'The widow and the phoenix: Dido, Carthage, and Tunis in *The Tempest*', *Harvard Library Bulletin*, XXVII, 1979, pp. 389–433.

55 For the relevant historical background, see Jamil M. Abun-Nasr, *A History of the Maghrib*, Cambridge, 1975.

56 On Sycorax, see James Smith, pp. 223–7. On some – but by no means all – of the multiple doubles and parallelisms that fill the play, see A.H. Gilbert, '*The Tempest*'s parallelism in characters and situations', *Journal of English and Germanic Philology*, XIV, 1915, pp. 63–74.

57 On the distinctions between 'white' and 'black' magic, see W.C. Curry, *Shakespeare's Philosophical Patterns*, Gloucester, Mass., 1968, chapter 6; and Kermode, pp. xl–xli, and xlvii–li; on Medea as the prototype of Sycorax, Kermode, p. xl; and cf. Kermode's 'Appendix D' (pp. 147–50), which reprints the relevant Ovid and Golding's translation.

58 Kermode's case, p. 149. On the graves he notes, 'There seems to be no occasion for this' (Note to V.i.48).

59 See Kahn, p. 238.

60 Kermode, p. lxxvi; and see Daniel C. Boughner, 'Jonsonian structure in *The Tempest*', *Shakespeare Quarterly*, XXI, 1970, pp. 3–10.

61 Kermode, p. lxxv.

62 See Glynne Wickham's point that the disappearing banquet is the true anti-masque rather than, as is sometimes supposed, the routing of the conspirators. His general argument is interesting but totally at odds with mine since he sees *The Tempest* itself as almost, if not entirely, a court entertainment produced for a particular occasion ('Masque and anti-masque in *The Tempest*', *Essays and Studies*, n.s. XXVIII, 1975, pp. 1–14). An excellent, and congruent, reading of the chess scene, is Bryan Loughrey and Neil Taylor, 'Ferdinand and Miranda at chess', *Shakespeare Survey*, XXXV, 1982, pp. 113–18.

63 Enid Welsford, *The Court Masque: A Study in the Relationship between Poetry and the Revels*, New York, 1962, p. 340. She recognizes Prospero as masque inductor, but does not distinguish between the masque and the play as a whole.

64 J. Middleton Murray, 'Shakespeare's dream' (from his *Shakespeare*, 1936), reprinted in *The Tempest: A Casebook*, ed. D.J. Palmer, London, 1968, p. 120. Murray goes on to say: 'It is not the plot against his life which has produced this disturbance. It is the thought

of what the plot means: the Nature on which Nurture will never stick' (p. 121).

65 Berger quotes Erikson to good effect on his theory of the microsphere:

> 'the small world of manageable toys' which the child establishes as a haven 'to return to when he needs to overhaul his ego'. There he constructs a model of his past experiences which will allow him to 'play at doing something that was in reality done to him'. (Berger, p. 261, quoting Erik Erikson, *Childhood and Society*, New York, 1963, pp. 198–9)

'Prospero's play' can therefore bear both meanings. His pastoral romance is a dream of wish-fulfilment, a fantasy of omnipotence come true. In one sense (to be explored further in Chapter 5) it is a Utopia, a crucible in which the essentials of the colonial paradigm are laid bare. The classic Utopian literature often began with a ship-wreck: for instance Johann Valentin Andreae's *Christianopolis* (1619).

66 The earliest, most trenchant, example is probably Clifford Leech, who called Prospero's behaviour 'pathological' (*Shakespeare's Tragedies and Other Studies in Seventeenth Century Drama*, London, 1950, pp. 137–58). Philip Mason notes the unquestioning admiration for Prospero during the era of British colonialism (*Prospero and Caliban: Some Thoughts on Class and Race*, London, 1962, pp. 92–3).

67 Daniel Wilson, *Caliban: The Missing Link*, Toronto, 1873.

68 Sharp, p. 276.

69 Sundelson, p. 46.

70 Kahn, pp. 236–40.

71 Taylor, p. 143.

72 Taylor, p. xi.

73 Cf. the manner in which Prospero expresses his eclipse by Antonio: 'now he was / The ivy which had hid my princely trunk, / And suck'd my verdure out on't' (I.ii.85–7); and Miranda's literal reading of Prospero's subsequent rhetorical question: '*Pros.* . . . tell me / If this might be a brother. *Mir.* I should sin / To think but nobly of my grandmother' (I.ii.117–19).

74 Prospero's inability (sloth?) calls to mind the Jamestown colonists who would not 'step into the Woods a stones cast off from them, to fetch other fire-wood' (quoted on p. 103).

75 John Nicholl, 'An Houre Glasse of Indian News' (1607), ed. Rev. C. Jesse, *Caribbean Quarterly*, XII, no. 1, 1966, p. 49. Nicholl speaks of dissension between the 'sea-men' and the 'land-men', 'which rested not only in the common sort, but rather and most chiefly in our captains' (p. 48).

76 Nicholl, pp. 49–50. Cf. Ripley Bullen, 'The first English settlement on St Lucia', *Caribbean Quarterly*, XII, no.2, 1966, pp. 29–35.

77 Compare George Percy's account of the stop-over on Dominica of the first Jamestown contingent. He describes the natives coming on board 'bringing us many kindes of sundry fruites, as Pines, Potatoes, Plantons, Tobacco, and other fruits', yet later in the same paragraph they are 'Canibals, that eate mans flesh', 'they are continually in warres and will eate their enemies when they kill them, and any stranger if they take them' ('A Discourse of the Plantation of the Southern Colonie in Virginia', in *New American World: A Documentary History of North America to 1612*, ed. D. Quinn, 5 vols, London, 1979, V, p. 267).

78 Nicholl, p. 52.

79 Nicholl, p. 53.

80 Nicholl, p. 59.

81 See pp. 163–4.

82 L.T. Fitz comments rather tartly that 'for all that has been said in favour of Prospero's "art" as symbolizing civilisation, it seems that in twelve years on the island he has succeeded in establishing no more than what anthropologists would call a "hunting and gathering" economy' ('The vocabulary of the environment in *The Tempest*', *Shakespeare Quarterly*, XXVI, 1975, pp. 42–9).

83 There is an enormous hinterland of work on the psychology of domination relevant here, which would have to begin with the Master and Slave dialectic developed by Hegel in *The Phenomenology of Mind*, chapter 4.A.: see, for example, Albert Memmi, *The Colonizer and the Colonized*, New York, 1965. Mannoni's use of the Prospero figure is interesting (pp. 97–121) but see the critique by Frantz Fanon of his ahistoricism (*Black Skin, White Masks*, trans. Charles Lam Markham, New York, chapter 4).

Erlich's analysis of this moment of the play is excellent (pp. 62–3); see also Leininger, p. 127. The moment is of course repeated in *Robinson Crusoe*: see p. 205.

84 See Bernard Knox, '*The Tempest* and the ancient comic tradition', in *English Stage Comedy*, ed. W.K. Wimsatt, New York, 1955, pp. 52–73.

85 G. Wilson Knight, 'The Shakespearian Superman' (from *The Crown of Life*, 1947), reprinted in *The Tempest: A Casebook*, ed. D.J. Palmer, London, 1968, p. 147.

86 Bartolomé de Las Casas, *The Spanish Colonie, or Brief Chronicle of the Acts and gestes of the Spaniardes in the West Indies, called the newe World, for the space of xl. yeeres*, trans. M.M.S., London, 1583, p. 3. Cf. William S. Maltby, *The Black Legend in England: The Develop-*

ment of Anti-Spanish Sentiment, 1558–1660, Durham, 1971. The English used dogs to hunt the Jamaican maroons in the eighteenth century: see p. 324n.51.

87 This final ambivalence could be looked at in structural terms: whether Caliban's is to be seen as a true 'countervoice' of the *platea* tradition or as an element within the 'literary' development of the multiple plot structure. Robert Weimann's remarks on this, although not directed at *The Tempest*, are of great interest: *Shakespeare and the Popular Tradition in the Theatre*, ed. Robert Schwartz, Baltimore, 1978, pp. 159 and 241.

4   John Smith and Pocahontas

1 Shirley Graham, *The Story of Pocahontas*, London, 1953, p. 171.

2 Morton Luce, 'Introduction' to the Arden edition of *The Tempest*, London, 1938, p. 169.

3 John Smith, *A Trve Relation* (1608), quoted from his *Works 1608–1631*, ed. Edward Arber, Birmingham, 1884, p. 38.

4 In Smith's *The Generall Historie of Virginia, New England, and the Summer Isles* (1624), facsimile edn, Cleveland, 1966.

5 *Narrative and Dramatic Sources of Shakespeare*, ed. Geoffrey Bullough, 8 vols, London, 1975, VIII, p. 241.

6 Perry Miller, *Errand into the Wilderness*, New York, 1964, p. viii.

7 Narrative histories have little option but to begin with Virginia; intellectual histories prefer to juggle with chronology in the interests of 'coherence'. Edward Saveth's anthology, *Understanding the American Past: American History and its Interpretation*, Boston, 1954, begins with 'The Puritan tradition'; and Daniel Boorstin's influential *The Americans: The Colonial Experience*, New York, 1968, has as its Part One 'A city upon a hill: the Puritans of Massachusetts Bay', Virginia not appearing until Part Four.

8 For the historical background to English settlement in America, see notes 1 and 2 to Chapter 3.

9 Smith, *The Generall Historie*, p. 49. Pocahontas's father was chief of the Pamunkey indians and paramount chief of a larger confederacy. I will simply call him Powhatan (which was in fact his title), and avoid the lengthy 'indians of the Powhatan confederacy' by referring simply to 'the Algonquian' – a more general classification and language family – unless mentioning one of the particular groups within the confederacy. Because of the clan system the nomenclature does not always correspond to our usage so, for example, Opechancanough may not have been Powhatan's consanguineal brother: it

probably suited the English to have him as Pocahontas's 'wicked uncle'. Pocahontas herself would, if she had survived, have been of little political significance as daughter of the Powhatan: in that sense Rolfe would have been better off marrying the Powhatan's sister. On the tidewater Algonquian and their neighbours see: Charles Hudson, *The Southeastern Indians*, Knoxville, 1976; and Christian Feest's three articles: 'Powhatan: A study in political organization', *Wiener Volkkundliche Mitteilungen*, XIII, 1966, pp. 69–83; 'The Virginian Indian in Pictures', *Smithsonian Journal of History*, II, no. 1, 1967, pp. 1–30; and 'Virginia Algonquians', in *Handbook of North American Indians*, vol. 15, ed. Bruce G. Trigger, Washington, DC, 1978, pp. 254–70. It may well be that the confederacy was a response to European presence on the Atlantic coast. For an interesting assessment of the extent of this presence during the sixteenth century, see J. Leitch Wright jun., *The Only Land They Knew: The Tragic Story of the American Indians in the Old South*, New York, 1981, chapter 2. Two good selections of the contemporary English material are: *The Jamestown Voyages under the First Charter*, ed. Philip Barbour, 2 vols, London, 1969; and *New American World: A Documentary History of North America to 1612*, ed. David Beers Quinn, 5 vols, London, 1979, V, Part XXIII. The relations between the English and the Virginia Algonquian are studied in: Wilcomb Washburn, 'The moral and legal justification for dispossessing the Indians', in *Seventeenth-Century America: Essays in Colonial History*, ed. J.M. Smith, Chapel Hill, 1959, pp. 15–32; Gary Nash, 'The image of the Indian in the southern colonial mind', *William and Mary Quarterly*, 3rd series, XXIX, 1972, pp. 197–230; Karen O. Kupperman, *Settling with the Indians: The Meeting of English and Amerindian Cultures in America, 1580–1640*, London, 1980; Bernard Sheehan, *Savagism and Civility: Indians and Englishmen in Colonial Virginia*, Cambridge, 1980; and J. Leitch Wright jun., *The Only Land They Knew*, chapter 3.

10 Bradford Smith, *Captain John Smith: His Life and Legend*, Philadelphia, 1953; and Philip Barbour, *The Three Worlds of Captain John Smith*, London, 1964. For a more sceptical account of Smith, see Ronald Sanders, *Lost Tribes and Promised Lands: The Origins of American Racism*, New York, 1978, chapters 23 and 24.

11 Purchas has a long account of Pocahontas's visit to London (*Purchas His Pilgrimes* (1625), 20 vols, Glasgow, 1905–7, XIX, pp. 117–19). The best modern 'biographies', although they inevitably include much speculation, are: Philip Barbour, *Pocahontas and her World*, London, 1971; and Frances Mossiker, *Pocahontas: The Life and the Legend*, London, 1977.

12 Most comprehensively studied in Philip Young, 'The mother of us all: Pocahontas reconsidered', *Kenyon Review*, XXIV, 1962, pp. 391–415; and Jay Hubbell, 'The Smith–Pocahontas literary legend', in his *South and Southwest: Literary Essays and Reminiscences*, Durham, NC, 1965, pp. 175–204; although the most penetrating analysis is Leslie Fiedler's in *The Return of the Vanishing American*, New York, 1968.

13 Smith, *The Generall Historie*, p. 121. The 'romantic' explanation is the commonest. Another has Pocahontas as the daughter of Virginia Dare, the first English child born on American soil, but part of the lost colony. So Pocahontas, though brought up an Indian, has white blood, which supposedly explains her compassionate (i.e. Christian) gesture (Mary Wall, *Daughter of Virginia Dare*, New York, 1908). The explanation is so satisfactory that it hardly seems to matter that Virginia Dare would have had to have given birth at the age of about 8.

Pocahontas's subsequent actions are open to a variety of explanations. She may have taken her role as intermediary to heart, encouraged by her father. But it does seem possible to suggest a genuine curiosity about, and vulnerability to, the attractions of European culture – such as they were in early Jamestown. It is difficult to disentangle the confluence of the literary topos of the 'enamoured princess' from the historical examples, of whom Pocahontas and Malinche are only the best known. Much can be put down to male fantasy, but some of the cases are well attested. Perhaps within certain Amerindian societies women of a particular social standing were, for reasons to do with their education, relative lack of manual labour, and so on, more likely to show an interest in alien cultures. The evidence is in need of reassessment. On the 'enamoured princess' topos, see: F.M. Warren, 'The enamoured Moslem princess in Orderic Vital and the French epic', *PMLA*, XXIX, 1914, pp. 341–58; Dorothy Metlitzki, *The Matter of Araby in Medieval England*, New Haven, 1977, pp. 136–77; and George A. Starr, 'Escape from Barbary: A seventeenth-century genre', *Huntington Library Quarterly*, XXIX, 1965–6, pp. 35–52.

14 Grace Steele Woodward, *Pocahontas*, Norman, Okla., 1968, p. 6.

15 On Opechancanough see Carl Bridenbaugh, *Early Americans*, New York, 1981, chapter 1; and J. Frederick Fausz, 'Opechancanough: Indian resistance leader', in *Struggle and Survival in Colonial America*, ed. Gary Nash and David Sweet, Berkeley, 1981, pp. 21–37. On the mission see Clifford M. Lewis and Albert J. Loomie, *The Spanish Jesuit Mission in Virginia 1570–72*, Chapel Hill, 1953.

16 See Nicholas P. Canny, 'The permissive frontier: The problem of social control in English settlements in Ireland and Virginia 1550–1660', in *The Westward Enterprise: English Activities in Ireland, the Atlantic, and America 1480–1650*, ed. K.R. Andrews, N.P. Canny and P.E.H. Hair, Liverpool, 1978, pp. 17–44. In 1612 English deserters to the Algonquian who had been recaptured were tortured and executed by order of the governor, Thomas Dale: 'all theis extreme and crewell tortures he used and inflicted upon them to terrify the reste· for Attempting the Lyke' (George Percy, 'A Trewe Relacyon of the Procedeinges and Occurrentes of Momente which had hapned in Virginia' (1612), quoted in Edmund S. Morgan, *American Slavery American Freedom: The Ordeal of Colonial Virginia*, New York, 1975, p. 74). On trans-culturation in general, see James Axtell, 'The white Indians of colonial America' (chapter 7 of his *The European and the Indian: Essays in the Ethnohistory of Colonial North America*, New York, 1981). In 1782 St John de Crevecoeur noted that '*thousands* of Europeans are Indians and we have no examples of even one of those Aborigines having from choice become Europeans!' (*Letters from an American Farmer*, London, 1962, p. 215).

17 'Copy of John Rolfe's Letter to Sir Thomas Dale Regarding His Marriage to Pocahontas', in Philip Barbour, *Pocahontas and her World*, Appendix III, pp. 247–52.

18 Purchas, XIX, p. 118.

19 See Wyndham Robertson, *Pocahontas and her Descendants* (1887), Baltimore, 1968. According to Mossiker (*Pocahontas*, p. 319) two million Americans can now claim consanguinity or affinity with Pocahontas.

20 Rolfe, in Barbour, *Pocahontas*, p. 247.

21 Frances Mossiker argues persuasively that Smith's general reticence about his relationship with Pocahontas was governed by the unmentionable subject of miscegenation (pp. 84, 109–14). It is quite possible that their relationship included sexual intercourse, especially after the extraordinary 'masque' that Smith describes, without this necessarily involving the European notion of romantic love that has generally dictated the story's motivations, even in Mossiker's more sophisticated version. On the 'masque' see John Smith, *A Map of Virginia* (1612) in *Works*, ed. Arber, pp. 123–4.

22 Rolfe, in Barbour, p. 247.

23 Rolfe, in Barbour, p. 251.

24 Smith, *The Generall Historie*, pp. 122–3.

25 Marshall Sahlins, 'The spirit of the gift', in his *Stone Age Economics*, London, 1974, p. 169. I have depended heavily in this section on

Sahlins's brilliant essay. Reference is to the English translation of Mauss: *The Gift: Forms and Functions of Exchange in Archaic Societies*, trans. Ian Cunnison, London, 1970, substituting 'pre-state' for Mauss's 'archaic'.

26 The gap is indicated by the very title of Robert Frost's deeply offensive poem, 'The gift outright' (1941), about the relationship between Euroamericans and 'their' land (*Complete Poems*, London, 1961, p. 378).

27 Mauss, pp. 79–80. He calls the system one of 'total prestation' (p. 3).

28 Sahlins points out (p. 175) how Mauss's word 'traiter' catches 'the double meaning of peace and exchange [that] perfectly epitomizes the primitive contract'.

29 Cf. for the relevant anthropological tradition: Arnold van Gennep, *The Rites of Passage*, trans. Monika B. Vizedom and Gabrielle L. Caffee, London, 1977; Victor Turner, *The Ritual Process: Structure and Anti-Structure*, Ithaca, 1969; and Mary Douglas, *Purity and Danger: An Analysis of the Concepts of Pollution and Taboo*, London, 1978. I am not aware of any work on the particular questions of hospitality and strangers.

30 'We were entertained with all love, and kindness, and with as much bountie . . . as they could possibly devise' (Philip Amadas (1584), in *New American World*, III, p. 279); 'where we were entertained by them very kindly', and 'to releeve us with victuals . . . otherwise we had all perished' (George Percy (1607), in *New American World*, V, pp. 269, 273). Ralph Lane's account (1586) makes clear the utter dependence of the Roanoke colony on supplies of Indian food (*New American World*, III, pp. 295–306). Sheehan (chapter 4) chronicles Jamestown's dependence on native food supplies. Washburn (p. 19) concludes: 'Nothing is so frequently recorded in the earliest chronicles as the warmth of the reception accorded the first colonists'.

31 See Mossiker, p. 26. It was the Paspahegh who first attacked the English fort, possibly on their own initiative.

32 Smith, *The Generall Historie*, p. 121.

33 Smith, *Works*, ed. Arber, p. 20.

34 Most recent commentators now accept this explanation: see, for example, Barbour, *The Three Worlds*, pp. 443–4, n. 4; and Mossiker, pp. 81–5.

35 The best general study of *compadrazgo* is still Sidney W. Mintz and Eric R. Wolf, 'An analysis of ritual co-parenthood (compadrazgo)', *Southwestern Journal of Anthropology*, VI, 1950, pp. 341–68. There are numerous studies of its contemporary importance in Latin America (for example, Hugo Nutini and Betty Bell, *Ritual Kinship*, Princeton, 1980), but consideration of its establishment probably under-

states the similarity of native institutions: cf. Claude Lévi-Strauss, 'The social use of kinship terms among the Brazilian Indians', *American Anthropologist*, XLV, 1943, pp. 398–409.

36 Powhatan's behaviour at their subsequent meeting supports such an interpretation: 'he proclaimed me *Awerowanes* of *Powhaton*, and that all his subjects should so esteeme vs, and no man account vs strangers nor Paspaheghans, but Powhatans, and that the Corne, weomen and Country, should be to vs as to his owne people' (Smith, *Works*, ed. Arber, pp. 25–6).

37 Smith, *Works*, ed. Arber, p. 19.

38 *Odyssey*, IX, ll. 250–86. Quoted from Richmond Lattimore's translation, *The Odyssey of Homer*, New York, 1975.

39 *Odyssey*, IX, ll. 131–9. Cf. in particular Robert Johnson, 'Nova Britannia: offering most excellent fruites by planting in Virginia', (1609) in *New American World*, V, pp. 235–48.

40 *Odyssey*, IX, l. 176.

41 *Odyssey*, IX, ll 478–9. Odysseus's traditional canniness could well be defined as his skill at improvisation, a protean quality useful in colonial contexts but morally ambiguous at home: see my 'Polytropic man: Tropes of sexuality and mobility in early colonial discourse', in *Europe and Its Others*, ed. Francis Barker, Peter Hulme, Margaret Iversen, and Diana Loxley, 2 vols, Colchester, 1985, II, pp. 17–32; and cf. Stephen Greenblatt, 'The improvisation of power', in his *Renaissance Self-Fashioning: From More to Shakespeare*, Chicago, 1980, pp. 222–54.

42 George Sandys, *Ovids Metamorphosis Englished, Mythologized, and Represented in Figures*, London, 1640, p. 263; and cf. R.B. Davis, 'America in George Sandys' "Ovid"', *William and Mary Quarterly*, 3rd ser., IV, 1947, pp. 297–304. Kermode's abbreviation: 'more salvage . . . are the *West Indians* at this day' ('Introduction' to *The Tempest*, London, 1962, p. xxxvi) has the West Indians more rather than less savage than Polyphemus through failing to read 'then' as 'than'. There is a hint in this passage, as in the *Odyssey*, of the Utopian topos that accompanies and subverts the political critique. On this aspect of the Cyclops episode see G.S. Kirk, *Myth: Its Meaning and Function in Ancient and Other Cultures*, Cambridge, 1970, pp. 162–71; and Pierre Vidal-Naquet, 'Land and sacrifice in the *Odyssey*', in *Myth, Religion and Society* ed. R.L. Gordon, Cambridge, 1981, pp. 80–94.

43 N.M. Crouse, *French Pioneers in the West Indies, 1624–1664*, New York, 1940, p. 14.

44 Thomas Morton of Merrymount perhaps put his finger on something when he implied that what the colonists objected to was that

the Indians' habits looked so much like those of the English aristocracy; they 'remoove for their pleasures ... after the manner of the gentry of Civilized nations' (*New English Canaan* (1637), quoted in Axtell, p. 48). Certainly the idea that hunting was recreation influenced the colonists' attitude towards the Indians, however dissimilar the two activities may have been in practice. It would be interesting to compare in detail the two different hunting techniques, one based on stealth and patience, the other on noise and the speed and ferocity of dogs. See the quotation at the end of this chapter; and cf. Francis Jennings, *The Invasion of America: Indians, Colonialism and the Cant of Conquest*, New York, 1976, p. 61.

45 See Morgan, pp. 56–8; J. Leitch Wright jun., chapter 1; and Jennings, pp. 61 (and n. 11), 62 (and n. 14), and 67.

46 *Letter from Port Royal in Acadia* (1612), quoted in Jennings, p. 80.

47 'Virginia's Verger' (1625), in Purchas, XIX, p. 231.

48 John Winthrop, 'General Consideration for the Plantation in New England' (1629), quoted in Jennings, p. 82.

49 Robert Johnson, *Nova Britannia* (1609), in *New American World*, V, p. 240.

50 Robert Gray, *A Good Speed to Virginia* (1609), facsimile edn, Amsterdam, 1970, p. C3v.

51 Nomadic patterns of life, however highly structured, have always appeared threatening to those settled in one place, but it is probably right to *implicate* into these arguments the perceptions and legislation concerning 'vagabondage' in Tudor and Stuart England. The structure of the argument is remarkably similar. Vagrancy was an economic threat because the landless were supposed to work for wages in the new organization of the economy. This threat was perceived in terms of a dangerous severance of the individual from ties of place ('parish'), although of course it was the enclosure of common lands ('waste') – which, because communal, did no particular wrong to any individual – that in fact broke those very ties and caused vagrancy in the first place. Only later would 'vagrancy' be redefined as 'social mobility' so that capitalism could shuffle its workforce more efficiently. James Boon (*Other Tribes, Other Scribes: Symbolic Anthropology in the Comparative Study of Cultures, Histories, Religions, and Texts*, Cambridge, 1982, p. 171) suggests the use of the word 'implication' in this argument in an attempt to flatten out the gap that Jennings perceives between Purchas's 'inventions' about the Amerindian way of life, and what he 'knew perfectly well' – 'that the Virginia Indians were sedentary and agricultural' (Jennings, p. 80). The issue is important, although Boon does not perhaps do it full justice. Jennings certainly implies that Purchas was setting out to

deceive, withholding information that he 'knew perfectly well', and thereby 'reifying metaphor into purported actuality' (Jennings, p. 82). Boon is, if you like, better aware of the power of symbolic representations to mould vision itself; but his monocular approach tends to divest the contradictions of all significance. The point is to comprehend the power of symbolic representations to articulate and defuse contradictory evidence as well as to simply 'not see it'.

The still expanding 'internal frontier' of Britain is one of the great themes of Angus Calder's *Revolutionary Empire: The Rise of the English-Speaking Empires from the Fifteenth Century to the 1780s*, London, 1981. On the 'masterless men' see Christopher Hill, *The World Turned Upside Down: Radical Ideas during the English Revolution*, Harmondsworth, 1975, pp. 39–56. Paul Brown has interesting remarks on the connections between the discourses of 'savagism' and 'masterlessness' ('"This thing I acknowledge mine": *The Tempest* and the discourse of colonialism', in *Political Shakespeare: New Essays in Cultural Materialism*, ed. Jonathan Dollimore and Alan Sinfield, Manchester, 1985, pp. 50–6). Michael Walzer points out that because, for Puritanism, life was a journey through alien country, nothing was more despised and hated than a 'vagabond', who travelled unprepared and without destination ('Puritanism as a revolutionary ideology', *History and Theory*, III, 1963–4, pp. 59–90.

52 S.E. Morison, *Admiral of the Ocean Sea: A Life of Christopher Columbus*, Boston, 1942, p. 308. Two otherwise valuable studies of this myth manage not to mention the native inhabitants at all: Henry Nash Smith, *Virgin Land: The American West as Symbol and Myth*, Cambridge, Mass., 1970; and Annette Kolodny, *The Lay of the Land*, Chapel Hill, 1975.

53 Walter Ralegh, 'The Discoveries of the Large, Rich, and Beautiful Empire of Guiana', in Richard Hakluyt, *The Principal Navigations, Voyages, Traffiques, & Discoveries of the English Nation* (1598–1600), 12 vols, Glasgow, 1903–5, X, p. 428.

54 George Chapman, 'De Guiana carmen Epicum' (1596), in Hakluyt, X, p. 447.

55 Purchas, XIX, p. 220.

56 Purchas, XIX, p. 229.

57 Purchas, XIX, p. 231.

58 Albertus Magnus, *Politicorum*, quoted in Anthony Pagden, *The Fall of Natural Man: The American Indian and the Origins of Comparative Ethnology*, Cambridge, 1982, pp. 20–1. I have drawn freely on Pagden's excellent discussion of these issues. Also relevant are: J.B. Scott, *The Discovery of America and its Influence on International Law*, Washington, 1928; Otto Gierke, *Natural Law and the Theory of*

Society 1500–1800, trans. Ernest Baker, Cambridge, 1958; J.A. Fernández-Santamaria, *The State, War and Peace: Spanish Political Thought in the Renaissance, 1516–1559*, Cambridge, 1977; Michael Wilks, *The Problem of Sovereignty in the Middle Ages*, Cambridge, 1964; Quentin Skinner, *The Foundations of Modern Political Thought*, 2 vols, Cambridge, 1978, II, pp. 135–73; James T. Johnson, *Ideology, Reason, and the Limitations of War: Religious and Secular Concepts, 1200–1740*, Princeton, 1975; and James Muldoon, *Popes, Lawyers, and Infidels: The Church and the Non-Christian World, 1250–1550*, Liverpool, 1979. And see note 62.

59 Vitoria, *Relectio 'De Indis'* (1539), quoted by Pagden, p. 77. This was the standard Spanish justification, the basis of the famous *requerimiento*, although it came under increasing strain during the early decades of the sixteenth century. In the important 'Carta de provisión' of August 1503, permitting the reduction to slavery of the 'canibales', their chief crime was refusing to 'rescebir e acoxer' (receive and welcome) the Spaniards ('Provisión para poder cautivar a los Canibales rebeldes', in *Colección de los viajes y descubrimientos, que hicieron por mar los españoles desde fines del siglo XV*, ed. M. Fernández de Navarrete, 5 vols, Madrid, 1825–37, II, p. 416).

The labour structure of Hispaniola likewise collapsed because the Amerindians refused to work in the mines; therefore, because 'se partan de la conversación y comunicación de los cristianos', they had to be *forced* into paid labour – a position only with subtlety distinguished from slavery: see Antonio Rumeu de Armas, *La política indigenista de Isabel la Católica*, Valladolid, 1969, p. 399.

60 *Aeneid*, I, 386, quoted from *The Eclogues, Georgics and Aeneid of Virgil*, trans. C. Day Lewis, Oxford, 1966.

61 *Aeneid*, I, 539–40.

62 Purchas, XIX, p. 223. Purchas always supports his arguments from the Bible but one of his key essays ('Of the proprietie which Infidels have in their Lands and Goods', I, pp. 38–45) mentions Vitoria, and he must have known such important works as: Matthew Sutcliffe, *The Practise, Proceedings and Lawes of Armes*, London, 1593; Alberico Gentile, *De iure belli*, London, 1588–9; and William Fulbecke, *The Pandectes of the Law of Nations*, London, 1602.

63 George Peckham, 'True Reporte of the Late Discoveries by Sir Humphrey Gilbert' (1583), in *New American World*, III, p. 43.

64 'A True Declaration of the Estate of the Colonie in Virginia' (1610), in *New American World*, V, p. 250.

65 Purchas, XIX, p. 230.

66 'Treacherousness' got the better of the alternative explanation, which was to have God making the natives act out of character: 'It pleased God ... to send those people which were our mortall enemies to

releeve us with victuals . . . otherwise we had all perished' (George
Percy, 'A Discourse of the Plantation of the Southern Colonie in
Virginia' (1607), in *New American World*, V, p. 273). See
pp. 128–31 and cf. Karen O. Kupperman, 'English perceptions of
treachery, 1583–1640: The case of the American "savages"', *The
Historical Journal*, XX, 1977, pp. 263–87.

67 Gabriel Archer, 'The Discription of the Now Discovered River and
    Country of Virginia' (1607), in *New American World*, V, p. 276.

68 In Barbour (ed.), *The Jamestown Voyages*, p. 438.

69 In *The Records of the Virginia Company of London*, 4 vols, Washing-
    ton, 1906–35, III, p. 165. See, for many other examples, the entries
    on 'inconstancy' and 'treacherousness' (under 'indians') in the useful
    index to H.C. Porter, *The Inconstant Savage: England and the North
    American Indian, 1500–1660*, London, 1979.

70 Purchas speaks of their 'greatest pretended amity' (XIX, p. 224).

71 Alexander Brown, *The First Republic in America* (1898), quoted in
    Washburn, p. 20.

72 According to John Smith it was around this time that Powhatan
    made his important statement that includes the words: 'many do
    informe me, your comming is not for trade, but to invade my people
    and possesse my Country' (Smith, *A Map of Virginia* (1612), in
    Works, ed. Arber, p. 134).

73 See Morgan, pp. 92–8. The rhetoric now becomes tougher. William
    Symonds, for example, advises that

    in a strange Countrey, we must looke for enemies; euen cursing
    enemies, vnder whose tongues is the poyson of Aspes, and whose
    right hand is a right hand of iniquitie . . . . This our Sauiour
    foretelleth to his holy Apostles, *In the world you shall haue trouble*. A
    thing which if the children of Israel had knowen as they ought,
    they would neuer haue refused to enter the land which God
    commanded them to possesse: because there were cursing and
    killing enemies, no better than Canibals. (William Symonds,
    Virginia: A Sermon Preached at White-Chapel (1609), facsimile edn,
    Amsterdam, 1968, p 42)

    The tidewater Algonquians were never openly accused of anthro-
    pophagy by the English, but 'cannibalism' is part of a constant
    referential sub-text.

74 Richard Hakluyt (the elder), 'Inducements to the lykinge of the
    voyadge' (1584), in *New American World*, III, p. 63.

75 Ingram's account was included in the first edition of Hakluyt's
    Principal Navigations (1589) but left out of subsequent editions,
    presumably on the grounds that its authenticity was suspect.
    Peckham also made much of Ingram's reports of cannibalism (*New*

American World, III, p. 44). Ingram's report is included in *Voyages and Colonizing Enterprises of Sir Humphrey Gilbert*, ed. David Beers Quinn, 2 vols, London, 1940, II, pp. 283–96.

76 It is interesting to note that Spanish violence (i.e. Hakluyt and Gray, in *New American World*, III, p. 92; and V, p. 240 respectively) looks much the same to English eyes as cannibalistic violence: the process of denial does not discriminate between objects of projection. See James Smith's pertinent remarks on the English colonists:

> Rather than waiting until they shall see, they must immediately make use of their blindness as a seeing. The use they make of it is of an appropriately fantastic kind. Ignorant of their own motives, they miscall both these motives, the actions which result therefrom, and the objects upon which the motives are directed. They reprove the conduct of the Spaniards in the Indies, and at the same time imitate that conduct. Filled with a Christian charity towards the natives, at a slight provocation they overflow with a diabolic hate. Aspiring to exalt the crude earth of the natives to the purest gold, they are ready to stamp it beneath their feet and scatter it to the winds. Like hoodwinked men they keep on no steady course, but lurch from one side to the other of the path in which it never occurs to them to halt, because they have no notion of being unable to walk down it. (*Shakespearian and Other Essays*, ed. E.M. Wilson, Cambridge, 1974, pp. 248–9)

At points such as this in the colonial discourse (which may well have to do with Ingram's 'imagination') it becomes clear how cannibalism quite simply *is* nothing other than the violence of colonialism incarnate beyond the pale. Roy Harvey Pearce's brief formulation is still to the point: 'Civilisation had created a savage, so to kill him' (*The Savages of America: A Study of the Indian and the Idea of Civilization*, Baltimore, 1965, p. 242).

77 See Barbour (ed.) *The Jamestown Voyages*, pp. 51–2.

78 See Peckham, *New American World*, III, p. 44.

79 'Instructions for Sir Thomas Gates for the Government of Virginia', *New American World*, V, pp. 215–16.

80 In other words, the behaviour that psychoanalysts refer to as 'disowning projection' (H.B. and A.C. English, *A Comprehensive Dictionary of Psychological and Psychoanalytical Terms*, London, 1958 – under 'Projection'). On the importance of disavowal for colonial discourse see Homi Bhabha, 'Signs taken for wonders: Questions of ambivalence and authority under a tree outside Delhi, May 1817', in *Europe and Its Others*, pp. 89–106.

81 Morgan, p. 90.

82 Cf. Hulme, 'Polytropic Man', pp. 19–23.

83 It is quite proper to condemn this process and to highlight what Francis Jennings calls its 'cant'. But it is even more important to understand its mechanisms so that we can intervene more effectively in its contemporary manifestations. The central mechanism is parallel to the way in which witch-hunting transferred society's 'guilt' at the breakdown of social conventions of mutual support to the victims of that breakdown: see Keith Thomas, *Religion and the Decline of Magic: Studies in Popular Beliefs in Sixteenth and Seventeenth-Century England*, Harmondsworth, 1978, chapter 17. The connection between *werowances* and witches was sometimes made (see Alexander Whitaker, *Good Newes from Virginia* (1613), quoted in Porter, p. 396); and the two processes overlapped in the infamous New England witchhunts where, at Salem in 1692, the instigator was claimed to be a woman called Tituba, a Caribbean Amerindian (possibly a Black Carib) brought as a slave from Barbados to Massachusetts (see Marion L. Starkey, *The Devil in Massachusetts: A Modern Enquiry into the Salem Witch Trials*, Garden City, New York, 1961, p. 23). In psychoanalytical terms it is quite clear that the 'masculine thrust' of European colonialism acted, as masculine thrusts do, as compensation for fairly radical internal problems and anxieties. A valuably wide perspective on these problems is provided by Brian Easlea's books, *Witch-Hunting, Magic and the New Philosophy: An Introduction to Debates of the Scientific Revolution 1450–1750*, Brighton, 1980, and *Fathering the Unthinkable: Masculinity, Scientists, and the Nuclear Arms Race*, London, 1983.

84 See W.F. Craven, *The Dissolution of the Virginia Company*, New York, 1932.

85 John Rolfe, *A True Relation of the State of Virginia Left by Sir Thomas Dale Knight in May last 1616* (1616), Charlottesville, 1971.

86 Purchas, XIX, p. 118.

87 Purchas, XIX, pp. 117–19.

88 See Margaret Holmes Williamson, 'Powhatan hair', *Man*, n.s. XIV, 1979, pp. 392–413; and James Axtell, pp. 59–62, who connects the Puritan dislike of the Amerindians' long hair with the key notion of 'reduction'.

89 John G. Chapman, *The Picture of the Baptism of Pocahontas Painted by Order of Congress, for the Rotunda of the Capitol*, Washington, 1840, p. 6.

90 Edward Waterhouse, *A Declaration of the State of the Colony in Virginia* (1622), facsimile edn, Amsterdam, 1970, pp. 22–3. Inevitably the 'massacre' drew forth implications of cannibalism:

> there fell vnder the bloudy and barbarous hands of that perfidious and inhumane people, contrary to all lawes of God and men, of

Nature and Nations, three hundred forty seven men, women, and children, most by their owne weapons; and not being content with taking away life alone, they fell after againe vpon the dead, making as well they could a fresh murder, defacing, dragging, and mangling the dead carkasses into many pieces, and carrying some parts away in derision, with base and bruitish triumph. (Waterhouse, p. 14)

The experience of 1622 also brought the English closer to their traditional European enemies (cf. note 76): Oviedo's opinion of the West Indian natives could be quoted with approval to show 'how farre, it agrees with that of the Natiues of VIRGINIA' (Waterhouse, p. 30).

91 Waterhouse, p. 24.

5   Robinson Crusoe and Friday

1 Derek Walcott, 'Crusoe's Journal', *The Castaway and Other Poems*, London, 1965, p. 51.
2 Daniel Defoe, *The Life and Adventures of Robinson Crusoe* (1719), ed. Angus Ross, Harmondsworth, 1965, p. 172. All subsequent page references are to this edition and are, where appropriate, included parenthetically in the text.
3 See pp. 68-9.
4 For the relevant geography see also *The Farther Adventures of Robinson Crusoe* (1719), London, 1925, pp. 33-4. Defoe may well have used the map in William Dampier, *A New Voyage Round the World*, 2 vols, London, 1697-9, I, facing p. 24.
5 Ian Watt, *The Rise of the Novel: Studies in Defoe, Richardson and Fielding*, Harmondsworth, 1963.
6 Watt, p. 68.
7 The first phrase is Pat Rogers's in his *Robinson Crusoe*, London, 1979, p. 51; the second is Watt's, p. 84. The two main studies usually invoked for this spiritual motif are G.A. Starr, *Defoe and Spiritual Autobiography*, Princeton, 1965; and J.P. Hunter, *The Reluctant Pilgrim: Defoe's Emblematic Method and the Quest for Form in Robinson Crusoe*, Baltimore, 1966.
8 Cf. Watt, p. 248.
9 Watt, p. 264.
10 Watt, p. 108.
11 Watt, p. 23.
12 Watt, p. 28.

13 Watt, p. 140.

14 Watt, p. 216 (my italics).

15 Georg Lukács, *The Theory of the Novel* (1920), trans. Anna Bostock, London, 1971, p. 88. Lukács's analysis of this philosophical dimension of the novel form is still unparallelled: cf. Jay Bernstein, *The Philosophy of the Novel: Lukács, Marxism and the Dialectics of Form*, Brighton,1984.

16 See Mark Kinkead-Weekes, '*Clarissa* restored?', *Review of English Studies*, n.s. X, 1959, pp. 156–71. The antinomy is explored by Terry Eagleton, *The Rape of Clarissa: Writing, Sexuality and Class Struggle in Samuel Richardson*, Oxford, 1982, pp. 17–39.

17 Watt, p. 98. The phrase is Clara Reeve's from *The Progress of Romance* (1785).

18 Cf. Watt, pp. 77–82. The providential sea narrative had continued to flourish over the century between the *Sea Venture* and Alexander Selkirk's story, which circulated in 1712 under the title *Providence Displayed*. See, for examples, James Janeway's collection, *Tokens for Mariners, Containing Many Famous and Wonderful Instances of God's Providence in Sea Dangers and Deliverances*, London, 1708.

19 Watt, p. 15. It might be said that Defoe is 'deliberately' exploiting the ambiguity that Richardson had tried to avoid – but how could we tell? He speaks *Robinson Crusoe*, as it were, deadpan, with the straight face that could be dry humour or humourless seriousness, but is not going to let us know.

20 Respectively Ian Watt, '*Robinson Crusoe* as a myth', *Essays in Criticism*, I, 1951, pp. 95–119; and Maximilian Novak, *Economics and the Fiction of Daniel Defoe*, Berkeley, 1962.

21 Stephen Hymer, 'Robinson Crusoe and the secret of primitive accumulation', *Monthly Review*, XXIII, no. 4, 1971–2, pp. 11–36. Cf. Karl Marx, *Capital: A Critique of Political Economy, Volume One*, chapters 26–33 (trans. Ben Fowkes, Harmondsworth, 1976, pp. 873–940); and André Gunder Frank, *World Accumulation 1492–1789*, London, 1978.

22 Hymer, p. 13. Cf. *Capital*, chapter 31.

23 Hymer, p. 12.

24 Diana Spearman, *The Novel and Society*, London, 1966, p. 154.

25 Hymer, pp. 16–17.

26 Hymer, p. 22.

27 Hymer, p. 13.

28 See for example Peter Earle, *The World of Defoe*, Newton Abbot, 1977; and Isaac Kramnick, *Bolingbroke and His Circle: The Politics of Nostalgia in the Age of Walpole*, Cambridge, Mass., 1968. J.G.A. Pocock brilliantly defuses oversimplistic readings of the economic

debates of the period by insisting on a recognition of the 'highly ambivalent rhetoric' in which all participants were to a large extent entrapped (*The Machiavellian Moment: Florentine Political Thought and the Atlantic Republican Tradition*, Princeton, 1975, pp. 423–61). For the economic history of the period the standard work is P.G.M. Dickson, *The Financial Revolution in England: A Study in the Development of Public Credit 1688–1756*, London, 1967. A particularly clear account of the South Sea Bubble affair is given in chapter 6 of Howard Erskine-Hill, *The Social Milieu of Alexander Pope*, New Haven, 1975; see also John Carswell, *The South Sea Bubble*, London, 1960.

29 There are early plans in the 1690s and 1703 (see J.R. Moore, *Daniel Defoe: Citizen of the Modern World*, Chicago, 1958, pp. 77–8); the 1711 memorandum to Harley (see *The Letters of Daniel Defoe*, ed. G.H. Healey, Oxford, 1955, pp. 338–49); a newspaper article of 1719 (partially reproduced in Maximilian Novak, *Realism, Myth, and History in Defoe's Fiction*, Lincoln, Nebr., 1981, p. 26) followed in the same year by *An Historical Account of the Voyages and Adventures of Sir Walter Raleigh*, the 1724 *A New Voyage Round the World* and, finally, the 1727 *The History of the Principal Discoveries and Improvements in the several arts and sciences*. On Defoe's South American project see: J.R. Moore, 'Defoe and the South Sea Company', *Boston Public Library Quarterly*, V, 1953, pp. 175–88; J.A. Downie, 'Defoe, imperialism and travel books', *The Yearbook of English Studies*, XIII, 1983, pp. 66–83; Jane H. Jack, '*A New Voyage Round the World*: Defoe's Roman à Thèse', *Huntington Library Quarterly*, XXIV, 1960–1, pp. 323–36; and B.J. Fishman, 'Defoe, Herman Moll and South America', *Huntington Library Quarterly*, XXXVI, 1972–3, pp. 227–38.

30   We expect, in two or three Days, a most flaming Proposal from the South Sea Company ... for erecting a British Colony on the Foundation of the South-Sea Company's Charter, upon the Terra Firma, or the northernmost Side of the Mouth of the great River Oronooko. They propose, as we hear, the establishing a Factory and Settlement there ... and they doubt not to carry on a Trade there equal to that of the Portuguese in the Brazils, and to bring home an equal quantity of Gold, as well as to cause a prodigious consumption of our British Manufactures. This, it seems, is the same Country and River discovered by Sir Walter Rawleigh, in former Days, and that which he miscarried in by several Mistakes, which may now easily be prevented. (*Weekly Journal*, 7 February 1719, p. 56; quoted by Novak, *Realism, Myth, and History*, p. 26)

Cf. Defoe's *Atlas Maritimus & Commercialis; or, a General View of the World*, London, 1728, p. 313, where he extols the potential of the land between Popayán and the mouth of the Orinoco. According to Moore (*Daniel Defoe*, p. 293) Defoe actually owned some of Ralegh's manuscripts and charts.

31 See Kenneth R. Andrews, *The Spanish Caribbean: Trade and Plunder 1530–1630*, New Haven, 1978, and *Elizabethan Privateering: English Privateering during the Spanish War, 1585–1603*, Cambridge, 1964; and S.A.G. Taylor, *The Western Design: An Account of Cromwell's Expedition to the Caribbean*, London, 1969.

32 Defoe opens his *Essay on Projects* (1697, facsimile edn, Menston, 1969, pp. 15–16) by referring to Phips's 'voyage to the wreck'. An excellent modern study of Phips's adventure is Peter Earle, *The Wreck of the Almiranta: Sir William Phips and the Hispaniola Treasure*, London, 1979. The importance of Phips's bullion is stressed by J.M. Keynes, *A Treatise on Money*, 2 vols, London, 1930, II, pp. 150–1; and by John Clapham, *The Bank of England I: 1694–1797*, Cambridge, 1944, pp. 13–14.

33 See Novak, *Economics and the Fiction of Daniel Defoe*, pp. 60–2.

34 See C.R. Boxer, *The Portuguese Seaborne Empire*, London, 1969, pp. 155–8; and Pierre Vilar, *A History of Gold and Money 1450–1920*, trans. Judith White, London, 1976, pp. 222–31. It was this Brazilian gold that helped stabilize England's currency after the bursting of the South Sea Bubble. Defoe's defence of the Methuen Treaty is in his *Considerations of the Eighth and Ninth Articles of the Treaty of Commerce and Navigations*, London, 1713. In his *Atlas Maritimus & Commercialis* Defoe speaks of how, just to the west of Bahia – where Crusoe has his plantation – 'they find so much gold that it is incredible' (p. 315).

35 Cf. Martin Green's definition: 'In general, adventure seems to mean a series of events, partly but not wholly accidental, in settings remote from the domestic and probably from the civilized (at least in the psychological sense of remote), which constitute a challenge to the central character' (*Dreams of Adventure, Deeds of Empire*, London, 1980, p. 23).

36 *Essay on Projects*, p. 15. Cf. his comparison between highwaymen and stockjobbers (in the highwaymen's favour because they rob 'at the Hazard of their Lives') in *The Anatomy of Exchange Alley*, London, 1719, p. 8.

37 Archives Nationales, Paris, K 1349, fols 14 and 15, quoted by Fernand Braudel, *The Wheels of Commerce*, trans. Sian Reynolds, London, 1982, p. 453 and n. 248. The voyage which results in Crusoe's shipwreck in the Caribbean would have made him an adventurer in this sense, the Brazilian planters being keen to avoid

the high prices charged by the licensed slavers; by this time much of the slave trade to South America was contraband (J.H. Parry, *The Spanish Sea-borne Empire*, London, 1966, p. 268).

38 What might seem a contradiction, namely the coupling of Crusoe's rationalistic book-keeping outlook on life – even down to what Weber calls the 'systematization of ethical conduct' (*The Protestant Ethic and the Spirit of Capitalism*, trans. Talcott Parsons, London, 1930, p. 123) – with his, according to some accounts, 'irrational', 'impulsive' urge to wander, can be made some sense of through the full connotations of the word 'adventure'. The 'spiritual' reading would readily introduce the term 'puritanism' here, but it will not quite do. It certainly suggests the requisite concern with the individual, and puritanism – *vide Pilgrim's Progress* – is not averse to the probationary qualities of adventure. But Crusoe's adventures – as the etymology suggests – are much more Odyssean improvisations than they are moral pilgrimages into the unknown: he is, simply, more John Smith than John Winthrop. The problem in discussing these facets of Crusoe's character is in a way – a presumably symptomatic way – the same as the problem in discussing the relationship between colonialism and capitalism. Certainly the rationalism that Marx and Weber both saw behind capitalism is only attributable to the phase of primary accumulation through the invocation of some 'rational' Hegelian world-spirit: it is hardly there in the historical record.

39 In his *History of the Principal Discoveries* part of Defoe's defence of his proposed South American colony is that Sir John Narborough landed on that part of the coast (now southern Argentina)

> and in order to obviate the Pretences of any other Nation, as far as those Pretences may be grounded upon Possession, took a formal Possession of this very Country in the Name of King *Charles* the Second, his then reigning Sovereign; declar'd he found the same uninhabited by any *European* Nation, and fixing up a Cross of Wood, with an Inscription cut in Brass fixt upon it, he proclaim'd King *Charles* Sovereign of the Country: This I mention (not that I think any Body has a Right to dispossess the Natives of a Country) to intimate, that at *least* the *English* have as good a Title to it as any other *Nation* whatsoever. (p. 298)

Crusoe is a literal cross (*Kreutz*nauer).

40 John H. Parry, 'A Secular Sense of Responsibility', in *First Images of the New World: The Impact of the New World on the Old*, ed. F. Chiappelli, 2 vols, Berkeley, 1976, I, p. 289, Cf.

> For supposing a Man, or Family, in the state they were, at first peopling of the World by the Children of *Adam*, or *Noah*; let him

plant in some in-land, vacant places of *America*, we shall find that
the *Possessions* he could make himself upon the *measures* we have
given, would not be very large, nor, even to this day, prejudice
the rest of Mankind, or give them reason to complain, or think
themselves injured by this Man's Incroachment, though the Race
of Men have now spread themselves to all corners of the World,
and do infinitely exceed the small number [which] was at the
beginning. (John Locke, *Two Treatises of Government*, ed. Peter
Laslett, New York, 1965, p. 335 (II, 37))

For Locke America was uncultivated and therefore not possessed. See
pp. 157–8.

41 Owen Lattimore, *Studies in Frontier History*, London, 1962, p. 27.
And cf. John McVeagh's analogous point that '*Robinson Crusoe* is
only seemingly a realistic novel, more truly an abstraction, the myth
of western development cast into story form' (*Tradeful Merchants:
The Portrayal of the Capitalist in Literature*, London, 1981, pp. 59–60).

42 A good account of this method is given by C.B. MacPherson in
his introduction to Hobbes, *Leviathan*, Harmondsworth, 1968,
pp. 25–9. Contrast Marx's account of his method in the *Grundrisse:
Foundations of the Critique of Political Economy (Rough Draft)* trans.
Martin Nicklaus, Harmondsworth, 1973, pp. 100–8.

43 *Capital Volume 1*, pp. 169–77; Watt, '*Robinson Crusoe* as a myth',
pp. 111–19. Cf. Michael White, 'The production of an economic
Robinson Crusoe', *Southern Review*, XVI, 1982, pp. 115–41; and John
J. Richetti, *Defoe's Narratives*, Oxford, 1975, pp. 15–16.

44 Christopher Hill, 'Robinson Crusoe', *History Workshop*, 10, 1980,
p. 12.

45 Hobbes, *Leviathan*, p. 187 (chapter 13); Locke, *Two Treatises*, p. 336
(II, 37), p. 338 (II, 41), p. 343 (II, 49); Jean-Jacques Rousseau,
'Discourse on the origin and basis of inequality', in *The Essential
Rousseau*, trans. Lowell Bair, New York, 1974, p. 168.

46 For Roldán, see Carl Sauer, *The Early Spanish Main*, Berkeley, 1966,
p. 93; for Stephen Hopkins and Bermuda, see pp. 103–4: Defoe
knew this story, possibly from John Smith's *Generall Historie of
Virginia*, and repeats it in the text of his *Atlas Maritimus &
Commercialis*, pp. 307–9 (Novak, *Economics*, p. 164, n. 6, suggests
that it provided Defoe with the main source for the development of
Crusoe's colony in *The Farther Adventures*); on Madagascar, see
Defoe's *A General History of the Pyrates* (1724–8), London, 1972; on
Christian and the fate of his Utopian ideal, see Richard Hough,
Captain Bligh and Mr. Christian: The Men and the History, London,
1972. More's narrator in *Utopia*, Hythloday, supposedly travelled
with Vespucci to the Caribbean.

47 René Descartes, *Discourse on Method*, trans. F.E. Sutcliffe, Har-

mondsworth, 1968, pp. 51–2. Cf. 'Everything revolves in our minds by innumerable circular motions, all centering in ourselves . . . . Hence man may be properly said to be alone in the midst of crowds and the hurry of men and business' (Daniel Defoe, *Serious Reflections of Robinson Crusoe*, London, 1720, p. 2).

Descartes' autobiography is of course 'real' as opposed to Crusoe's fictional life story but this makes little difference to the narrative strategies involved. On the rhetoric of the *Discourse* see: Jean-Luc Nancy's two articles, 'Larvatus pro Deo', *Glyph*, 2, 1977, pp. 14–36, and 'Mundus est fabula', *MLN*, 93, 1978, pp. 635–53; David Simpson, 'Putting one's house in order', *New Literary History*, IX, 1977–8, pp . 83–101; and Bernstein, *The Philosophy of the Novel*, chapter 5. Descartes' realization of his intellectual task was heralded by a dream: see Jacques Maritain, *The Dream of Descartes*, London, 1946. On solitude as a recurrent image in much of Defoe's fiction, see Homer Brown, 'The displaced self in the novels of Daniel Defoe', *English Literary History*, XXXVIII, 1971, pp. 562–90.

48 Descartes, *Discourse on Method*, pp. 33–4.

49 Descartes, p. 78. As Gilson points out, this is 'l'idéal baconien de la science' (René Descartes, *Discours de la méthode: Texte et commentaire*, ed. Etienne Gilson, Paris, 1976, p. 446).

50 The best discussions of these issues are in Homer Brown, 'The displaced self'; Thomas Kavanagh, 'Unraveling Robinson: The divided self in Defoe's *Robinson Crusoe*', *Texas Studies in Language and Literature*, XX, 1978, pp. 416–32; and James H. Maddox, 'Interpreter Crusoe', *English Literary History*, LI, 1984, pp. 33–52.

51 Brown, p. 569. One of the providential narratives that flourished around the turn of the century recounts the deliverance of a ship's company 'from the Devouring Waves of the Sea; amongst which they Shipwrack: and also, From the cruel Devouring Jaws of the Unhumane Canibals of Florida' (Jonathon Dickenson, *God's Protecting Providence*, Philadelphia, 1700, title page; quoted by Hunter, p. 61).

52 Kavanagh, making a similar point, speaks about the 'optics of compensation'; 'an obsessive repetition of the claim to a unity and identity of the self coming to grips with the obvious proofs of its arbitrariness and insufficiency' (p. 418).

53 Descartes, pp. 78–9. Cf. Francis Barker, *The Tremulous Private Body: Essays on Subjection*, London, 1984. An emblem of such a body is Crusoe within the walls of his cave: 'The wall that he builds is an integument that reinforces the boundaries of the self – it is a metaphorical psychic skin' (Elihu Hessel Pearlman, 'Robinson Crusoe and the cannibals', *Mosaic*, X, 1976, p. 52).

54 Cf. Edmund Morgan's remark quoted on pp. 167–8.

55 The next two paragraphs are closely based on Maddox, pp. 38–9.

56 Maddox sees a hint here of Protestant distaste for the 'cannibalistic' Eucharist.

57 Hymer, p. 26.

58 Hymer, pp. 27–9.

59 Watt, *The Rise of the Novel*, p. 14.

60 Dewey Ganzel suggests that the whole episode is a late interpolation ('Chronology in *Robinson Crusoe*', *Philological Quarterly*, XL, 1961, pp. 495–512). This would be striking evidence of textual disturbance. The arguments are complex, based on five chronological references to a 28+ year cycle (rather than the predominant 27+ cycle); but there are also two anticipatory remarks of Crusoe's – to a meeting with cannibals in his twenty-fourth year on the island, and to the usefulness of his fortifications – that apply only to the dream events.

61 This follows closely Locke's phrasing in paragraph 23 of the Second Treatise (*Two Treatises*, p. 325).

62 In this very precise sense Crusoe is in a 'state of nature' according to Hobbesian theory. The motif of 'rescue' continues from the previous chapters. The Algonquian response operates in terms of 'gift'; Europeans (*viz* Prospero and Crusoe) in terms of forced labour; between Europeans there must be a written contract. Hobbes specifically contrasts 'gift' with 'contract' (I, 14 (p. 193)).

63 Fredric Jameson, 'Magical narratives: On the dialectical use of genre criticism', in his *The Political Unconscious: Narrative as a Socially Symbolic Act*, London, 1981, pp. 140–1.

64 Jameson, p. 141.

65 For a discussion of Defoe's own use of the term 'romance', see M.E. Novak, 'Defoe's theory of fiction', *Studies in Philology*, LXI, 1964, pp. 650–68.

66 Northrop Frye, *Anatomy of Criticism*, Princeton, 1971, p. 186. See also Frye's *The Secular Scripture: A Study in the Structure of Romance*, Cambridge, Mass., 1976.

67 There were no goats native to the Caribbean (though Selkirk had goats on Juan Fernández), but the islands had a variety of small edible mammals.

68 On the European fetishism of technology see my essay 'Polytropic man: Tropes of sexuality and mobility in early colonial discourse', in *Europe and its Others*, ed. Francis Barker, Peter Hulme, Margaret Iversen, and Diana Loxley, 2 vols, Colchester, 1985, II, p. 17–32.

69 See Douglas Taylor, 'Spanish *canoa* and its congeners', *International Journal of Linguistics*, XXIII, 1957, pp. 242–4. The island Caribs were

renowned for their boatmanship although it is still a matter of dispute whether they used sails before 1492: see M.B. McKusick, 'Aboriginal canoes in the West Indies', in *Papers in Caribbean Anthropology*, comp. Sidney Mintz, New Haven, 1960.

70 'The virtual absence of dishonest or imprudent business transactions in his novels is remarkable' (Michael Shinagel, *Daniel Defoe and Middle-Class Gentility*, Cambridge, Mass., 1968, p. 134). Hymer notes the 'elaborate social network of capitalist intercommunications' presupposed by this series of transactions (p. 15). And cf. John McVeagh, 'Defoe and the romance of trade', *The Durham University Journal*, n.s. XXXIX, no. 2, 1978, pp. 141–7.

71 See Pat Rogers, 'Crusoe's home', *Essays in Criticism*, XXIV, 1974, pp. 375–90.

72 He has, in that Rousseauesque paradox, to learn his unalienation – hence the importance of *Robinson Crusoe* as a model for *Emile*. And unalienated he was an ideal model for the marginal economists: see note 43.

73 Rogers, 'Crusoe's home', p. 386; quoting Pope's 'Epistle to Burlington', 1. 56.

74 The phrase is Kavanagh's (p. 417). Hunter (p. 99) makes the point that Puritanism sought the reassurance of an earlier, internally consistent world of space and time to allay the anxieties produced by 'the challenge of modernity'. Crusoe's psychosis is an index of how little, or how unsuccessfully, he was solaced by a Puritan world-view.

> Mercurial, hastily constructed from the ruins of a once universal notion of hierarchy relating man as species to all orders above and below him, the sense of an individual as an unfissured touchstone of experience must be seen far more as an act of faith than as an immediate given of experience.

The providential pattern is then 'but one of a series of crumbling timbers thrown across the chasm of the fissured self as it seeks to achieve some coincidence of consciousness with existence' (Kavanagh, pp. 417 and 421).

75 Descartes, p. 62.

76 Descartes, p. 79.

77 James Joyce, 'Daniel Defoe', trans. Joseph Prescott, *Buffalo Studies*, I, 1964, pp. 3–25. Leslie Stephen made a similar point in 1868, calling Crusoe 'the typical Englishman of his time' (*Defoe: The Critical Heritage*, p. 176).

78 For all their differences of style and language the parallels between *The Tempest* and *Robinson Crusoe* are many and startling, and have

the colonial encounter at their root. See: J.R. Moore, '*The Tempest and Robinson Crusoe*', *Review of English Studies*, XXI, 1945, pp. 52–6; Jeffrey Meyers, 'Savagery and civilization in *The Tempest, Robinson Crusoe*, and *Heart of Darkness*', *Conradiana*, II, 1970, pp. 171–9; and Jeanne de Chantal Zabus, '*The Tempest* and *Robinson Crusoe*: A structuralist "attention"', *English Studies in Canada*, IX, pp. 151–63. I am particularly indebted at various points in this chapter to Diana Loxley, '"A play of shadows": Slaves and strangers in *The Tempest, Robinson Crusoe*, and *Victory*', MA Dissertation, University of Essex, 1982. To speak of *Robinson Crusoe* as a 'romance' is clearly to bring it generically closer to *The Tempest* than it would be as 'realist novel'.

79 Maddox, p. 36.
80 Maddox, p. 43.

6   Inkle and Yarico

1 Quoted from *The Aeneid of Virgil*, ed. T.E. Page, 2 vols, London 1926.
2 For the eighteenth-century history of the European powers in the Caribbean see the contemporary account by Bryan Edwards, *The History, Civil and Commercial, of the British Colonies in the West Indies*, 3 vols, London,1794–1801; and: Nellis Crouse, *The French Struggle for the West Indies 1665–1713*, New York, 1943; L.J. Ragatz, *The Fall of the Planter Class in the British Caribbean 1763–1833*, New York, 1963; Alan Burns, *History of the British West Indies*, New York, 1965; Cyril Hamshere, *The British in the Caribbean*, Cambridge, Mass., 1972; Richard S. Dunn, *Sugar and Slaves: The Rise of the Planter Class in the English West Indies 1624–1713*, New York, 1973; and D.L. Niddrie, 'Eighteenth century settlement in the British Caribbean', *Transactions of the Institute of British Geographers*, XL, 1966, pp. 67–80.
3 Nellis Crouse, *French Pioneers in the West Indies, 1624–1664*, New York, 1940, p. 258.
4 Bryan Edwards, writing before the Second Carib War, had noted indignantly: 'By the 9th article of the peace of Paris, signed the 10th of February, 1763, the three islands of Dominica, St Vincent, and Tobago were assigned to Great Britain . . . the Charaibes not being once mentioned in the whole transaction, as if no such people existed' (vol. 1, p. 391).
5 I.E. Kirby and C.I. Martin, *The Rise and Fall of the Black Caribs of St Vincent*, Kingstown, St Vincent, 1972, pp. 12–20. The Black Caribs had already resisted attempts to breach that line.

6 David Brion Davis, *The Problem of Slavery in Western Culture*, Ithaca, 1966, pp. 10–11.

7 The standard study is Lawrence Price, *Inkle and Yarico Album*, Berkeley, 1937. See also Wylie Sypher, *Guinea's Captive Kings: British Anti-Slavery Literature of the XVIIIth Century*, New York, 1969, pp. 122–37.

8 On 13 October 1766 Goethe wrote to his sister Cornelia: 'J'ai commencé de former le Sujet d'Yncle et d'Jariko pour le Théatre' (quoted by Price, p. 97); Mary Wollstonecraft, *Vindication of the Rights of Woman*, Harmondsworth, 1982, p. 212.

9 See Price's full chronological bibliography, pp. 155–68.

10 These details are taken from Price's bibliography. Apart from Ligon and Steele I refer principally to the three anonymous poems: 'The Story of Inkle and Yarico. From the 11th *Spectator*,' *The London Magazine*, III, 1734, pp. 257–8; *Yarico to Inkle, an Epistle*, London, 1736 – reprinted in Price, following p. 18; and *The Story of Inkle and Yarico*, London, 1738 – reprinted in Price, following p. 18 (referring to these three by their dates); and also to Edward Jerningham, *Yarico to Inkle, an Epistle*, London, 1766; and George Colman, *Inkle and Yarico* (1787), in *The British Drama*, vol. II, London, 1826, pp. 1448–65.

11 See in particular: R.F. Brissenden, *Virtue in Distress: Studies in the Novel of Sentiment from Richardson to Sade*, London, 1974; Jean Hagstrum, *Sex and Sensibility: Ideal and Erotic Love from Milton to Mozart*, Chicago, 1980; Paul Hazard, *La Crise de conscience européenne*, Paris, 1935; Geoffroy Atkinson, *The Sentimental Revolution: French Writers of 1690–1740*, Seattle, 1965; and D.G. Charlton, *New Images of the Natural in France: A Study in European Cultural History*, Cambridge, 1984.

12 *Discourse on the Origin and Basis of Inequality among Men* (*The Essential Rousseau*, trans. Lowell Bair, New York, 1974, p. 140).

13 In, respectively, Dryden's *All for Love* (1677); Aphra Behn's *Oronooko* (1688); Pope's *Eloisa to Abelard* (1717); Richardson's *Clarissa* (1749); Bernardin de Saint-Pierre's *Paul et Virginie* (1788); and John Davis's *The First Settlers of Virginia: an historical novel* (1806).

14 *Lettres d'une religieuse portugaise* (1669) and Dryden's *Aeneis* (1697). On both of these see Hagstrum, pp. 106–17. Around the *Lettres* – whose 'authenticity' is still disputed – gathered the same accretion of translations, imitations, sequels, answers, etc. as 'Inkle and Yarico' attracted.

15 The standard study is B. Bissell, *The American Indian in English Literature of the Eighteenth Century* (1925), New Haven, 1968. See also: Hoxie Fairchild, *The Noble Savage: A Study in Romantic Naturalism*,

New York, 1928; Lois Whitney, *Primitivism and the Idea of Progress in English Popular Literature of the Eighteenth Century*, Baltimore, 1934; and Margaret M. Fitzgerald, *First Follow Nature: Primitivism in English Poetry 1725–1750*, New York, 1947.

16 See Winthrop Jordan, *White Over Black: American Attitudes towards the Negro, 1550–1812*, Chapel Hill, 1968, pp. 3–43.

17 Jean-Baptiste du Tertre, *Histoire générale des Antilles habitées par les Français*, 4 vols, Paris, 1667–71; Jean-Jacques Rousseau, *Discours sur l'origine et les fondements de l'inegalité parmi les hommes*, (1754); Guillaume Raynal, *Histoire philosophique et politique des établissements et du commerce des européens dans les deux Indes* (1770).

18 Du Tertre, II, pp. 365–7.

19 J.B. Labat, *Voyage aux isles d'Amérique* (1714), quoted by Edwards, I, pp. 33–4.

20 *The Essential Rousseau*, p. 168 and 179. Cf. G. Pire, 'Jean-Jacques Rousseau et les relations du voyage', *Revue d'histoire littéraire de la France*, LVI, 1956, pp. 355–78.

21 Guillaume Raynal, *A Philosophical and Political History of the Settlements and Trade of the Europeans in the East and West Indies*, trans. J. Justamond, 5 vols, London, 1776, IV, p. 311.

22 Wylie Sypher is right to make the point that just because works like *Oronooko* and 'Inkle and Yarico' have a slave as protagonist does not mean that they are in any straightforward sense 'anti-slavery literature' (Sypher, p. 137). An enslaved Yarico or Oronooko remain individuals wrongly enslaved rather than condemnations of the institutions of slavery. This would be true even of the most famous 'anti-slavery' work of all, Bicknell and Day's *The Dying Negro* (1773), which celebrates an exceptional and sentimental individual as the continuation of its title makes clear: 'a Poetical Epistle Supposed to be written by a Black, (who lately shot himself on board a vessel in the river Thames); to his intended wife'. So in general it might be more accurate to think of certain portions of the literature of sentiment being put to use by the anti-slavery movement as part of its campaign. For a general survey: Eva Beatrice Dyke, *The Negro in English Romantic Poetry*, Washington, 1942. And on the wider context see: David Brion Davis, *The Problem of Slavery in the Age of Revolution, 1770–1823*, Ithaca, 1975; James Walvin (ed.), *Slavery and British Society 1776–1846*, London, 1982; Gordon K. Lewis, *Slavery, Imperialism and Freedom: Studies in English Radical Thought*, New York, 1978, chapter 1; Gordon K. Lewis, *Main Currents in Caribbean Thought*, Baltimore, 1983, chapter 4; and Edward Seeber, *Anti-Slavery Opinion in France During the Second Half of the Eighteenth Century*, Baltimore, 1937.

23 See Richmond P. Bond, *Queen Anne's American Kings*, Oxford,

1952; and more generally, C.T. Foreman, *Indians Abroad 1493–1938*, Norman, 1943.

24 Steele, *The Tatler*, 171, 13 May 1710; Addison, *The Spectator*, 50, 27 April 1711.

25 As Bond suggests, pp. 137–9.

26 On Tomochichi see Helen Todd, *Tomochichi*, Atlanta, 1977; on Omai, Michael Alexander, *Omai: 'Noble Savage'*, London, 1977.

27 *The Gentleman's Magazine*, XIX, 1794, p. 89. There is also a shorter report in *The London Magazine*, XVIII, 1749, p. 94.

28 Anthony J. Barker, *The African Link: British Attitudes to the Negro in the Era of the Atlantic Slave Trade, 1550–1807*, London, 1978, pp. 27–8.

29 Richard Ligon, *A True and Exact History of the Island of Barbados*, London, 1657, pp. 54–5.

30 Quoted from *The Spectator*, ed. Donald P. Bond, 5 vols, Oxford, 1965, I, pp. 47–51.

31 The 1738 poem, in Price. Olympe de Gouges amended her *Zamore et Mirza, ou l'heureux Naufrage* (1786) by transforming its Caribbean protagonists into negroes and renaming it *L'Esclavage des noirs, ou l'heureux Naufrage* (1789): see Seeber, p. 178. There also exists *The Prince of Angola, a Tragedy; altered from the play of Oronooko, and adapted to the Circumstances of the present Time*, by J. Ferriar, Manchester, 1788.

32 Cf. Hayden White, 'The noble savage theme as fetish', in his *Tropics of Discourse: Essays in Cultural Criticism*, Baltimore, 1978, pp. 183–96; and Anthony Pagden, 'The savage critic: Some European images of the primitive', *The Yearbook of English Studies*, XIII, 1983, pp. 32–45.

33 George Guffey, 'Aphra Behn's *Oronooko*: Occasion and accomplishment', in *Two English Novelists: Aphra Behn and Anthony Trollope*, Los Angeles, 1975.

34 Aphra Behn, *Oronooko: or, the Royal Slave*, in *Shorter Novels: Seventeenth Century*, London, 1930, p. 154. Cf. the description of Friday referred to on p. 205.

35 Ernest Bernbaum's attack ('Mrs Behn's biography, a fiction', *PMLA*, 28, 1913, pp. 432–53) seems refuted by H.G. Platt ('Astraea and Celadon: An untouched portrait of Aphra Behn', *PMLA*, 49, 1934, pp. 544–59) and J.A. Ramsaran, '*Oronooko*: a study of the factual elements', *Notes and Queries*, VII, 1960, pp. 142–5. See also Maureen Duffy, *The Passionate Shepherdess: Aphra Behn 1640–89*, London, 1977; and Angeline Goreau, *Reconstructing Aphra: A Social Biography of Aphra Behn*, New York, 1980.

36 Aphra Behn, *Oronooko*, p. 151.

37 The two most important contemporary sources on the Carib Wars, apart from the Colonial Office papers (henceforth CO) and the Parliamentary reports (*The Parliamentary History of England from the Earliest Period to 1803*, ed. William Cobbett and T.C. Hansard, 36 vols., London, 1806–20, XVII, pp. 565–635 and 722–41), are William Young, *An Account of the Black Charaibs in the Island of St Vincent*, London, 1795 – the papers of the elder William Young put together by his son of the same name; and Charles Shephard, *An Historical Account of the Island of St Vincent*, London, 1831. Apart from Kirby and Martin (see note 5) the best modern accounts are: Bernard Marshall, 'The Black Caribs – Native resistance to British penetration into the windward side of St. Vincent 1763–1773', *Caribbean Quarterly*, 19, 1973, pp. 4–19; Charles Gullick, 'The Black Caribs in St Vincent: The Carib war and its aftermath', *Actes du XLIIe Congrès International des Américanistes*, VI, 1976, pp. 451–65; and Michael Craton, *Testing the Chains: Resistance to Slavery in the British West Indies*, Ithaca, 1982, chapters 12 and 15.

38 According to Craton (p. 147) the Black Carib community numbered more than 5000 at this period.

39 'Memorial of William Young, 11th April 1767', *Parliamentary History*, XVII, p. 576; CO 101/16 (Memorial of the Council and Assembly of St Vincent).

40 Young, *An Account*, p. 22.

41 Emerich de Vattel, *The Law of Nations; or Principles of the Law of Nature*, 2 vols, London, 1760–59, I, pp. 37–8. Cf., on Black Carib agricultural practices, Charles Gullick, 'The ecological background to the Carib wars', *Journal of Belizean Affairs*, VI, 1978, pp. 51–61.

42 'Memorial of William Young', p. 577.

43 CO 101/13 (Governor Fitzmaurice to Hillsborough, 18 December 1768).

44 Young, *An Account*, pp. 54–6.

45 *Parliamentary History*, XVII, p. 609.

46 *Parliamentary History*, XVII, p. 607.

47 CO 101/16 (Memorial of the Council and Assembly of St Vincent).

48 *Parliamentary History*, XVII, p. 609.

49 Young, *An Account*, pp. 6–9.

50 See Craton, p. 147; and the excellent study by Charles Gullick, 'Black Carib origins and early society', in *Proceedings of the Seventh International Congress for the Study of the Pre-Columbian Cultures of the Lesser Antilles*, ed. Jean Benoist and Francine-M. Mayer, Montreal, 1978, pp. 283–90.

51 'Black Carib', in other words, was an awkward category that the British tried hard to refuse. For one thing it compromised their

ability to distinguish their colonial practice from that of the Spaniards, a distinction seen in the last chapter to be of great importance to Robinson Crusoe (see pp. 199–200). The indigenous Caribbean population found their place within British colonial discourse as the victims of Spanish cruelty: Bryan Edwards even sees the rebellion of St Domingue as providential retribution for the sixteenth-century genocide of the Hispaniolan natives (III, chapter XII). Blacks did not have this protected status so that, for example, when the importation of bloodhounds and chasseurs from Cuba to hunt down the Jamaican maroons was condemned in parliamentary debate by Sheridan and others (quoting Las Casas in support), Edwards could defend the practice – with a great display of sophistry and historical quotation – by maintaining that the maroons 'were not an unarmed, innocent and defenceless race of men, like the ancient Americans; but a banditti of assassins: and tenderness towards such an enemy was cruelty to all the rest of the community' (III, p. 346). So it helped if the Black Carib were regarded as *really* black and only *falsely* Carib.

52 CO 101/16 (Hillsborough to Governor Leybourne, 18 April 1772).
53 CO 101/16 (quoted by Marshall, p. 12).
54 Young, *An Account*, p. 51.
55 The letter is quoted from Prince Hoare, *Memoirs of Granville Sharp, Esq.*, London, 1820, pp. 109–11.
56 'Probus', 'Injustice of the Proceedings at ST VINCENT represented', *The Scots Magazine*, XXXIV, 1772, p. 588.
57 *Parliamentary History*, XVII, pp. 389–90 and 728–31.
58 CO 101/16 (Leybourne to Hillsborough, 9 October 1772). Shephard (p. 30) speaks of a parliamentary inquiry, initiated by opponents of Lord North, which attempted to embarrass the government by resolving that the expedition was founded on injustice, and ordered the immediate negotiation of a treaty. Given the time-scheme involved it is difficult to see how this inquiry could have been responsible for halting the war. Cf. Marshall, p. 14; and Craton, pp. 150–1.
59 The treaty is reprinted in Kirby and Martin, pp. 33–8. Cf. the surveyors' map and accompanying notes: John Byers, *References to the Plan of St Vincent as surveyed from the years 1765–1773*, London, 1777. The treaty was based on the 1738 settlement with the Jamaican maroons.
60 The translation used is by C. Day Lewis, *The Eclogues, Georgics and Aeneid of Virgil*, Oxford, 1966.
61 Edward Jerningham's version of the story had already amalgamated Yarico and Dido by introducing a new ending: 'This Poniard by my

daring Hand imprest / Shall drink the ruddy Drops that warm my Breast'.

62 *The Oxford Companion to Classical Literature*, ed. Paul Harvey, Oxford, 1959, p. 7.

63 My paragraphs on Dido draw extensively on Monti's argument: Richard Monti, *The Dido Episode and the Aeneid: Roman Social and Political Values in the Epic*, Leiden, 1981.

64 Monti, p. 3. The reference is to Richard Heinze, *Virgils epische Technik*, Darmstadt, 1965, p. 134, n. 1.

65 See Chapter 3, p. 117.

66 'The possibility of joining the emotional and the political in such a curious blend is one open especially to a Roman poet because of the peculiarities of Roman social institutions' (Monti, p. 35).

67 Monti, p. 5. The reference is to Arthur Pease, *Publi Vergili Maronis Aeneidos Liber Quartus*, Cambridge, Mass., 1935.

68 'The Aeneis', I.805; in *The Poems of John Dryden*, ed. James Kinsley, Oxford, 1958, vol. III, p. 1085.

69 Bengal is the subject of one of Raynal's sentimental set-pieces (I, pp. 475–6); on the Somerset case see, for example, Peter Fryer, *Staying Power: The History of Black People in Britain*, London, 1984, pp. 120–7. What did survive, however, was the evangelical morality to be found, for example, in one of the sub-texts of *Mansfield Park*, which implies that that there can be no moral economy *in absentia*, a symptomatic rejection of the kind of slave system on which the first British Empire was built.

70 CO 71/3. The sentiment, though not the exact phrase, can be traced back to Pliny, *Natural History*, 10 vols, London, 1968, IV, XV, p. xx. Young's letter, which is not in fact totally sympathetic to the planters' position, is of the greatest interest.

71 *Plutarch's Lives*, trans. Bernadotte Perrin, London, vol. II, 1914, pp. 382–3. Cf. Charles E. Little, 'The authenticity and form of Cato's saying "Carthago delenda est"', *The Classical Journal*, XXIX, 1934, pp. 429–35; and Sylvia Thurlemann-Rapperswil, '"Ceterum censeo Carthaginam esse delendam"', *Gymnasium*, LXXXI, 1974, pp. 465–75.

Cf. 'An article in yesterday's *Washington Post* extolled the fashion among right-wing pundits here of impressing their audiences with a smattering of Latin – as in "Delenda est Carthago", which means "Nicaragua must be flattened"' (*The Guardian*, 30 April 1985, p. 1).

72 Jean Mocquet, *Travels and Voyages*, trans. Nathaniel Pullen, London, 1696. See Gilbert Chinard, *L'Amérique et le rêve exotique dans la littérature française au XVIIe et au XVIIIe siècle*, Paris, 1913, pp. 25–7.

73 Mocquet, pp. 124–7. For the original French, see Jean Mocquet,

Voyages, 2nd edn, Rouen, 1645, pp. 148–50, quoted by Sypher, pp. 122–3.

74 Though it had at one time been settled by native Caribbeans: see Ripley Bullen, 'Barbados and the archaeology of the Caribbean', *Journal of the Barbados Museum and Historical Society*, XXXII, 1966, pp. 16–19. The geographical touchstone of Barbados may also hint at a historical residue since there is a well attested story of thirty Arawak indians going voluntarily to Barbados only to be made slaves after having become involved, it seems, in the wrangles between the two English factions disputing control of Barbados: see Jerome Handler, 'The Amerindian slave population of Barbados in the seventeenth and early eighteenth centuries', *Caribbean Studies*, VIII, no. 4, 1969, pp. 38–64.

75 1738 poem, in Price, p. 9.

76 Kirby and Martin, pp. 41–5. See Valentine Morris, *A Narrative of the Offical Conduct of Valentine Morris*, London, 1787; and cf. Ivor Waters, *The Unfortunate Valentine Morris*, Chepstow, 1964.

77 Thomas Coke, *Some Account of the Late Missionaries to the West Indies; in Two Letters from the Rev. Dr. Coke, to the Rev. J. Wesley*, London, 1789, p. 11.

78 William Young, *A Tour through the several Islands of Barbadoes, St. Vincent, Antigua, Tobago, and Grenada, in the years 1791 and 1792*, in Edwards, III, pp. 275, 279 and 301.

79 Thomas Coke, *History of the West Indies*, 3 vols, Liverpool, 1808–11, II, pp. 264–5.

80 Shephard, p. 51.

81 Shephard, p. 22.

82 On all the above, see Craton's magnificent *Testing the Chains, passim*; and Richard Price (ed.), *Maroon Societies: Rebel Slave Communities in the Americas*, New York, 1973.

83 Shephard, pp. 53–4.

84 Craton, p. 190.

85 See Gullick, 'Black Carib Origins'.

Afterword

1 M.J. Chapman, *Barbadoes and Other Poems*, London, 1833, p. 7.

2 See, respectively, Charles Gullick's *Exiled from St Vincent: The Development of Black Carib Culture in Central America up to 1945*, Malta, 1976; his 'The Black Caribs in St Vincent: The Carib war and its aftermath', *Actes du XLIIe Congrès International des Américanistes*, Paris, 1976, VI, pp. 451–65; Anthony Layng, *The Carib Reserve:*

Identity and Security in the West Indies, Washington, 1983; Nancy Owen, 'Land, politics, and ethnicity in a Carib Indian community', *Ethnology*, XIV, 1975, pp. 382–93; and 'Conditions in the Carib reserve and the disturbance of 19th September 1930', *Report of a Commission Appointed by His Excellency the Governor of the Leeward Islands*, London, 1932.

3 Referring to the practices of the Jacobins he wrote:

> To all this let us join the practice of *cannibalism*, with which, in the proper terms, and with the greatest truth, their several factions accuse each other. By cannibalism, I mean their devouring, as a nutriment of their ferocity, some part of the bodies of those they have murdered; their drinking the blood of their victims, and forcing the victims themselves to drink the blood of their kindred slaughtered before their faces. By cannibalism, I mean also to signify all their nameless, unmanly, and abominable insults on the bodies of those they slaughter. ('Letters on a Regicide Peace', in *The Works of Edmund Burke*, 12 vols, London, 1815, VIII, pp. 177–8)

> In the earlier *Reflections on the Revolution in France* (1790) he had quoted Lally Tollendal's letter describing the entrance into Paris of the King and Queen surrounded by 'ces perfides janissaires, ces assassins, ces femmes cannibales' (*Reflections*, Harmondsworth, 1979, p. 167).

4 On Edwards, Frankenstein and Canning see the interesting note in Darko Suvin, *Metamorphoses of Science Fiction: On the Poetics and History of a Literary Genre*, New Haven, 1979, pp. 135–6. Saint-Marc Girardin is quoted from his *Souvenirs d'un journaliste*, Paris, 1859, pp. 144–5: cf. my 'Balzac's Parisian mystery: *La Cousine Bette* and the writing of historical criticism', *Literature and History*, XI, 1985, pp. 47–64.

5 Michel de Montaigne, 'Of the caniballes', *Essays*, trans. John Florio (1603), 3 vols, London, 1892, I, p. 231.

Bibliography

Section **A** lists the colonial texts up to 1850 on which the previous pages have offered any kind of comment. **Section B** lists those books and articles which (i) have been particularly valuable in the writing of this book, and (ii) could be seen as contributing to the study of colonial discourse, especially as it pertains to the Caribbean.

Section A

Behn, Aphra, *Oronooko: or, the Royal Slave* (1688), in *Shorter Novels: Seventeenth Century*, London, 1930.

Breton, Raymond, *Dictionaire Caraibe-François* (1665), 2 vols, Leipzig, 1892.

(Butler, Nathaniel), *The Historye of the Bermudaes or Summer Islands*, ed. J.H. Lefroy, London, 1882.

Byers, John, *References to the Plan of St. Vincent as surveyed from the years 1765–1773* (with map), London, 1777.

Chanca, Diego Alvarez, 'Letter of Dr Chanca' (1494), in Christopher Columbus, *Four Voyages to the New World: Letters and Selected Documents*, bi-lingual edition, trans. and ed. R.H. Major, New York, 1961, pp. 18–68.

Chapman, George, 'De Guiana carmen Epicum' (1596), in Hakluyt, *The Principall Navigations*, X, p. 447.

Chapman, J.G., *The picture of the baptism of Pocahontas painted by order of Congress, for the Rotunda of the Capitol*, Washington, 1840.

Coke, Thomas, *History of the West Indies*, 3 vols, Liverpool, 1808–11.

Coke, Thomas, *Some Account of the late Missionaries to the West Indies; in Two Letters from the Rev. Dr. Coke, to the Rev. J. Wesley*, London, 1789.

Colman, George, *Inkle and Yarico* (1787), in *The British Drama* vol. II, London, 1826, pp. 1448–65.

Colonial Office Papers 71/3, 101/13, 101/16.

Columbus, Christopher, *La carta de Colón anunciando la llegada a las Indias*, ed. Carlos Sanz, Madrid, 1958.

Columbus, Christopher, *The Journal of Christopher Columbus*, trans. C. Jane, revised and annotated by L.A. Vigneras, London, 1960.

Columbus, Christopher, 'Letter of Columbus', in *The Journal of Christopher Columbus*, pp. 191–202.

Columbus, Christopher, *Diario de Colón*, ed. Carlos Sanz, Madrid, 1962.

'Concerning Hurricanes and their Prognosticks – & observations of my owne Experience thereupon' (*c.* 1669), Egerton Manuscripts, 2395/619–24 (British Library).

Defoe, Daniel, *An Essay on the South Sea Trade*, London, 1712.

Defoe, Daniel, *An Historical Account of the Voyages and Adventures of Sir Walter Raleigh*, London, 1719.

Defoe, Daniel, *The Life and Adventures of Robinson Crusoe* (1719), ed. Angus Ross, Harmondsworth, 1965.

Defoe, Daniel, *The Farther Adventures of Robinson Crusoe Being the Second and Last Part of His Life* (1719), London, 1925.

Defoe, Daniel, *The Serious Reflections of Robinson Crusoe*, London, 1720.

Defoe, Daniel, *The History of the Principal Discoveries and Improvements in the several arts and sciences*, London, 1727.

Defoe, Daniel, *Atlas Maritimus & Commercialis; or, a General View of the World*, London, 1728.

Defoe, Daniel, *The Letters of Daniel Defoe*, ed. G.H. Healey, Oxford, 1955.

Descartes, René, *Discours de la Méthode: Texte et Commentaire* (1637), ed. Etienne Gilson, Paris, 1976; *Discourse on Method and the Meditations*, trans. F.E. Sutcliffe, Harmondsworth, 1968.

Du Tertre, Jean-Baptiste, *Histoire générale des Antilles habitées par les Français*, 4 vols, Paris, 1667–71.

Edwards, Bryan, *The History, Civil and Commercial, of the British Colonies in the West Indies*, 3 vols, London, 1794–1801.

Figueroa, Rodrigo de, 'Información hecha por el licenciado Rodrigo de Figueroa acerca de la población india de las islas E costa de Tierra Firma, E sentencia que dió en nombre de Su Majestad' (1520), in *Colección de documentos inéditos relativos al descubrimiento, conquista, y organización de las antiguas posesiones españolas de América y Oceanía*, 42 vols, Madrid, 1864–84, I, pp. 379–85.

Gray, Robert, *A Good Speed to Virginia* (1609), facsimile edn, Amsterdam, 1970 (The English Experience no. 253).

Hakluyt, Richard (the elder), 'Inducements to the lykinge of the voyadge intended to that parte of America which lyethe betwene 34. and 36. degree' (1584), in *New American World: A Documentary History of North America to 1612*, ed. David Beers Quinn, 5 vols, London, 1979, III, pp. 62–4.

Hakluyt, Richard, *The Principall Navigations, Voyages, Traffiques, And Discoveries of the English Nation* (1598–1600), 12 vols, Glasgow, 1903–5.

Homer, *The Odyssey*, trans. Richmond Lattimore, New York, 1975.

Jerningham, Edward, *Yarico to Inkle, An epistle*, London, 1766.

Jourdain, Silvester, 'A Discovery of the Bermudas, Otherwise Called the Isle of Devils' (1610) in *A Voyage to Virginia in 1609*, ed. L.B. Wright, Charlottesville, 1964.

Las Casas, Bartolomé de, *The Spanish Colonie or Briefe Chronicle of the Acts and gestes of the Spaniardes in the West Indies, called the newe World, for the space of XI. yeeres*, trans. M.M.S., London, 1583.

Las Casas, Bartolomé de, *Historia de las Indias*, ed. A. Millares Carlo, 3 vols, Mexico City, 1951.

Ligon, Richard, *A True and Exact History of the Island of Barbados*, London, 1657.

Locke, John, *Two Treatises of Government* (1689), ed. Peter Laslett, New York, 1965.

Martyr, Peter (Pedro Martir de Anglería), *Décadas del nuevo mundo* (1493–1525), trans. A. Millares Carlo, 2 vols, Mexico City, 1964.

Mocquet, Jean, *Voyages en Afrique, Asie, Indes Orientales et Occidentales*, Paris, 1616; *Travels and Voyages*, trans. Nathaniel Pullen, London, 1696.

Nicholl, John, 'An Houre Glasse of Indian News' (1605), ed. Rev. C. Jesse, *Caribbean Quarterly*, XII, no. 1, 1966, pp. 46–67.

Pané, Fray Ramón, *Relación acerca de las antigüedades de los Indios* (1498), ed. J.J. Arrom, Mexico City, 1974.

The Parliamentary History of England from the Earliest Period to 1803, ed. William Cobbett and T.C. Hansard, 36 vols, London, 1806–20, vol. XVII.

Price, Lawrence M., *Inkle and Yarico Album*, Berkeley, 1937.

'Probus', 'Injustice of the Proceedings at ST VINCENT represented', *The Scots Magazine*, XXXIV, 1772, p. 588.

Purchas, Samuel, *Purchas His Pilgrimes* (1625), 20 vols, Glasgow, 1905–7.

Purchas, Samuel, 'Virginia's Verger' (1625), in *Purchas His Pilgrimes* XIX, pp. 218–67.

(Queen Isabella of Castile), 'Provisión para poder cautivar a los Caribales rebeldes' (1503), in *Colección de los viajes y descubrimientos, que hicieron por mar los españoles desde fines del siglo XV*, ed. M. Fernández de Navarrete, 5 vols, Madrid, 1825–37, II, pp. 414–16.

Raynal, Guillaume, *Histoire philosophique et politique des établissements et du commerce des européens dans les deux Indes* (1667), 4 vols, Amsterdam, 1770; *A Philosophical and Political History of the Settlements and Trade of the Europeans in the East and West Indies*, trans, J. Justamond, 5 vols, London, 1776.

Rolfe, John, 'Copy of John Rolfe's Letter to Sir Thomas Dale Regarding His Marriage to Pocahontas' (1614), in Philip Barbour, *Pocahontas and her World*, London, 1971, Appendix III, pp. 247–52.

Rousseau, Jean-Jacques, *Discours sur l'origine et les fondements de l'inégalité parmi les hommes* (1754); 'Discourse on the origin and basis of inequality among men', trans. Lowell Bair in *The Essential Rousseau*, New York, 1974, pp. 125–201.

Sandys, George, *Ovids Metamorphosis Englished, Mythologized, And Represented in Figures*, London, 1640.

Shakespeare, William, *The Tempest* (1611), ed. Frank Kermode, The Arden Shakespeare, London, 1958.

Sharp, Granville, 'Letter to Lord Dartmouth' (1772), in Prince Hoare, *Memoirs of Granville Sharp, Esq.*, London, 1820, pp. 109–11.

Shephard, Charles, *An Historical Account of the Island of St. Vincent*, London, 1831.

Smith, John, *A Trve Relation of such occurrences and accidents of noate as hath hapned in Virginia since the first planting of that collony* (1608), in Smith, *Works*, pp. 1–40.

Smith, John, *Works 1608–1631*, ed. E. Arber, Birmingham, 1884.

Smith, John, *The Generall Historie of Virginia, New England, and the Summer Isles* (1624), facsimile edn, Cleveland, 1966.

Steele, Richard [Inkle and Yarico], *The Spectator*, 11, Tuesday 13 March 1711 (in *The Spectator*, ed. D.F. Bond, 5 vols, Oxford, 1965, I, pp. 47–51).

The Story of Inkle and Yarico (1738), reprinted in Price, *Inkle and Yarico Album*, following p. 18.

'The Story of Inkle and Yarico. From the 11th *Spectator*', *The London Magazine*, III, 1734, pp. 257–8.

Strachey, William, 'A True Reportory of the Wracke' (1610), in Purchas, XIX, pp. 5–72.

Symonds, William, *Virginia: A Sermon Preached at White-chapel* (1609), facsimile edn, Amsterdam, 1968 (The English Experience no. 52).

Taylor, John, *New and strange News from St. Christophers*, London, 1638.

Vespucci, Amerigo, *El nuevo mundo. Cartas relativas a sus viajes y descubrimientos. Textos en italiano, español, e inglés*, Buenos Aires, 1951.

Virgil, *The Aeneid*, ed. T.E. Page, 2 vols, London, 1926; *The Eclogues, Georgics and Aeneid of Virgil*, trans. C. Day Lewis, Oxford, 1966.

Waldseemüller, Martin, *The Cosmographiae Introductio in facsimile. Followed by the Four Voyages of Amerigo Vespucci, with their Translation into English*, ed. C.G. Herbermann (1907), New York, 1969.

Waterhouse, Edward, *A Declaration of the State of the Colony in Virginia*

(1622), facsimile edn, Amsterdam, 1970 (The English Experience no. 276).

Yarico to Inkle, an Epistle (1736), reprinted in Price, *Inkle and Yarico Album*, following p. 18.

Young, William, *An Account of the Black Charaibs in the Island of St. Vincent*, London, 1795.

Section B

Abellán, José-Luis, 'Los orígenes españoles del mito del "buen salvaje"', *Revista de Indias*, XXXVI, 1976, pp. 157–80.

Alegría, Ricardo E., *Las primeras representaciones gráficas del indio americano 1493–1523*, San Juan, 1978.

Allen, D.C., *The Legend of Noah*, Urbana, 1949 (Illinois Studies in Language and Literature, vol. XXXIII, nos. 3 and 4).

Anderson, A.R., *Alexander's Gate, Gog and Magog, and the Inclosed Nations*, Cambridge, Mass., 1932.

Andrews, Kenneth R., *Elizabethan Privateering: English Privateering during the Spanish War, 1585–1603*, Cambridge, 1964.

Andrews, Kenneth R., *The Spanish Caribbean: Trade and Plunder 1530–1630*, New Haven, 1978.

Andrews, Kenneth R., *Trade, Plunder, and Settlement: Maritime Enterprise and the Genesis of the British Empire 1480–1630*, Cambridge, 1984.

Andrews, Kenneth R., Canny, N.P. and Hair, P.E.H. (eds), *The Westward Enterprise: English Activities in Ireland, the Atlantic, and America 1480–1650*, Liverpool, 1978.

Arens, W., *The Man-eating Myth: Anthropology and Anthropophagy*, Oxford, 1979.

Arrom, José Juan, *Mitología y artes prehispánicas de las Antillas*, Mexico City, 1975.

Asad, Talal (ed.), *Anthropology and the Colonial Encounter*, London, 1973.

Axtell, James, *The European and the Indian: Essays in the Ethnohistory of Colonial North America*, New York, 1981.

Barbour, Philip, *The Three Worlds of Captain John Smith*, London, 1964.

Barbour, Philip, *Pocahontas and her World*, London, 1971.

Barbour, Philip (ed.), *The Jamestown Voyages Under the First Charter*, London, 1969.

Baritz, Loren, 'The idea of the West', *American Historical Review*, LXVI, 1960–1, pp. 618–40.

Barker, A.J. *The African Link: British Attitudes to the Negro in the Era of the Atlantic Slave Trade, 1550–1807*, London, 1978.

Barker, Francis and Hulme, Peter, 'Nymphs and reapers heavily vanish: The discursive con-texts of *The Tempest*', in *Alternative Shakespeares*, ed. John Drakakis, London, 1985, pp. 191–205.

Baudet, F., *Paradise on Earth: Some Thoughts on European Images of non-European Man*, trans. E. Wentholt, New Haven, 1965.

Berkhofer, Robert F. jun., *The White Man's Indian: Images of the American Indian from Columbus to the Present*, New York, 1978.

Bernheimer, R., *Wild Men in the Middle Ages*, Cambridge, Mass., 1952.

Bhabha, Homi K., 'Difference, discrimination and the discourse of colonialism', in *The Politics of Theory*, ed. Francis Barker, Peter Hulme, Margaret Iversen, and Diana Loxley, Colchester, 1983, pp. 194–211.

Bhabha, Homi K., 'Of mimicry and man: The ambivalence of colonial discourse', *October*, 28, 1984, pp. 125–33.

Bissell, B., *The American Indian in English Literature of the Eighteenth Century* (1925), New Haven, 1968.

Boas, G., *Essays on Primitivism and Related Ideas in the Middle Ages*, Baltimore, 1948.

Boas, G. and Lovejoy, A.O., *A Documentary History of Primitivism and Related Ideas in Antiquity*, Baltimore, 1935.

Boon, James A., *Other Tribes, Other Scribes: Symbolic Anthropology in the Comparative Study of Cultures, Histories, Religions, and Texts*, Cambridge, 1982.

Brotherston, Gordon, 'Towards a grammatology of America: Lévi-Strauss, Derrida and the native New World text', in *Europe and Its Others*, ed. Francis Barker, Peter Hulme, Margaret Iversen, and Diana Loxley, 2 vols, Colchester, 1985, II, pp. 61–78.

Brown, Paul, '"This thing of darkness I acknowledge mine": The Tempest and the discourse of colonialism', in *Political Shakespeare: New Essays in Cultural Materialism*, ed. Jonathan Dollimore and Alan Sinfield, Manchester, 1985, pp. 48–71.

Calder, Angus, *Revolutionary Empire: The Rise of the English Speaking Empires from the Fifteenth Century to the 1780s*, London, 1981.

Canny, Nicholas P., 'The ideology of English colonization: From Ireland to America', *William and Mary Quarterly*, 3rd ser., XXX, 1973, pp. 575–98.

Canny, Nicholas P., 'The permissive frontier: the problem of social control in English settlements in Ireland and Virginia 1550–1650', in *The Westward Enterprise*, ed. K.R. Andrews, N.P. Canny and P.E.H. Hair, pp. 127–44.

Canny, Nicholas P., 'Dominant minorities: English settlers in Ireland and Virginia, 1550–1650', in *Minorities in History*, ed. A.C. Hapburn, London, 1978, pp. 51–69.

Carneiro, Robert L., 'A theory of the origin of the state', *Science*, 169, 1970, pp. 733–8.

Carneiro, Robert L., 'From autonomous villages to the state, a numerical estimation', in *Population Growth: Anthropological Implications*, ed. Brian Spooner, Cambridge, Mass., 1972, pp. 65–77.

Carneiro, Robert L., 'The chiefdom: Precursor of the state', in *The Transition to Statehood in the New World*, ed. G. Jones and R. Kautz, Cambridge, 1981, pp. 37–79.

Chiappelli, F. (ed.), *First Images of America: The Impact of the New World on the Old*, 2 vols, Berkeley, 1976.

Chinard, G., *L'Amérique et le rêve exotique dans la littérature française au XVIIe et au XVIIIe siècle*, Paris, 1913.

Clifford, James, 'On ethnographic authority', *Representations*, 1, 1983, pp. 118–46.

Cohn, Norman, *Europe's Inner Demons*, London, 1976.

Craton, Michael, *Testing The Chains: Resistance to Slavery in the British West Indies*, Ithaca, 1982.

Destins du cannibalism (*Nouvelle Revue de Psychoanalyse* (Paris), no. 6, Autumn 1972).

Detienne, Marcel, 'Entre bêtes et dieux', in *Destins du cannibalisme*, Paris, 1972, pp. 231–46; 'Between beasts and gods', in *Myth, Religion and Society*, ed. R.L. Gordon, Cambridge, 1981, pp. 215–28.

Diamond, Stanley, *In Search of the Primitive: A Critique of Civilization*, New York, 1974.

Douglas, Mary, *Purity and Danger: An Analysis of the Concepts of Pollution and Taboo*, London, 1978.

Drummond, Lee, 'On being Carib', in *Carib-speaking Indians: Culture, Society and Language*, ed. E.B. Basso, Tucson, 1977, pp. 76 88.

Dudley, E. and Novak, M. (eds.), *The Wild Man Within: An Image in Western Thought from the Renaissance to Romanticism*, Pittsburgh, 1972.

Dunn, Richard S., *Sugar and Slaves: The Rise of the Planter Class in the English West Indies 1624–1713*, New York, 1973.

Elliott, J.H., *The Old World and the New, 1492–1650*, Cambridge, 1970.

Evans, W.M., 'From the land of Canaan to the land of Guinea: The strange odyssey of the sons of Ham', *American Historical Review*, LXXXV, 1980, pp. 15–43.

Fairchild, H.N., *The Noble Savage: A Study in Romantic Naturalism*, New York, 1928.

Fanon, Frantz, *Black Skin, White Masks*, trans. Charles Lam Markmann, New York, 1967.

Fernández Retamar, Roberto, *Caliban: Apuntes sobre la cultura en nuestra América*, Mexico City, 1971.

Fiedler, Leslie, *The Return of the Vanishing American*, New York, 1968.

Fiedler, Leslie, 'The New World savage as stranger: or "Tis new to thee"' in his *The Stranger in Shakespeare*, London, 1973, pp. 199–253.

Frey, Charles, '*The Tempest* and the New World', *Shakespeare Quarterly*, XXX, 1979, pp. 29–41.

Friedman, J.B., *The Monstruous Races in Medieval Art and Thought*, Cambridge, Mass., 1981.

Gerbi, Antonio, *The Dispute of the New World: The History of a Polemic, 1750–1900* (1955), trans. J. Moyle, Pittsburgh, 1973.

Gliozzi, Giuliano, *Adamo e il nuovo mondo. La nascita dell'anthropologia come ideologia coloniale: dalle genealogie bibliche alle teorie razziali (1500–1700)*, Florence, 1977.

Góngora, Mario de, *Studies in the Colonial History of Spanish America*, Cambridge, 1975.

Goveia, Elsa V., *A Study on the Historiography of the British West Indies to the End of the Nineteenth Century*, Mexico City, 1956.

Greenblatt, Stephen, 'Learning to curse: Aspects of linguistic colonialism in the sixteenth century', in *First Images of America*, ed. F. Chiappelli, I, pp. 561–80.

Greenblatt, Stephen, *Renaissance Self-Fashioning From More to Shakespeare*, Chicago, 1980.

Greenblatt, Stephen, 'Invisible bullets: Renaissance authority and its subversion, *Henry IV* and *Henry V*', in *Political Shakespeare: New Essays in Cultural Materialism*, ed. Jonathan Dollimore and Alan Sinfield, Manchester, 1985, pp. 18–47.

Hanke, Lewis, *Aristotle and the American Indians*, Bloomington, 1959.

Harlow, V.T. (ed.), *Colonising Expeditions to the West Indies and Guiana, 1623–1667*, London, 1925.

Hartog, François, *Le Miroir d'Herodote: Essai sur la représentation de l'autre*, Paris, 1980.

Hay, Denys, *Europe: The Emergence of an Idea*, Edinburgh, 1957.

Hodgen, Margaret T., *Early Anthropology in the Sixteenth and Seventeenth Centuries*, Philadelphia, 1964.

Honour, Hugh, *The New Golden Land: European Images of America from the Discoveries to the Present Time*, New York, 1975.

Hsu, Francis L., 'Rethinking the concept "primitive"', *Current Anthropology*, V, 1964, pp. 169–78.

Hulme, Peter, 'Columbus and the cannibals: A study of the reports of anthropophagy in the Journal of Christopher Columbus', *Ibero-Amerikanisches Archiv*, N.F. IV, 1978, pp. 115–39.

Hulme, Peter, 'Hurricanes in the Caribbees: The constitution of the discourse of English Colonialism', in *1642: Literature and Power in the Seventeenth Century*, ed. Francis Barker, Jay Bernstein, John Coombes, Peter Hulme, Jennifer Stone, and Jon Stratton, Colchester, 1981, pp. 55–83.

Hulme, Peter, 'Polytropic man: Tropes of sexuality and mobility in early colonial discourse', in *Europe and Its Others*, ed. Francis Barker, Peter Hulme, Margaret Iversen, and Diana Loxley, 2 vols, Colchester, 1985, II, pp. 17–32.

Johnson, James E., *Ideology, Reason, and the Limitation of War: Religious and Secular Concepts, 1200–1740*, Princeton, 1975.

Jameson, Fredric, *The Political Unconscious: Narrative as a Socially Symbolic Act*, London, 1981.

Jennings, Francis, *The Invasion of America: Indians, Colonialism and the Cant of Conquest*, New York, 1976.

Jordan, W.D., *White Over Black: American Attitudes towards the Negro, 1550–1812*, Chapel Hill, 1968.

Kavanagh, Thomas M., 'Unraveling Robinson: The divided self in Defoe's *Robinson Crusoe*', *Texas Studies in Language and Literature*, XX, 1978, pp. 416–32.

Kermode, Frank, 'Introduction' to the Arden edition of *The Tempest*, London, 1958, pp. xi–xciii.

Kleinbaum, Abby Wettan, *The War Against the Amazons*, New York, 1983.

Kott, Jan, 'La tempête ou la répétition', *Tel Quel*, 70, 1977, pp. 136–62.

Lamming, George, 'A monster, a child, a slave', in his *The Pleasures of Exile*, London, 1984, pp. 95–117.

Landucci, Sergio, *I filosofi e i selvaggi 1580–1780*, Bari, 1972.

Levin, Harry, *The Myth of the Golden Age in the Renaissance*, London, 1970.

Lewis, Gordon K., *Main Currents in Caribbean Thought: The Historical Evolution of Caribbean Society in its Ideological Aspects, 1492–1900*, Baltimore, 1983.

Loxley, Diana, '"A play of shadows": Slaves and strangers in *The Tempest, Robinson Crusoe* and *Victory*', MA dissertation, University of Essex, 1982.

Macherey, Pierre, *A Theory of Literary Production*, trans. Geoffrey Wall, London, 1978.

Maddox, James H., 'Interpreter Crusoe', *English Literary History*, LI, 1984, pp. 33–52.

Maltby, William S., *The Black Legend in England: The Development of Anti-Spanish Sentiment, 1558–1660*, Durham, NC, 1971.

Mannoni, Octave, *Prospero and Caliban: The Psychology of Colonization*, trans. Pamela Powesland, New York, 1964.

Marshall, P.J. and Williams, G., *The Great Map of Mankind: British Perceptions of the World in the Age of Enlightenment*, London, 1982.

Mauss, Marcel, *The Gift: Forms and Functions of Exchange in Archaic Societies*, trans. Ian Cunnison, London, 1970.

Morgan, Edmund S., *American Slavery American Freedom: The Ordeal of Colonial Virginia*, New York, 1975.

Morison, Samuel Eliot, *Admiral of the Ocean Sea: A Life of Christopher Columbus*, Boston, 1942.

Mossiker, Frances, *Pocahontas: The Life and the Legend*, London, 1977.

Muldoon, James, *Popes, Lawyers, and Infidels. The Church and the non-Christian World, 1250–1550*, Liverpool, 1979.

O'Gorman, Edmundo, *The Invention of America: An Inquiry into the Historical Nature of the New World and the Meaning of its History*, Bloomington, 1961.

Oliva de Coll, Josefina, *La resistencia indígena ante la conquista*, Mexico City, 1974.

Pagden, Anthony, *The Fall of Natural Man: The American Indian and the Origins of Comparative Ethnology*, Cambridge, 1982.

Parker, John, *Books to Build an Empire*, Amsterdam, 1966.

Parry, John H., *The Age of Reconnaissance: Discovery, Exploration and Settlement 1450–1650*, London, 1973.

Parry, John H. and Keith, Robert G. (eds.), *New Iberian World: A Documentary History of the Discovery and Settlement of Latin America to the Early 17th Century*, 5 vols, New York, 1984.

Pearce, Roy Harvey, *The Savages of America: A Study of the Indian and the Idea of Civilization*, Baltimore, 1965.

Poliakov, Leon, *The Aryan Myth: A History of Racist and Nationalist Ideas in Europe*, trans. E. Howard, London, 1974.

Porter, H.C., *The Inconstant Savage: England and the North American Indian*, London, 1979.

Price, Lawrence M., *Inkle and Yarico Album*, Berkeley, 1937.

Quinn, David Beers (ed.), *New American World: A Documentary History of North America to 1612*, 5 vols, London, 1979.

Rogers, Pat, *Robinson Crusoe*, London, 1979.

Rouse, Irving, 'The Arawak', and 'The Carib', in *Handbook of South American Indians*, ed. J.H. Steward, 6 vols, New York, 1948, IV, pp. 507–65.

Ryan, Michael T., 'Assimilating new worlds in the sixteenth and seventeenth centuries', *Comparative Studies in Society and History*, XXIII, 1981, pp. 519–38.

Said, Edward, *Orientalism*, London, 1978.

Sanders, Ronald, *Lost Tribes and Promised Lands: The Origins of American Racism*, New York, 1978.

Sauer, Carl Ortwin, *The Early Spanish Main*, London, 1966.

Shepherd, Simon, *Amazons and Warrior Women: Varieties of Feminism in Seventeenth-Century Drama*, Brighton, 1981.

Smith, James, 'The Tempest', in *Shakespearian and Other Essays*, ed. E.M. Wilson, Cambridge, 1974, pp. 159–261.

Stocking, George W., *Race, Culture, and Evolution: Essays in the History of Anthropology*, Chicago, 1982.

Sued Badillo, Jalil, *Los caribes: realidad o fábula*, Río Piedras, 1978.

Sypher, Wylie, *Guinea's Captive Kings: British Anti-Slavery Literature of the XVIIIth Century*, New York, 1969.

Taylor, Douglas M., *Languages of the West Indies*, Baltimore, 1977.

Verlinden, Charles, *The Beginnings of Modern Colonization*, trans, Yvonne Freccero, Ithaca, 1970.

Vilar, Pierre, *A History of Gold and Money 1450–1920*, trans. Judith White, London, 1976.

Wallerstein, Immanuel, *The Modern World-System: Capitalist Agriculture and the Origins of the European World-Economy in the Sixteenth Century*, New York, 1974.

Wallerstein, Immanuel, *The Modern World-System II: Mercantilism and the Consolidation of the European World-Economy 1600–1750*, New York, 1980.

Washburn, Wilcomb E., *Red Man's Land/White Man's Law: A Study of the Past and Present Status of the American Indian*, New York, 1971.

Watt, Ian, *The Rise of the Novel: Studies in Defoe, Richardson and Fielding*, Harmondsworth, 1963.

White, Hayden, *Tropics of Discourse: Essays in Cultural Criticism*, Baltimore, 1978.

Williamson, James A., *A Short History of British Expansion*, 2 vols, London, 1930.

Wittkower, R., 'Marvels of the East: A study in the history of monsters', *Journal of the Warburg and Courtauld Institutes*, V, 1942, pp. 159–97.

Wolf, Eric, *Europe and the People without History*, Berkeley, 1982.

Index

Abercromby, General Sir Ralph 263
Abraham, Karl 81
Addison, Joseph 231
Africa 35, 36, 112, 139, 161, 185,
    229, 232–3, 239, 245, 247, 252,
    255
Albertus Magnus 161
Alexander the Great 100
Algonquian 90, 107, 137, 140, 141,
    142, 146, 147–52, 157, 158, 160,
    164, 168, 169, 170, 172, 209,
    298n.9
Althusser, Louis xv, 7, 11
Alvarez Chanca, Dr Diego 68–9,
    175
Amazons 21, 43
America xii–xiii, 1, 2, 3, 6, 18, 20,
    28, 34, 35, 62, 83, 89, 90, 91–2,
    93, 94, 105, 107, 109, 128, 139,
    158, 186, 187, 197, 229; Central 6,
    265; Meso- 51; North 4, 242, 246;
    South 4, 47, 49, 51, 52, 53, 59, 61,
    66, 68, 76, 181, 238
Andes air crash, 81–2
Anson, Admiral George 70
anthropology: as discipline 54–7, 80,
    83, 278n.19; South American, 46,
    50, 64, 73, 275n.2; see also
    chiefdom, culture-area, culture,
    ethnography, ethnology, ethnic
    ascription, historical linguistics,
    prehistory
Anthropophagi 21, 67, 68, 70
anthropophagy 15, 19, 21, 43,
    79–87, 100
Antigua 59, 97
Antilia 24, 38

Antilles, Greater 60; see also names of
    individual islands
Antilles, Lesser 48, 49, 61, 62, 63, 68,
    90; see also names of individual
    islands
anti-semitism 85
Araucanian 57
Arawak 16, 19, 20, 22, 24, 25, 27,
    29, 32, 45, 46, 47, 48–50, 53, 60,
    61–6, 71, 72, 74, 246
archaeology 34, 46, 55, 56
Archer, Gabriel 163
Arens, W. 80, 83
Argall, Samuel 140
Arnold, Matthew 54
Arrom, José Juan xv
Asia 20, 24, 36, 39, 161
Atlantic discourse 106–9, 128, 133
Augustine, St 250
Avila, Bishop of 1
Azores 38

Bacon, Francis 10
Bahamas 22, 29, 58, 225
Bahia 4, 184, 213, 219
Ballantyne, R.M. 184
Barbados 4, 90, 97, 224, 227, 234,
    236–7, 238, 245, 258–9
Barbour, Philip 140
Batela, Fray Gregorio 60
Behn, Aphra 229, 232, 240–2
Bequia 245
Bermuda Pamphlets 91, 92; see also
    Strachey, William
Bermudas 4, 90, 91, 96–7, 100, 102,
    103, 104, 106, 182, 185, 188
Bernardin de St Pierre, Jacques

342 INDEX

Henri 229
Biard, Pierre 157
Bible, the 96–7, 145–6
Black Carib xiii, 226, 242–9, 255, 259–63, 265, 323n.51
Black Carib wars 226, 242, 247–9, 254, 260, 261, 262–3, 323n.37
Bligh, Captain William 188
Bobadilla, Francisco de 94–5
Bolingbroke, Henry St John 181, 213
Bougainville, Louis Antoine de 229
Brant, Joseph 232
Brathwaite, Edward vii
Braudel, Fernand de 37, 183
Brazil 4, 6, 180, 182, 184, 185, 213, 214, 218, 220, 221, 256
Breton, Raymond 61, 62–3, 230
Brinton, Daniel 60
Brizan, George 48
Brontë, Charlotte 220
Brown, Alexander 163
Brown, Homer 193
Buchan, John 183
Bullough, Geoffrey 138
Bunyan, John 179
Burke, Edmund 265

Cabot, Sebastian 37
cacicazgo: see chiefdom
Caliban xiii, 3, 88, 106, 107, 108, 109, 113, 114, 116, 119, 120, 121, 122–8, 131–4, 138, 160, 161, 163, 168, 195, 202, 220, 294n.46
Calvin, John 145
Canary Islands 26, 27, 29, 37
canibal: see cannibal
cannibal xiii, 15, 16–17, 19, 22, 33, 34, 38, 41, 44, 47, 48, 49, 50, 68, 69, 70, 86, 90, 95, 100, 101, 107, 108, 129, 130, 165, 166, 170, 175, 176, 193, 194, 196, 198, 199, 200, 201, 202, 204, 205, 209, 210, 216, 217, 218, 219, 221, 227, 230, 259
'cannibalism': as trope within colonial discourse 3, 14, 15, 48, 54, 68, 78–87, 108, 150, 154, 175, 198, 200, 211, 239, 265, 285n.78,

287n.88, 287n.89
Canning, George 265
capitalism 37, 155, 176, 180–1, 183, 219, 222
Carib 10, 15, 16, 40, 41, 42–3, 45, 46, 47, 48–51, 53, 58, 60, 61–72, 77, 78, 100, 129–30, 149, 155, 174, 176, 186, 187, 195, 196, 206, 209, 210, 211, 225, 226, 227, 230–1, 245–6, 259, 263
Caribbean xiii, 3–5, 6, 9, 15, 16, 18, 22–3, 26, 34, 42, 44, 45, 46, 47, 48, 49, 53, 56, 58, 65, 68, 69, 70, 72, 74, 75, 89, 90, 94, 97, 98, 107, 125, 176, 181, 182, 184, 185, 186, 187, 195, 196, 206, 215, 216, 225, 230, 232, 233, 238, 239, 241, 242, 256, 258, 262, 265 (*see also* Antilles, Greater, Antilles, Lesser, *and individual islands*); native cultures of xiv, 3, 8, 34, 42, 43, 45, 45–87, 89, 148–9, 176, 194, 195, 205, 225, 226, 254, 266 (*see also* Arawak, Black Carib, Carib, Ciboney, Ciguayo, Lucayan, Taino, sub-Taino)
Carneiro, Robert 74–5
Carthage 35, 110–12, 162, 249, 252–3, 255, 258, 259
Castile: *see* Spain
Cathay 20, 21, 24, 26, 28, 29, 30, 31, 33, 35, 37
Cato, Marcus Porcius 255
Catullus 250
Chamfort, S.-R.-N. 227
Chanca, Dr: *see* Alvarez Chanca, Dr Diego
Chapman, George 159
Chapman, John G. 170, 171
Chapman, M.J. 265
Charles II 240
Charles V 71
Chatoyer, Joseph 242, 244, 261, 263
chiefdom 73–6, 282n.68
Chile 57
China 36, 38
Chinard, Gilbert 255–6, 257
Choanik 57

Christian, Fletcher 188
Christianity 3, 28, 84–6, 102, 105, 146, 160, 202; see also Bible, the, Providence
Ciboney 58, 63
Cicero 156
Ciguayo 40, 50, 69
Cipangu (Japan) 24, 25, 37, 38
Cipolla, Carlo M. 36
Clermont-Ferrand, Council of 84
Cohn, Norman 84
Coke, Thomas 260
Collingwood, R.G. 10–11
Colman, George 241
colonial discourse xiii-xiv, 1–3, 5, 7, 8, 9, 34, 35, 45, 46, 71, 73, 81, 84, 85, 86, 89, 106, 108, 145–6, 152, 156, 157–66, 172, 193, 196, 200, 209, 242, 246, 253, 266, 309n.83; see also 'cannibalism', 'savagery', 'treachery'
colonial triangle 1, 159, 160, 170
Columbus, Christopher xiii, 8, 13–43, 44, 45, 46, 47, 53, 63, 68, 69, 79, 83, 89, 94–5, 181, 185, 187; Journal 3, 9, 10, 16–17, 18, 20–34, 36, 37, 38, 39–43, 46, 47, 48, 50, 60, 69, 72, 108, 125; Letter 3, 28, 32, 37, 41–3, 68
Constantinople, fall of (1453) 36
Cook, Captain James 229
Corrente, John 233
Cosa, Juan de la 70
Cotubano 71
Croce, Benedetto 94
Cromwell, Oliver 181
Crusades 84
Crusoe, Robinson xiii, 4, 174, 175, 176, 179, 180, 181, 183, 184–5, 186–7, 188–9, 190–222, 246, 258, 266
Ctesias 21
Cuba 4, 23, 24, 25, 26, 28, 29, 31, 33, 37, 39, 42, 47, 58, 59, 68, 75, 142, 225
Cudjoe 261
culture 54–5, 79
culture-area typology 51–3, 54, 73,

227n.16
Cynocephali 21

D'Ailly, Pierre 21
Dale, Sir Thomas 143
Dartmouth, Earl of 247–8
Davis, David Brion 227
De Bry, Theodore 14, 113, 136
Dee, John 90
Defoe, Daniel 104, 176, 177, 178, 179, 180, 181, 182, 183, 184, 185, 192, 195, 205, 206, 210, 213, 216, 221, 255; Robinson Crusoe 9, 10, 35, 174, 176, 178–81, 184–222, 226, 254, 259
De La Warr, Lord Thomas 102, 164
Derrida, Jacques 5
Descartes, René 179, 188–9, 196, 215
Diderot, Denis 229
Divisament dou Monde 21
Dominica 4, 61, 63, 149, 225, 226, 262, 265
Dominican Republic 50
Douglas, Mary 82
Drake, Sir Francis 139, 181, 182, 183
Drummond, Lee 64–6
Dryden, John 107, 229, 249, 250, 252
Du Tertre, Jean-Baptiste 229, 230

Eden, Richard 70, 95
Edwards, Bryan 265
Elizabeth I 159
England: as colonial power 6, 10, 35, 59, 89–90, 91, 94–8, 105, 155, 160, 162–4, 168, 182, 196, 205, 216, 226, 232–3, 242–9, 254, 261–3
Enriquillo: see Guarocuya
Ercilla, Alonso de 57
Esquivel, Juan de 71
ethnic ascription 57–73
ethnography 7, 15, 16, 19, 55, 67
ethnology 51, 54, 55, 68
Euripides 250, 251
Europe xii-xiv, 3, 8–9, 18, 20, 21, 35, 36, 45–7, 65–8, 73, 77–8, 81, 82–6, 89, 109, 112, 152, 155–6,

161, 167, 183, 185, 186, 194, 199, 201, 202, 206, 211, 215, 217, 225, 228, 229, 242, 253, 257, 265, 288n.93

Evans-Pritchard, E.E. 78

Ferdinand, King of Aragon 2, 26, 27–8, 29, 32, 37, 38
Fernández de Oviedo, Gonzalo 63, 95
Fernández Retamar, Roberto xv
Fiedler, Leslie 109
Fielding, Henry 176–7, 179, 220
Figueroa, Rodrigo de 71–2
Foucault, Michel 6, 7, 8
Freud, Sigmund 31, 81, 82, 254
Frey, Charles 93
Friday xiii, 174, 175, 176, 185, 194–6, 200, 201–2, 205, 206–7, 209–11, 212, 215, 217, 227
Frye, Northrop 208–9, 213
Fuseli, Henry 88

Galileo 186
Galván, Manuel 50
García Márquez, Gabriel 13
Gates, Sir Thomas 96, 104, 158, 166, 168, 185
Gellert, C.F. 227
Genoa 35–9
Geraldini, Bishop of Santo Domingo 101
Gibbon, Edward 138
Gilbert, Humphrey 90
Girardin, Saint-Marc 266
Goethe, J.W. von 227
Graham, Shirley 2, 137
Gramsci, Antonio 7
Grand Khan (of Cathay) 20, 21–2, 24, 25, 26, 28, 29, 30, 32, 33, 39
Gray, Robert 158
Greece 3, 21
Grenada 48, 226, 262, 263
Grenville, Sir Richard 139
Guadeloupe 69
Guanahani xiii, 23
Guanche 37
Guarocuya 50

guatiao 71–2, 150, 170, 195, 209
Guiana 4, 60, 61, 65, 90, 94, 128, 159, 181, 182
Guyana 64–6
Gwyneth, Owen 89

Haiti 225, 254
Hakluyt, Richard 165–6
Hakluyt, Richard (the younger) 89–90, 95
Halifax, Earl of 232
Handbook of South American Indians 49–53, 57–8, 73, 79
Hariot, Thomas 142
Harrington, M.R. 58, 60
Hawkesworth, John 241
Hawkins, John 166
Heinze, Richard 251
Henry VII 89
Herder, J.G. von 54
Herodotus 21, 22, 32, 33, 36, 41, 108, 270n.9
Hill, Christopher 187
Hillsborough, Lord 246, 247, 248, 255
Hispaniola 4, 5, 23, 39, 42, 47, 50, 58, 60, 69, 75, 182, 185, 187, 231
historical linguistics 7, 15, 51, 67, 72
history 6, 7, 10–13, 56, 155
Hobbes, Thomas 149, 161, 186, 187, 207, 217, 218
Homer: Odyssey 108, 153–6, 162, 187, 258
Honduras 263
Hopkins, Stephen 103, 187
hospitality 131, 148–52, 153–5, 161, 167, 195, 238, 246, 249, 251–3, 258–9, 302n.30
Hugues, Victor 262
Humboldt, Alexander von 101
hurricane 5, 94–101, 102
Hutcheson, Francis 228
Hymer, Stephen 180, 202

Im Thurn, E.F. 45
India 2, 3
Ingram, David 166, 257
Inkle, Thomas 227–9, 232, 234–6,

238, 239, 249, 258, 259, 261; *see also* 'Inkle and Yarico'
'Inkle and Yarico' xiii, 10, 225, 227–8, 230–42, 246, 249–50, 251, 253, 254, 255, 259
Innocent III, Pope 85
Iroquois 231
Isabella, Queen of Castile 1, 2, 26, 27–8, 29, 32, 37, 38, 70
Islam 3, 35, 37, 185
Island Carib: *see* Carib
Island Carib language 61, 62, 265

Jamaica 4, 59, 68, 261
James I 143
Jameson, Fredric xv, 11–12, 208
Jamestown 4, 89, 96, 102, 103, 143, 149, 154, 163, 164
Jane, Cecil 37
Japan: *see* Cipangu
Jennings, Francis 84, 157
Jerningham, Edward 229
Johnson, Robert 158
Johnson, Samuel 101
Joyce, James 216

Kahn, Coppélia 126
Kari'na 61, 63, 76
Kermode, Frank 92–3, 105, 115, 117, 163, 251
Kirchhoff, Paul 51
Kotzebue, A.F.F. von 229

Labat, Père 230
Lamming, George 106
Las Casas, Bartolomé de 17, 19, 20, 27, 29, 30, 32, 58, 71, 133
Lateran Council, Fourth 85
Lattimore, Owen 186
Lawrence, D.H. 109
Leavis, F.R. 54
Leigh, Charles 128
Leith, Major 263
Lettres d'une religieuse portugaise 229
Lewis, Gordon W. xv
Leybourne, Governor 248
Ligon, Richard 227, 231, 233–4, 236–7, 238, 239, 241, 255, 257,

258
Lloyd's List 183
Locke, John 158, 186, 187, 205–6
Lokono 60
López de Velasco, Juan 60
Loven, S. 60
Lucayans 225
Luce, Morton 107–8, 137, 138
Lukács, George 177

Macherey, Pierre xv, 11, 12, 81
Maddox, James 200, 217, 220
Madoc 89
Maitland, Richard 245
Marmontel, J.F. 229
Marryat, Captain Frederick 184
Martyr, Peter (of Anghera) 69, 101
Marx, Karl 8, 180, 186, 266
Marxism 5, 8, 11–12, 75, 152
Mauss, Marcel 147–8, 150
Mediterranean discourse 3, 35, 47, 96–101, 105, 106, 108–15, 133, 155; *see also* Bible, the, Herodotus, Homer, Ovid, Virgil
Medvedev, P.N. 34
Methuen Treaty (1703) 182
Mexico 5, 48, 78, 248
Miller, Perry 138–9
Milton, John 179
Mocquet, Jean 256–8
Monckton, General 242, 243
Montaigne, Michel de 199, 230, 266
Montesquieu, Baron de 231
Monti, Richard 250–1
Montserrat 97
More, Sir Thomas 188
Moreau le Jeune, Jean-Marie 224, 231
Morgan, Edmund 167–8
Morison, Samuel Eliot 29, 30, 158
Morris, Valentine 259
Münster, Sebastian 70

Namontack 151
Nanny 261
Navarrete, Rodrigo de 60
Nevis 97
Newport, Captain Christopher 150,

151, 153
Nicholl, John 128–31
Nietzsche, Friedrich 38
Nuestra Señora de la Concepción 182

Olive Branch 90, 128–30
Olsen, Fred 59
Omai 232
Opechancanough 140, 142, 164, 170, 261
Orient, discourse of 18, 21, 22, 24, 26, 31, 33, 35, 36, 38, 39
Ovid 154
Oxford English Dictionary 15, 16–17, 34, 70, 95

Pané, Fray Ramón 55
Paris, Treaty of (1763) 226, 242, 262
Parry, John 186
Paterson, William 181
Paul VI, Pope 82
Paul, St 96–7, 102
Pease, Arthur 251
Peckham, George 162
Peru 56, 78, 159
Phips, William 182
Pinzón, Martín Alonso 26
Pius II, Pope 84
Pliny 21
Plutarch 255
Pocahontas xiii, 4, 10, 90–1, 137, 138, 139, 140–52, 156, 168–72, 195, 206, 227, 229, 231, 238, 252, 253, 255, 300n.13
Polo, Marco 21, 22, 30, 31, 37
Pope, Alexander 109, 181, 213, 214, 229
Powhatan 137–8, 140, 146, 149, 150, 151, 152, 155–6, 161, 164, 215
prehistory 55, 56, 278n.20
Price, Lawrence 227, 255
'Probus' 248
Prospero xiii, 3, 88, 102, 103, 105, 106, 109, 113, 114, 115–28, 131–4, 160, 168, 195, 202, 212, 216–17, 220, 221, 251, 258
Providence 96, 102, 104, 105, 106, 128, 163, 177–9, 203, 204, 318n.74

psychoanalysis 11–12, 81, 83, 106, 126, 167, 228
Puerto Rico 4, 40, 47, 58, 68, 75
Pullen, Nathaniel 256
Purchas, Samuel 90, 95, 102, 141, 143, 158, 159–60, 162, 169–70, 246

Rafinesque, Cornelius 60
Ralegh, Sir Walter 90, 95, 142, 159, 181, 182, 183, 184
Raynal, G.-F.-T. 224, 229, 231
Razilly, Pierre 256
Reagan, Ronald 6
Reid, Captain Mayne 183
Richardson, Samuel 176–8, 179, 220, 229
Rogers, Pat 214
Roldán, Francisco 187
Rolfe, John 138, 140, 141, 143, 144–5, 146, 168, 169, 170
Rolfe, Thomas 141
Rouse, Irving 55, 59
Rousseau, Jean-Jacques 186, 187, 228, 229, 230–1

Said, Edward xv
St Christopher's: see St Kitts
St Domingue 262, 265, 266
St Kitts 90, 97, 100, 155
St Lucia 129, 244, 263
St Vincent xiii, 4, 10, 35, 225, 226, 231, 242, 245, 248, 254, 255, 259, 260, 262, 263, 265
Sandys, George 154, 155
San Salvador: see Guanahani
Sauer, Carl Ortwin xv, 28, 31
Savage, Thomas 142, 151
'savagery', as trope within colonial discourse 3, 21, 22, 32, 33, 36, 38, 99–100, 139, 156–7, 172
Sea-Venture 90, 91, 95, 96, 100, 104, 182, 187–8
Sesarakoo, William Ansah 232–3
Shaftesbury, 3rd Earl of 228
Shakespeare, William 70, 91, 92, 93, 95, 105, 107, 112, 115, 117, 212, 240; The Tempest 3, 9, 10, 35, 89,

90, 91–4, 95, 101–2, 103, 104,
105–28, 130, 131–4, 137–8, 141,
155, 164, 167, 173, 186, 189–90,
202, 212, 217, 220, 255, 257,
292n.42
Sharp, Granville 247–8, 254
Shephard, Charles 260–1, 263
Sheridan, Richard 229
Sidney, Sir Philip 109
Smith, Bradford 140
Smith, James 93
Smith, John xiii, 4, 9, 10, 90, 137,
138, 140–1, 142, 143, 146–7,
149–52, 153, 155, 160, 172, 215,
229, 258
Solinus 21
Somers, Sir George 96, 102, 158,
185, 187
Somerset, James 254
Southerne, Thomas 241
Southey, Robert 229
Spain: as colonial power 6, 36–9, 85,
86, 89, 199–200, 248, 261
Spenser, Edmund 109
Staden, Hans 79
Steele, Richard 227, 228, 231,
234–9, 257, 258
Sterne, Laurence 193
Steward, Julian 51, 53, 73
Stoll, E.E. 91
Strachey, William 91, 92, 93, 95,
96–7, 101- 4, 142
Straet, Jan van der xii-xiii, 1, 3, 8
Sub-Taino 58, 59
Sundelson, David 126
Surinam 240, 241
Swift, Jonathan 181, 213
Sylvius, Aeneas 21
Sypher, Wylie 256, 257

Taino 40, 60, 61, 63, 69, 70, 71, 73,
77, 86–7, 150, 209, 225
Taylor, John 97–101, 102, 104
Taylor, Mark 126
Tegreman 155
Thousand and One Nights 241
Tierra del Fuego 57
Tobago 226, 262

Tomochichi 232
Torres, Luís de 20, 29
Toscanelli, Paolo 24, 37
'treachery', as trope within colonial
discourse 131, 132, 133, 163–4,
167, 172, 306n.66
Trinidad 4, 49, 176
True Declaration of Virginia, A 103–4,
162
Tupi, 266
Tylor, Edward 54, 55

United States of America 4, 6,
138–9, 141, 143, 144, 170
Urban II, Pope 84
Uttamatamakin (Tomocomo) 146,
169–70

Vattel, Emerich de 242
Venice 35
Vespucci, Amerigo de xii, 8
Vignaud, Henry 37
Virgil: Aeneid 109–12, 114, 161–2,
225, 249–53, 255, 258, 259
Virginia 5, 9, 90, 91, 94, 96, 104,
136, 137, 139, 141, 142, 149, 154,
155–6, 159, 160, 167, 168, 169,
170, 171, 173, 246; 1622 'massacre'
136, 139, 160, 171–3
Vitoria, Francisco de 156, 161

Walcott, Derek 175
Wallerstein, Immanuel 3
Warner, Thomas 155
Warton, Joseph 229
Waterhouse, Edward 172–3
Watt, Ian 176–9, 180, 186, 188, 204
Welsford, Enid 117
Wesley, John 260
West Indies: see Caribbean
White, John 139
Wilson, Daniel 125
Wilson Knight, G. 133
Winthrop, John 158, 159
Wollstonecraft, Mary 227
Wordsworth, William 229

Yahgan 57

Yamaná 57

Yarico 9, 224, 227–9, 231, 234, 236,
　237, 238, 239, 241, 252, 257, 258,

261; *see also* 'Inkle and Yarico'

Young, Sir William 242, 243–4,
　245–6, 247, 254, 255

Young, William (the younger) 260